Pelican Books
The Pelican Guide to Modern Theology
Editor: R. P. C. Hanson

Volume 2
Historical Theology

JEAN DANIÉLOU was born at Neuilly-sur-Seine on 14 May 1905. Educated at the Sorbonne, he graduated in 1927. Two years later he entered the Order of Jesus (Compagnie de Jésus). He obtained a Doctorate in Theology in 1943, and became a Doctor of Letters the following year. He has been Professor of the History of Early Christianity at the Faculty of Catholic Theology in Paris since 1944, and Dean of the Faculty since 1962. A member of the Societas Novi Testamenti, he is also a corresponding member of the Greek Society for Byzantine studies at Athens. Daniélou, a Chevalier of the Legion of Honour, has also given a course of lectures at Oxford. He has recently been made a Cardinal.

A. H. COURATIN was born in 1902. He was educated at Dulwich College and at Corpus Christi College, Oxford. He was trained for ordination at St Stephen's House, Oxford, and finally ordained in 1926. After doing parish work for nine years he returned to St Stephen's House, Oxford, to teach; he was Principal for twenty-five years. At the moment he is Canon Librarian of Durham Cathedral. He has given lectures on liturgy in the Universities of Oxford and Durham, and he has been a member of the Archbishops' Liturgical Commission for ten years.

JOHN KENT, PH.D., was born in 1923. He read History at Emmanuel College, Cambridge, where he later taught. He worked for the B.B.C. before entering the Methodist ministry in 1950. Since then he has taught church history in the Methodist theological colleges in Leeds, Cambridge and Mancheste[illegible] lecturer in Ecclesiastical History and Doctrine in th[illegible] Dr Kent, who has many connexion[illegible] *Disunity* (1966), an essay [illegible] Conscience in *Essays in* [illegible] *Darwin to Blatchford*, t[illegible]

[illegible] He has been a [illegible] the University of Bristol since [illegible] with America, has published *The Age of* [illegible] H. P. Hughes and the [illegible] *Church History* (1960), and [illegible] the Dr Williams's Library Lecture for 1960.

J. Daniélou
A. H. Couratin
John Kent

Historical Theology

Penguin Books

Penguin Books Ltd, Harmondsworth,
Middlesex, England
Penguin Books Inc, 7110 Ambassador Road,
Baltimore, Maryland 21207, U.S.A.
Penguin Books Australia Ltd, Ringwood,
Victoria, Australia

First published 1969
Reprinted 1971

Made and printed in Great Britain by
Hazell Watson & Viney Ltd,
Aylesbury, Bucks
Set in Linotype Times

Contents

Introduction to The Pelican Guide to Modern Theology 7

Introduction to Volume 2 9

Patristic Literature by J. Daniélou

Introduction 25

1 Judeo-Christian Patristic Literature 33
2 The Birth of Greek Patristic Literature 43
3 Origen 53
4 The Origins of Latin Patristic Literature 64
5 Literature Associated with the Council of Nicaea 79
6 The Age of Theodosius 92
7 The End of Greek Patristic Literature 104
8 Augustine and the West 116

Liturgy by A. H. Couratin

Introduction 131

1 The Origins of the Liturgy 136
2 The Pre-History of the Liturgy 141
3 Baptism before the Middle Ages 157
4 The Eucharist before the Middle Ages 172
5 Baptism in the Middle Ages 198
6 The Eucharist in the Middle Ages 215
7 The Liturgical Movement and its Background 231

The Study of Modern Ecclesiastical History since 1930 by John Kent

Introduction 243

1 General Histories of the Modern Church 249
2 The History of Christian Missions in the Modern Era 255

Contents

3 The Reformation and the Sixteenth Century 271
4 The Seventeenth Century: America and England 287
5 The European Church, 1550–1789 292
6 The Eighteenth Century in England 296
7 The Eighteenth-Century Evangelical Revival and the Rise of Methodism 302
8 The Nineteenth Century in England: The Anglican Mythology 307
9 Anglo-Catholicism, J. H. Newman, and Catholic Modernism 316
10 The Evangelical Tradition 330
11 Liberal Protestantism and Christian Socialism 337
12 The Social Gospel in America 344
13 Europe in the Nineteenth and Twentieth Centuries 346
14 The Sociological Approach and Popular Religion 351
15 American Revivalism 362
16 The Ecumenical Movement 366
Conclusion 367

Index of Names 370
Index of Subjects 378

Introduction to The Pelican Guide to Modern Theology

Theology used to claim to be able to give authoritative information about all the phenomena in the universe, or at the least to share this privilege with philosophy. Now through the vicissitudes of the history of thought theology usually occupies a lowly place in those institutions which exist to train men and women in all the important intellectual disciplines, and in some it does not appear at all. And its sister, philosophy, has fared little better. Theology has been chastened by adversity, by discovering that its claims were disputable, and in many cases manifestly false. The brash confidence sometimes displayed by the newer disciplines may encounter a similar experience. In consequence of this development it is thought by some that theology is dying: theology is the scientific study of religion, and religion is dying. The answer to this suggestion is simply that theology is not dying as long as there are people who believe it worth while to practise it. There are still plenty of people interested enough in theology to study it and to contribute to it.

Theology is the science of thinking about God. It has to cover a vast field, including ancient history, ancient languages, Church history, philosophy of religion, literary criticism (including textual criticism of two or three different types), the history of Christian thought and comparative religion. Men have always thought about God, often passionately; some of the best minds in history have been devoted to thought about God. Theology has therefore behind it a long, varied and fascinating history.

But what and how is God? This is one of the first questions handled by *The Pelican Guide to Modern Theology*. A guide of this sort should explain how people today think and in the past have thought about God. And as this is a Christian country (or at least a post-Christian one) this guide has thought it right to explain how Christians think about God. This has involved devoting a volume to the philosophy of religion (the interaction of Christian thought and philosophy), a volume to the Bible, describing how it is studied today, and a volume to historical theology, demonstrating in three different fields how scholars today handle the tradition which Christianity has formed in the course of its journey through history. We have not covered the whole field; we have had to omit, for instance, a treatment of the medieval period and we have made no reference to comparative religion. But this series will have done enough if it causes its readers to understand how it is that some people find theology the most attractive, the most exacting and the most satisfying intellectual pursuit of all.

R. P. C. HANSON

Introduction to Volume 2

It might seem to many readers that historical theology, whatever it is, has got nothing to do with modern theology. Modern theology should be about modern times and contemporary affairs and living issues. It should not be concerned with remotely past events. We do not, after all, hear of historical medicine or historical sociology, and even historical philosophy is at the moment rather under eclipse.

But in this respect Christianity (and with it Judaism and Islam) is in a peculiar position. It claims to have originated in a recognizable series of historical events and in some sense to regard those events as normative for its message and its significance. It must not therefore allow those events to be forgotten. This, if nothing else, should justify Christian theologians in having a special concern with history. But the argument cannot be left there, because it is in fact impossible, not to say undesirable, to move from the period of the Old and the New Testaments directly to our own day, to 'confront' the men of the twentieth century with the Bible, as if nothing had happened to the Christian religion between the first and the twentieth centuries. Christianity is 'the religion of a book', but the religion is not the book. The Bible supplies the source and the norm for Christian doctrine, but Christianity is a historical phenomenon, a religion which has made its way through history accompanied by its sacred book. And as a religion it has both formed history and has been formed by history. History has left its mark on Christianity. It has brought out its weak points and revealed its strength. It has tested Christianity in numberless different situations and moulded it to many different societies and cultures. It has both made Christians realize the limitations of Christianity and brought home to them its unexpected resources and potentialities. Christianity has during the last nineteen centuries undergone expansion and reduction, success and failure, corruption and reform, attack and adjustment. We regard one particular period of history as normative, but all Christian history must be illustrative. Christianity has not just been an idea, but an active force in history, impressing itself on its surroundings and in turn influenced by them.

It would therefore be absurd to ignore Christian history, to assume that it can throw no light on what the Christian faith is about, on the activity and character of God as seen in Christianity, or by Christians. We may want to try to isolate the ordinary Christian at one particular moment in history, the fifth-century monk in an Egyptian *laura*, the Western medieval peasant at mass, the godly apprentice in the England of Oliver Cromwell, the charismatic leader of a contemporary African Independent church and so on. Or we may turn our attention to the great figures of Christian history, to Athanasius, Augustine, Aquinas, Luther, Wesley, Kierkegaard. A properly conducted investigation of any period or any aspect of Christian history cannot fail to tell us something important about Christianity.

But why should such historical investigation be called theology? Because it needs a theological understanding to carry it out properly. It needs *logos* about *theos*, thought about God. We do not imagine that economic historians need no knowledge of economics if they are to write about their subject; we expect art historians to know something about art. It is therefore not a very arrogant claim to suggest that professional theologians are the best people to write about theological history. Three examples of the contemporary study of aspects of Christian history are given here.

The first example of historical theology which is provided here consists of an account of contemporary research and opinion concerning patristic literature. We do not here supply a history of dogma; instead we give an account of how experts in this field work when they study the literature through which we can see how the classic primary dogmas of the Christian faith came to be formed, the intellectual pressures which the earliest Christian writers had to face, the problems which they attempted to solve and the means they used to solve them.

This may at first sight seem the most recondite of subjects – dogma, ancient ecclesiastical dogma produced by theologians writing in three different dead languages, Greek, Latin and Syriac, in situations and for publics totally removed from the conditions which form our society and our life, in a remotely pre-scientific era, relying for the most part upon systems of thought which are admitted by almost everybody to be quite out-of-date. But this view must always seem superficial to those who have penetrated any distance beneath the surface of the Christian faith. It must first be recognized that no group of Christians in the whole history of Christianity has ever succeeded in confining its doctrine to the Bible and the Bible alone. Many groups at different times have made serious and valiant attempts to do this. The slogan of 'the Bible without notes', 'the Bible without the creed', 'the Bible and the Bible only' has often exercised strong attraction upon simple-minded, and sometimes even upon more intellectual, souls. This was the cry of a well-meaning anti-dogmatic group in Rome and elsewhere at the beginning of the fourth century. It was the principle which brought the eminent Anglican divine Illingworth out of the Church of Rome in the middle of the seventeenth century; it is a principle written into the Westminster Confession; it was the cry of the Free Church leaders who opposed the education policy of the Church of England at the beginning of this century. It is one of the reasons for the existence of the Churches of Christ, that numerous and respectable church in the USA. But it is a self-evidently impossible principle.

In the first place, no institution can exist in history without creating a tradition, be it a cricket club, a bird-watching society, a parliament, a police force or a literary clique. Those institutions which attempt to reject tradition merely succeed in establishing a tradition of rejecting tradition. Every intelligent person must recognize the existence of Christian tradition, because, for good or ill, it is an inescapable ingredient of historical Christianity (as Islamic tradition is of Islam and Shaman tradition is of Shamanism, etc.). It is simply a given fact. This is not to say that it is necessary to canonize tradition, to give it absolute value, to defend it to the last ditch in the teeth of every sort of criticism. It may be quite proper in some circumstances to cut back tradition, to reform and remould it, to abandon parts of it, to bring other parts hitherto neglected into prominence. But it is ludicrous to behave as if Christian tradition has not existed and does not exist. It certainly does. In fact, Christianity would not be alive as a recognizable contemporary phenomenon today if there had not been any tradition. The formation of tradition is the sign of a living Church, as it is of a living political party or a living university.

In the second place, every intelligent person ought to realize that the Bible does not interpret itself. This is meant in the simplest and directest way. If any reader were to take a modern printed copy of the Bible and place it, open, in Trafalgar Square, it would not begin either to read itself aloud or to preach itself. Indeed, the process of interpretation by the Church has begun even before the open Bible is placed in Trafalgar Square, for the Church originally put the Bible together, decided the order of its books, and more recently the Church translated it into English, and more recently still the Church printed it and published it. All this is a rudimentary form of interpretation. In fact no Christian communion, as far as I know, has been content with presenting the Bible, and the Bible alone, in complete deferential silence, to the world, confident that the book will make its own impact unaided by any human interpretation. Even the Society of Friends publishes posters putting forward their views with Bible texts or references annexed, which is of course a form of interpretation.

But when we once realize that the Bible needs an interpreter, we are forced to go further than merely saying that the Bible must be read and must be expounded. The decision has to be made as to what the Bible is saying, what its message is. The

New Testament, for instance, consists of twenty-seven books, at least nine of which give quite separate interpretations of the significance of Jesus Christ, each distinct from the others, some of them incompatible with each other in at least some of their details. Do those who believe believe in the Jesus of Mark, or of Matthew, or of John, of Paul, or of the Epistle to the Hebrews? Do they believe in Jesus as the Marcan Son of God, but not as the Pauline Second Adam, or as the Johannine Word of God, but not as the Eternal High Priest of the Epistle to the Hebrews? Manifestly not. Christian believers believe in a Christ who is in some sense witnessed to in all these books but is not restricted to any of them, nor is a mere aggregate or amalgam of all the texts in the New Testament about him. This is only another way of saying that the Christ of faith is the Christ of the Bible as interpreted by the Church. No believing Christian ever believes nakedly the Bible and nothing but the Bible without any interposition of an interpreting Church, even though he may think that he does.

The fact is that the Bible was written for a community that was already living in a tradition of belief, of worship and of life and that it was designed to function in such a context. The Bible was not written in order to be examined by objective, dispassionate historical scholarship. I do not say that the Bible should not be subjected to scholarship of this sort. But it was not designed to form a field of study for scholarship, it was designed to nourish and instruct faith in God; in other words, it was designed to be interpreted in one particular way, in one particular context, and not in others. Some years ago there was brought out a volume called *The Bible Designed to be Read as Literature*. This undertaking was not unlike bringing out an edition of *Hamlet* called *Hamlet Designed to be Read as a Manual for Gravediggers*. Gravediggers could presumably learn something from the play, and people learning how to act could learn even more, but manifestly the book was not intended for such uses. When the Christian Church took over the Old Testament and canonized the New Testament there already existed a lively and complex Jewish tradition of exegesis which, quite unreflectingly, the Church took over, even though in taking it over it added much and altered much in the course of time. One of the most important elements in that tradition was that the Bible was to be used in order to kindle and to nourish faith in a living God who had manifested himself in history. The question facing the Church at the beginning was not how it was going to preserve the Bible intact, without notes, insulated from creeds or doctrines, but how it was going to continue the tradition of expounding the Bible which it had inherited. At no point has the Church faced the Bible with its mind a *tabula rasa*. It was not a question of whether tradition would appear to corrupt the Bible, but of what tradition would be formed by the Church's interpretation of the Bible.

Those people whom we call the Fathers of the Church answered this question. They were the first Christian writers, the first Christian theologians, the first people to attempt to apply the Christians' sacred book to life, to ethics, to philosophy. They were the first people to form doctrine and later dogma out of the Biblical text. We can follow the process as it takes place. Until the middle of the second century doctrine consists of little more than strings of texts and of longer passages from the Bible (mainly the Old Testament). The second and third centuries see the gradual formation of a body of doctrines, not particularly well coordinated or knit into a tight system. The Apostles' Creed in its string-of-sausages or washing-line form vividly mirrors this phase. The fourth and fifth centuries witness the great doctrinal controversies in which doctrinal problems which have for long exercised the minds of Christian theologians come to a head and urgently demand decision. The decisions are only reached by the Church after convulsive struggles. The whole process of forming doctrine is inevitably one of struggle and conflict, trial and error, experiment. The process is deeply involved with the cultural background and the philosophical assumptions of the period during which it is taking place, of course. If it had not been so, it would not have been a real, open-ended, struggle. The decisions reached as a result of these struggles and conflicts in the fourth and fifth centuries are usually called dogmas, the dogma of Trinity, the dogma of the union of divine and human natures in the incarnate Lord. They came to be regarded as permanent achievements, and were given an authority corresponding to the cruciality and intensity of the struggles which preceded them. But, when all is said and done, they were examples of the Church interpreting the Bible.

This interpretative achievement must, by the very facts of history, be regarded as in some sense irreversible. It is in fact this Bible-thus-interpreted and not just the Bible which today forms what we today call Christian doctrine and which underlies what we today call Christian faith. 'The Christ of the Church's faith' means the Christ of the faith of the Church of the first five centuries, not the Christ of the faith of the Church as it faces the Bible unaffected by Christian history, Christian tradition. The Fathers were, quite simply, those who first formed, or reflected the formation of, Christian tradition, who first made Christian doctrine, who first decided what the Bible meant, its drift, its burden, its main impression, its message. We cannot stand apart from, emancipate ourselves from, loftily ignore, this primary tradition. Either we accept it, or we modify it, or we react against it. What we cannot do is behave as if it had never occurred. It must be the point from which all subsequent consideration of Christian doctrine starts.

Very few people throughout the long reaches of Christian history have even attempted to start from the Bible and the Bible alone without any consideration of this primary Christian tradition. Certainly none of the great Reformers, Luther, Zwingli or Calvin, made any serious attempt to do so. Those who have done so are easily named – the Christian Scientists, the Mormons, the Witnesses of Jehovah. By their fruits they can be known. All modern discussion of Christian doctrine, from the early nineteenth century onwards, starts from this classical tradition. It has had no alternative.

We should therefore have no doubts about the importance of this patristic literature. In the essay dealing with it here a description is given of the useful and vigorous activity of international scholarship in this field of historical theology.

The second example of historical theology which is provided here is an account of the development of liturgy. Once again, this is a field which may strike the reader at first sight as totally irrelevant. At the words 'the history of liturgy' a picture is conjured up of ageing priests in archaic garments murmuring words in a forgotten tongue at ornate altars surrounded by the smoke of incense. We remember Browning's lines,

> To hear the blessed mutter of the Mass
> And see God made and eaten all day long.

Or we recall a picture of ineffectual Anglican clergy mouthing obsolete sentiments couched in Elizabethan English while the congregation drowses. 'Liturgy' suggests to many people everything that is remote, abstruse, obscurantist and pedantic in religion. It suggests a field of study that is the preserve of sacerdotally-minded clergy and academic-minded laity.

But, once again, if we were to surrender to these impressions and dismiss the history of liturgy as not worthy of attention we would be missing something both interesting and important in theology. The history of Christian doctrine is not simply the history of ideas, like the history of a philosophic school or of a literary or political movement. It is also the history of worship. We make a great mistake if we think that we can ignore the existence of Christian worship throughout history. While the theologians were forming their doctrines, while the doctrinal controversies were raging, while the commentaries and treatises were being written, Christians were offering worship to God, Sunday by Sunday, day by day, in unbroken continuity with their fellow-worshippers from the very beginning. This practice of worship strikes some people today as curious, indeed unaccountable, but it is *there*, and it always has been there. It is inconceivable that it should not have had some influence on Christian belief. The most elaborate, the most uncompromisingly dogmatic and intellectualist of the ancient creeds contains the words: 'And the Catholic faith is this, that we *worship* one God in Trinity and Trinity in unity.'

Belief and worship have always been closely related to each other. At least three of the major denominations regularly include a creed in their Eucharistic worship. The Church of England, apparently more credally-minded than any other group, requires her laity to say a creed at every service which they attend on Sundays and her clergy to repeat a creed twice a day every day of their lives. And just as creeds have made their impress on liturgy so liturgy is likely to have made its impress on creeds. We take the history of the Arian controversy as an example. This complex, thorny and confused controversy pursued its wearisome way for at least sixty years of the Church's history during the fourth century. It was a controversy over one of the most vital and central of theological questions, how divine is Jesus Christ? Every possible method of solving it was tried and every possible method failed. Theologians met and denounced each other, then retired to write books against each other. Councils of bishops met again and again, both large ecumenical councils and smaller local ones, all in vain. The Popes of Rome made pronouncements, one Pope on one side, his successor on the other, and solved nothing. Emperors used persuasion, and then coercion, and then persuasion again, and then coercion again. The ordinary Christian in the pew, when he was given a chance to speak, as he occasionally was, usually expressed himself by rioting. The modern historian, looking narrowly into the violent and agitated behaviour of these fourth-century Christians, will probably conclude that what finally settled the controversy in the sense that became the orthodox doctrine of the divinity of Christ was not the Popes, the Emperors, the councils and the theologians, but the steady pressure of the fact that Christ was worshipped as God by all Christians and that he had been so worshipped from the very earliest times of the Church. The law of prayer here decided the law of belief.

This is not to say that Christian doctrine has always been controlled by Christian cultic and devotional practice. There have indeed been periods when the theologians appeared to be simply following in the wake of the fancies of the devout. The medieval doctrine of Purgatory was partly built up by this process. But there have been other times when doctrine has led worship. The Reformed traditions in the sixteenth century drastically altered their worship because they had drastically altered their doctrine; much of the indignation expressed by the Reformers in their works is directed against late medieval liturgical and devotional practice, because it was thought to embody and rest upon, and also to encourage, false doctrine. Worship and belief interact, just as tradition and Scripture interact. But if we want to understand Christian thought, to leave out the consideration of Christian worship is to deprive ourselves of one of our main sources of information.

When we trace the development of patristic literature we discover something of how the intellectuals thought. But when we trace the development of Christian worship we are seeing theology at its grass-roots, theology from the inside, the theology of the ordinary man. We are coming as near as we can to seeing, not how people thought, but how they felt. What is more directly personal, what more existential, than prayer? Individuals often reveal themselves more fully in prayer than in conversation. The Pharisee no doubt impressed those who met him on the ordinary occasions of social intercourse as a grave, worthy and honest man, but when in his prayer he said, 'I thank thee, God, that I am not as other men', he revealed his odious inner character. Walter Scott in *Quentin Durward* with a very sure touch represents Louis XI of France exposing in his prayer to the statue of the Madonna his crafty bargaining soul as he asks her to forgive his murder of his brother in consideration of the expensive presents which he has given to her cult. Similarly Churches reveal in their worship their true ethos, whatever they may say in their confessions of faith and manuals of doctrine. If anyone wants to understand what the Eastern Orthodox Church, or the French Calvinists, or the Salvation Army are like, it is not enough for him merely to read their professions of faith. He must attend their worship.

The amazing atmosphere of being at home in the liturgy, the remarkable and touching informality within formality, of Orthodox worshippers, and likewise the appealing spontaneity, casualness and warmth of the Salvationists at worship, tell us as much about the real character of these bodies as any theological exposition could do.

There is therefore a good case to be made for studying the history of liturgy, not just contemporary liturgical practice (interesting though that is) but liturgy in its development through history. Liturgy, even contemporary liturgy, is often a mirror of history. Religion does, it must be admitted, tend to be intensely conservative. The Romans of the time of Augustus in the first century A.D. were still formally and publicly practising a religion which for its sacrificial cult used flint knives, because when metal knives were invented the rest of society moved on but religion kept to the old practice. The reason why the Jewish Passover ritual used (and still uses) unleavened bread is perhaps because this ritual went back to a period so early that the use of leaven had not yet been invented, and when it was invented it was thought best to retain the old type of bread in religious practices. The Irish Church in the ninth century was, as the Stowe Missal witnesses, still in its liturgy praying for 'the *two* emperors and their armies', even though it was then three centuries or more since there had ceased to be more than one Roman Emperor. Those members of the Church of England who use the 1662 Prayer Book still pray in their Communion Service for the governing authorities of England as they existed in the time of Queen Elizabeth I, for the Queen and her Privy Council, making no mention of Parliament, Cabinet or Prime Minister. Liturgy can sometimes become a kind of fossilized or petrified history.

But liturgy can also be an interesting guide to history as it moves and develops. In a sense the history of any religious body is the history of its worship. The Church is always at its most representative when it worships. The medieval congregation at mass is a kind of miniature of the medieval Church, with its hierarchically ordered society, its religious materialism, its sense of mystery. The early Victorian congregation gathered in its box-pews, with the poor occupying the free unfenced seats in the nave, listening, or not listening, to a long sermon from the black-gowned parson in his three-decker pulpit, such as we see depicted in illustrations to Dickens' early novels, is a cross-section of the early Victorian Church, with its strong consciousness of social distinctions, its sense, too, of the Church as an agent of social cohesion, and its concentration upon the sermon to the neglect of the sacrament. Worship is indeed a reflection of changing ideas, of the climate of religious opinion, of social and intellectual pressures; it is a kind of slow barometer of Christian opinion or prejudice. If we could reconstruct, as we probably could after some research, the kind of prayers which a Congregationalist minister would have used in 1868 and then contrast them with the prayers used by Congregational ministers in 1968, we would have a world of information about the development of Christian thought, opinion and prejudice during those hundred years, which could not be fully supplied by any theological works of the same period.

The scientific study of liturgy and of worship is a comparatively recent discipline. The significance of worship was scarcely fully understood until the middle of the last century. There had been liturgiologists before that, but they had been ill-informed and had had only inefficient tools to use, as the efforts towards comparative liturgiology of such figures as Cranmer and Laud witness. Liturgiology is still a young discipline. It is scarcely forty years since it first began to receive proper recognition in the theological schools of universities. There are still places, like Scotland and Germany, where it is little known in the universities. The study of liturgy has its own methods, its own terminology and, it must be conceded, sometimes (like other disciplines) its own pedantry. It has received little publicity and it is still virtually unknown to the man in the street. This adds to the reasons for including an account of the history of liturgy in a volume devoted to historical theology. Here is in a sense the history of experienced religion, religion as it is done.

The third essay in historical theology needs very little introduction. In this critical account of how the writing of recent Church history has been conducted for the last few hundred years the reader will discover not only a mine of information but also an arsenal of rockets. Here we are in a very different situation from that which faces us in other areas of historical theology. When we try to trace the history of Christianity in the ancient and in the medieval world, we are usually able to sketch the social and political background only faintly, though we would be most unwise to ignore it altogether. We can in these cases often only guess at the prevailing contemporary presuppositions, attitudes and prejudices, of the 'image' which people or institutions presented to the public of their day, those forces which, we know, must have influenced theological ideas and ecclesiastical institutions. In some cases (as often when we are dealing with the fifth and sixth centuries) our sources are fragmentary and indirect and leave large lacunae which we can scarcely fill even by guessing. But when we come to deal with recent Church history the sources which we can use are abundant. We are often presented with an *embarras de richesse*. We can much more readily imagine ourselves in the situation of those whose actions we are studying. We can look more deeply into their characters, there is even some excuse for employing conjectures about their psychology. Again, the study of recent Church history runs up into our own day. Some of the issues debated in it may run through our own hearts. It often involves us and becomes part of contemporary discussion. We can feel the history as living and as relevant in a way which we cannot experience when investigating earlier history. Both this fulness of material and this relevance are well illustrated in the last essay in this volume.

But it should be pointed out that the study of recent history suffers from one inevitable disadvantage. Our very involvement in it means that we do not know how it is going to end, and therefore, paradoxically, we have not all the means of judging it objectively. We are involved in many of the movements which are traced in it. We do not know where they will lead in the future. Here we can only guess, and study of past history suggests that our guesses are likely to be wrong. Bishop Joseph Butler in the middle of the eighteenth century appeared to think that the Church of England would collapse within a few generations. He could not appreciate the Evangelical nor foresee the Tractarian revivals. Gladstone at one point prophesied majestically that in generations to come men would recall a small town in West Cork where the Royal Irish Constabulary had fired upon a rioting crowd, and cry 'Remember Mitchelstown!' But who raises that cry now? The writing of the history of the recent past must involve much more tentative and provisional judgements than the writing of long past history. Curiously, but in fact logically, the last essay is the most subjective of the three.

Inevitably there is an element of arbitrariness about the choice of the subjects of these essays. This volume is not attempting to cover a field systematically. It is hoped that the reader will be satisfied if he feels that he has encountered three typical examples of how historical theology is conducted today, and if he is stimulated to delve further into the subject.

R. P. C. HANSON

Patristic Literature
by J. Daniélou

Translated by R. P. C. Hanson

List of Abbreviations

AC	*L'Antiquité Classique*
Ant	*Antonianum*
BLE	*Bulletin de Littérature Ecclésiastique*
BZ	*Byzantinische Zeitschrift*
Greg	*Gregorianum*
HTR	*Harvard Theological Review*
JTS	*Journal of Theological Studies*
MSR	*Mélanges de Science Religieuse*
OCP	*Orientalia Christiana Periodica*
RAM	*Revue d'Ascétique et de Mystique*
R Ben	*Revue Bénédictine*
RE Aug	*Revue des Études Augustiniennes*
REG	*Revue des Études Grecques*
RHPR	*Revue d'Histoire et de Philosophie Religieuses*
RSR	*Recherches de Science Religieuse*
Rev SR	*Revue des Sciences Religieuses*
SC	*Sources Chrétiennes*
Schol	*Scholastik*
SDB	*Supplément au Dictionnaire de la Bible*
SP	*Studia Patristica*
ST	*Studia Theologica*
VC	*Vigiliae Christianae*
ZKT	*Zeitschrift für Katholische Theologie*
ZNW	*Zeitschrift für Neutestamentliche Wissenschaft*
ZTK	*Zeitschrift für Theologie und Kirche*

Introduction[1]

The patristic period of Christian theology is regarded as that which coincides with the age of the Fathers of the Church. This definition involves several criteria of different sorts. In one sense it has a chronological meaning. It indicates the most ancient period of Christian theology, that which extends from the New Testament to the beginning of the Byzantine age in the East and to the High Middle Ages in the West. It also has a meaning for dogma. The Fathers of the Church are the witnesses of the belief of the ancient Church and enjoy in this respect a special authority in all Christian confessions. Finally the word 'patristic' has a literary reference: it indicates a certain type of theology which is different both from scholastic theology and from modern theology, but which can still be pursued today by some theologians. In the pages which follow we adopt these different points of view at times. But this procedure requires some further explanation. In a primary sense patristic theology denotes the Christian literature of the first six centuries as a whole, apart from the New Testament. Here the criterion is entirely concerned with accurate description. This literature embraces all Christian writers without paying any attention to their doctrinal authority. It includes the heterodox writers just as much as the orthodox. The task is nevertheless simplified by the fact that heterodox works have almost completely disappeared from the manuscript tradition. In this respect ancient Christian literature constitutes a branch of the history of types of ancient literature, Greek, Latin or Syriac.

1. The bibliographical references in the footnotes of this essay are the work of the author. The rest have been added by the translator, with the kind help of Mr G. Robinson.

It is only because of a particular dogmatic presupposition that the custom of dealing with it separately is maintained. All the same a work like the *Cambridge History of Philosophy* prints alternate chapters on the pagan philosophers like Plotinus and Porphyry and on the Christian theologians like Origen and Gregory of Nyssa.

The writing of the history of Christian literature started early in Christian antiquity. People such as Eusebius of Caesarea in the fourth century and Jerome in the fifth century busied themselves with preserving records of the earliest ecclesiastical writers. The Latin Middle Ages, preoccupied by dogmatic problems, showed only a modified interest in literary history. But at Byzantium the patriarch Photius has left us in his *Library* accounts, which are sometimes extended summaries, of a large number of pagan or Christian writings of which many have now disappeared. The Renaissance gave a new and important impulse to the process. The humanists, in the course of hunting out and editing the manuscripts of Classical authors, turned up and published the manuscripts of many Christian writers. The work of publishing manuscripts was continued in the seventeenth and eighteenth centuries by the labours of people like Fronton du Duc, Combefis and Montfaucon.

But it was in the nineteenth century that the study of ancient Christian literature developed into a science. While investigators like Maï or Pitra continued to turn up texts, the concern to produce critical editions made itself felt. This found expression in such great compilations as the *Corpus Scriptorum Ecclesiasticorum Latinorum*, published in Vienna since 1866, and *Die griechischen christlichen Schriftsteller der ersten drei Jahrhunderte*, published in Berlin since 1897. At the same time histories of ancient Christian literature by Adolf von Harnack and by Bardenhewer were appearing. The interest which had hitherto been confined to the great Christian authors was extended to the whole period of ancient Christianity. Particular interest was shown in the apocrypha of the New Testament preserved in Coptic, in Syriac and in Armenian. The series

Texts and Studies, published from 1891 onwards by J. A. Robinson, played an important part in these.

In our own time patristic studies are flourishing in many countries. Since 1951 the International Congress of Patristic Studies, founded by F. L. Cross, has been bringing together every four years the patristic experts of the whole world. W. Schneemelcher in Bonn publishes every year a *Bibliographia Patristica*. Werner Jaeger had before his death gathered at Harvard a team of scholars who were editing the works of Gregory of Nyssa. The collection *Sources Chrétiennes* has given a new impulse in France to patristic studies. Italy possesses lively centres of research into the ancient Christian writers in Turin, Milan and Rome. In Holland Christine Mohrmann has demonstrated the originality of Christian Latin. Amazing discoveries have opened new fields of research. The chief of these is the discovery of the Gnostic library at Nag Hammadi, of which only a meagre part has been actually edited. Unknown works of Origen and of Didymus the Blind have been unearthed, also in Egypt, at Toura.

This study of ancient Christian literature is one aspect of the history of culture. Its aim is to place the works of the Christian writers of antiquity on their chronological and environmental background. This applies to the literary aspects also. Origen or Augustine were influenced in their exegesis by the methods of literary criticism used by the grammarians of their time. Gregory of Nyssa or John Chrysostom are listed among the representatives of the Second Sophistic era. Gregory of Nazianzus or Prudentius observe the poetic literary forms of the ancient world. The links of Justin and of Clement of Alexandria with Middle Platonism have been traced. Basil of Caesarea and Gregory of Nyssa were aware of both Plotinus and neo-Stoicism. In certain respects this study makes us realize that the Fathers of the Church belonged to a world of culture different from our own. It makes us aware of their distance from us. But at the same time it enables us to distinguish the enduring content of their message from this cultural wrapping.

This brings us to a second aspect of patristic theology, and here the interest is not its literary side, but its doctrinal authority. We have just been speaking of ancient Christian literature. We are now speaking of the Fathers of the Church. The two fields only partly overlap. Antiquity, as such, is no criterion of authority. It is obvious, as Walter Bauer has well shown, that in the first period of the Church's life it is very difficult to distinguish between orthodoxy and heterodoxy. Some doctrines were professed by the first generations of Christians, such as millenniarism, which were not endorsed by later teaching. The ideas of the Trinity which we meet in the second and the third century are almost all infected with error. It is equally true that the great teachers are not the writers of the second and the third century, Tertullian, Clement of Alexandria and Origen, but those of the fourth and fifth centuries, Athanasius, Basil, the two Gregories, Jerome, Augustine. And this is easily understandable. It should be clear that if the faith of the Apostles, enshrined in the Scriptures, is the norm of belief, the articulation of this given faith, called forth as problems present themselves, cannot but be a developing one. Consequently the Trinitarian theology of St Gregory of Nazianzus is more orthodox than that of St Justin. This is what is called the development of dogma.

Where then are we to place the authority of these old theologians who are called the Fathers of the Church? What sort of authority will it be, if they were only the witnesses of an obsolete theology? At this point we must explain what the term 'Father' means in ancient Christian literature. The word does not primarily have any connexion with a man's personal quality. The word denotes essentially the bishops in as far as they are the witnesses of tradition. The word was used in this sense in the fourth century. St Basil writes about the bishops who met at Nicaea: 'What we teach is not at all the outcome of our own thoughts, but what we have learnt from the holy Fathers' (*Epistles* 140.2). And Gregory of Nyssa in his turn says, 'Recall the holy Fathers to mind, those whose tradition we too by the grace of God have been judged worthy to preserve. Walk in the ancient rule of faith' (*Epistles* 3).

Here we have reached the first element in the definition of the Fathers'. Taken in this sense, the expression does not denote writers who enjoy an unusual personal reputation, but the bishops in as far as they enjoy an authority bound up with their function. They are the Fathers in that they are the witnesses of the common faith of the Church. This faith is the ancient faith, in accordance with the fact that their function is to transmit the faith received from the Apostles. This is just where there is a link with primitive Christianity. But what constitutes the authority of the Fathers is not, as is sometimes thought, the fact that they are nearer the origins. We have shown that this criterion is invalid. R. P. C. Hanson has proved how deceptive in this respect was the earliest Christian literature. What constitutes their authority is a divine gift bound up with their function which guarantees that their concrete teaching is consistent with the doctrine of the Apostles. It is impossible to define the authority of the Fathers of the Church without appealing to the concept of tradition, not in the popular sense which means the inheritance of the past, but in the Biblical sense of divine aid safeguarding against error in the handing on of the faith.

This first characteristic is not enough of itself to define the Fathers in the usual meaning of the word. It has happened that as a matter of fact some bishops held personal opinions which do not form part of the tradition. Some have even held heresies and have consequently abandoned the faith shared in common. This is the case with figures such as Apollinaris, Eunomius or Nestorius. Bishops are therefore regarded as Fathers as long as they witness to the common faith. In this respect it is not the individual quality of their work which counts, but on the contrary their sharing of the faith in common with other bishops. It is on this score that the Councils, whether local or ecumenical, will appear as the expression *par excellence* of the faith of bishops and that there will be attributed to them an authority which each bishop does not possess individually.

It is on the basis of these facts that it is possible to explain what is meant by 'the Fathers of the Church' in the meaning which we give to this expression. It does involve the kind of authority which we have defined but it also takes account of the more outstanding quality of certain figures. Accordingly all the bishops of Christian antiquity will not be called Fathers of the Church, but those who may appear as the great witnesses of the faith of the Church. The expression consequently could even be extended to ecclesiastical writers, such as Jerome or Ephrem, who only had lesser responsibilities in the Church. Some great Christian teachers, such as Origen or Theodore of Mopsuestia, are not regarded as Fathers of the Church, because some of their doctrines have been made the subject of condemnation after their death. They join the number, according to Prestige's epigram, of 'those who entered the Church of Heaven before being excluded from the Church on earth'. But this does not prevent the possibility of a part of their work being appealed to as witnessing to the common faith, just as conversely the most authoritative Fathers are not exempt from sometimes producing errors. The term 'Father of the Church' has in this respect to be used with some flexibility.

There remains a third element contributing to the character of patristic theology, and one which is certainly the most impressive: it is that which represents the idea of Christian understanding, in which Biblical exegesis, speculative reasoning and mystical contemplation were fused in a synthesis which has never been fully recovered. This is the reason why the Fathers of the Church have at all periods exercised an attraction. We can observe one of these renewals of interest in the twelfth century, centring in St Bernard and William of St-Thierry. In the seventeenth century the 'solitaries' of Port-Royal, in France, and the 'Caroline divines' in England learnt at the feet of the Fathers. It was their influence which people such as Moehler and Newman felt anew at the beginning of the nineteenth century. And much of contemporary theology has been revitalized from patristic sources.

Patristic theology is primarily a way of looking at the Bible. Scriptural commentaries form the largest part of it. Writers like Origen or Jerome wrote commentaries on the whole of Scripture. This aspect of the Fathers has often been neglected; it has achieved its proper place in our day. The Fathers did not neglect the methodical study of Biblical texts. But their interest is principally theological. The Bible gives its witness to the history of salvation. Their interpretation consists in explaining the analogies between the Old and the New Testaments, and in showing that it is the same divine activity which is contained in the life of the Church and in the Christian life. There are basic analogies between the crossing of the Red Sea, the Resurrection of Christ, and Christian baptism. This is what is called typology. This process, whose validity had been misunderstood and which had been confused with the use of allegory, has today taken its place in the development of the theology of history.

I have said that the Fathers placed the Bible in the context of the Christian life. Another characteristic of their theology is that it is involved in the life of the Church. Almost all the Fathers of the Church, as we have pointed out, were bishops. Their pastoral work put them in contact with the life of Christian communities. For them preaching is the action of the Word of God in the Christian congregation. The explanation of the sacraments is one of their special privileges in teaching. But the Christian life is also a call to holiness. A large number of the Fathers of the Church, John Chrysostom, Basil, Augustine, Jerome, had previously been monks. Theological speculation was not separated in their minds from contemplation. The same men at this period were great bishops, great theologians and great saints. Those who read them meet not only ideas but also encounter a living experience.

But this practical side of the writings of the Fathers does not in the least exclude theological rigour. The age of the Fathers of the Church is the one in which the problem arose of the right statement of the realities involved in the events of Christ's life. The Bible witnessed that Christ was man and that he was God, that beside the Father there were the Son and the Spirit, but it was necessary to state clearly in detail what this meant. The Fathers of the Church are those who by the style of their theology have chiefly contributed to the correct formulation of the data of the faith. They were exegetes and men of prayer, but they also were theologians in the most precise meaning of the word. Yet this theology was never separated in their minds from Scripture and from experience. And it is this impressive cohesion which explains the attraction which they continue to exert and the paradigmatic quality of their work.

We have stated that the study of the Fathers of the Church is today in full swing. Rather than supplying general ideas about the principles of the Fathers of the Church, I have attempted in the pages which follow to give a sketch of the actual state of research in this field. This is why I have concentrated particularly upon some writers and upon some lesser-known problems. Rather than placing the emphasis exclusively upon some outstanding figures, I have preferred to show the complexity of the movements of thought and so to give an idea of the richness and diversity of the Patristic age of theology. Placed in this way in their context, the Fathers of the Church perhaps lose something of their 'stained-glass' character, but they appear closer to us, and doubtless can consequently assist us the better to solve our own problems.

One

Judeo-Christian Patristic Literature

Christianity was born in a Jewish environment, and it was in the Jewish environments of Asia Minor, of Alexandria and of Rome, that it proceeded to grow. Its first expressions, then, were related to the Jewish culture, Aramaic or Greek, of the first century of our era. This Judeo-Christian period of patristic literature for a long time remained difficult to identify. On the one side few complete works survived, and what did survive was mainly fragments. On the other, we knew little of the Judaism of this period. That is why there is no mention of this Judeo-Christian literature in the older accounts of patristic literature.

This is undoubtedly the field in which patristic studies have during the last twenty years made the most amazing progress.[1] This progress is mainly due to the fact that we now know the Jewish background of the period much better. The discovery of the Dead Sea Scrolls has here been the decisive factor in supplying the means of an exact comparison.[2] The *Manual of Discipline*, for instance, included a treatise about the Two Ways[3] which supplied the background to the ethical part of the *Didache*, and the *Psalms of Thanksgiving* supplied something with which the *Odes of Solomon* could be compared.

At the same time, mainly during the last ten years, studies in Rabbinic literature have made great steps forward which enable us to discern for the future the different stages of the redaction of this literature and to identify that which is rele-

1. *Aspects du Judéo-christianisme*, Paris, 1965; Bellarmino Bagatti, *L'Église de la circoncision*, Jerusalem, 1965.

2. See Matthew Black, *The Scrolls and Christian Origins*, London, 1961.

3. Life and Death.

vant to the Judaism of about the Christian era. Here again discoveries like that of the Neofiti Codex, which gives us an archaic Targum, have played an important part.[4] These discoveries, added to the Jewish works of this period which we already knew, such as the *Book of Enoch* and the Jubilees, have given Judeo-Christian literature its *Sitz im Leben*.[5]

A third type of investigation has enabled us to throw light on Judeo-Christian literature. These are the investigations concerned with Gnosticism. Gnosticism is a dualist[6] religion which appears in the second century in Syria and in Egypt. Its origins are much debated.[7] But it is certain that this religion appears in a Jewish and in a Judeo-Christian milieu. It borrowed a number of features from the Jewish and Judeo-Christian culture of the time.[8] It therefore constitutes a new source of knowledge for this last subject. Till very recently we knew Gnosticism almost exclusively from the accounts of its Christian opponents. The discovery of the Gnostic library of Nag Hammadi, which has given us original texts, allows us to draw much firmer conclusions.[9]

Judeo-Christian literature reproduces the literary forms of the Judaism of its time. Expositions of the Old Testament inspired by Rabbinic methods are to be found in it. The Old Testament remained the unique Bible for the earliest Christian community. Christian teachers expounded it just as other Jewish rabbis did. But their exegesis had this peculiarity, that it demonstrated in the events of Christ's life the accomplishment of what the prophets had declared. One of the forms of Jewish exegesis was the *Targum*, that is the translation into Aramaic of a Hebrew text, but this translation constituted at the same time a kind of commentary.

It is possible that there was a kind of Christian version of

4. See Roger le Déaut, *La Nuit pascale*, Rome, 1963, pp. 19–71.

5. Situation in life from which it evolved.

6. A theory explaining the universe as having two absolute but opposed elements in it, for example spirit and matter.

7. See *Recherches sur le Gnosticisme*, Leiden, 1967.

8. R. M. Grant, *Gnosticism and Early Christianity*, New York, 1959.

9. Jean Doresse, *Les Livres secrets des gnostiques d'Égypte*, Paris, 1958.

some books of the Bible, especially the Psalms and Isaiah. This is what a phrase of Justin[10] seems to imply (*Dial.* LXXI.2). But this Targumic interpretation is only preserved for us in the collections of *Testimonia*. The Christians, following the example of the Jews, used to make collections of quotations relevant to particular subjects, for example passages critical of ceremonial observances, Messianic prophecies, etc. There can be observed in these quotations a great flexibility in using the Biblical text: quotations are abridged; quotations from different places are conflated; above all, certain additions give the text a more explicitly Christian meaning.[11]

Another literary form is well known to us from the Dead Sea Scrolls. It is the 'pesher'. It consists of a commentary in which after each phrase of the Biblical text the writer explains how it ought to be interpreted in the light of its fulfilment. A certain number of expositions of this type have been preserved in the *Epistle of Barnabas*. Finally, Jewish literature of the time used to employ the 'midrash', which is a very free development of the text of Scripture – the *Book of Jubilees*, for instance, or the *Genesis Apocryphon* reproduces this form. The *Epistle of Barnabas* gives us fragments of a midrash on Exodus, particularly on the rites connected with the festivals.[12] A long fragment of a midrash on Ezekiel has been found, which is quoted elsewhere by various writers.[13]

Besides the exegesis of Scriptures, Jewish literature of the time included works of different literary form, apocalypses, testaments, parables, psalms, lists of rules. These writings were sometimes gathered together in composite works. Thus the *Book of Enoch* collects together three apocalypses and a book of parables. The *Manual of Discipline* of Qumran contains a

10. See pages 44ff.

11. E. Earle Ellis, *Paul's Use of the Old Testament*, Edinburgh, 1957; Jean Daniélou, *Études d'exégèse judéo-chrétienne*, Paris, 1966.

12. *Barnabas and the Didache, A New Translation and Commentary*, by Robert A. Kraft, New York and London, 1965.

13. 'Some Fragments of the Apocryphal Ezekiel', edited by Campbell Bonner, in *Studies and Documents*, XII, London, 1940, pp. 183–90.

part devoted to regulations, a catechetical part and a liturgical part. This composite character reappears in Judeo-Christian writings. The *Didache* includes a liturgical portion, an ethical portion and an apocalypse; the *Epistle of Barnabas* an exegetical section and an ethical section; the *Ascension of Isaiah* an account of a martyrdom and an apocalypse; the *Epistle of the Apostles* a testament, a catechism and an apocalypse; the *Shepherd* of Hermas an apocalypse, an ethical part and parables.

Most of the Jewish literary forms reappear in Judeo-Christian literature. Above all there was the apocalypse, which is the unveiling of the secrets of the heavenly world and of the epochs of history. We possess an apocalypse of this sort in the second part of the *Ascension of Isaiah*, which describes for us first the ascension of the prophet through the seven heavens and shows us what he saw there, and then shows us the descent of the Beloved (that is, the Son of God) and his ascension. There has been found at Akem an *Apocalypse of Peter* which describes the punishments of the damned and the rewards of the elect. Codex V of Nag Hammadi contains an *Apocalypse of Paul* which is not Gnostic.[14] Papias[15] has handed down to us fragments of primitive Christian apocalypses. The *Visions* in the *Shepherd* of Hermas reproduce the apocalyptic form.

The Testament form is represented above all by the *Testament of the XII Patriarchs*. Here the Judeo-Christian character is obvious. In this we possess a Jewish work – and apparently Essene – worked over by the Christians.[16] The first part of the *Epistle of the Apostles*, which exists also in an independent form, is a Testament of Jesus in Galilee. The *Apocryphon of James*, found at Nag Hammadi, reproduces the same literary form. Another form, well known from the Gospels, is that of parables. According to Eusebius,[17] Papias recounted

14. See *RSR* 54 (1966), pp. 285–6.
15. Papias of Hierapolis, *c.*130; only fragments of his work survive.
16. M. de Jonge, *The Testament of the Twelve Patriarchs*, Assen, 1953.
17. See Chapter 5.

'curious parables' (*Ecclesiastical History*, III.39.11), attributing them to the Lord. The third part of the *Shepherd* of Hermas is a collection of parables.

One of the most precious inheritances of Judeo-Christianity is that of the liturgical texts and hymns. They appear at the very end of the first century and are connected with Edessa.[18] The *Didache*, at the same time as it informs us about the Judeo-Christian liturgy, has handed down to us three Eucharistic prayers whose Jewish basis is obvious.[19] Otto Knoch has shown that the liturgical parts of the *First Epistle of Clement* were earlier than the work itself, indeed come from the middle of the first century, and that they are indebted in their style to the liturgy of the Hellenistic synagogue of Rome.[20] Finally the ethical catechetical works, presented under the form of the Two Ways, which are to be found in the *Didache*, the *Epistle of Barnabas* and the *Shepherd*, are influenced according to all the evidence, if not by the Essene *Manual*, at least by the Jewish catechetical tradition founded upon Deuteronomy.

But Judeo-Christian literature does not only include works of a Jewish literary form. It also includes compositions which are characteristically Christian, but which originate nevertheless from a Jewish background. It is in this class that a certain number of primitive Gospels and Acts must be placed. As far as the Gospels are concerned, we possess, thanks to Clement of Alexandria,[21] Eusebius of Caesarea and St Jerome[22] in particular, fragments which are certainly Judeo-Christian coming from works of different sorts. The *Gospel of the Nazarenes* is an orthodox text of an avowedly Jewish character; the *Gospel of the Hebrews*, Egyptian in origin, has

18. J. de Zwaan, 'The Edessene Origin of The Odes of Solomon', *Quantulacumque* (Studies Presented to Kirsopp Lake), London, 1937, pp. 285–302.

19. Jean-Paul Audet, *La Didachè. Instructions des apôtres*, Paris, 1958.

20. *Eigenart und Bedeutung der Eschatologie im theologischen Aufriss des ersten Clemensbriefes*, Bonn, 1964, pp. 56–64.

21. See Chapter 2.

22. See Chapter 8.

Encratite[23] features; the *Gospel of the Ebionites* comes from a heterodox sect.

The most important text is the *Gospel of Peter*; it was read in some churches; the fragments of it which survive include a passage of apocalyptic character on the resurrection. In addition the papyri of Egypt have yielded fragments which are related to our Synoptic Gospels, but which are not found in them, particularly Pap. Egerton 2 and Oxyrhynchus v, 840. The question of ascertaining whether the *Gospel of Thomas*, found at Nag Hammadi, which is certainly Gnostic, uses non-canonical Judeo-Christian traditions has been raised by Quispel.[24] But it seems in fact to have been answered in the negative.[25] The *Gospel of James*, which describes the infancy of Christ and mixes legendary elements with it, comes from the middle of the second century and has Encratite features reminiscent of certain Judeo-Christian circles.[26]

We possess a group of apocryphal Acts of the Apostles, *Acts of Peter*, *of John*, *of Thomas*, *of Andrew*. These works come from the end of the second century. They present Judeo-Christian traits, particularly in their hostility to marriage and in their mystique of the Cross.[27] But some traditions about the Apostles go back to an earlier date, especially those which derive from Papias, mainly concerned with Philip and John, and those which Clement of Alexandria has preserved in his *Hypotyposes*. The traditions about James of Jerusalem[28] are particularly important, preserved by combining the accounts

23. Encratites are persons who abstain from flesh and wine and from marriage. They were to be found in various sects.

24. 'The Gospel of Thomas and the New Testament', *VC* 11 (1957), pp. 189–207.

25. Wolfgang Schrage, *Das Verhältnis des Thomas Evangeliums zur synoptischen Tradition und zur den Koptischen Evangelienübersetzungen*, Berlin, 1964; R. McL. Wilson, *Studies on the Gospel of Thomas*, London, 1960.

26. See Émile de Strycker, *La Forme la plus ancienne du protévangelie de Jacques*, Brussels, 1961.

27. See Erik Peterson, *Christentum Judentum und Gnosis*, Freiburg, 1959, pp. 183–220.

28. The brother of the Lord.

of Hegesippus,[29] of the pseudo-Clementine writings[30] and the second *Apocalypse of James* in Codex V of Nag Hammadi. Similarly we are justified in regarding the *Epistles of Ignatius* of Antioch and the *First Epistle of Clement* of Rome as works related to the literary forms of the New Testament.

It is worth observing that, in contrast to the anonymous literature with which we have been dealing hitherto, these writings are connected with easily recognized people. We have here works of an official character which derive their authority from the fact of their being connected with bishops, as the New Testament Epistles are connected with the Apostles. Just as much as the New Testament Epistles, they have the moral welfare of the churches as their object. The *First Epistle of Clement* of Rome is concerned with the divisions in the Church of Corinth. By its interests, which are ethical rather than eschatological, and by its concept of ecclesiastical order, it shows the influence of the Hellenistic Judaism of the synagogues of Rome. The *Epistles of Ignatius* of Antioch manifest by their unwearied emphasis upon the unity of the Churches round their bishop the continuance of conflicts between Judeo-Christians and Gentile Christians in the Churches of Asia Minor at the beginning of the second century. They are the most precious witness in this period to the Christian experience of a life which is already transformed by union with the risen Christ and which hopes for its consummation in glory.

Finally we can perceive manifesting itself at this period a Judeo-Christian missionary literature directed towards the poor and influenced by the missionary literature of Hellenistic Judaism. Just as the Jews had initiated the Greek *Sibylline Oracles*, so the Christians were influenced by the Jewish

29. A second-century Church historian, his work only survives as fragments quoted by Eusebius.

30. Forgeries including letters from Clement to James; probably written in the fourth century, but using sources that may go back to the second.

Sibylline Oracles, and put into the mouth of pagan Sibyls[31] prophecies about Christ, the Church and the Last Judgement. Book V of the collection of *Sibylline Oracles* is a Jewish production worked over by the Christians in the time of Vespasian.[32] Book VI is completely Christian and dates from the beginning of the second century. We possess on the other hand some fragments of a *Preaching of Peter* which is a presentation of the Christian message to the Greek world.

We have now given a full list of the Judeo-Christian literature which can be regarded as representing the expression of the common faith. But it would be giving an incomplete picture of Judeo-Christianity not to mention some marginal movements which were connected with it. It is difficult, however, to demarcate the limits. In the works which we have mentioned there are many features which will later on be regarded as heterodox; this applies, for instance, to the representation of the Son and the Spirit as angels, to dualistic tendencies in Christology, against which Ignatius of Antioch is already reacting, to the claim to 'gnosis' (knowledge) of heavenly secrets, and to the radical asceticism which disparages marriage. There are however in addition some circles which teach doctrines which are in conflict with the common faith on essential points and which form peripheral sects. This is the case with the Ebionites, who acknowledged in Jesus the last of the prophets but rejected his divinity.[33] They are a kind of preliminary sketch for what will later be Islam. The Helcesaites were devotees of a revelation which was attributed to someone called Elksai, and were related to Ebionism. But the most important phenomenon is the appearance, with Simon Magus, Menander and Satorninus, of a dualism which looked like the expression

31. Originally there was only one Sibyl, from Marpessus near Troy (*c.* 700 B.C.), a prophetess of Apollo. But as her fame spread so did her identities. One Roman historian, Varro, lists ten Sibyls.

32. Roman Emperor A.D. 69–79.

33. Hans Joachim Schoeps, *Theologie und Geschichte des Judenchristentums*, Tübingen, 1949.

of a revolt against Yahweh within Judaism, but which tried to turn to its advantage the Christians' break with Israel.

As we look at this account of the Judeo-Christian literary heritage it is possible to disentangle some of its features which enable us to be more exact about it. We have noticed the use of Rabbinic methods in exegesis and the Two Ways pattern in ethics. But the importance of certain theological patterns borrowed from the Judaism of the time must be underlined.[34] This applies to some titles given to Christ which have a markedly Jewish ring: the Name, the Day, the Covenant, the Law. We have also referred to the use of angel-categories to denote the Son and the Spirit. All this goes back ultimately to Jewish speculations about the divine Names, the divine Powers and the angels in which the Judeo-Christians quarried to find there tools for expressing their Trinitarian faith.

But the most remarkable feature of Judeo-Christian theology is the way in which it was influenced by the structures of Jewish apocalyptic. This consisted of a gnosis, a knowledge of hidden secrets about sacred space and time, that is the heavens and the people who live there and the events at the end of time. One cannot help noticing the place which these speculations about heavenly and hellish dwelling places, about angels and devils, occupy in Judeo-Christian literature. And it is precisely in the context of these images that the mystery of Christ is expressed: it is the descent of the Son through successive heavens in the Incarnation. The Descent into Hell takes a large place. And the Ascension, rather than the Resurrection, is the Judeo-Christian mystery, as the exaltation above all angelic worlds of the human nature which the Son has united to himself.

Further, Judeo-Christianity expresses itself in the categories of the theology of history to be found in the apocalypses. All history is written in advance in the heavenly books. In particular Christ and the Church pre-existed in the design of God. Their appearance ushers in the End of Time. A typical feature

34. Jean Daniélou, *A History of Early Christian Doctrine I. The Theology of Jewish Christianity*, London, 1964.

of all these Judeo-Christian documents is the return of Christ to reign for a thousand years on the earth, restoring the terrestrial paradise, before the inauguration of the eternal kingdom.[35] Here once more the Christian faith has looked for means of expression in contemporary Jewish speculations. Judeo-Christianity is the reflection of the Christian faith in the categories of Jewish apocalyptic.

35. This belief is called millenarianism.

Two

The Birth of Greek Patristic Literature

The Gospel came into contact with the Greek world from the very beginnings of the apostolic period. But it is only after the close of the first period that it was really confronted with Hellenistic culture. This confrontation had already been achieved earlier by the Jews. The work of Philo of Alexandria[1] in the first century of our era witnesses to this. But the Christians had to make this confrontation in their turn. It occupied the second and the third centuries. During this period the Christians will have to win their place in society and in Greco-Roman culture. In the fourth century their success will be assured and Christian Hellenism will be able to spread its wings freely in a society and a culture which is henceforward Christian.

Here once again patristic studies have achieved considerable progress during the last thirty years, owing to a better knowledge of the cultural background, which is that of the Hellenism of the age of the Antonines.[2] The most important question is that of Middle Platonism, that is to say the period of Platonic thought which runs from Antiochus of Ascalon at the beginning of the first century B.C. to Ammonius Sakkas at the opening of the third century, and which is represented in the second century A.D. mainly by Numenius, Maximus of Tyre and Albinus. The labours of R. E. Witt,[3] of Willy Theiler,[4]

1. *c.* 30 B.C. to *c.* A.D. 45. He produced a synthesis of Hebrew and Platonic thought, and is famous for the allegorical interpretation of the Old Testament which he used to achieve this.

2. A.D. 138–92.

3. *Albinus and the History of Middle Platonism*, Cambridge, 1937.

4. *Die Vorbereitung des Neuplatonismus*, Berlin, 1930.

of J. H. Waszink,[5] of A. M. J. Festugière,[6] of Philip Merlan[7] and of Hendryk Kraemer[8] have completely revolutionized our knowledge of this philosophical background.

Another field has been revolutionized, that of the influence of the works of Aristotle's youth, in particular the *Protreptikos*, the *De philosophia* and the *Eudemus*. The influence of these works, now lost, on the Christian apologists of the second century, has been established especially by Luigi Alfonsi.[9] The question of Stoic thought in the second century is more difficult to decide. It is represented primarily by the moralists, like Epictetus and Marcus Aurelius. The continuance of the Middle Stoicism of Panetius and Posidonius, contemporaries of Antiochus of Ascalon, has been both asserted and denied. It is sure however that Stoicism had also exerted an influence on Christian thought, as M. Spanneut[10] has shown.

We have a picture of this philosophical background at the beginning of the *Dialogue with Trypho the Jew* of Justin.[11] Justin is the first great figure of Hellenistic Christianity. He was born in Samaria, but of a pagan family. He tells us that in his search for wisdom he approached in turn a Stoic, an Aristotelian, a Pythagorean and a Platonist. It was to the Platonist that he finally attached himself before his conversion to Christianity. When he became a Christian he continued to wear the philosopher's cloak and founded a school at Rome. Only three works of his have come down to us: an *Apology* addressed to Antoninus,[12] a second *Apology* and the *Dialogue with Trypho*. Now Carl Andresen has shown that in his

5. 'Der Platonismus und die altchristliche Gedankenwelt', in *Recherches sur la tradition platonicienne*, Geneva, 1936, pp. 137–79.

6. *La Révélation d'Hermès Trismégiste*, 4 vols., Paris, 1954–64.

7. *From Platonism to Neoplatonism*, The Hague, 1960.

8. *Der Ursprung der Geistmetaphysik*, Amsterdam, 1964.

9. See in particular 'Motivi tradizionali del giovane Aristotele in Clemente Alessandrino e in Atenagora', *V C* 7 (1953), pp. 133–5.

10. *Le Stoicisme des Pères de l'Église*, Paris, 1957.

11. Died A.D. 165.

12. Roman Emperor A.D. 138–61.

theology of the Word particularly Justin was influenced by the Middle Platonism of Albinus.[13]

Justin's chief disciple was Tatian.[14] He came from Adiabene, and was a pupil of Justin at Rome. He is well known for his *Diatessaron*, a kind of synopsis of the four Gospels with extra-canonical elements, which he produced for the Church of his native country after his return from Rome. His chief interest for us is his *Address to the Greeks*. It is a violent piece of propaganda against paganism. In contrast to Justin, Tatian attacks not only the Greek cults but also the philosophers. It is nevertheless true, as Martin Elze has shown, that his thought contains elements of Middle-Platonic philosophy.[15] It does not seem likely, in spite of the articles of R. M. Grant[16] and of R. McL. Wilson,[17] that he had Gnostic leanings.

It is again with Middle Platonism that Athenagoras was connected. He addressed a *Petition* on behalf of the Christians to the Emperors Marcus Aurelius[18] and Commodus,[19] between 177 and 180. Athenagoras however seems to be closer to Plutarch and to Numenius than to Albinus because of the emphasis he places on the evil world-soul in connexion with matter. It is also with Middle Platonism that the more philosophical sections of a work dedicated in the reign of Marcus Aurelius by the bishop of Antioch, Theophilus, to someone called Autolycus are connected. In contrast, the anonymous author of the *Epistle to Diognetus* seems rather more influenced by Stoic views. At the same time a certain philosophical eclecticism is a feature of Christian writers from this period onwards. 3

Recent investigations on this period have been able to restore to his proper importance Melito, bishop of Sardis under

13. 'Justin und der mittlere Platonismus', *Z N W* 44 (1952–3), pp. 157–95.

14. *c.* 120–after 174.

15. *Tatian und seine Theologie*, Göttingen, 1960.

16. 'The Heresy of Tatian', *J T S* 5 (1954), pp. 62–8.

17. 'The Early Exegesis of Gen. 1, 26', *S P* 1 (1957), pp. 427–8.

18. A.D. 161–80.

19. A.D. 180–92.

Marcus Aurelius. Eusebius attributes a certain number of works to him, among them two books on the Easter festival. One of the most important of contemporary discoveries is that of a *Homily on the Passion* of which we possess the complete text; F. L. Cross sees in this one of the most valuable recoveries of Christian antiquity.[20] Some fragments should be added to this whose evidence has been studied by R. M. Grant.[21] Eusebius quotes a fragment of Melito's *Apology* addressed to Marcus Aurelius and gives a list of the books of the Old Testament which formed part of his *Eclogae*. But there must certainly be added to these a short Paschal hymn, edited among the Bodmer papyri, which Othmar Perler attributes to him,[22] and a fragment of a work *On Baptism* which R. M. Grant regards as authentic.

Other texts are more uncertain. It is quite possible that the 'distinguished' man to whom Irenaeus[23] refers in several passages is Melito and that chapters xxv–xxx of the *Adversus haereses* Book V are influenced by him, as Widmann has suggested.[24] This influence of Melito on Irenaeus could specially affect his view of history as a progressive development, which derives from Stoicism. Melito appears to be specially influenced by Stoicism. The last section of the *Epistle to Diognetus* is a kind of sermon whose resemblances to the Homily are striking. Finally a work *Against the Jews* wrongly attributed to Cyprian,[25] which is earlier than Tertullian,[26] is a kind of Latin translation of Melito, as Erik Peterson has suggested.[27]

The encounter with Hellenism which distinguishes the middle

20. *The Early Christian Fathers*, London, 1960, pp. 103–9.

21. 'The Fragments of the Greek Apologists and Irenaeus' in *Special Print of Biblical and Patristic Studies in Memory of Robert Pierce Casey*, New York, 1964, pp. 192–201.

22. *Ein Hymnus zur Ostervigil von Meliton?*, Fribourg, 1960.

23. See below, pages 47–8, 51.

24. 'Irenäus und seine theologische Väter', *Z T K* 24 (1957), p. 167.

25. See pages 74–7.

26. See pages 64–70.

27. 'Ps.-Cypriani Adversus Judaeos und Melito von Sardes', *V C* 6 (1959), pp. 33–41.

of the second century also affected the heterodox versions of Christianity. The opponents of heresy, Irenaeus and Hippolytus[28] in particular, go as far as seeing in the heretical sects the persistence of the Greek schools of philosophy. We have already said that Gnosticism is Judeo-Christian in origin. But it is still true that it too drew its inspiration in the second century from Greek philosophy in order to seek there the tools to make a system. The task was all the easier because Platonism itself implied a cosmological dualism. This dualism was quite different from the Gnostic dualism. It was based on the original opposition between the divine monad and matter. But it was easily capable of providing ingredients for the anti-cosmic dualism of Gnosticism.

The great exponent of this Hellenistic Gnosticism was one of the most eminent minds of the second century, Valentinus. He was born in Egypt, but he also betook himself to Rome, where he seems to have taken part in the life of the Church. Till recently his work, apart from short fragments, was only known to us by the accounts of the opponents of heresy. The manuscripts of Nag Hammadi include several works which appear to be capable of being assigned to him. The most important is the *Gospel of Truth*. The treatise *On the Resurrection* should also be mentioned, and that *On the Three Natures*. It is not entirely certain that they are by Valentinus himself. They could be by one of his Alexandrian disciples, Heracleon or John Cassian.[29] Valentinian Gnosticism produced a reaction in the Church. The most important evidence of this reaction is the work of Irenaeus,[30] bishop of Lyons. Irenaeus's life has been studied in recent years by Pierre Nautin.[31] He came from Asia Minor, and was priest of the church of Lyons, and on the death of Pothinus became its bishop. His chief

28. See pages 70–74 for Hippolytus.

29. H.-Ch. Puech, G. Quispel, W. C. van Unnik, *The Jung Codex*, London, 1955; Sasagu Arai, *Die Christologie des Evangeliums Veritatis*, Leiden, 1964.

30. *c.* A.D. 130–200.

31. *Lettres et écrivains chrétiens des IIe et IIIe siècles*, Paris, 1961, pp. 92–104.

Irenaeus Clement of Alexandria

work, the *Adversus haereses*, is directed against the Valentinians. It has only been preserved in a Latin translation for the greater part of its extent. Irenaeus refutes the claim of the Gnostics to base their doctrine on the tradition of the Apostles. He declares that the true tradition of the Apostles is only to be found in the succession of the bishops. A number of studies have brought to light the originality of his work on this point, especially those of Henri Holstein [32] and of R. P. C. Hanson.[33] To the dualism of the Valentinians Irenaeus opposed the unity of the Word who is both Creator and Redeemer. He was thus led to construct a theology of history. In this theology he was influenced by the Stoic view of the development of the human race. It is not therefore simply a witness to the common faith, as André Benoit [34] has declared. Widmann [35] and R. M. Grant [36] have shown that he is indebted to the philosophy of his time.

This is even truer of Clement of Alexandria,[37] whose work is at the same time a reply to Gnosticism and an encounter with Hellenism. In his *Protreptikos*, whose title is suggested by Aristotle's, he continues the work of the apologists of presenting the Christian message in a Hellenistic guise. Though he is strongly critical of the Greek cults, especially of the mystery religions,[38] he constantly relies on Greek mythology to present Christ as the true Orpheus, who is building the City of God. Justin had already compared the Word to Hermes, and Valentinus to Hercules and Ulysses. All these writers were influenced

32. 'La tradition des Apôtres chez Saint Irénée', *R S R* 36 (1949), pp. 129–270.

33. *Tradition in the Early Church*, London, 1962.

34. *Saint Irénée. Introduction à l'étude de la théologie*, Paris, 1960.

35. loc. cit., pp. 161–8.

36. 'Irenaeus and Hellenistic Culture', *H T R* 42 (1949), pp. 41–51.

37. He was head of the catechetical school of Alexandria and may have been a presbyter. He died in Asia Minor *c.* A.D. 214.

38. A long and involved initiation during which the mysteries or secrets of the particular sect were revealed to the initiate characterized these religions. Often they embodied a high moral code and an emphasis on personal religion.

in this point by the allegorization of the Homeric poems made by the Middle Platonists.[39] The same re-interpretation is to be found in Christian iconography. It is not only on the level of ideas but also on that of images that Christianity was separating itself from the Semitic matrix in order to express itself in Hellenistic imagery.

The second great work of Clement is unique of its kind. The *Paidagogos* is a book on Christian ethics. It represents a unique document about the customs of Alexandrian society of the time as far as concerns food and clothes, public entertainments and sport, domestic and economic life. It gives an account of Christian Hellenism at the level of ordinary life.[40] Finally, the *Stromateis* are a summary of Christian *Gnosis*. In this Clement brings together the inheritance of both Judeo-Christianity and Middle Platonism. The work reaches its climax in Books VI and VII, where the ideal of the Gnostic Christian is depicted as one who is at the same time initiated into the knowledge of heavenly truths and who realizes the perfection of spiritual liberty. The study of Clement has been revolutionized by the labours of André Méhat.[41]

The essential question which the Christians of the second century had to answer was the determination of Christianity's relationship to Hellenism. The fundamental objection which it encountered was that it was in fact introducing a new religion which was subversive as much in relation to the philosophy of the intellectuals as to the religion of the urban populations. The task before the Christians was to give an interpretation of Christianity as a successor to Platonism. The problem had already been raised by the parallel succession of Christianity to Judaism. The Judeo-Christians had met this problem by pointing to a preparation for the New Testament in the Old.

39. Jean Daniélou, *Message évangélique et culture hellénistique*, Paris, 1961, pp. 73–101.

40. H.-I. Marrou, 'Humanisme et christianisme chez Clément d'Alexandrie d'après le Pédagogue', in *Recherches sur la tradition platonicienne*, Geneva, 1956, pp. 183–200.

41. *Le Plan des Stromates de Clément d'Alexandrie*, Paris, 1966.

In Clement of Rome, as Knoch has shown, this succession had already been established in a vision of a progressive revelation of the Logos.[42] It is this theology of the progressive revelation of the Logos as Revealer and Saviour which represents the essential substance of the Patristic Literature of the second century.

This is observable in Justin's work, as Carl Andresen has shown.[43] Already in his thought, according to a view of things which will be dominant right up to the Council of Nicaea,[44] the immanent Logos of the Father has achieved an individual existence for the purpose of the Creation and government of the world. He revealed himself to the holy men of the Old Testament. But it was also he who inspired the wise men of Greece, Heracleitus and Socrates: 'All those who have lived according to the Word are Christians' (I *Apol.* 46. 1–4). This revelation is however only in part. It is only in a rudimentary form that the Logos was given to the wise men. The question of whether this rudimentary form ought to be understood as a gift of the moral sense or already as a supernatural assistance has been debated between Holte[45] and Waszink.[46] With the Incarnation, it is the fulness of the Logos which is communicated.

Clement of Alexandria takes up and develops the ideas of Justin. He recognizes in human reason the capacity to know God. But in addition he sees in the pagan wise men a special activity of the Logos, parallel to his activity in the Jewish

42. God's activity seen in abstraction from himself. This concept origin ated in Philo and was greatly developed in Christian thought. For the Stoic the Logos was the rational principle immanent in reality. Literally it means word or reason.

43. *Logos und Nomos: Die Polemik des Kelsos wider das Christentum.* Berlin, 1955.

44. Held in A.D. 325, it was the birthplace of the Nicaean Creed. See Chapter 5.

45. 'Logos Spermatikos. Christianity and Ancient Philosophy according to St Justin's Apologies', *S T* 12 (1958), pp. 109–68.

46. 'Bemerkungen zur Justins Lehre vom Logos Spermatikos', *Mullus* (Festschrift Theodor Klauser), Münster, 1964, pp. 380–91.

prophets. But for him the wise men are not the Greek philosophers. They are the ancient sages, Orpheus, Pythagoras, Musaeus. This wisdom had first been given to the non-Greeks. Clement lists the magi and the Druids, the brahmans and Buddha, whom he is the first to name. This precedence of the non-Greeks over the Greeks reappears in Theophilus of Antioch and in Tatian. But the concept comes from the Greek philosophy of the time, which was more interested in the ancient religious traditions than in formal philosophy.[47] The theory even appears that the truths which are to be found among the Greek philosophers are borrowings from the ancient wisdom of the Jews. This is why Theophilus and Tatian evince a concern to demonstrate by chronological research the priority of Moses to Orpheus.

This view of history takes the form in Irenaeus of a progressive education of the human race. The race had been created as a child, and this was to conform to the principle that beginnings ought to have a childish character. The Jewish law corresponds to the adolescence of a human race which needed to be educated by external restraints. It is only with the Incarnation that the human race became adult and was able to obey the law of liberty. At the same time this is the same Logos of God who had originally created Adam, who had never deserted the human race even when it sinned and who came to recover full possession of this human race in Christ. In this theology the stages of the religious history of the human race form themselves into a vision of progress which makes development a law of creation. These ideas seem to be influenced by Stoicism.

It must be emphasized all the same that this concept of progress is opposed by another, which is complementary to it. It is that of a progressive decline beginning from the origins. Sin continues to increase. This view is particularly observable

47. Jean Daniélou, *Message évangélique et culture hellénistique*, pp. 50–72; J. H. Waszink, 'Some Observations on the Appreciation of the Philosophy of Barbarians in Early Christian Literature', in *Mélanges offerts à Mademoiselle Christine Mohrmann*, Utrecht, 1968, pp. 51–7.

in the *Epistle to Diognetus*. The writer raises the subject of the reasons for the late arrival of the Incarnation. He thinks that he has the answer in the need to wait until evil should reach its height. This idea will be taken up by Origen and by Gregory of Nyssa.[48] This concept of history as a decline also has its Hellenistic ancestry, in the succession of ages starting with the Golden Age. The subject of the ages of the world has been studied by A. Luneau.[49] The essential point is that even when they used patterns of thought borrowed from Hellenism the Christians interpreted them in relation to the Incarnation of the Logos considered as forming the turning-point of history.

48. See Chapter 3 and pages 99–100.

49. *L'Histoire du salut chez les Pères de l'Église. La doctrine des Âges du Monde*, Paris, 1964.

Three

Origen [1]

The work of Origen in the middle of the third century marks the transition of Greek patristic literature from its childhood to its maturity. It coincides with the period when contact with the oral tradition of the primitive Church had been lost and when Christianity became a religion of the Book. Similarly on the purely theological level, as R. P. C. Hanson has well observed, tradition gives place to speculation.[2] Contemporary research has thrown into relief the importance of Origen's work. It has on the one hand noticed, with Prestige,[3] de Lubac [4] and Crouzel,[5] all that was positive and the progress which his work made possible especially in the field of theology and of spirituality. But research has also underlined, with Koch,[6] Von Ivanka [7] and Cornelis,[8] the questionable features which were to lead to the condemnation of Origen in the sixth century.

Origen is first and foremost an exegete, and he is so in all the meanings of the word. He first occupied himself with the establishment of the text of Scripture. The need for this task

1. A.D. 186–255.

2. *Origen's Doctrine of Tradition*, London, 1954, p. 87.

3. *Fathers and Heretics*, London, 1948, pp. 43–66.

4. *Histoire et Esprit, L'intelligence de l'Écriture d'après Origène*, Paris, 1950.

5. *Origène et la connaissance mystique*, Paris, 1960.

6. *Pronoia und Paideusis. Studien über Origenes und sein Verhältnis zum Platonismus*, Berlin, 1932.

7. 'Zum Geistesgeschichtlichen Einordnung des Origenismus', *B Z* 44 (1951) pp. 291–303.

8. *Les Fondements cosmologiques de l'eschatologie d'Origène*, Paris, 1959.

arose out of the arguments with the Jews about the Old Testament. But this concern signalized an important milestone in the Christian attitude to the Old Testament. Up till then it had been regarded as accepted in the tradition and interpreted by the tradition. In imitation of the Jewish *targums*, the Christians used to handle the text freely, and used not to hesitate to alter, to add, to suppress words. The *testimonia* are the valuable evidence of just this primitive exegesis. It is with Origen that devotion to the letter of Scripture and concern to refer to the original text come to take on a new importance. Science will gain from this. But the living relationship between Scripture and tradition is on the way to being compromised.

The great critical work of Origen, the *Hexapla*, which gave different versions of Scripture in parallel columns, has formed the subject of much research. The second column, which was a transliteration of the Hebrew into Greek letters, has been explained, by Paul Kahle in particular,[9] by the custom in the churches of always reading the Hebrew text before the Greek translation, and so by the need to have a transliteration in those churches where Hebrew was not known. The character of the different Greek translations which occupy the four other columns creates some difficult questions. Barthélemy has shown that it is not necessary to take literally the attribution of these versions to Aquila, to Theodotion or to Symmachus,[10] and that some columns may give us translations from a different origin.[11] Origen applied to the text of Scripture the method which the Alexandrian grammarians used to employ to establish the text of Homer, with the diacritical signs, the obelus and the asterisk. He was concerned with scientific exegesis of a Greek sort which was substituted for the living exegesis of the Semitic sort; grammarians took the place of teachers.

9. *The Cairo Geniza*, Oxford, 1959, pp. 147–54.

10. Aquila came from Sinope; according to Epiphanius he was an ex-communicated Christian. He produced his version *c.* A.D. 140. Theodotion may have been a sectarian Christian; he wrote in the second century A.D. Symmachus was an Ebionite, perhaps from Samaria; and he wrote late in the second century A.D.

11. *Les Devanciers d'Aquila*, Leiden, 1963.

But Origen's intention was not only to establish the text (*exetasis*), but to interpret it (*hermeneia*). Origen is the first Christian who wrote continuous commentaries on *all* the books of the Bible. We can find some sort of an analogy earlier among the Jews of Alexandria with Philo's *Quaestiones in Genesim et Exodum.* Origen first disciplined himself to establish the literal meaning. He displays considerable learning in this field. He appeals to Greek science. He uses the dictionaries of his time, as Cadiou has shown.[12] But he also went to the Jewish Rabbis for information. Hanson has effectively studied these different sources. Origen's books are a mine of information. They were destined to be plundered by his successors, Eusebius and Didymus,[13] Ambrose[14] and Jerome.[15]

The questions which concern allegorical interpretation present greater difficulty. This subject is one of those where different sides have been taken in the discussion during the last few years, particularly by de Lubac and Hanson. The debate has however made it possible to register progress in the subject and to reach some conclusions. It is certain, to begin with, that Origen inherited a Biblical typology which formed part of tradition and which was based on the analogy between the two Testaments. Origen's originality shows itself in this field by the manner in which he develops this typology to cover new subjects, by his handling of it as he demonstrates the successive designs in which a master pattern unfolds itself on the level of the different stages of the history of salvation, and in his success in reaching the genuinely theological meaning, the work of the Holy Spirit, which is included within the actual events. He deploys this exegesis in a terminology which distinguishes the typical, the spiritual and the mystical, each kind expressing one aspect.[16]

12. 'Dictionnaires antiques dans l'œuvre d'Origène', *R E G* (1932), pp. 270–83.

13. *c.* A.D. 313–98; although blind, he headed the catechetical school at Alexandria. Several of his works survive.

14. See pages 101–2.

15. See Chapter 8.

16. See Jean Daniélou, *Origen*, New York, 1955, pp. 139–74.

But here once again Origen was anxious to place at the service of the Bible the hermeneutical methods which the pagan philosophers, Stoics or Pythagoreans, used to apply to the Homeric poems. Jean Pépin has effectively shown this.[17] It could be said that Origen did this in two ways. On the one hand he took up Philo's task. Philo saw in the Old Testament symbols either of cosmic realities, or of elements in the soul, or of the mysteries of the heavenly world. These kinds of interpretation can be found in Origen, which threaten to interfere with his Biblical typology, so much so that sometimes it is difficult to distinguish the tangled threads of this tapestry. Moreover, the principle of verbal inspiration is to be found in his work, as Hanson[18] and Grant[19] have well shown. All these passages of Scripture hold a hidden message. Consequently, when he applies, following the grammarians, the technique of *kataskeuē* and of *anaskeuē*, Origen will attempt to detect in Scripture that which is historical and that which is not, and will look for a hidden meaning in the improbable events, and even takes literal absurdity as a sign of the existence of a hidden sense, as Pépin has shown.[20]

The same dichotomy of respect for tradition and of the influence of philosophy reappears in his dogmatic theology. We can be assured that he was a witness to tradition by the ecclesiastical tasks with which he never ceased to be entrusted: he was a catechist at Alexandria, a preacher at Caesarea, a controversialist against Celsus. A new proof of this was given by the discovery in 1948, at Toura in Egypt, of two works of his on the Easter festival, and above all of a discussion with an Arab bishop, Heracleides, who was holding doctrines that were theologically suspect, and whom his colleagues had invited

17. *Mythe et Allégorie, Les origines grecques et les contestations chrétiennes*, Paris, 1958, pp. 453–61.

18. *Allegory and Event, A Study of the Sources and Significance of Origen's Interpretation of Scripture*, London, 1959, pp. 190–210.

19. *The Earliest Lives of Jesus*, New York, 1961, pp. 54, 96.

20. 'À propos de l'histoire de l'exégèse allégorique: l'absurdité signe de l'allégorie', *S P* 1, Berlin, 1957, pp. 105–22.

Origen to refute.[21] On many points he brought about an advance in theological knowledge, thanks to his speculative genius. Even though he maintained a subordinationist[22] concept of the Word he is the first to have produced the doctrine of the eternal generation of the Word.[23] He continued Justin's and Irenaeus's theology of history, starting from the same idea of history as education.[24] He strongly asserted the existence of a human soul in Christ. His theology of salvation as a victory over the powers of evil is purely in the line of tradition. Karl Rahner has gathered together the threads of his teaching about penance.[25]

But at the same time a theological system is to be found in his works. The point of departure is his observation of the inequality of the circumstances of human beings. Since this inequality is contrary to God's justice it can only arise from the freedom of his creatures. Origen therefore postulates that at the beginning all spirits were created equal and immaterial; it is a doctrine of pre-existence, and is Platonic. They all cooled off in different degrees from their attachment to God. Corresponding to these degrees, God has placed them in different conditions of existence in a body. The structure of the universe is therefore a secondary datum, created by God, but for the purpose of dealing with sin. The problem is to know how these spirits will be restored to their original condition. To the extent to which they turn towards God they raise themselves up the ladder of promotion, becoming men from being devils and angels from being men. This progressive return is carried out

21. *Entretien d'Origène avec Héraclide.* Introduction, text, translation and notes by Jean Scherer, *S C* 67, Paris, 1960.

22. That is, he regarded the word or Logos as subordinate to the Father.

23. That is, the doctrine that the Father did not bring the Son into existence at one point in time, even an immeasurably remote one, but has always from eternity been generating him.

24. See Marguerite Harl, *Origène et la fonction révélatrice du Verbe incarné*, Paris, 1958.

25. 'La Doctrine d'Origène sur la pénitence', *RSR* 37 (1960), pp. 47–97, 152–266, 422–56.

through successive existences. At the end of innumerable existences it will finish up with the total restoration of all spirits, including devils, in the original perfection of pure spirits, for God must completely conquer evil.[26]

This system raises several problems. First, some writers, such as Henri Crouzel,[27] have disputed the existence of this system in Origen himself, asserting that the texts condemned by the Second Council of Constantinople do not represent his doctrine, but that of his disciples at the end of the fourth century, especially Evagrius.[28] But this position is untenable. Even if it is true that the texts condemned by the Council of Constantinople of 553 reflect the views of Evagrius, the text which the anathemas of 543 envisage are genuinely Origen's, as Antoine Guillaumont has proved.[29] Further, Origen's errors were attacked well before the Origenism of the end of the fourth century by Methodius of Olympia,[30] Epiphanius,[31] Gregory of Nyssa and Jerome. On the other hand, Crouzel has likewise disputed the view that Origen wished to set up a system. But this too cannot withstand the arguments of Ivanka, of Jonas and of Kern.[32]

Once it has been proved that there was an Origenist system and that this system certainly is the one condemned by Justinian,[33] the next task is to investigate its origins. Origen's philosophic background is Middle Platonism of the second century. The connexions of his thought with that of Albinus, Maximus of Tyre and Numenius have been pointed out.[34]

26. See Jean Daniélou, op. cit., pp. 209–20, 271–310.

27. 'Origène est-il un systématique?' *BLE* (1959), pp. 81–116.

28. A.D. 346–99. He spent the latter half of his life as a monk in the Nitrian desert. Few of his writings survive. See pages 112–14.

29. *Les 'Kephalaia gnostica' d'Évagre le Pontique et l'histoire de l'origénisme chez les Grecs et chez les Syriens*, Paris, 1962, pp. 146–50.

30. Bishop in Cappadocia, died *c.* A.D. 311. See pages 62–3.

31. Bishop of Salamis, *c.* A.D. 315–403.

32. *The First Systematic Theologian: Origen of Alexandria*, Princeton, 1958.

33. Byzantine Emperor A.D. 527–65.

34. See Jean Daniélou, op. cit., pp. 73–98.

But Origen does nevertheless belong to another generation. He is only a little earlier than Plotinus,[35] and he supplies some firm analogies with Plotinus's thought. He belongs to the world of Neo-Platonism, not of Middle Platonism. Now these similarities seem to be explained by the fact that Origen and Plotinus were both, with an interval of twenty years between them, disciples of the same master, Ammonius Sakkas.[36] This last figure is then the true father of Neo-Platonism. Unfortunately, he appears to have written nothing. We know his thought directly only from two references, one of Nemesius[37] and the other of Photius.[38] This is why the pictures of him which scholars have attempted to give contradict each other. Heinemann sees in him a Greek philosopher, Seeberg a missionary from India, Dörries a Pythagorean wonder-worker, Langerbeck a Christian theologian. It seems that with Dodds we must acknowledge our ignorance.[39] But Willy Theiler has shown that it is possible to recover Ammonius's teaching by means of Origen's works as one source and as another the work of Hierocles, a Neo-Platonist of the fifth century.[40]

The problems of the relations of Origen and Plotinus have been complicated by the existence of a Neo-Platonist also called Origen. Porphyry[41] seems to have deliberately conflated the two persons in order to make out that our Origen was a deserter from paganism. Some modern writers, such as Cadiou[42] and Hanson,[43] have asserted their identity. But this theory is today generally abandoned. It could have been made possible by the fact that both Origens were disciples of

35. *c.* A.D. 205–75.

36. A.D. 175–242.

37. *c.* A.D. 390. Bishop of Emesa (in Syria).

38. *c.* A.D. 810–95, Patriarch of Constantinople.

39. 'Numenius and Ammonius', in *Les sources de Plotin*, Entretien sur l'Antiquité Classique V, Geneva, 1960, pp. 1–63.

40. *Forschungen zum Neuplatonismus*, Berlin, 1966, pp. 1–45.

41. *c.* A.D. 232–303. A Neo-Platonist philosopher who wrote against Christianity, as well as many other works.

42. *La Jeunesse d'Origène*, Paris, 1936, pp. 231–62.

43. *Origen's Doctrine of Tradition*, London, 1954, p. 10.

Ammonius. K. O. Weber has studied the thought of Origen the pagan.[44] He has effectively shown that he was the inheritor of Ammonius's thought, in his faithfulness to Plato as representing the ancient tradition, and in his concept of the identity of the supreme God and the Creator. The vigorous personality of Plotinus produced a different system. It was this system which was continued by Porphyry, Iamblichus[45] and Proclus,[46] while the original thought of Ammonius survived in the two Origens, and was destined to be picked up by Hierocles in the fifth century.

Origen was an exegete and a theologian, and he was also a great master of the spiritual life. This is the aspect of his work which has evoked the greatest number of works during the last thirty years, in particular that of W. Völker.[47] In Origen, however, exegesis, theology and spirituality are not in fact separable. The same basic structure is to be found in all three fields, the structure of gradations. Urs von Balthasar[48] and Gerhard Gruber[49] have established this fact. Just as there is a movement onward from the literal meaning to the allegorical meaning, so there is a transition from the common faith to gnosis and there is a progress from the ordinary Christian life to perfection. Spirituality forms the inward dimension of this ladder. But this ladder itself corresponds to reality in the order of being. This close connexion between the inward disposition and the structure of the order of being brings Origen close to Plotinus.

The basic theme of Origen's mystical thought is the relatedness of man to the Logos, as Lieske[50] has shown. Man has been

44. *Origen der Neuplatoniker. Versuch einer Interpretation*, Munich, 1962.

45. Died *c.* A.D. 333.

46. *c.* A.D. 412–85.

47. *Das Volkommenheitsideal des Origenes*, Tübingen, 1931.

48. 'Le Mysterion d'Origène', *R S R* 26 (1936), pp. 513–68; 27 (1937), pp. 38–64.

49. *A P X H. Wesen, Stufen und Mitteilung des wahren Lebens bei Origenes*, Munich, 1962.

50. *Die Theologie des Logosmystik bei Origenes*, Münster, 1938.

made in the image of the Logos who is himself the image of the Father. Because of this affinity to the Logos, man is capable of knowing him, and through him the Father. But sin has obscured this image. The spiritual life consists in restoring it. It henceforward follows that man should know himself in his true reality, that is as an image of the Word, and not in his fleshly reality, which represents the devil's image. He must gradually free himself from slavery to his passions which is also slavery in subjection to devils. Origen's ascetic thought is very noticeable in its parallel between the devils and the passions, in the manner in which the Judeo-Christians, the author of the *Testaments of the XII Patriarchs* and Hermas had developed it. The doctrine of the spiritual warfare is one of the essential aspects of his spirituality, as Bettencourt [51] has rightly observed. Athanasius [52] will later interpret the life of Anthony,[53] the first eremite, from this viewpoint.

To this departure (*ekstasis*) from the demonic prison of the passions there corresponds the entry into the spiritual world, which is the real world. The powers of the soul darkened by the passions awake. This is the doctrine of the spiritual senses, parallel to the fleshly senses, a doctrine which expresses the empirical manner of laying hold of spiritual realities. All through this experience it is the Logos himself who draws the soul to an ever-increasing union with him. Origen is the first who ever wrote a commentary on the *Song of Songs* so as to interpret it as this mystical marriage. In this tradition also his influence on later spirituality was destined to be immense. The Logos reveals himself to the soul in proportion to its degree of development, as physician, then as master, then as friend, then as husband; the titles of the Logos evince these successive *epinoiai* (aspects). As the abyss of the Logos is unfathomable anyway, the soul can always make progress in it; it is the doctrine of *epectasis*, of unending progress, to which Gregory of Nyssa was destined to give its supreme expression.

51. *Doctrina Ascetica Origensis*, Stud. Anselm. 13, Vatican, 1965.

52. See pages 84–6.

53. A.D. 251?–356. Known as the Father of Monasticism.

An achievement as powerful as this could not fail to arouse reactions. Greek patristic literature of the end of the third century is dominated by the disturbance which it provoked. Origen had many followers. A large proportion of the bishops of Egypt, of the East and of Asia were directly or indirectly his disciples. This was true of Dionysius of Alexandria, of Gregory of Neo-Caesarea, of Firmilian of Caesarea in Cappadocia and of Theotecnus of Caesarea in Palestine. It was this group which condemned Paul of Samosata[54] at the Council of Antioch in 264. As a successor to the headship of the school of Caesarea in Palestine Origen had Pamphilus[55] who defended him in an Apology. At the head of the school of Alexandria were to be found his disciples Theognostus and Pierius.

But if Origen's work aroused an understandable enthusiasm, it also provoked no less understandable criticism. At Alexandria bishop Peter, who succeeded Dionysius, attacked the Origenistic doctrines of the pre-existence of souls, and their return to the condition of pure spirits. The most important opponent of Origen was Methodius of Olympia. His attitude towards Hellenism was quite different from that of the Alexandrians. He adopted its literary forms, and his *Dialogue of the Virgins*, an imitation of Plato, represented a new event in its own kind, like the invention of a new style. But he is, in contrast, hostile towards the influence of Greek philosophy which he detected in Origen. He criticizes Origen's ideas in his dialogue *On the Resurrection.* He remains faithful to the Asiatic tradition of Irenaeus and to his realism. He defends the traditional doctrine of the millennial reign which he found in Justin, in Irenaeus and in Nepos,[56] against the spiritualization of which he accuses the Alexandrians. So it was that on the morrow of Origen's death

54. A heretical bishop of Antioch; the exact form of his Trinitarian heresy is not known. He held his post for some years through the influence of the ruler of Antioch, the Queen of Palmyra, who was not overthrown until A.D. 272.

55. *c.* 240–309. Eusebius was his disciple.

56. An Egyptian bishop in the middle of the third century whose naïve literalist and millernniarist ideas were attacked by Dionysius of Alexandria.

a dispute about his work was sparked off which will crop up again repeatedly at the end of the fourth century, and at the beginning of the sixth century particularly, and which will be one of the permanent features of Greek patristic literature.

Four

The Origins of Latin Patristic Literature

The growth of Christianity in the West is evidenced from the time of the Apostles. The coming of Peter and Paul to Rome is already witnessed to by Clement of Rome. The importance of the Church in Africa at the time of Tertullian prompts the conclusion that it had been planted there very early. But it is above all in places of Greek origin that it first grew. It is with the Hellenistic synagogue that works like that of Clement of Rome are connected. Many of the Greek writers whom we have mentioned had lived at Rome; this is true of Justin, Tatian, Valentinus and Irenaeus. Even in Africa we shall find Tertullian writing his earliest works in Greek. It was only gradually that a Christianity expressing itself in Latin was destined to be formed, and only gradually that this Christianity would produce literary works. For this to happen it would have to create its own language. This process was slower at Rome, which was a cosmopolitan city. It was in Africa that there first appeared a Latin offshoot of Christianity with a more consistent character.

Towards the end of the second century, Christian Africa comes into view in the form of a work of genius, that of Tertullian. Since we scarcely possess one document about Christian Africa before his day, the majority of scholars up till very recently have hailed him as the creator of Christian Latin. But research on the origins of Christian Latin, especially that done in the school of Nijmegen by Mgr Schijven and Christine Mohrmann, has shown that Tertullian was writing at a time when Christian Latin was already in existence. These writers have even maintained that it is not simply a question of the invention of a few new words, but that the Christian

Tertullian

community, which consisted of a recognizable social entity, had created its own language, including elements which have nothing to do with anything specifically Christian, such as syntax.[1] This theory has been qualified by more recent studies, especially those of René Braun and of C. Becker. They attribute an important role to Tertullian.[2] Still, he had had the advantage of an earlier literary heritage which has been reconstructed. The Latin versions of the Bible must be included in this heritage. They appeared in Africa and in Rome towards the beginning of the second century and they can be partly reconstructed by means of quotations of them. It is even possible that these Christian translations were preceded in Africa and in Rome by Jewish translations of the Old Testament. Further, some Christian writings, the *First Epistle of Clement*, the *Epistle of Barnabas*, the *Shepherd* of Hermas, the *Didache*, had been translated into Latin at Rome in the second century. It is possible that a work *Adversus Judaeos* preserved under the name of Cyprian may be the oldest original piece of Christian Latin literature that we possess.[3]

It is none the less true that Christian Latin had produced no important work before Tertullian. The sources of his thought must consequently be sought elsewhere. Contemporary research has set itself to establish these sources. On one side, Tertullian is dependent on the Greek Christian writers who lived before him. In this respect he indicates an important link between Greek and Latin Christianity, as Stephen Otto has rightly seen.[4] We have already noted that he could speak both languages. We can discover some of the Greek authors whom he had read. We can be certain about Justin, whom he quotes in his book against the Valentinians. In addition Pierre Prigent

1. See Christine Mohrmann, *Essai sur le latin des chrétiens*, Rome, 1958.

2. *Deus Christianorum. Recherches sur le vocabulaire doctrinal de Tertullien*, Paris, 1962; *Tertullians Apologeticum. Werden und Leistung*, Munich, 1954.

3. See D. van Damme, 'Pseudo-Cyprian Adversus Judaeos: the Oldest Sermon in Latin', *S P* 7 (1966), pp. 299–307.

4. *'Natura' und 'Dispositio'. Untersuchung zum Naturbegriff und zur Denkform Tertullians*, Munich, 1960.

has attempted to prove that he had used Justin's lost *Adversus Marcionem*[5] in his works against the Jews and against Marcion. But this does not exclude the possibility of his having known the *Dialogue*, whatever Prigent may say.[6] He certainly used Theophilus of Antioch in his book against Hermogenes. His Trinitarian vocabulary is derived from Tatian. It looks as if in the second part of his life the influence of the Asiatic writers, Melito and Irenaeus, had taken on more and more importance; this is why he produced a theology of history under their guidance. This fact should lead us to correct the assertion that it was Montanism[7] alone which shaped the later form of his thought.[8]

It is true, all the same, that Tertullian also knew Greek writers belonging to peripheral movements of thought. His work is in part a polemic against different heresies, which implies a knowledge of the offending writings. He had read Praxeas[9] and Hermogenes.[10] Two examples are particularly important. First, the question arises of the influence of Valentinian Gnosticism on his theological vocabulary. René Braun has studied this subject and has shown that the effect of this influence was negative.[11] The fact that he was attacking the Valentinians causes Tertullian to avoid certain words which

5. Marcion died *c.* A.D. 160. He established a sect which almost rivalled the Church in size in the late second century. He preached the Gospel as Love to the exclusion of Law, which for him the Old Testament represented. The Old Testament God was the cruel creator God, whom Jesus overthrew.

6. *Justin et l'Ancien Testament*, Paris, 1964.

7. An apocalyptic movement in the later part of the second century based on one Montanus, who lived in Phrygia. It daily expected the coming of the Holy Spirit on the Church, as shown by the prophets and prophetesses of the movement. The movement imposed a rigorous morality on its adherents.

8. See J. Daniélou, 'Bulletin d'Histoire des Origines chrétiennes, III, Tertullien', *R S R* 49 (1961), pp. 593–4.

9. A heretic *c.* A.D. 200. He maintained the unity of the Godhead to the extent that God suffered; as Tertullian said, 'He crucified the Father'.

10. A Gnostic teacher of the second half of the second century.

11. op. cit., pp. 39–65.

Latin writers will adopt later. For instance, he does not reproduce expressions involving a doctrine of God expressed in negatives, so dear to Greeks contemporary with him. If he uses the term *incomprehensibilis*, it is in a very different sense from the Greek term *akatalēptos*. Similarly he avoids using *salvator* because of the misuse of the word *sotēr* by the Gnostics. The other example is Montanism, the only marginal movement of thought which influenced Tertullian, and to this he finally attached himself. It is to this source that he owes the description of the third Person of the Trinity as the *Paraclete*, which occurs often in his latest works. He also found here the justification for his rigorism.

Tertullian is above all a convert who had received a wide pagan culture. The Latin classics were very familiar to him. He quotes Cicero and Vergil. But it would be wrong to say that he was their disciple in literary composition. The influence of Greek philosophy is stronger with him. In the earlier part of his work he seems mainly indebted to Middle Platonism, as were his Greek predecessors. Waszink has proved his dependence upon Albinus in his book *De anima*.[12] The texts of Plato which he quotes are those which were cherished by Middle Platonism. The doctrine of the natural knowledge of God to be found in his *De testimonio animae* suggests to Tibiletti that its origin is Platonic.[13] But the influence of Stoicism in his work continually increases, parallel with the influence of the Asiatic theologians, who in their turn were influenced by Stoicism. Waszink has shown the influence on him of the Stoic physician Soranus already present in the *De anima*. The concept of *natura*, which is crucial in his work, derives from the Stoic concept of *physis*.[14] This Stoicism came to him from Greek writers, Zeno and Cleanthus. But he also knew Seneca, whom he calls *Seneca noster*. These Stoic leanings are characteristic of the Latin world of his time and mark

12. *Tertullian. De anima*, ed. with a commentary, Amsterdam, 1947.

13. *Q. S. F. Tertulliani. De testimonio animae*, introduction, text and commentary by Carlo Tibiletti, Turin, 1959.

14. Stephan Otto, op. cit.

Tertullian off from the Greek apologists. It is noticeable too that he has had a legal education. But Braun reckons that the legal character of his vocabulary has been over-estimated.

Tertullian's work is almost entirely controversial. It was in the course of facing his opponents that he was led to express his personal ideas. This controversy is directed first towards paganism. Tertullian is here to a large extent indebted to the apologists who went before him. One of his constant traits is a pessimism greater than Justin's. Not only does he condemn popular religion, in which he sees worship given to devils, but he is also critical of the philosophers. He relies on Varro[15] in dividing paganism into mythical, physical and political theology. He here foreshadows St Augustine. He is also the first to tackle the argument which had no doubt been raised in the circle surrounding Marcus Aurelius, according to which the Christians were the cause of the disasters of the Empire by refusing to worship the gods who were protecting it. He answers by pointing out that the troubles of the Empire were earlier than the arrival of the Christians. He contrasts the Emperors who had left the Christians undisturbed with the Emperors who had persecuted. His criticism of paganism affects its morals as well as its teaching. Many of his works are occupied with this subject, especially *De spectaculis* and *De corona militis*.

Tertullian's attitudes in the matter of Biblical interpretation come to light mainly in his works *Adversus Iudaeos* and *Adversus Marcionem*. The first of these has been the subject of much discussion. Its authenticity has been disputed in whole or in part. Its date has been variously estimated. Its latest editor believes in its authenticity and sees in it a work of the beginning of his career which was to be used again in *Adversus Marcionem*.[16] Against the contrary views of the Jews who reject the New Testament and of the Marcionites who reject the Old, Tertullian emphasizes the unity of the two. In this he

15. Roman antiquarian, *c.* 116–29 B.C.

16. Hermann Tränkle, *Q. S. F. Tertullian Adversus Judaeos*, with introduction and critical commentary, Wiesbaden, 1964.

does no more than continue the work of Justin and Irenaeus. We can find cropping up again in his work the *Testimonia* which have for the most part been already used by Justin. These *Testimonia* can be detected by their primitive form, for example of Deuteronomy 28.66, 'You will see your life hung *upon a tree*', where the last words are a Christian addition. It is possible similarly to find the traditional typology reappearing with him. *De baptismo* especially includes a list of types of baptism drawn either from the Old Testament, such as the flood and the crossing of the Red Sea, or from the New, such as the marriage at Cana and the pool of Bethesda. On the other hand, no trace of Alexandrian allegorization can be found in him. This point is an important one, for Tertullian both expressed and gave direction to the Western tradition, which was destined to remain faithful to this exegesis until the Alexandrian influence made itself felt in the fourth century.

Finally, Tertullian's work in the field of theology was very great. His work *Against Praxeas* formulated a Trinitarian theology which was in many respects more articulated than that of his Greek contemporaries.[17] He brought out very well both the unity (*unitas*) of the divine being (*substantia*) and the Trinity (*trinitas*) of the Persons (*persona*). This vocabulary was destined to be continued in Latin literature. Some other expressions were to be less fortunate, such as the distinction of *status* to denote the dimension of divine existence common to the three Persons, and of *gradus* to indicate the order of succession which distinguishes them.[18] One more point to note is that the generation of the Son as an individual *persona* still seems in Tertullian's work to be connected with the creation of the world. The other field where his thought is noteworthy is eschatology.[19] He emphasizes the importance of the resurrection of the dead against the Gnostics. The body is so necessary

17. J. Moingt, *Théologie Trinitaire de Tertullien*, 4 vols., Paris, 1966–9.
18. See R. Braun, op cit., pp. 141–243.
19. That part of theology which deals with the final destiny of the individual and of mankind in general.

in his view to the wholeness of the man that he allows neither development nor punishment in the intermediate state that precedes the resurrection. He appears to have corrected these ideas in his last works, for in them, under Stoic influence, he admits that the soul has materiality and consequently the possibility of suffering or being happy in the intermediate state between death and resurrection.[20] The words *refrigerium* and *requies* which later become important in the office of the dead in the West owe to him, not their origin, but their career. His depicting of the other world seems to be influenced by Judeo-Christian apocalyptic images. In Rome, the first piece of Latin literature is the *Octavius* of Minucius Felix, which represents a pagan and a Christian meeting each other in a polite discussion. The *Octavius* betrays some connexions with Tertullian's *Apologeticum.* But the question of which of the two books appeared first has not been decided. Though the contents are admittedly the same, the tone is quite different. The attacks on paganism in the *Octavius* are carefully moderated and do not rule out a certain understanding of it. The language, too, has a quite different character from Tertullian's. Minucius Felix is influenced by the Classical writers, especially by Cicero and Seneca. He does not possess Tertullian's originality and harshness. In all these points Minucius Felix represents Roman Christians of the ruling classes. People of this sort are anxious to be loyal to the Latin literary tradition and seek to preserve good relations with those who wield political power. It is the spirit that will show itself in the Roman hierarchy of the period.

While Latin Christians were producing their first writings, the separate existence of the Greek Christians in the West continued. This is what we observe in the work of Hippolytus. Few writings of Christian antiquity present more problems. On the one hand we must distinguish this Hippolytus from other people of the same name, a martyr of Antioch, an eastern bishop, an official whose name occurs in the *Ager Veranus,* and

20. See Heinz Finé, *Die Terminologie der Jenseitsvorstellungen bei Tertullian*, Bonn, 1958, pp. 77–9.

this has been effectively established by Hanssens.[21] On the other hand, scholars appeared to have reached agreement in identifying the author of the collection of works preserved under the name of Hippolytus, especially the *Commentary on Daniel*, a Roman priest who was in opposition to Pope Callistus[22] and who attacked him in the *Elenchos*, somebody represented by a statue near the Via Tiburtina, and a Roman priest exiled with Pope Pontianus in 235 and buried after his return near this same Via Tiburtina. This identification has been challenged in its entirety by Pierre Nautin,[23] who distinguishes three different people: the writer of the *Elenchos*, who was the same as the person represented by the statue, was not Hippolytus, but someone called Josippus; the author of the Biblical commentaries was an Easterner, perhaps the Syrian bishop mentioned by Eusebius; the Roman priest found near the Via Tiburtina was a third person. This theory has not received universal acceptance. It has to face the objections of Marcel Richard,[24] of J.-M. Hanssens and of A. Amore.[25] The argument for holding on to the unity of Hippolytus's personality, then, seems to be stronger.

Hippolytus's work is primarily concerned with exegesis. He is the first Christian writer whose continuous commentaries on books of the Bible we possess: the *Commentary on Daniel*, the *Blessings of Isaac and Jacob* and the *Commentary on the Song of Songs*. Hippolytus's exposition is a development of the primitive typology. No influence from Alexandrian allegorization is to be found there. It witnesses above all to the traditional Roman catechetical teaching. The subjects which are beginning to appear in the catacombs can be found in it, Daniel in the den of lions, Susanna and the elders, the three young men in the furnace, Jonah vomited up by the whale. Hippolytus's typology is directed specially to the Church and

21. J.-M. Hanssens, *La Liturgie d'Hippolyte*, Rome, 1959.

22. A.D. 217–23.

23. *Hippolyte et Josippe*, Paris, 1947.

24. 'Comput et chronographie chez Saint Hippolyte', *MSR* 7 (1950), pp. 237–68.

25. 'La personalità dello scrittore Ippolito', *Ant* 36 (1961), pp. 3–28.

the sacraments. The story of Susanna receives a baptismal interpretation, where Susanna stands for the Church, her bath for baptism, the elders for the Jews and the pagans. There are also to be found in his work the symbols of the Church which are destined to remain dear to the Roman church: the ship whose pilot is Christ, and whose mast is the Cross; the vine whose branches are the saints and whose clusters are the martyrs; the Paradise whose trees are the righteous and whose four rivers are the preaching of the gospel.[26] Hippolytus's exegesis is as traditional as Tertullian's but it is still connected with a different tradition. It is less influenced by the Greek apologists and it is rooted in the original Judeo-Christian Roman background, affected by Jewish apocalyptic, as his work on the Blessings of Isaac and Jacob testifies.[27]

The striking feature of Hippolytus is his interest in eschatology. His earliest work is a discussion of the Anti-Christ. He wrote a book on the Apocalypse listed on the statue from the Via Tiburtina. The *Commentary on Daniel* indulges in speculation about the weeks and years.[28] His interest in chronology which made itself evident in the *Chronicle* mentioned on the statue, and in the *Computation of Easter* which is inscribed on it, is connected with his desire to fix the date of the Second Coming. This interest in eschatology was not unusual in the earliest Roman community. We can find an echo of it in Hermas. But it does not represent the spirit of the Church of Rome in the time of Hippolytus. The Roman priest Gaius[29] had written a work against the genuineness of the Johannine authorship of the Apocalypse. Since the time of Clement, the bishops of Rome were more interested in the development of the Church in the Roman Empire. In this case, what we en-

26. See Jean Daniélou, H. I. Marrou, *The Christian Centuries*, I, London, 1964, p. 147.

27. See Manlio Simonetti, *Note su antichi commenti alle Benedizioni dei Patriarchi*, Cagliari, 1961.

28. Based on Daniel, 9.24.

29. *c.* A.D. 210.

counter in Hippolytus is the influence of Asiatic 'prophet' cults. Photius represented him as a disciple of Irenaeus. He draws on him in his doctrine of the recapitulation[30] of Adam by Christ. He shares the millennial hopes of the Asiatics. He thinks that the End of the Ages is imminent. His rigorism, too, is motivated by this expectation. Without going as far as Tertullian and adopting Montanist notions, he approximates to him in his apocalyptic literalism, which was very different both from the spiritualization of eschatology of the Alexandrians and from the tendency to see it realized in the present world on the part of the bishops of Rome.

This particular divergence of doctrine was expressed in practical terms by the quarrel between Hippolytus and the bishops of Rome, Zephyrinus and Callistus, to which the *Elenchos* testifies. In this book, which is a refutation of heresies, Hippolytus relies upon Irenaeus in his description of the Gnostics. He finishes off this account by a description of some groups whom we know only through him. This is consistent with the existence at Rome of Gnostic sects, which has been confirmed for us by the discovery of a Naasene[31] shrine in the Viale Manzoni.[32] But Hippolytus, whose Trinitarian theology is related to that of Tertullian, seizes as his main theme upon the modalism of Noetus,[33] as Tertullian had that of Praxeas, and accuses Callistus of showing favour to this heresy. In fact behind this accusation, which does not seem to be well grounded, it is Hippolytus's quarrel with the Papacy of his time that is finding expression. It represents the resistance of the ancient Roman system of government by presbyters to the development of monarchical episcopacy.[34] His devotion to the

30. Recapitulation for Irenaeus was the bringing back of mankind to God through Christ's obedience; and the summation of all previous revelations of God, in the Incarnation.

31. Gnostics who worshipped the serpent in opposition to the Old Testament God (Genesis 3.14 f.).

32. See Jérôme Carcopino, *De Pythagore aux Apôtres*, Paris, 1956, pp. 85–224.

33. A heretic, *c.* 200; for his teaching see note 9, p. 66.

34. One town or area being ruled by one bishop.

Greek language here comes into full play against the use of the Latin tongue which the bishops of Rome were encouraging. Similarly the *Apostolic Tradition* is perhaps, as Hanssens thinks, a liturgical manifesto against the innovations in the sphere of discipline with which Hippolytus charged Callistus.

Hippolytus was the last of the Western writers who wrote in Greek. In the next generation Rome had a writer in Latin, Novatian. He was a priest of the Church of Rome, and separated himself from the community at the time of the election of Pope Cornelius in 251, taking a rigorist position on the question of the reconciliation of the *lapsi*, those who had apostatized during the persecution. On this subject he was the representative of the same tradition as Tertullian and Hippolytus. The schismatic sect of the Novatians, which spread particularly in Asia Minor, was later to represent the persistence of this tendency. It is nevertheless true that Novatian was a distinguished member of the Roman Church. This is clear from his writings that have been preserved, though it is uncertain whether they are earlier or later than his act of schism. In his theology, Novatian continues the work of Tertullian and Hippolytus in his *On the Trinity*. He is similarly connected with Tertullian in his books *On Chastity* and *On Public Entertainments* too. His minor exegetical works are written against the Jews and consist of a criticism of their ritual observances which he interprets in a spiritual sense, following a tradition which goes back to Hellenistic Judaism and is continued by the apologists. He is also influenced by the Stoicism of Seneca. But from a literary point of view he is more indebted to Classical Latin literature, to Vergil specially, than to Tertullian.

It is true nonetheless that it was at Carthage that the brightest light of patristic Latin shone in the middle of the third century and at its end. Two great writers appeared there. The first is Cyprian.[35] He was an admirer of Tertullian. He continued some of his tendencies. But he was altogether more

35. Bishop of Carthage, A.D. 248–58.

restrained. His style did not have the brilliance of that of his predecessor. It is more Classical, like Novatian's. He too shows clear signs of Stoic influence, in the spheres of philosophy and ethics. Two of his works are particularly important. First, he put together a selection of the main collections of *Testimonia*, referring to the Christian sacraments and Christian ethics. This selection is the first of this type which we possess. But it brings together material which we find scattered among earlier writers. And it leads us to assume the existence of smaller collections of quotations used by these authors. Another work of Cyprian, the *Ad Fortunatum*, consists of a collection of *Testimonia* about martyrdom. And Michel Reveillaut has shown that, though Cyprian in his *De oratione* was influenced by Tertullian's book on prayer, he has only seven Biblical quotations out of sixty-six in common with him. This leads us to assume that here he was once again using a particular collection of *Testimonia*.[36] These collections are valuable for our knowledge of the text of ancient Latin translations of the Bible in Africa.

The other piece of writing by which Cyprian has left his mark on history is the *De unitate ecclesiae*. This work arose out of the disputes which first threw Cyprian and Novatian into opposition to each other over the reconciliation of the *lapsi*, and then embroiled Cyprian and Felicissimus[37] over the validity of baptism performed by heretics. It is difficult to determine to which of these disputes he is directly referring. The purpose of the book is to condemn schism and to demonstrate the necessity of unity. Cyprian is the first great teacher of the collegiality of the episcopate in communion with the bishop of Rome. But in addition Cyprian later fell into dispute with Stephen, bishop of Rome, on the question of baptism by heretics. On this occasion he established the importance of the local episcopate. Consequently Cyprian's theology had two poles, which testify to the existence of two movements of

36. *Saint Cyprien. 'L'oraison dominicale'*, text, translation, introduction and notes, Paris, 1964.

37. A deacon in Carthage, a consistent opponent of Cyprian.

thought which had not yet been integrated. J.-P. Brisson tried to prove that the sources of Donatism[38] can be found in him.[39] But André Mandouze has rightly disproved this.[40] As Maurice Bévenot has proved, the alternative version of Chapter IV of the *De unitate ecclesiae*, where the importance of the bishop of Rome is reduced, corresponds in all probability to an alteration introduced into his work by Cyprian himself as a result of this dispute with Stephen.[41]

Among Cyprian's works there is a book, *Ad Demetrianum*, which answers the charge by the pagans against the Christians of being the cause of Rome's ill fortune. The refutation of this charge had already appeared in the *Ad nationes* of Tertullian. The subject was destined to crop up continually in African literature up to the time of St Augustine. It is this charge which caused Arnobius's work *Adversus nationes* at the end of the century. Arnobius had first been converted from paganism when he wrote his book. An echo of the pagan mysticism of Porphyry can be detected in it, and the manifestation of an interest in Orphism and the Hermetic tradition, in the *Chaldaean Oracles* and in Mithraic papyri.[42] In this respect he signalizes the arrival of a Neo-Platonic Latin Christianity which will reappear in the fourth century in the work of another convert, Marius Victorinus, and which will achieve its widest expression with Augustine. But Arnobius has not yet achieved a

38. Schismatic movement in the African Church whose members refused to accept Caecilian (bishop of Carthage A.D. 311) as bishop, since one of his consecrators had handed over the Scriptures during the Diocletianic persecution. They were rigorists and persisted until the seventh century A.D. as a group.

39. *Autonomisme et christianisme dans l'Afrique romaine de Septime Sévère à l'invasion vandale*, Paris, 1958.

40. 'Encore le donatisme', *A C* 29 (1960), pp. 61–107.

41. *The Tradition of Manuscripts. A Study in Transmission of St Cyprian's Treatises*, Oxford, 1961.

42. See A. M. J. Festugière, 'Arnobiana', *V C* 6 (1952), pp. 208–54. The Hermetic literature and the *Chaldaean Oracles* reflect theosophical and philosophical semi-religious movements of pagan thought typical of the period. The cult of Mithras was one of the most popular of the mystery religions.

synthesis, for his Christianity manifests a dualism consisting of a transcendant God and a demiurge Creator scarcely consistent with the Christian faith. In the account of Greek religion which he gives he relies on Varro, as Tertullian had already done in his *Ad nationes*. The continuity of the African school in this point is striking.

The creativity of African literature at this period showed itself in a certain number of anonymous works usually attributed to Cyprian but in fact written by African bishops of the time. They have special interest because they acquaint us with the spirit of Latin Christianity of the period. The work *De Pascha Computus* testifies to a curious taste for the symbolism of numbers and for eschatological speculations. It includes traditions of Jewish origin. The book *De Montibus Sina et Sion* contrasts the Jewish people with the Church and has some interesting typological features, especially that which concerns the living water springing from the Temple at Jerusalem. The work *De Centesimo, Sexagesimo et Tricesimo*, a little later in date, is an exposition of the Parable of the Sower. A development of Judeo-Christian origin on the clothing of Christ during his descent with the nature of the different orders of angels appears here. The impression given by these works is of the close contact preserved by Latin Christianity, at Carthage and at Rome, with a Jewish Rabbinic and apocalyptic tradition which was still very much alive and against which it was reacting, as the various works called *Adversus Iudaeos* show, but to whose influence it was also open.[43] This marks one difference from the East which was more influenced by Hellenistic Judaism.

With these writings two authors can be associated whose tendencies are related to them, Victorinus of Pettau[44] and Commodian. Both wrote in Latin. There has come down to us a commentary *On the Apocalypse* by the first of these and a book *On the Creation of the World* in which a typology of the epochs of world history appears. The source of these specula-

43. See Marcel Simon, *Verus Israël*, second ed., Paris, 1964.
44. Died A.D. 304.

tions is to be found in Jewish apocalyptic.[45] Victorinus of Pettau shares the millenniarist doctrine which is one of the ingredients of these speculations. As for Commodian, who has left us two collections of poems, the *Instructions* and the *Carmen Apologeticum*, the dating of his work is much disputed.[46] But the primitive literary and doctrinal expression of the work leaves no doubt about its early date. It is a valuable witness to traditional typology. It is influenced by Jewish apocalyptic. The eschatological breath which blows through his work and his rigorism place him firmly in the same world as Tertullian and Hippolytus.

45. See A. Luneau, *L'Histoire du salut chez les Pères de l'Église*, Paris, 1964.

46. See H. A. M. Hoppenbrouwers, 'Commodien poète chrétien' in *Graecitas et latinitas christianorum primaeva*, Supplementa Fascicula II, Nyjmegen, 1964, pp. 47–89.

Five

Literature Associated with the Council of Nicaea

The beginning of the fourth century marks a turning-point in the history of patristic literature. Constantine's[1] conversion had consequences which were not confined to politics. When he allowed Christianity to come out into the daylight and gave it an official standing, he also created the conditions for a cultural expansion. The building of numerous churches, the development of Christian feast-days and the rise in fashion of the cult of martyrs gave rise to new literary forms, speeches made on public occasions, eulogies on the saints, catechetical teaching in preparation for the sacraments. But though this association with political power made possible new activity, it had its dangers too. As Edward Schwartz has shown,[2] the Emperors claimed the right to interfere in ecclesiastical questions, and a dangerous involvement of movements of theological thought with political causes made itself evident.

But this was not the only concern that marked the beginning of the fourth century. This period coincided with a critical time for theology. After the creative age which had produced Origen, a period of decline set in at the end of the third century. The formulae which defined the relation of the Father and the Son in the Trinity continued to be characterized by the subordinationism which marks most of the Christian thinkers of the pre-Nicene period. This kind of subordinationism was not seriously meant by these writers. But the most radical form of it found expression at the beginning of the fourth century

1. Emperor A.D. 306–37.

2. 'Zur Kirchengeschichte des 4. Jahrhunderts', *ZNW* 34 (1935), pp. 129–213.

in the form of Arianism.[3] Other forms were more restrained. A different definition, however, was produced which better emphasized the unity of being of the Father and the Son. It followed the theological tendencies of the Roman Church. It met support in an anti-Arian reaction. The Council of Nicaea gave it its sanction. The conversion of Constantine and the Council of Nicaea are the two poles between which the patristic literature of this age gravitates.

The great representative of the traditional theology of the Apologists and of Origen at the beginning of the fourth century is Eusebius of Caesarea. Eusebius is first and foremost a historian. His work is dominated by the meeting of theology and history and by Constantine's miraculous patronage of the Church. It was primarily his learning that made Eusebius a historian. He was bishop of Caesarea in Palestine, and he laboured at the library which Origen and Pamphilus had founded. Pierre Nautin[4] has effectively demonstrated how the version which he gives of the history of the first three centuries is dictated by the documentation which was available to him at Caesarea. If his idea of how to write history is compared with those of earlier pagan historians, it will be realized, as Modigliano has seen,[5] that its main features are 'the importance attached to the most recent past, the place given to doctrinal controversies, and the careful use of documents'. The part assigned to the martyrs, which W. Völker[6] has brought out, is also remarkable. Eusebius had experienced the persecution of Diocletian,[7] and wanted to recall the times of the first Christian centuries.

3. Founded by Arius, a presbyter of Alexandria (died 335), it was condemned at Nicaea in 325 but survived long afterwards as a sect.

4. *Lettres et écrivains chrétiens des IIe and IIIe siècles*, Paris, 1961, pp. 9–11.

5. 'Pagan and Christian Historiography in the Fourth Century A.D.', in *The Conflict between Paganism and Christianity in the Fourth Century*, Oxford, 1963, p. 91.

6. 'Von welchen Tendenzen liess sich Eusebius bei Abfassung seiner Kirchengeschichte leiten?', *V C* 4 (1950), pp. 163–7.

7. Emperor A.D. 284–305.

But this history implied a philosophy which Jean Sirinelli[8] has studied to good purpose. This philosophy is particularly set forth in the first chapters of the *Demonstration of the Gospel*. Eusebius's aim was to write a religious history of the human race. Christianity is the natural and primitive religion both by its monotheism and by its morality. This primitive religion, with the exception of some wise men, has degenerated into idolatry under the influence of the devils. The primitive tradition was, however, preserved among the Jews. In most respects these ideas recall Clement of Alexandria in their concern to give a comparative account of the history of the religious traditions of different nations. Christ appeared as he who had come to vanquish the devils and so to bring back the original monotheism. This work reached its fulfilment with the conversion of Constantine. In his Address to the *Congregation of Holy People* which expresses Eusebius's political and religious thought, Constantine is represented as the man who has effected the religious and political unity of the world by destroying polytheism, which was the cause of division among the nations.[9] The complete absence from Eusebius's work of concern for calculation of the time of the Second Advent is remarkable; it had engrossed the attention of earlier Christian historians, Hippolytus or Hegesippus. Eusebius's interest is turned towards the Kingdom of God on earth. Eusebius's mind, in contrast to Origen's, might be compared to the mind of Marx in contrast to that of Hegel.

Eusebius's theology of the Word is related to this view of history. In the continuation of the theology of history which is already visible in Clement of Rome and which persists throughout the whole ante-Nicene period, the Word is thought of primarily in his function in the universe. He is the agent of the Father in his ordering of the history of the universe. The action of the Word is co-extensive with the action of the Father. The Word has already manifested himself in the Old

8. *Les Vues historiques d'Eusèbe de Césarée durant la période prénicienne*, Dakar, 1961.

9. See Erik Peterson, *Theologische Traktate*, Munich, 1951, pp. 45–51.

Testament. The New Testament only represents a further stage of this manifestation. By this doctrine the Incarnation is reduced. Moreover, in Eusebius's subordinationism the emphasis is laid upon monotheism. It is the Father who is God in the absolute sense of the term. Christianity is not different from primitive monotheism. The political structure corresponding to this subordination is visible in the parallel between the Father, the original Monad, like Plotinus's One; the Word, the being that holds all things of the intellect in a unity; and the Emperor, the being that binds all things of the senses in a unity.

This theology of the Word was not only important as far as it affected Eusebius, but because it stood for the thought of most of the bishops of the East on the eve of the Council of Nicaea, especially those who were devotees of Origen. This was the doctrine of Dionysius of Alexandria[10] and Gregory of Neo-Caesarea.[11] This was what was to persist in the 'Homoean' tradition of the disciples of Eusebius, Akakius of Caesarea, Eusebius of Emesa and Meletius of Antioch.[12] This theology is not Arian, because it confesses, with Origen, the eternal generation of the Word. But it makes this generation the result of a free decision of God, related to creation and revelation. The doctrine of the Word has not succeeded in freeing itself from its associations with a theory of the universe.

Eusebius was to have as his successor at Caesarea his disciple Akakius who was to continue his theological work and to emerge as one of the leaders of the 'Homoean' party. Akakius was an exegete like his teacher. Fragments of his *Commentary on the Octateuch* have been identified by Robert Devreesse in the *catenae*.[13] This discovery is interesting because of the tendencies which this work displays. Akakius rejects Origen's

10. Bishop A.D. 248–65.

11. Gregory the Wonder-Worker, *c.* A.D. 213–70.

12. Died 366, 359 and 381 respectively. They were called 'Homoeans' because they supported the view that the Son was 'like' the Father (Greek *homoios*), but no more.

13. *Les Anciens Commentateurs grecs de l'Octateuque et des Rois*, Vatican, 1959, pp. 55–103, 105–22.

allegorical exegesis, just as he rejects his ideas about the pre-existence of souls. But neither does he use literal exegesis as the exegetes of Antioch did, as did Eustathius of Antioch,[14] the supporter of Nicaean doctrine, or Eusebius of Emesa, the Homoean, whose fragments Devreesse has also published. What interests Akakius is the harmonization of the Biblical narrative with the facts of the science of his time. It is a new interest.[15] We shall find it again in the works of St Basil and St Gregory of Nyssa's work on the *Hexameron*. It is not impossible that on this point these last writers belonged to the school of Caesarea, seeing that they originally had links with Homoean circles.

Eusebius's chief controversial work is his essay *Against Marcellus*. On the eve of the Council of Nicaea Marcellus of Ancyra[16] looked in fact like the champion of the theological revolution which was to break with the subordinationist tradition and prevail at Nicaea. His work has almost completely disappeared as a result of the condemnations which were passed on by him in the second half of the fourth century. But we must not forget the resistance which Athanasius and the bishops of Rome were for a long time to put up against this condemnation, which was extracted from them by the bishops of the East in exchange for the acceptance by those bishops of the *homoousios*.[17] For these reasons, the importance of Marcellus of Ancyra has scarcely been recognized. The labours of Weber[18] and of Simonetti[19] have begun to restore his importance to him.

The difference between Marcellus of Ancyra and earlier

14. Bishop *c.* A.D. 324–30.

15. See Jean Daniélou, 'Bulletin d'histoire des origines chrétiennes', *RSR* 61 (1949), pp. 146–7.

16. Died A.D. 374.

17. 'Of the same substance', the crucial word in the Nicene formula which was used to refute the subordinationism of the Arians.

18. *Archè. Ein Beitrag zur Christologie des Eusebius von Cesarea*, Neue Stadt, 1964, 132–8.

19. *Studi sull'arianesimo*, Rome, 1965, pp. 38–42. See *RSR* 54 (1966), 308–12.

theology lies in the importance given to the Incarnation. This emerges as something completely new. The texts of the Old Testament which the earlier Fathers used to apply to the eternal generation such as Proverbs 8.22, 'The Lord created me the beginning of his ways', or Psalm 110.3, 'I have begotten thee before the daystar', are applied by Marcellus to the Incarnation. It is through the Incarnation that the Logos became the centre of the creation's unity. As eternal Logos he has no closer relation to it than the Father. These emancipating views were destined to prevail in later theology. The weakness of Marcellus's theology lies in the absence of clear assertions about the eternal generation of the Logos as a separate Person. But it must be realized that this assertion had always hitherto been linked with a subordinationist concept, that it was so in the thought of his opponents, and consequently that even if he did not hold this doctrine himself it is owing to him that it had been made feasible.

But though contemporary research gives back an important part to Marcellus of Ancyra in the Nicaean revolution, it is not the less true that the most significant representative of this revolution is Athanasius of Alexandria. As far as his personality is concerned, one of the most valuable contributions of contemporary research is the publication by Th. Lefort of his spiritual books, in Coptic.[20] In this there appear more clearly the links that connect him with the monastic tradition of Anthony and Pachomius.[21] He was a deacon of Alexandria, and accompanied his bishop Alexander to the Council of Nicaea. He became Alexander's successor and emerged as the great champion of the faith of Nicaea and on this score the target of the persecution of the Arians. They deposed him from his episcopal see three times. During his battle against Arianism, he found a powerful support in the West and especially in the Church of Rome, where the subordinationist theology

20. See A. Aubineau, 'Les Écrits de Saint Athanase sur la virginité', *R A M* 31 (1955), pp. 151–73.

21. *c.* 290–346. The founder of coenobitic monasticism, a system whereby monks live in a community but occupy separate dwellings.

had never found an enthusiastic response. When his successor, Peter, was exiled in his turn he too sought refuge in Rome.

Athanasius's significance in Trinitarian theology lies in his ability to separate wholly the generation of the Word from a theory about the universe and consequently reject all subordinationism, as Marcellus had done, but at the same time asserting the existence as a separate Person of the Word, with the traditional theologians, something which Marcellus had not done. By this achievement he made possible a reconciliation of the movements of thought which were opposing each other while retaining whatever of value each possessed. This new doctrine is evident in the fact that he is the first to apply the word Pantocrator (Almighty) to the Word, a term hitherto reserved for the Father,[22] and to assert as a consequence the entire equality in the Godhead of the Father and the Son, while at the same time subscribing to the eternal existence as a Person of the latter. This formula alone expressed realistically the Christian datum. But it formed a paradox from the point of view of the philosophic tradition, because for it existence as a person implied limitations. This is why earlier definitions had been inadequate. The intellectual tools capable of formulating the datum of the faith had not yet been invented.

But Athanasius is also not less important as a theologian of the Incarnation and the Atonement. Here again he comes close to Marcellus of Ancyra, in that he is a very definite innovator. Following Marcellus, it is to the Incarnation that he applies Proverbs 8.22. In his book *On the Incarnation of the Word*, which is his most important work, he emphasizes this innovation by linking the Incarnation consistently with the Atonement and in placing Christ's conquest of death at the centre of his theology. The interest is thus firmly shifted from the Word as Creator to the Word as Redeemer, without, however, the doctrine of the original creation of man in the image of God being played down. On the contrary, Athanasius sees in

22. See Per Beskow, *Rex Gloriae. The Kingship of Christ in the Early Church*, Uppsala, 1962, pp. 295–313.

the image of God in man, which he does not distinguish from the likeness, man's calling to share the life of God.[23] On one point his theology of the Incarnation has recently given rise to disputes: it is the problem of determining whether he recognized a human soul in Christ. Marcel Richard sees in him a representative of the 'Logos/sarx' theory which his disciple Apollinarius of Laodicea[24] was to push to the point of formally denying the existence in Christ of a human *nous* (mind).[25] It seems that Athanasius did not formally ask this question.

Besides Athanasius, the great champion of Nicaea in the East was the bishop of Antioch, Eustathius. The fragments of his work which survive have been gathered together by M. Spanneut.[26] Like Athanasius and Marcellus, he interprets Proverbs 8.22 of the Incarnation. His theology of the Incarnation, as indeed that of Marcellus, is very orthodox and presents no difficulties such as that of Athanasius does. But though Eustathius attacks Arianism as far as his theology goes, he stands for a very different mentality which contrasts the Antiochene tradition with the tradition of Alexandria. Whereas the latter, continuing Hellenistic Judaism, is notable for its taste for allegory, its liking for philosophical speculation and its passion for the intellectual, the Antiochene tradition, whose great representative at the beginning of the fourth century is Eustathius, is closer to Rabbinic Judaism. He employs a literal exegesis. Eustathius is an opponent of Origen in his essay on the Witch of Endor. Besides Eustathius, Eusebius of Emesa, a good Semitic scholar, consulted the original Hebrew of the Bible. Literary studies were pursued at Antioch rather than

23. See Régis Bernard, *L'Image de Dieu d'après Saint Athanase*, Paris, 1952, pp. 25–9.

24. *c.* A.D. 310–90. See pages 95–6. The 'Logos/sarx' theory saw Jesus Christ as the result of a direct assumption of the human physical frame (but not the human mind) by the Word of God.

25. 'Saint Athanase et la psychologie du Christ selon les ariens', *M S R* 4 (1947), pp. 5–54.

26. *Recherches sur les écrits d'Eustathe d'Antioche*, Lille, 1948, pp. 93–132.

philosophy. We have one example of these in the *Homilies on the Psalms* of the Arian Asterius,[27] the whole of which have been reconstructed by Marcel Richard; they are characteristic of the second Sophistic period.[28] Finally, the spiritual tradition of Antioch has a more realistic and empirical colour.

Antioch has its own cultural structure corresponding to that of Alexandria. But whereas at Alexandria there was also a consistent doctrinal tradition, Antioch in the fourth century was destined to be the clearing-house for the most contrary movements of thought. Since the third century the Origenists of Antioch had been cheek by jowl with the modalism[29] of Paul of Samosata. But Lucian,[30] a priest of Antioch of the same era, is the father of Arianism. Eustathius, who stood for the Nicaean revolution, was destined to be deposed in 326 and replaced by an Arian bishop. The most important school remained the Homoean tradition of Eusebius of Caesarea. It is at Antioch too that Monophysitism[31] first made its appearance, and with Antioch that the origins of Nestorianism[32] are connected. For certain periods Antioch was to have four bishops at the same time, corresponding to the four separated communities, Eustathian, Apollinarian, Arian and Homoean. Just as Alexandria during all the fourth century was to be the great centre of Nicaean orthodoxy and was to remain controlled by Athanasius's spirit, so Antioch was for long to be controlled by Arian and Eusebian tendencies and the community founded by Eustathius was only to consist of a small minority.

The contrast between Eusebius and Athanasius repeated

27. Died after 341.

28. *Asterii Sophistae Commentariorum in Psalmos quae supersunt*, ed. Marcel Richard, Oslo, 1956.

29. Modalism is the view that Jesus Christ is not a separate entity or person within the Godhead but simply one expression of, or one recipient of, a mode or aspect of the activity of God the Father.

30. Died 312.

31. The doctrine that in Christ there was but a single nature and that divine, rather than a double nature divine and human.

32. The doctrine that in Christ there were two *separate* natures, divine and human, carried to the point of almost identifying two persons in him.

itself in the West in the contrast between Lactantius[33] and Hilary.[34] The former represents at the beginning of the fourth century a reproduction of Eusebius in Latin. He has a view of history very much like his. For him it is a decline from primitive monotheism under the impulsion of devils. Only the Jewish people preserved the original religion (*Institutions* II.14 (*PL* VI, 328)). Christ came to restore the true religion. Further, in his *De mortibus persecutorum* Lactantius sees in the pagan Emperors who persecuted the Church the agents of devils who opposed the spread of Christianity,[35] and hails in Constantine, who summoned him to his side at Nicomedia, the alliance between the Roman Empire and the Christian faith. All the same it is noteworthy that, precisely opposite to the theology of Eusebius, his theology of history achieves its end by millenniarism. In this point he is faithful to Tertullian's African theology, whereas Eusebius had come under Origen's influence. Finally, Lactantius's theology, like that of Eusebius, is primarily monotheistic. The Son, who is more or less identified with the Spirit, is put forth by the Father for the purpose of teaching the human race. He appears to be greater than the angels but exists on the same level of being as they. Here Lactantius is reproducing a primitive theology of the Word, akin to that of Tertullian, and one which has not profited, as the theology of Eusebius has, from Origen's intellectual achievement.

Lactantius's theology is the end result of that of the apologists. Christianity in his thought is presented neither as one religion among all the religions nor as something other than a religion. But it is the true and unique religion of which the various form of paganism are distortions. This religion was that of the primitive human race, and it remained that of the Jews. Some wise men among the pagans knew it. Lactantius, like Justin and Clement of Alexandria, saw in the wise men of Greece or of India the witness of a genuine religion which they

33. *c.* A.D. 240–320.

34. *c.* A.D. 315–67, Bishop of Poitiers.

35. See Lactance, *De la mort des persécuteurs*, I, Introduction by J. Moreau, Paris, 1954, p. 29.

contrasted with the idolatrous cults. This idea, borrowed from the apologists, takes on a new reality in the period of Eusebius and of Lactantius. It fits into an age when the forms of paganism were in the process of dying and when Christianity was about to replace them as virtually the religion of the Mediterranean world. But in Lactantius's manner of thought the essential Christian dogmas, the Trinity and the Incarnation, were reduced. Just as Athanasius faced Eusebius, so Hilary was destined to stand for the Nicaean revolution against Lactantius.

Hilary's work is primarily expository. He wrote three important books of this kind, the *Commentary on Matthew*, the *Treatises on the Psalms* and the *Book of Mysteries*. Hilary's exegesis is essentially typological. In this sense he continues the Western tradition, that of Irenaeus of Lyons, of Tertullian of Carthage and of Hippolytus of Rome. Here he represents the common tradition of the Church.[36] He takes no notice of either the allegorization of Alexandria or the literalism of Antioch. It is in the next generation, with Ambrose and Jerome, that these two traditions will begin to make themselves felt in the West. On this reckoning Hilary's work must be thought of as close to that of other Western authors, the *Tractatus* of Gregory of Elvira[37] and the *Sermons* of Zeno of Verona.[38] The great subjects of this typological exegesis, Noah and the Flood, the sacrifice of Isaac, Moses and the crossing of the Red Sea, Joshua and the crossing of Jordan, David playing on his harp, are those which we also find at the same period in the paintings of the catacombs and the carvings on the sarcophagi. We have in it the richest collection of common Christian symbolism.

On the theological level, Hilary adopts positions close to those of Athanasius. He breaks with the subordinationism of

36. See J. Daniélou, *Sacramentum Futuri. Essai sur les origines de la typologie biblique*, Paris, 1950, pp. 40–1. (Trans. *From Shadows to Reality*, London. 1960.)

37. Died after A.D. 392. A very strong opponent of Arianism.

38. An African who was Bishop of Verona from 362 until his death in 375.

Tertullian and Lactantius, as Athanasius had with that of Origen and Eusebius. He too understands Proverbs 8.22 of the birth of Christ according to the flesh. He also underlines the new move represented by the Incarnation. He is not interested in an original affinity of men with the Word which the Word only came to restore. But he is concerned with a human race deprived of the life of God to which the Word of God came to impart this life. Hilary always attempted in his *De Trinitate* to bring his ideas closer, as Athanasius had in the East, to the views which corresponded in the West to those of the followers of Eusebius and Marcellus. In this respect he was opposed to the extreme Nicaeans, such as Ossius of Cordova[39] and Lucifer of Cagliari.[40] In the strength of his theological thought he represents the most important stage of Latin Trinitarian theology between Tertullian and Augustine.

Latin theology is also represented at this period by Marius Victorinus. This man had been previously a Neo-Platonic philosopher, before he became a Christian. He is the first great representative of Latin Christian Neo-Platonism. His thought has been examined in noteworthy fashion by Pierre Hadot.[41] His Neo-Platonism, related to that of Porphyry and Iamblichus, joined the influence of Plato, especially in the *Parmenides*, to Aristotelian logic and a mysticism indebted to the *Chaldaic Oracles*. When Victorinus was converted he integrated this Neo-Platonism into Christian theology. By this achievement, his work foreshadows what the Pseudo-Areopagite[42] will achieve in relation to Proclus a century later. Victorinus's Trinitarian thought is original. He starts off from the contrast, common in the pre-Nicene period, between the Father, who is the infinite and unconditioned Being, that is, the substance, and

39. *c.* A.D. 257–357, for a time he may have acted as ecclesiastical adviser to Constantine.

40. Died *c.* A.D. 370. A fiercely anti-Arian theologian.

41. In his introduction to *Traités théologiques sur la Trinité*, Paris, 1960.

42. A mystical theologian writing probably in Syria *c.* A.D. 500. His writings were attributed by the Monophysites to Dionysius of Athens (Act 17.34). See pages 114–15.

the Son who is form and condition, that is, a Person. But he overcomes this opposition by showing that the Father is also a Person inasmuch as he is an unrevealed form, and that the Son is of one substance with the Father inasmuch as he is the revelation of his form. Marius Victorinus was destined to exert a decisive influence upon Augustine. He opens the second epoch of Latin theology.

Six

The Age of Theodosius

It was in the second half of the fourth century that patristic literature attained its zenith. The union of the Greco-Roman civilization and the Christian faith, hallowed by the conversion of Constantine, began at this point to bear fruit. Once it had become the religion of the Empire, Christianity drew to itself the living forces of society. The activity of the Church was evident in every sphere, on the religious level, on the social level, on the cultural level. At the same time theology outstripped the tentative explorations of its beginnings, found out the formulae which accurately expressed its belief, and canonized them in the great councils which followed Nicaea, those of Constantinople, Ephesus and Chalcedon.[1] Finally, the powerful spiritual drive of the age of the martyrs continued under a new form in the monastic movement which attracted countless followers of Anthony and Pachomius from Mesopotamia to Gaul.

It is impossible during this period, short as it is, to make distinctions between the East and the West, so much are their characteristics common to both. In fact the East at this period shone with an extraordinary brilliance, and the West became its pupil. Ambrose is much more the disciple of Origen and of Basil than of Tertullian or Lactantius. Rufinus[2] translated Origen into Latin. Soon Jerome will be learning exegesis with Didymus of Alexandria, Apollinarius of Laodicea and Gregory of Nazianzus. The reaction was destined to make itself felt swiftly. It would appear already in Jerome's reversal of attitude towards Origen. With Augustine the West was destined to re-

1. Which took place in 381, 431 and 451 respectively.

2. *c.* 345–410. A presbyter of Aquileia.

turn to its own spirit and cut itself off from the East for long centuries. And this cultural break would correspond to a political break within the Empire. But the age of Theodosius[3] was exactly the fortunate moment when political unity encouraged cultural unity. The fact that the Emperor resided as much at Constantinople as at Milan has its parallel in the kinship between the bishop of Constantinople and the bishop of Milan, between Gregory of Nazianzus and Ambrose. The only sub-division we can follow here is a geographical sub-division which keeps our interest moving between the great centres of the Empire. At Alexandria Athanasius's successors were first his two brothers, Peter and Timothy; Theophilus succeeded these. They continued to make Alexandria the centre of Nicene orthodoxy. But they did not possess Athanasius's genius and we have very few writings from their pens. By way of contrast the school of Alexandria had an important head at this period, Didymus the Blind. The only remains of his exegetical work used to be fragments preserved in the *Catenae*. But the library found at Toura, which has been mentioned in connexion with Origen, includes several of his works, especially on the Psalms, Zachariah, Genesis and Ecclesiastes. Only a part of this has been published. He is concerned with an exposition of texts, in the scholarly sense of the word, following the methods of the Alexandrian grammarians.[4] In these Didymus seems to be a disciple of Origen, whose distant successor he was at the head of the school. He employs, like him, an allegorical method of interpretation. He shares his doctrines too, especially the pre-existence of souls and the *apokatastasis* (universalism),[5] as his *Commentary on Zachariah*[6] proves. This discovery then explains the reasons for which Didymus was included in the condemnation of Origenism in 553.

3. Emperor A.D. 379–95.

4. See Aloys Kehl, *Der Psalmenkommentar von Tura*, Quaternio IX, Cologne, 1964, pp. 19–40.

5. In its simplest form, the belief that every soul ultimately attains union with God, or reaches heaven.

6. See Jean Daniélou, 'Bulletin d'histoire des origines chrétiennes', *R S R* 51 (1963), pp. 162–3.

In Palestine the most important figure is Cyril of Jerusalem.[7] He had been consecrated by his metropolitan Akakius of Caesarea.[8] He was therefore connected by his origins with the Eusebian and Homoean tradition. But he ranged himself firmly with Nicene orthodoxy and was an object of Akakius's persecutions, for Akakius remained faithful to Homoeanism. We possess a catechetical collection of his corresponding to the different stages of the final preparation for baptism during Lent. After the inaugural catechetical class which corresponds to the taking down of names, five addresses had to be given to a congregation on each of the five first Sundays in Lent (which lasted eight weeks in the East). Then twelve catechetical lectures giving a commentary on the creed corresponded to the daily meetings of the sixth and seventh week. Finally five 'mystagogic catacheses' explaining the sacramental rites were given during Holy Week. It is possible that these last are those of Cyril's successor, John of Jerusalem.[9] We have in this a unique collection which has nothing comparable to it except in the *Catechetical Homilies* of Theodore of Mopsuestia.[10] Many allusions to the Holy Places can be noticed in Cyril's catecheses. These took a new importance for Christian piety during the fourth century and were visited by numerous pilgrims. We have a little later a valuable document about a pilgrimage of this kind, the *Travel Journal* of Etheria.[11]

The episcopal see of Antioch at the Council of 381 was occupied by Meletius. Meletius is one of the greatest figures of his time. By his origins he was connected with Homoean circles. He had in competition with him at Antioch a Eustathian bishop Paulinus, who was supported by Alexandria and Rome. But Meletius was a man of conciliatory spirit. It was owing to him that at the Synod of Antioch of 379 a great step forward was taken towards reconciling opposed parties. Antioch was first

7. *c.* A.D. 315–86.

8. Died A.D. 366.

9. W. A. Swaan, 'À propos des catéchèses mystagogiques attribuées à Cyrille de Jérusalem', *Museon* 55 (1942), pp. 1–43.

10. See pages 104–6.

11. Probably a Spanish nun.

and foremost in the reign of Theodosius a great centre of Biblical scholarship. Its master was Diodore of Tarsus,[12] a friend of Meletius. He was a pupil of Eusebius of Emesa. His work is almost completely lost. Louis Mariès has collected the fragments preserved in the catenae of his *Commentary on the Psalms*.[13] Diodore appears in these as a typical example of Antiochene literalism. He attacks Alexandrian allegorization. Antioch was also a great centre of literary culture. The rhetorician Libanius included Christians among his pupils there, among them John Chrysostom and Theodore of Mopsuestia,[14] who are mentioned below.

The neighbouring town of Laodicea also possessed a famous man, but of very different views, Apollinarius.[15] His father, Apollinarius the elder, was a rhetorician and had attempted to endow Christianity with its own literature, by writing epic poems and tragedies on Biblical themes. His son was primarily a great exegete. Jerome was later to come to work under him. The task of reconstructing a part of his literary remains by means of fragments preserved in the *Catenae* has been started.[16] In these Apollinarius seems to be a disciple of Origen, but a moderate one. In the theological field he belongs to the Nicene party of Athanasius and Eustathius. But his theological thought has presented difficulties on two points. In the first place, pushing Athanasius's positions to extremes, he disputed the existence of a human *nous* (mind) in Christ, for he reckoned that otherwise Christ's unity could not have existed.[17] These ideas

12. Died *c.* A.D. 390.

13. *Études préliminaires à l'édition de Diodore de Tarse* 'Sur les Psaumes', Paris, 1933.

14. See especially A. M. J. Festugière, *Antioche païenne et chrétienne*, Paris, 1959.

15. *c.* A.D. 310–90.

16. See especially Joseph Reuss, *Matthäus – Kommentare aus der griechischen Kirche*, Berlin, 1957; R. Devreesse, *Les Anciens Commentateurs grecs de l'Octateuque et des Rois*, Paris, 1959; Henri de Riedmatten, 'Le texte des fragments exégétiques d'Apollinaire', *RSR* 44 (1956), pp. 560–6.

17. See R. A. Norris, *Manhood and Christ. A Study in the Christology of Theodore of Mopsuestia*, Oxford, 1963.

of Apollinarius were later to be vigorously challenged by Diodore, who in reaction tended to exaggerate the independence of Christ's human nature. This dispute was to be at the bottom of long debates which would set Monophysites and Nestorius in opposition to each other and would result in the Councils of Ephesus and of Chalcedon. Antioch therefore, which was already divided on the Trinitarian question, was also to become divided on the Christological question. Apollinarius in addition is one of the last millenniarists. He believed that at the End of Time Jerusalem would become the capital of a Messianic Kingdom.

Epiphanius, bishop of Salamis[18] in the island of Cyprus, represents a type which Irenaeus and Hippolytus had exemplified before him, that of the controversialist against heretics. He is a fanatical defender of the Nicene dogma. His chief enemy is Origen. In 392 he attacked him publicly in the presence of John of Jerusalem, at a moment when Origenistic theories were circulating in monastic communities in Palestine. This attack lay behind a whole series of controversies, in which Jerome and John Chrysostom in particular took part. Epiphanius's great work, the *Panarion*, or 'Medicine-chest', listed all the heresies since the beginning. Many in this list are only known from it. It is a mine of valuable information, especially on certain Gnostic groups and Judeo-Christian movements of thought.

But in the period which we are examining the chief centre of patristic thought is to be found neither at Alexandria nor at Antioch, but in Cappadocia. It is there that the works of greatest genius saw the light and also where Eastern theology overcame its tensions and worked out a common Trinitarian doctrine. The man who started this was St Basil.[19] He belonged to a senatorial family of rich landed proprietors.[20] This accounts for the very intense studies which he pursued at

18. *c.* A.D. 315–403.

19. *c.* A.D. 330–79.

20. See Barnim Trencke, *Politische und Sozialgeschichtliche Studien zu den Basilius-Briefen*, Munich, 1961.

Athens and at Antioch. He was converted to the monastic ideal by Eustathius of Sebaste, and became the founder of Cappadocian coenobitic monasticism. Dom Gribomont has studied the chronology of his work as a legislator for monastic communities and has shown that the *Moral Rules*, which is mainly composed of Biblical quotations, is the older work, and that the *Quaestiones*, which consists of answers to questions on particular points, was added to later by successive editions.[21] Basil became bishop of Caesarea in Cappadocia in 371 and devoted the eight years of his episcopacy to reconciling the different movements of Trinitarian thought. His immense correspondence testifies to this endeavour. He was in communication with Athanasius of Alexandria, with the bishop of Rome and with Meletius of Antioch.[22] This valiant struggle was crowned with success just after his death by the Council of Constantinople of 381. Basil's greatest trial was to have to see opposed to him his master and friend Eustathius of Sebaste, who at the head of a small sect led a secession on the subject of the Holy Spirit.

As far as theology and exposition are concerned, Basil had originally been a disciple of Origen. This is explained, among other reasons, by the links between Origen and Cappadocia. This area has been evangelized by Gregory the Wonder-Worker in the third century, who had been a pupil of Origen's at Caesarea. It was Gregory who had converted Basil's grandparents. Firmilian, bishop of Caesarea[23] in the third century, was also a pupil of Origen. During his time as a monk, Basil had composed a book of selections from Origen, the *Philocalia*. His work must have been intended to preserve from decay the better parts of Origenism, while separating the extreme doctrines. As far as exegesis goes, Basil is connected with the heirs of Origen's tradition at Caesarea, Eusebius and Akakius,

21. *Histoire du texte des ascétiques de Saint Basile*, Louvain, 1963.

22. See Emmanuel Amand de Mendieta, 'Basile de Césarée et Damase de Rome', in *Special Print of Biblical and Patristical Studies in Memory of Robert Pierce Casey*, Freiburg, 1963, pp. 122–66.

23. Died A.D. 268.

rather than with his Alexandrian successors. He is above all concerned to transpose Scripture into a literary and scientific language suitable for his time. As far as theology is concerned, he preserved Origen's theological patterns, especially that which relates to the doctrine of the Holy Spirit, but he brings them into conformity with the Nicene doctrine of the Son being of one substance with the Father.[24]

By the side of Basil must be set two figures whose work is of the same standard as his. First there is his friend Gregory of Nazianzus.[25] They had been students together at Athens. Together they had been led towards the monastic ideal. But Gregory's predilections urged him more towards a hermit's life and he never returned to the world of Basilian monasticism and its communal life. His personality and his character as a writer represent a unique case which has never been completely delineated. He never wrote any work of exegesis; but Jerome regarded him, with Didymus, and Apollinarius, as one of the three great masters of exposition of his time. He never wrote a work of controversial theology; yet he is considered to be the theologian of the Trinity *par excellence*. He never wrote a work of spirituality; yet he is thought to be the spiritual master above all others by Evagrius and by Maximus.[26] He had been a bishop; but he never was able to remain in the three sees which he filled.

Gregory is essentially a literary man, a type who would have been called a 'sophist' or a rhetorician. From a cultural point of view he is to be classed with the great pagan rhetoricians of his time, such as Libanius, Themistius or Himerius. His work consists exclusively of addresses, poems and letters, in conformity with the literary conventions of his time. And he is a superb writer, concise, brilliant, arresting. His work is

24. See Hermann Dörries, *De Spiritu Sancto. Der Beitrag des Basilius zum Abschluss des trinitarischen Dogmas*, Göttingen, 1956; Alkuin Heising, 'Der Heilige Geist und die Heiligung der Engel in der Pneumatologie des Basilius von Cäsarea', *Z K T* 87 (1965), pp. 257–308.

25. A.D. 329–89.

26. 'The Confessor', *c.* 580–662, Greek theologian and ascetic writer.

soaked in the culture of antiquity, with allusions to Homer and to the tragedians. He has something like a contempt for the dull technical uniform of the Biblical commentators and polemical theologians. But at the same time, and in his own way, he contends for the same doctrinal, exegetical and spiritual values as Basil. And thanks to his literary skill he imparted to these values an effect on the educated society of his period which technical works could never have done. In his hands the charms of rhetoric, which had exercised so powerful an attraction towards decaying paganism that men of the stature of Theodore of Mopsuestia and Gregory of Nyssa had found it necessary to give way to it, were employed in the service of the Christian faith.

The third great figure from a Cappadocian background is the younger brother of Basil, Gregory of Nyssa, who continued the general tendencies of his brother's thought, but gave them an incomparable depth of theology and spirituality. His work, which has often been neglected, has been the centre of a new interest during the last thirty years. Werner Jaeger has instituted a new edition of his works, which is a monument of contemporary scholarship. It is difficult to fix the chronology of his life and of his work.[27] Jaeger has fixed with certainty 371 as the date of his earliest work, *De virginitate*, which is a propaganda piece for Cappadocian monasticism.[28] Elsewhere Gregory states that he is married.[29] He was bishop of the little town of Nyssa in 371, and began to assume a position of leadership after his brother's death in 379. He took part in the Synod of Antioch assembled by Meletius in 379. He spoke at the Council of Constantinople of 381 and delivered the funeral address on Meletius. He was entrusted by Theodosius with the task of implementing the decrees of the Council in the diocese

27. See J. Daniélou, 'La Chronologie des sermons de Grégoire de Nysse', *Rev S R* 29 (1955), pp. 346–72.

28. *Two Rediscovered Works of Ancient Christian Literature. Gregory of Nyssa and Makarius*, Leiden (1954), p. 24.

29. See J. Daniélou, 'Le Mariage de Grégoire de Nysse et la chronologie de sa vie', *R E Aug* 2 (1956), pp. 71–8.

of the Pontus (a large group of provinces) and he delivered the funeral addresses on the wife and daughter of Theodosius. The part he played as a counsellor of Theodosius is significant up to the Emperor's move to Milan in 385, where Ambrose was to play a similar part. He devoted the rest of his life to giving new spiritual life to Basilian monasticism, especially by the publication of the *Hypotyposis* which Jaeger has restored to him.[30]

In the field of exegesis, Gregory continues Basil's tradition in his works on Genesis, but with the special concern of giving a more methodical analysis, which was meant to bring out the logic of its development, the *akolouthia*,[31] and to be open to a confrontation by forms of pagan philosophy, in particular to Neo-Platonism. But in addition, in his books on *Exodus*, the *Psalms*, *Ecclesiastes* and the *Song of Songs*, he continues the allegorization of Origen, to whom he refers explicitly, in the task of seeking in the books of Scripture the laws of God's activity in order to apply them to the spiritual life. His exegetical work has consequently two sharply different tendencies, one more scientific and philosophic, in the tradition of Akakius of Caesarea, and the other more mystical. Both tendencies can claim Origen as their source.

In the field of theology Gregory's thought has two poles. On one side he stresses strongly the doctrine of the image of God, as the basic direction of human nature towards the vision of God. In this he preserves Origen's influence, but he rejects Origen's errors, the pre-existence of souls and the final return to the condition of pure spirit. But at the same time, in his controversy with the Arian Eunomius,[32] he establishes the absolute transcendence of God, whose essence he defines as the *apeiron*, the infinite. He is the first to define this fully, as E. Mühlenberg has shown.[33] Starting from these two facts he reaches a concept

30. op. cit.

31. See J. Daniélou, 'Acolouthia chez Grégoire de Nysse', *Rev S R* 27 (1953), pp. 219–49.

32. Bishop of Cyzicus in Mysia for a short period; died *c.* A.D. 395.

33. *Die Unendlichkeit Gottes bei Gregor von Nyssa*, Göttingen, 1966.

of human life as continual movement onwards (*epectasis*). Change is what constitutes man because his essence as a creature is to move from nothingness towards existence and this movement can never have an end, because he can never exhaust the divine infinity.[34]

To turn to Ambrose of Milan[35] is not so much to leave the cultural and theological *milieu* of the Cappadocians as to move from the Greek world to the Latin world. He resembles them first in belonging to senatorial society. He was chosen bishop when he was governor of the local province and not yet baptized. He exerted a deep influence on Theodosius when he made Milan his headquarters. He continued to perform important political tasks, especially in his diplomatic missions to Trèves. But he used his influence over the Emperor above all in the interests of the Church, particularly in the struggle against Arianism. His theological education, which necessarily took place late, shows that he knew the works of Tertullian and of Cyprian. But his knowledge of Greek, which formed part of the education of young men of the senatorial aristocracy, allowed him also to deepen his knowledge both of non-Christian writers like Plato and Plotinus, and also of Christian writers such as Origen and Basil.[36] In this respect his education is very similar to that of Gregory of Nyssa, his contemporary.

The chief work of Ambrose consists of the studies which he devoted to many books of the Bible. These works give a reproduction of his oral teaching, especially of his preaching during the first three weeks of Lent. We know what he was like by the personal testimony of St Augustine, who was brought by his mother to Ambrose's lectures on the *Hexameron*, even though Augustine was not yet a catechumen.[37] The most interesting part of Ambrose's work is his

34. See Jean Daniélou, *Platonisme et théologie mystique. La doctrine spirituelle de Saint Grégoire de Nysse*, second ed., Paris, 1954.

35. *c.* A.D. 339–97.

36. See P. Courcelles, *Les Lettres grecques en Occident de Macrobe à Cassiodore*, Paris, 1943.

37. A person undergoing training before baptism.

doctrine of man. In his doctrine of man's creation he is indebted to Basil's *Hexameron* in that he does not distinguish, as Philo and Gregory do, between the two narratives of Genesis as representing two different episodes. He combines a philosophic view of man, in which the body forms part of human nature, with a spiritual view in which the flesh wars against the spirit. One of his original ideas is to relate grace given to fallen man not to the vestiges of the original grace of Paradise, but to the anticipatory action of Christ's Resurrection. In this he recalls Tertullian and foreshadows Augustine.[38]

St Ambrose recalls Basil by his natural powers of leadership and Gregory of Nyssa by his mystical traits. An heir to Gregory of Nazianzus is found in the West in the poet Prudentius.[39] He was a Spaniard, an official under Theodosius, but above all a writer. His poetic output is considerable. But in contrast to the other Latin Christian poets of his time for whom poetry either remained something pagan, as with Ausonius,[40] or was a mere diversion, as with Paulinus of Nola,[41] he regarded the task of using Classical culture in the service of the praise of the true God as a vocation in him, as Italo Lana has effectively shown.[42] We have seen that this was precisely the intention of Gregory of Nazianzus. They were both the first examples of a new type which could only reach maturity in a Christian world, that of Christian literary men. They are the distant predecessors of Dante, of Milton, of Claudel.

At the other end of the Christian world, Syriac Christian literature produced a great writer at Edessa, Ephrem. Quite unlike Latin Christian literature, which relied to a great extent on Greek thought, Syriac Christian literature was connected with primitive Judeo-Christianity. It retained its forms of thought and of expression. Edessa, which was the centre of

38. See W. Seibel, *Fleisch und Geist beim Heiligen Ambrosius*, Munich, 1958.

39. *c.* A.D. 348–410.

40. *c.* A.D. 310–95. He was a native of Bordeaux.

41. *c.* A.D. 353–431. Also a native of Bordeaux.

42. I. Lana, *Due capitoli prudenziani*, Rome, 1962; Klaus Thraede, *Studien zum Sprache und Stil des Prudentius*, Göttingen, 1965.

Syriac Christianity, had seen the publication of the *Odes of Solomon* in the second century. In the third century Aphraates had published his *Treatises*. But it was in the fourth century that it reached its highest flight. Ephrem was born near Nisibis, was baptized there at the age of eighteen, then became a monk and finally a deacon. About 161 he established himself at Edessa. He retired to a hermit's dwelling near the city. But all the same he shared actively in the life of the local community, intervened in theological debates and encouraged charitable activities. In this respect the picture which A. Vööbus has drawn of him, of a hermit who has retreated into the mountains, without a fixed residence, living on grass and wild fruits, unkempt in appearance, seems exaggerated.[43] His work, which is entirely written in rhythmical prose, is a noteworthy example of a Semitic expression of Christianity, which naturally finds its place in the continuation of the thought of the Hebraic Bible without having to effect the transposition to the frame of reference of non-Semitic thought.

43. *Literary, Critical and Historical Studies in Ephrem the Syrian*, Stockholm, 1958.

Seven

The End of Greek Patristic Literature

The fifth and sixth centuries were to do no more than continue in the East what the fourth century had created. This is true as far as culture goes. The two great schools of Antioch and Alexandria, whose opposition began in the fourth century, were to continue to encounter each other. It is true also as far as theology goes. The Christological question was to be at the centre of the controversies of the century. It was destined to experience the persistence of the contrary traditions of Apollinarius and of Diodore of Tarsus in Monophysitism and Nestorianism. It was to form the subject of the two great councils of Ephesus and Chalcedon. Finally, the monastic movement would continue to expand and would give rise to a number of notable works, as many in Egypt as in Syria and in Asia Minor.

It was the school of Antioch, the more recent of the two, which was the more lively at the beginning of the fifth century and which produced the more notable works. Its great teacher was Theodore of Mopsuestia, who was to remain the master of the theology which is called Nestorian. He had been the disciple at Antioch of Diodore of Tarsus, whose tendencies in exegesis and in theology he carried forward. He had in addition been the pupil of Libanius,[1] at the same time as John Chrysostom was. Almost all of his vast writings have perished, as a result of the suspicion cast on him by the Second Council of Constantinople.[2] One of the results of contemporary re-

1. *c.* A.D. 314–393. A pagan rhetorician, he taught at Athens, Constantinople and Antioch.

2. A.D. 553.

search has been to reconstruct part of his work. The discovery of his *Catechetical Homilies* in Syriac by Mingana, of his commentary on St John's Gospel in Syriac by Vosté, of his commentaries on St Paul's epistles in a Latin translation by Swete, and the reconstruction from the *catenae* by Devreesse of the greater part of his commentary on the Psalms in Greek might be specially noted. The Syriac text of his famous book on the Incarnation, 'the most important of the theological works that ever emerged from the school of Antioch', as Quasten has written,[3] has been discovered by A. Scherer, but has been lost before it could be published.

In exegesis Theodore is the most typical example of the characteristics of the school of Antioch. His exegesis is very literalist. He takes the stories in Genesis in a historical sense. Paradise is a garden planted with beautiful trees. The tree of the knowledge of good and evil is a fig tree. The coats of skins are garments made of the bark of trees. Theodore's conception of the universe is of a Semitic kind, so he has no difficulty in accepting the Biblical picture of the universe, which is of the same kind. We know this picture of the universe through Cosmas Indicopleustes,[4] Theodore's disciple.[5] The universe has the form of a cube divided by the firmament fixed between the terrestrial sphere and the celestial sphere. Theodore interprets the Psalms by reference to the history of Israel and almost completely eliminates all Messianic references. He certainly has a critical spirit which causes him to interpret the texts of Scripture in the most scientific manner. In this he is the forerunner of the exegesis of the nineteenth century. But this literalism caused him to misunderstand the figurative character of some passages and the continuity in typology of the Old and New Testaments.

In the field of theology several scholars, especially Robert

3. *Patrology*, III, p. 576.

4. Cosmas the Indian Navigator; mid sixth century. He became a monk in later life.

5. Wanda Wolska, *La Cosmologie chrétienne de Cosmas Indicopleustès*, Paris, 1962.

Devreesse[6] and Marcel Richard,[7] have defended the Antiochene Christology against the condemnations of the Second Council of Constantinople, by showing that these condemnations were to some extent based on interpolated texts. But F. A. Sullivan has proved that Theodore's theology does beyond all denial hold dangerous possibilities.[8] It appears that for him God has placed man in his earthly condition, at odds with his passions, so that he can show what use he makes of his liberty. The moralistic character of his thought is very obvious. His contacts with Pelagius in the West have attracted notice. It is even possible that Pelagius[9] was influenced by him. John Chrysostom, his friend, testifies to the same moralism, but with a safer theology. Original sin appears to play no part in Theodore's thought. The function of man as the centre and bond of creation is to be noted.[10] Theodore's theology shows the effects of this view. He sees accordingly in Christ rather the man who uses his liberty perfectly than the saving activity of the Word. And it certainly seems as if by thus placing the emphasis on Christ's humanity he made this humanity the subject of Christ's actions as a man, and consequently distinguished two persons in him. Nestorius was destined later to give this doctrine a sharper form which would bring about his condemnation at the Council of Ephesus in 431.

John Chrysostom, the friend of Theodore of Mopsuestia, must be grouped with him. Like him, he was a pupil of Libanius and of Diodore of Tarsus. He led a monastic life with him and it has been proved that his writing *Ad Theodorum*

6. *Essai sur Théodore de Mopsueste*, Vatican, 1948.

7. 'L' introduction du mot hypostase dans la théologie de l'incarnation', *M S R* 2 (1945), pp. 21–9.

8. *The Christology of Theodore of Mopsuestia*, Rome, 1956.

9. Pelagius was a British monk who entered into a controversy with St Augustine as to the nature and extent of man's freewill and independence to attain or lose salvation without being guided by divine Grace. There were many repercussions from this dispute.

10. R. A. Norris, *Manhood and Christ. A Study in the Christology of Theodore of Mopsuestia*, Oxford, 1963.

Lapsum was addressed to the future bishop of Mopsuestia.[11] He was ordained priest at Antioch in 386, and then became bishop of Constantinople on the death of Nectarius in 397. In contrast to Theodore, who was primarily an exegete and a theologian, John Chrysostom was first and foremost a writer and an orator. The works of his youth show the relationship of his style to that of Libanius.[12] His work is made up essentially of addresses delivered at Antioch and at Constantinople. It consists mainly of commentaries on the New Testament. In these Chrysostom employs a literal exegesis of an Antiochene type. There is little original in his thought. He preserves throughout the moralizing tendencies of his Antiochene teachers. The ethics which he applies in his *Letters to Olympias* are more Stoic than Christian. The traditional nature of his theology, which did not engage in dogmatic discussions, saved him from the condemnations which struck Theodore and enabled his work to be preserved almost in its entirety. The efforts of modern criticism have not in his case taken the form of restoring to him works preserved under other names, but on the contrary in restoring to other authors the works which had been falsely attributed to him because of his reputation.[13] Exception should be made in the case of the rediscovery of his *Baptismal Catechetical Teaching* by A. Wenger.

The school of Antioch saw one more important figure in the next generation, that of Theodoret of Cyrus.[14] Theodoret is typical of an age when the creative period of Greek patristic literature was over. He drew up the balance-sheet of all that had been achieved. He is primarily a scholar and an editor. He belonged to the school of Antioch, he defended its Christology against Cyril of Alexandria, and he brought about the preservation of the best part of it at the Council of Chalcedon. But he had a comprehensive and eclectic mind which wel-

11. Jean Chrysostome, *À Théodore*, Introduction by Dumortier, Paris, 1965.

12. See Caius Fabricius, *Zu den Jugendschriften des Johannes Chrysostomus*, Lund, 1962.

13. A. de Aldama, *Repertorium pseudochrysostomicum*, Paris, 1965.

14. *c.* A.D. 393–460.

comed whatever was valuable in all traditions. Consequently his work represents rather the heritage of the whole of Greek patristic literature than the expression of the school of Antioch. His scholarly labours were extended into the most varied fields. It is the nature of Theodoret's work to be encyclopedic. He stands already on the threshold of the Byzantine world. To a small extent he did for the East what Isidore[15] would later do for the West. But Latin Christian literature, a plant of more recent growth, preserved in the fifth century its creative vitality which contemporary Greek patristic literature had already lost.

In his *Remedy for the Ills of the Greeks* Theodoret is the heir of earlier Christian apologists. He was acquainted with Justin, Clement of Alexandria and above all Eusebius of Caesarea, whom he often singles out. His knowledge of pagan writers and philosophers derives to a large extent from the anthologies which abounded in the Hellenistic world. Theodoret refers expressly to them, as Pierre Canivet has shown.[16] In the field of exegesis his eclecticism came to the surface, because he combines the literal system of the Antiochenes with the common tradition of typology, though he bans Alexandrian allegorization. On this subject he holds a very balanced view. As a historian he was anxious to write a sequel to the *Ecclesiastical History* of Eusebius of Caesarea. He is also indebted to writers like Socrates and Sozomen[17] who had already written accounts of this period. He also collected the traditions of Syrian monasticism in his *History of the Monks*, and on this subject his work very fortunately complements the work which Palladius[18] had already done in his *Lausiac History* for Egyp-

15. *c.* A.D. 560–636. A monk from Seville and later archbishop of that city, he was famous for his miscellaneous knowledge, to which his works, which all survive, testify.

16. *Histoire d'une entreprise apologétique au Ve siècle*, Paris, 1957.

17. They both flourished *c.* 420–40. Both wrote histories of the Church; Sozomen's work was based on Socrates but incorporated some additional material.

18. *c.* A.D. 365–425. He was a native of Galatia, and later became bishop of Helenopolis in Bithynia.

tian monasticism. Finally his letters provide an example of a literary form which had already been illustrated by the Cappadocians, and in this he displays no great originality.

The great representative of the school of Alexandria in the first half of the fifth century, corresponding to Theodoret who represents the school of Antioch, is Cyril of Alexandria.[19] The school of Alexandria does not in this case mean the tradition of Origen's school which Didymus continued, marked by its love of allegorization, but the continuation of the theological line pursued by Athanasius. This tradition, as we have already observed, displays a remarkable consistency. Cyril's theology stems directly from that of Athanasius. This doctrinal continuity was in addition supported by a family continuity. Athanasius's successors were his two brothers, Peter and Timothy, one after the other. Timothy's successor, Theophilus, was Cyril's uncle. The difference between the two Alexandrian traditions, the tradition of the teachers and the tradition of the bishops, was shown in a striking way when Theophilus displayed implacable hostility to the Origenist monks, whose defence was undertaken, paradoxically enough, by John Chrysostom.

Cyril of Alexandria's work is considerable both in the field of exegesis and in that of theology. The first two of these works, *Glaphyra* and *De adoratione*, are among the most important documents of Biblical typology. Both deal with the Pentateuch. But the exegesis of *De adoratione* is more concerned with the Church, that of *Glaphyra* more concerned with the significance of Christ. It is most instructive to compare the expository work of Cyril with Theodoret's. Just as Theodoret rejects the excesses of Antiochene literalism and gleans the best part of typology, so Cyril rejects the excesses of Alexandrian allegorization and only retains its typology.[20] Even though each of these two works is still affected by its own background, they nevertheless suggest a convergence

19. Patriarch of Alexandria, A.D. 412–44.

20. See A. Kerrigan, *St Cyril of Alexandria's Interpretation of the Old Testament*, Rome, 1952.

towards a common type of exegesis which was destined to become that of the Christian East. It is in the West that the opposite excesses of allegorization and literalism will make themselves more strongly felt.

In theology, Cyril's work is primarily significant in its treatment of the Incarnation. In contrast to the Antiochenes, who put the stress on Christ's humanity and show a liking for moralist ideas, Cyril, following Athanasius, is the great champion of the hypostatic union,[21] which emphasizes Christ's divinity. This was the doctrine that was to prevail at Ephesus, and it was thus enabled to retain at Chalcedon whatever positive value was possessed by the Antiochene doctrine. The strength of Cyril's theory lies in its emphasis upon the deifying activity of the Word. This conception of the deifying activity controls all Cyril's thought. The danger in Cyril's ideas lies in a lack of precision, an undue contempt for philosophical definitions. Cyril no longer disputes, as Apollinarius had done, the existence of a human soul in Christ, but the logical consequences of Christ's humanity are not followed up. As J. Lebon has well demonstrated,[22] it is the absence of precise definition which was destined after the Council of Chalcedon to result in the doctrine of Severus of Antioch,[23] which was no different from Cyril's, being regarded as Monophysite.

Alexandrian society produced as well as Cyril a very different figure, that of Synesius.[24] Synesius had at first been a pagan. He was a pupil at Alexandria of Hypatia, who was a Neo-Platonic woman philosopher, of the school of Porphyry. In his dialogue *Dion*, written when he was still a pagan, he delivers

21. The doctrine that the divine Word formed in union with the human being in Jesus Christ a separately existing single entity, and did not merely juxtapose or loosely link the human being with himself.

22. See Joseph Lebon, 'La christologie du monophysisme syrien', in *Das Konzil von Chalkedon*, I, 1951, pp. 421–580.

23. *c.* A.D. 465–538. Severus was the great theologian of the Monophysite view which had been formally rejected at the Council of Chalcedon in 451.

24. *c.* A.D. 370–414.

a eulogy on ancient humanism.[25] He shows his sympathy towards Christianity. But he is hostile towards what he considers its extravagances and specially towards monasticism. He was entreated by his fellow-citizens in Cyrene to become their bishop, and consented in spite of the intellectual difficulties which some doctrines gave him. But even when he was a Christian he remained loyal to the culture of the ancient world. This way of thinking was directly opposed to Cyril's, whose Christianity does not lack a certain fanaticism that sometimes took the form of violent invective against the Emperor Julian,[26] and through Julian against Hellenism, and of the exaltation of the monastic ideal. The tension reached its fullest point when Cyril's monks, in their anti-pagan rage, lynched Hypatia, to whom Synesius was always to remain loyal.

The interest of this comparison lies in the fact that it illustrates two kinds of relationship between Christianity and Hellenism, which was now dying. There was a Neo-Platonic tradition which was definitely anti-Christian. The source of this tradition was Iamblichus, Julian's master, and it continued in the school of Athens, under Syrianus and Proclus. It was the heir not only of Platonic philosophy but also of the pagan practice of divination and magic, and it made out of these a religion in the strict meaning of the word. Countering this paganism, Cyril was the champion of a similar tendency within the framework of Christianity. There was a complete incompatibility between the two. But Hypatia belonged to another Neo-Platonic tradition which was marked both by its purely philosophic nature and by a philosophical viewpoint which was nearer that of Christianity. One of the achievements of contemporary research is to have isolated this tradition. It was connected with Porphyry's teaching; even though he was a violent enemy of the Christians, he held philosophical views considerably closer to theirs. It is in this tradition that Hypatia stands. Lacombrade has brought out the influence of

25. See Kurt Treu, *Synesios von Kyrene, ein Kommentar zu seinen Dion*, Berlin, 1958.
26. Emperor A.D. 361–3.

Porphyry's thought on hers.[27] It is therefore this type of Neo-Platonic thought which Synesius had learnt under her. It is understandable that he did not have fundamental difficulty in reconciling it with Christianity. Marrou has shown that his objections dealt more with the sectarian Christianity of Cyril's type than with the basic dogmas.[28] In this respect the figure of Synesius is very like that of Marius Victorinus, who was himself also a converted pagan rhetorician and who kept on in his theology the best elements of Porphyry's Neo-Platonism, to be later enshrined by Augustine.

At the same time that Athanasius's tradition was persisting in Cyril, the tradition of the school of Alexandria, which Didymus represented in the middle of the fourth century, was persisting at the beginning of the fifth century in Evagrius. Evagrius's work was condemned at the same time as that of Didymus, on the grounds that it was Origenist, by the Second Council of Constantinople, and it had almost completely disappeared. One of the most significant results of contemporary research has been its reconstruction. Evagrius was born at Ibera in Pontus, that is in the area where Origen's tradition had been kept alive, as we have seen when considering the Cappadocians. Further, he had had contact with these theologians. He had been ordained deacon by Gregory of Nazianzus, and had gone with him to Constantinople during the time that he was bishop there. But Evagrius's Origenism was more thorough-going than the Cappadocians'. He first found more congenial company in Jerusalem with Melania[29] and Rufinus, the translator of Origen into Latin, than with Didymus at Alexandria. He settled down finally in the desert of Nitria, made famous by Anthony, in order to lead a life of solitary prayer there.

27. *Synésius de Cyrène, hellène et chrétien*, Paris, 1951.

28. 'Synesius of Cyrene and Alexandrian Neoplatonism', in *The Conflict between Paganism and Christianity in the Fourth Century*, essays edited by Arnaldo Momigliano, Oxford, 1963, pp. 126–50.

29. *c*. A.D. 345–410. A Roman lady who became an ascetic under Jerome's influence.

The reconstruction of Evagrius's writings has been the work of many scholars. Irenée Hausherr restored to him the book *On Prayer*,[30] which had been attributed to St Nilus.[31] Urs von Balthasar[32] and Marie-Josèphe Rondeau[33] have reconstructed his *Commentary on the Psalms* from the *catenae*. The *Gnostikos* has been recovered by Frankenberg in a Syriac translation. But the most important discoveries are concerned with his chief book the *Kephalaia Gnostica*. Frankenberg recovered a Syriac translation of it. But André Guillaumont proved that this is a translation of a text from which its Origenist elements have been removed, and has published another Syriac translation which gives the original text.[34] This discovery is of great importance. The texts which we previously possessed virtually prevented us understanding why Evagrius had been made the subject of a condemnation. From now on this has been fully explained by the fact that the text published by Guillaumont expressly contains all the errors of which Evagrius had been accused.

The *Kephalaia Gnostica* is a work of great importance both for the material which it contains and by reason of the influence which it had on Christian spirituality as much in the East as the West. In one direction, a development of the most questionable of Origen's speculations can be found in it. For Evagrius, as for Origen, all spirits have been created before time was. They have different natures according to the extent of their fall. They can pass from one nature to another through successive existences. They will all be restored after a certain time to the condition of pure spirits, and matter, which had been created in view of their fall, will be entirely destroyed. But through the *Kephalaia* there breathes at the same time a spirit of contemplation which makes it an unusually attractive

30. 'Le Traité de l'oraison d'Évagre le Pontique', *RAM* 15 (1934), pp. 34–93, 113–70.

31. Bishop of Ancyra. Died *c.* 430.

32. 'Die Hiera des Evagrius', *ZKT* 63 (1939), pp. 86–106, 181–206.

33. 'Le Commentaire sur les psaumes d'Évagre le Pontique', *OCP* 26 (1960), pp. 307–48.

34. *Les 'Kephalaia Gnostica' d'Évagre le Pontique*, Paris, 1962.

book. Evagrius is deeply convinced that life has no purpose except to purify the spirit so that it may become luminous in the light of the Trinity beyond both corporeal and incorporeal things. Evagrius's style, which is terse and uses Biblical symbols with amazing success, like that of his earliest teacher Gregory of Nazianzus, contributes to the attractiveness of this book.

The end of the fifth century brings into view one of the most mysterious works of Greek Christian antiquity, the writings of an author who takes the pen-name of Dionysius, the person who was converted by Paul when he spoke on the Areopagus. Research has established two connected facts about this person. The first is the identification of the author. The most diverse theories had been aired for half a century. To take them chronologically, the proposal had been made to identify the author with Ammonius Sakkas, Origen's teacher; with Dionysius of Alexandria, at the end of the third century; and with a contemporary of Gregory of Nazianzus. The most serious theories were those of Hönigmann, who assigned these texts to Peter the Iberian, a Palestinian monk at the end of the fifth century;[35] of Riedinger who gave them to Peter the Fuller, of the same period;[36] and of Stiglmayr, for whom the author of these writings was Severus of Antioch at the beginning of the sixth century.[37] What has been established by now is that the work of Pseudo-Dionysius is later than that of the Neo-Platonist Proclus, for Corsini has proved that it consists of a reply to Proclus,[38] and that its place of origin is Syria or Palestine.[39]

35. 'Pierre l'Ibérien et les écrits du Pseudo-Denys l'Aréopagite', Académie Royale de Belgique, Classes des Lettres et des Sciences Morales et Politiques, 47 (1952), fasc. 3.

36. 'Pseudo-Dionysios Areopagites, Pseudo-Kaisarios und die Akoimeten', *B Z* 52 (1959), pp. 276–96.

37. 'Der sogennante Dionysius und Severus von Antiochien', *Schol* 2 (1927), pp. 1–27, 161–207.

38. 410–85. A great teacher of the last phase of Neo-Platonic pagan philosophy; he was born in Constantinople and was later head of the pagan philosophical academy at Athens.

39. *Il trattato De divinis nominibus dello Pseudo-Dionigi e i commenti neoplatonici al Parmenide*, Turin, 1962.

The second fact reached by contemporary research on Dionysius concerns the question of deciding how far he is a Neo-Platonist and how far he is a Christian. Some scholars, especially Vanneste[40] and Hornus,[41] have maintained that his work is basically Neo-Platonic and that Christianity is distorted in it. But Völker has proved that in reality this writer is much more indebted to earlier Christian tradition, in particular to Gregory of Nyssa, than had been allowed.[42] Corsini has completed the proof by showing that though Pseudo-Dionysius certainly knew Proclus's work and has been influenced by it, his aim was precisely to reply to Proclus by rejecting what was incompatible with the Christian religion in his thought, and specially by showing that the world of ideas and of spirits has no eternal independent existence, but was produced by a creative act of the transcendent God. Pseudo-Dionysius is a genuinely Christian theologian, and this explains why his work exerted so deep an influence upon Western medieval thought.

40. *Le Mystère de Dieu. Essai sur la structure rationnelle de la doctrine mystique du pseudo-Denys l'Aréopagite*, Paris, 1959.

41. 'Les recherches dionysiennes de 1955 à 1960', *R H P R* 41 (1961), pp. 22–81.

42. *Kontemplation und Ekstase bei Pseudo-Dionysius Areopagita*, Wiesbaden, 1958.

Eight

Augustine and the West

While the fifth century in the East sees a definite decline, in the Christian West it is on the contrary the period of fullest maturity. Whereas the writers of the fourth century, Hilary and Ambrose, were always indebted, both from a literary and a theological point of view, to the Easterns, the West now found its true self in an original manner. Henceforward it was to take its own way and a deeper and deeper gulf between it and Eastern patristic literature would open. This cultural division was based on a political division. The West would be compelled to encounter the barbarian world which would upset the structures of ancient society and introduce a new spirit, while the Byzantine world would continue to exist in the cultural continuity of ancient society until the invasion of the Arabs. Two pieces of work, though of unequal compass, dominate this period, that of Jerome and that of Augustine.

Jerome always remained greatly influenced by Eastern thought. In this respect he is nearer Ambrose, whom he did not like, than to Augustine. He was born in Dalmatia, and received a very sound Classical education at Rome. But as early as 373 he moved to the East, where he was to stay until 382. This residence in the East left its mark on him in a significant way in two respects. In the first place he came into contact with the leaders of Eastern exegesis, and secondly in the East he found monasticism. He returned to Rome in 382, became secretary to Pope Damasus, and devoted himself to work on the Bible while at the same time gathering round him a group of devout people from Roman society. He went back to the East in 385 and finally settled down at Bethlehem, which he did not leave till his death. It is mainly during this last period that he produced a vast literary output, consisting primarily in his commentaries on Scripture.

In the course of his two periods of residence in the East, Jerome became involved in theological disputes. In this respect his work is interesting in that it allows us to see the East through Latin eyes and forms a source of information about the movements of thought of the time. When he made his move in 373 it was to Antioch that he went. But the circle that he joined was not that of the disciples of Meletius. He was a pupil of Apollinarius and was ordained priest by Paulinus. He attached himself consequently to the Nicene community of the friends of Athanasius. He was active in violent opposition to Meletius and contributed to no small extent to obstruct Basil's efforts at bringing about reconciliation, by denouncing Basil's Trinitarian formulae to Damasus. He was in the company of Gregory of Nazianzus at the Council of Constantinople of 381, and he can hardly have helped to calm Gregory when the problem of finding a successor to Meletius came up.[1] He took a more important part in the dispute about Origen during his second period in the East. He had a great admiration for Origen's work on the Gospels. But when the campaign against Origen was launched by Epiphanius, he became a violent partisan of Epiphanius, and found himself at odds with bishop John of Jerusalem and with his friend, Rufinus of Aquileia.[2] Finally when the Pelagian crisis broke out Jerome once again took sides, against Pelagianism, with his usual violence, and accused Evagrius in particular of having fallen into the heresy.[3]

Jerome's expository work has two sides to it. In one aspect he handed on to the Latin West by his commentaries the tradition of an Eastern school of exegesis. He had been a pupil

1. Meletius, bishop of Antioch, died during the course of the Council of Constantinople in 381. The Christians of Antioch had been deeply divided by both doctrinal and personal causes, and the attempt to make the choice of Meletius's successor an occasion of reconciliation between the warring parties unfortunately failed.

2. See Francis X. Murphy, *Rufinus of Aquileia. His Life and Works*, Washington, 1945.

3. See Antoine Guillaumont, op. cit., pp. 65–9.

of Apollinarius at Antioch. This influence on him appears to have been permanent. One aspect of Apollinarius, as of all the Antiochenes, was his concern to make the literal sense clear. At his school Jerome learnt Greek and Hebrew – an acquisition which was at that time unique for a Westerner. He took an interest in Rabbinic exegesis, as Braverman has well brought out.[4] But we have seen that another aspect of Apollinarius was faithfulness to Origen and to his allegorization. In this respect he differed in his exegetical theory from Diodore of Tarsus, as he differed from him in his theological views. Under the tutelage of Apollinarius, Jerome conceived an admiration for Origen. He was later to translate several of Origen's works into Latin. And even when he turned against Origen in theology he did not cease to use him in his exegetical methods. Later the other teachers under whom he was to study, Gregory of Nazianzus in 380/381 and Didymus the Blind in 385, were also followers of Origen. Jerome was thus to hand on to the Latin West both constructive gifts of great value, and also a very questionable allegorization.[5]

But Jerome's most important role in the history of culture is his function as translator. It is not without good cause that a modern writer, himself in contact with many different cultures, Valéry Larbaud, has devoted a book to him as the patron of translators.[6] There were translations of the Old and New Testament before Jerome's day. Many studies have been devoted to these ancient Latin versions.[7] But Jerome constitutes a turning-point in the history of the Latin Bible. Even if the Roman Psalter, used at Rome up to the sixteenth century, is not his work, as de Bruyne has shown,[8] it is he, surprisingly, who is the author of the *Psalterium Gallicanum*, which was

4. *Jerome as a Biblical Exegete in Relation to Rabbinic and Patristic Tradition as Seen in his Commentary on Daniel*, New York, 1966.

5. See Angelo Penna, *Principi et carattere dell'esegesi di San Girolamo*, Rome, 1950.

6. *Sous l'invocation de Saint Jérôme*, Paris, 1946.

7. See Bernard Botte, 'Latines (Versions) antérieures à Saint Jérôme', *S D B* 5 (1957), pp. 334–47.

8. 'Le problème du Psautier romain', *R Ben* 43 (1950), pp. 447–82.

Jerome: the Vulgate

first issued in Gaul and made mandatory upon the whole Church by Pius V.[9] It consists of a revision of the Old Roman Psalter following the Greek text. In addition Jerome translated the whole Old Testament directly from the Hebrew text. It is this text which is called the Vulgate and which has become the Bible of the West. Consequently the West was endowed with an original translation independent of the Septuagint.[10] Jerome also made a revision of the Latin translation of the Gospels in use at Rome. In one sense Jerome's work is an expression of the emancipation of the Latin world from the Greek world,[11] and further Jerome's Latin Bible has been one of the factors which created Western Latin culture first and later Roman culture.[12]

Apart from his work as a translator, Jerome is greatly indebted to the Greek world. With St Augustine, by way of contrast, we are faced with a new creation, where the Christian West is displayed in the mind of a genius. It is from Augustine onwards that Latin Christian thought definitely branches off to take its own course. The study of St Augustine has experienced a huge development in the last quarter of a century.[13] Investigation has concentrated first on the history of Augustine's education and on the analysis of the facts supplied to us by his *Confessions*. Augustine was first a teacher of rhetoric. H.-I. Marrou has studied his debt to the literary culture of his time.[14] The question of his knowledge of Greek has been debated. In contrast to Ambrose, who learnt Greek

9. A.D. 1504–72. Pope from 1566.

10. A Greek version of the Hebrew Bible probably the work of Alexandrian Jews. A Jewish tradition says that seventy-two scholars were actually commissioned to do it, hence the name Septuagint (Seventy), for which the symbol LXX, by which the translation is commonly known, stands.

11. Bleddyn J. Roberts, *The Old Testament Text and Versions*, Cardiff, 1951, pp. 258–59.

12. *Richesses et déficiences des Anciens Psautiers latins*, Rome, 1959.

13. See *Augustinus Magister*, Actes du Congrès International Augustinien, 21–24 September 1953, III, Paris, 1955.

14. *Saint Augustin et la fin de la culture antique*, Paris, 1938; *Retractatio*, Paris, 1949.

as part of the tradition of the Senatorial class to which he belonged, and to Jerome, who was taught Greek at Antioch, Augustine seems to have had only a superficial acquaintance with it. The stages of the spiritual pilgrimage which led him to Catholicism have been the main subject of the research of Pierre Courcelle.[15] His period in the Manichaean sect has been illuminated by the advance in our knowledge of Manichaeanism,[16] owing to the manuscripts of Turfan. His meeting after that with the *Libri Platonici* had a decisive effect upon him. He became a student of Neo-Platonism. But the problem of identifying these books is one of the most hotly debated among Augustinian subjects. Paul Henry thinks that he was handling some of the *Enneads* of Plotinus.[17] Willy Theiler asserts that he read only Porphyry.[18] Pierre Courcelle believes that he had both these works in his hands.[19] But R. J. O'Connell has returned to the position according to which Augustine would have read Plotinus only.[20] This problem, it must be understood, does not preclude later contact of Augustine with both these thinkers. He expressly mentions Porphyry in his *City of God*, and Jean Pépin has shown that he used Porphyry's *Zetemata*.[21]

The circumstances of St Augustine's conversion itself have formed a subject of close research. Pierre Courcelle has been able to fix a correlation between the allusions which Augustine makes to Ambrose's sermons and the chronology of these sermons. It was certainly in 387 during Lent that Ambrose preached his *Homilies on Genesis* and that Augustine was

15. *Recherches sur 'les Confessions' de Saint Augustin*, Paris, 1950.

16. A heresy founded by one Mani (*c.* A.D. 215–75), about whom little is certainly known. It was a dualistic heresy, with a system of religious knowledge, and an elite who were severe ascetics, among its ingredients.

17. *Plotin et l'Occident*, Louvain, 1934.

18. *Porphyrius und Augustin*, Halle, 1933.

19. 'Litiges sur la lecture des Libri platonicorum par Saint Augustin', *Augustiniano* 4 (1954), pp. 226–39.

20. 'Ennead VI, 4 and 5, in the Works of Saint Augustine', *R E Aug* 19 (1963), pp. 1–39.

21. 'Une nouvelle source de Saint Augustin : le zetema de Porphyre sur l'union de l'âme et du corps', *R E Aug* 66 (1964), pp. 53–107.

present at them. As for the scene of the conversion itself and the words *tolle, lege*, heard by Augustine, Pierre Courcelle has attempted to prove that it was intended as a symbolic account of a purely interior experience.[22] But this theory has been vigorously disputed by all the critics.[23] The narrative of the ecstasy at Ostia[24] has aroused just as much controversy. Paul Henry sees in it a Christian spiritual experience expressed in Neo-Platonic vocabulary,[25] while others give it a purely intellectual interpretation.[26]

It certainly is an exaggeration to say, as Prosper Alfaric does, that Augustine's conversion was rather to Neo-Platonism than to Christianity.[27] But it is clear that Augustine's thought at the time of his conversion was strongly influenced by Neo-Platonism, and very close in this respect to the Greek Christians who went before him.[28] This philosophy provided the problems which he was to encounter, the problems which would produce a development in his thought and lead him on to open new paths which were to be the paths of Latin theology. This is why the problem of chronology in the works of Augustine is a crucial one. The transition from one world to another takes place within Augustine's own evolution. Augustine himself recognized this evolution when he published his *Retractationes* at the end of his life in which he reconsidered the positions taken in his first books in order to correct them in the light of the final state of his thought.

22. 'Source chrétienne et allusion païenne de l'épisode du Tolle-Lege', *R H P R* 32 (1952), pp. 171–200.

23. See Franco Bolgiani, *La conversione di S. Agostino e l'VIIIo Libro delle Confessioni*. Turin, 1956.

24. In the ninth book of his *Confessions* Augustine describes an ecstatic or mystical experience enjoyed by his mother Monnica and himself while they were staying at Ostia, by the mouth of the river Tiber, a few days before Monnica's death.

25. *La Vision d'Ostie. Sa place dans la vie et l'œuvre de Saint Augustin*, Paris, 1938.

26. See P. Cavallera, 'La contemplation d'Ostie', *R A M* 20 (1939), pp. 181–96.

27. *L'Évolution intellectuelle de Saint Augustin*, Paris, 1918.

28. See Ragnar Holte, *Béatitude et sagesse*, Paris, 1962.

This evolution shows itself mainly in the field of his doctrine of man. The earliest works of Augustine are very much influenced by Neo-Platonism on this subject. The real man is the inner man, and this man has been made by God capable of knowing him. As E. von Ivanka has shown, Augustine is nearer the Neo-Platonists than even Gregory of Nyssa, for in Gregory the sense of God's transcendence is sharper.[29] The existence of man in a fleshly body is for Augustine, as for Plotinus, both the consequence of sin and one of the processes of the universe.[30] But the spirit has no rest until it has got beyond everything created and rests in the vision of the Trinity. These opinions are amazingly close to those of Gregory of Nyssa. The similarity could have come from a common indebtedness to Plotinus, from the influence of Gregory upon Augustine through Ambrose, who knew Gregory, or even a direct contact of Augustine with some of Gregory's works is not excluded. On this subject the investigation pursued by Altaner has not been followed up, and much remains to do.[31]

But his encounter with Pelagianism brought about a crisis in Augustine's thought. In the East Pelagianism continued Origen's doctrine of man, and we shall return to it. To Augustine it seemed to be a reduction of Christianity to a method of personal discipline and to be nullifying the Pauline doctrine of salvation by grace alone. In reacting to this peril Augustine produced the theology of grace with which his name is permanently connected, and which thenceforward was to form one of the characteristics of Western theology, whether in moderate forms, as in Thomas Aquinas, or in extreme forms, as in Luther and Jansen. The corollaries of this theology of grace were to be predestination to salvation, the damnation of infants who die without baptism, and the restriction of the

29. 'Vom Platonismus zur Theorie der Mystik', *Schol* 11 (1936), pp. 163–95.

30. See Robert J. O'Connell, 'The Plotinian Fall of the Soul in St Augustine', *Traditio* 19 (1963), pp. 1–34.

31. 'Augustinus und die griechisch Patristik', *R Ben* 62 (1952), pp. 201–15.

elect to a small number. From this position the bridges will henceforward be broken not only with Pelagianism, which was an exaggeration in the other direction, but with all Greek theology which had underlined, against the Gnostics, the value of freedom of will and the universal scope of salvation.

Augustine's personality made itself felt equally in other theological fields. While Greek theology was mainly interested in disentangling the doctrine of the Trinity from Platonic speculations which had led to Arianism, Augustine was able to combine a strictly orthodox Trinitarian theology with a flight of philosophical speculation derived from Neo-Platonism concerning the powers of the soul living in the life of God, by showing the analogy between the divine Persons and the powers of the soul when it is living in God's life.[32] Here once again Augustine opened new horizons to Latin thought by the depth of his interior experience. The same should be said of another field, that of the theology of history. In his *City of God* as well as in his *De catechizandis rudibus* Augustine depicts the whole of history, from the creation of angels to the Last Judgement, in the context of sin and salvation, by developing the Origenist doctrine of the two cities. In this interpretation all earthly realities, including political realities, are viewed in their relation to the Last Judgement.[33] As Grillmeier has clearly perceived, just as Eusebius's theology of history, by emphasizing the realization of the Kingdom of God in Constantine's Empire, prepared the way for Byzantine Caesarpapism,[34] so Augustine, by subordinating all earthly realities to that design for salvation of which the Church is the centre, prepared the way for the primacy of the Pope over the Emperor in medieval society.[35]

Augustine's essential significance lies in his theological synthesis in which he gathered and combined in a new system

32. See Charles Boyer, 'L'Âme à l'image de la Trinité chez Saint Augustin', *Greg* (1946), pp. 173–99, 333–52.

33. See Karl Lowith, *Meaning in History*, Chicago, 1947.

34. The system whereby the Emperor exercised complete authority over the Eastern Patriarch even in matters of doctrine.

35. *Augustinius Magister*, III, 211–12.

a vast culture both secular and sacred. This is why there is no point in distinguishing Scriptural and theological books in his work. His expository work virtually consists of his sermons on the Bible, especially on the Psalms and on St John's Gospel. The reconstruction of his genuine homiletic works and the chronology of his sermons have formed the subject of the labours of Dom Lambot especially. Augustine's exegesis is primarily indebted to his literary education, as H.-I. Marrou has clearly shown. This contributed a factor which was sometimes deceptive. He was also influenced by Ambrose – and from this source he was a devotee of Alexandrian allegorization,[36] which he defended against Faustus the Manichee.[37] And further, the depth of his spiritual experience and his pastoral responsibility often lent him a wonderful insight into Scripture deeper than did the academic methods upon which he relied.

Augustine's personality quickly produced disciples for him. One of the achievements of modern research has been the restoration of the work of Quodvultdeus, bishop of Carthage in 437. His name, like that of the deacon Deogratias to whom Augustine dedicated his *De catechizandis rudibus*, is typically African. It consists of a direct transposition into Latin of the old Punic names like Hannibal, Hasdrubal, etc. Apart from his sermons, we have a book of Quodvultdeus's, *De promissionibus et praedicationibus Dei*, which Braun has finally restored to him.[38] It is a list of the prefigurations and prophecies used in Africa at the beginning of the fifth century. Traditional typology dear to the heart of the East, and characteristic of, for example, Zeno of Verona or Gregory of Elvira, is to be found there. But in addition the influence of Augustine is expressly acknowledged. It was another disciple of Augustine,

36. See A. M. de la Bonnardière, 'Le Cantique des Cantiques dans l'œuvre de Saint Augustin', *R E Aug* 1 (1955), pp. 225–37.

37. A Manichaean propagandist who won fame as a rhetorician at Rome.

38. Quodvultdeus, *Livre des Promesses et des predictions de Dieu*, introduction by René Braun, Paris, 1964, pp. 88–113.

but in another direction, Paulus Orosius,[39] who took up again the project of the *City of God*; but he did so by seeking to justify the activity of Providence in the details of historical events and especially to demonstrate in Rome's disasters the working out of the just judgements of God, in an excessively systematic way.[40]

But Augustine's influence was not fastened upon the Latin West all at once. The Greek doctrine of man, which placed the stress on freedom and which had influenced Hilary and Ambrose in the West, persisted among a number of writers who stood for movements of thought contrary to those of Augustine. The most important was Pelagius. His work was condemned as a result of Augustine's attacks and had almost entirely disappeared. It has been reconstructed in large part by A. Souter and Georges de Plinval.[41] It has now been possible to estimate Pelagius's thought otherwise than through Augustine's criticism of it. He seems to be mainly indebted to Origen, whose *Commentary on the Epistle to the Romans* he knew, through the translation of it made by Rufinus.[42] Origen had been the great defender of freedom against the determinism of the Gnostics. Pelagius took up the task of defending it against Manichaeanism, which was heir to Gnosticism. Pelagius also was influenced by Origen through Hilary. Pelagius was to have as his disciple Julian of Eclanum,[43] who was destined to be the pupil of Theodore of Mopsuestia at Antioch. Julian's expository publications brought into the West the rigid literalism of the Antioch school and in this respect set itself in opposition to Jerome's exposition, for Jerome exemplified a restrained Alexandrian interpretation. Further, again follow-

39. Of the early fifth century, he played some part in the Pelagian controversy while Augustine was alive.

40. See Benoit Lacroix, *Orose et ses idées*, Montreal, 1965.

41. A. Souter, *Expositiones XIII epistularum Pauli, Texts and Studies*, IX, 1–2, Cambridge, 1922–6; Georges de Plinval, *Pelage. Ses écrits, sa vie et sa réforme*, Lausanne, 1943.

42. See Torgny Bohlin, *Die Theologie des Pelagius und ihre Genesis*, Uppsala, 1957.

43. *c.* A.D. 386–454.

ing Theodore's lead, Julian pushed Pelagius's ideas to the point of teaching a moralism which destroyed the doctrine of original sin. It was mainly the work of Julian which justified the Augustinian reaction.

It is again the Greek tradition that we meet in very different circumstances, those of the Gallic monasticism of Cassian.[44] The studies of Owen Chadwick[45] and of H.-I. Marrou[46] have thrown light on his early history. He was born in the Dobroudja and first was a monk in Palestine and in Egypt, where he knew Evagrius. When Theophilus's persecution of Origenism broke out, he took refuge at Constantinople under John Chrysostom. He finally settled down at Marseilles. He was to be the great intermediary between the spirituality of the monks of Egypt and Western monasticism. Traces of his influence on the Rule of Benedict can be detected. With Cassian the Origenist tradition is again visible in the West, but in the form which Evagrius had given to it; it placed contemplation foremost, and the contempt of the world. Cassian does not develop altogether as far as Evagrius the doctrine of the complete 'impassibility' of those who are perfect. To Evagrius's influence on Cassian we must add the more moderate effect of the *Hypotyposis* of Gregory of Nyssa;[47] here Jaeger has brought out the same emphasis on freedom derived from Origen.[48]

In spite of its continuation in monastic society the Origenist tradition looked like a survival from the past in the fifth and sixth centuries. It was certainly Augustine's thought which brought it into the West. But at least the various forms of resistance which it met were destined to lead to its excesses being corrected. The result was the appearance from the middle of the fifth century onwards of a moderate form of Augustinianism which was to be thenceforward the doctrine of the

44. *c.* A.D. 360–435.

45. *John Cassian, A Study in Primitive Monasticism*, Cambridge, 1950.

46. 'La Patrie de Jean Cassien', *O C P* 13 (1947), pp. 588–601.

47. See Kemmer, 'Gregorius Nyssenus estne inter fontes Jo. Cassiani numerandus?' *O C P* 21 (1955), pp. 454–5.

48. *New Rediscovered Works of Ancient Christian Literature*, Leyden, 1954, pp. 88–92.

Latin church. A crucial part was played in this result by Prosper of Aquitaine.[49] He was a monk of Marseilles who denounced to Augustine the dangerous Semi-Pelagianism of Cassian, but also defended against Augustine the doctrine of God's will to save everybody, and ended up with a synthesis which held grace and freedom in balance. He was to be the collaborator of the Pope St Leo[50] at Rome. Leo has left us his sermons for the liturgical feasts which are full of doctrine. He too was a follower of Augustine, and he introduced into Augustinianism the adjustments which Prosper had suggested. But above all in his sermons on Christmas and Epiphany he gives the doctrine of the Incarnation a noteworthy formulation in the sense which the Council of Chalcedon, which took place during his lifetime, made into a definition. The work of Caesarius of Arles is associated with the same tradition. He took part in the second synod of Orange in 519 which rejected at the same time Semi-Pelagianism and the Augustinian doctrine of predestination. Modern research has collected all his sermons, which were distributed among a variety of authors to whom they were assigned. He emerges as the great preacher of his century, both by the severity of the penances which he exacts in ethical matters, and also by his acceptance of Biblical typology, a typology handed down in the Latin tradition, the kind upon which Augustine had impressed its permanent form.

49. *c.* A.D. 390–463.
50. Pope A.D. 440–461.

Liturgy

by A. H. Couratin

Introduction

The late Dean of St Paul's,[1] so the story runs, was dining at a high table in Oxford, and was asked by his neighbour, a distinguished liturgist,[2] whether he was interested in liturgy. 'No,' said the Dean, 'neither do I collect postage stamps.' The Dean's estimate of liturgical study – that it is a trivial branch of archaeology – was typical of his period. The Dean himself was an exponent of personal religion, and was profoundly interested in mysticism, in its Christian and non-Christian forms. His period tended to overwork von Hügel's distinction between the institutional, the intellectual and the mystical elements in religion, and to undervalue the institutional as much as it overvalued the mystical. Liturgy was at best an exercise by means of which men might be led on to personal religion: at worst it was a sensuous pageant performed to impress the uneducated.

A good deal of water has passed under Folly Bridge since the days of the late Dean Inge. The type of society that he represented and the type of religion that he inculcated have dissolved under the influence of the two world wars, and of the social revolution which these have set in motion. Von Hügel's three elements are seen today in a fairer proportion. The practice of personal religion, and the mystical experience to which it may lead, is still thought to be of the highest value. The intellectual grasp of the Christian faith, which it is the business of the theologian to enlarge and to deepen, has gained an added importance in a post-Christian world. But the insti-

1. Dr W. R. Inge, popularly known as The Gloomy Dean.

2. The Rev E. C. Ratcliff, later Regius Professor of Divinity in the University of Cambridge.

tutional element has inevitably come into its own in modern society. For we are becoming more and more aware of ourselves as members of a group, whether family or class, trades-union or nation, which conditions our approaches and reactions to other groups and to the world as a whole. In this climate the Christian naturally tends to become conscious of himself as a member of a supernatural group, which, borrowing an idea from St Paul, he calls the Body of Christ.[3]

There are two ways, both of them legitimate, in which a Christian can think about the religious society to which he belongs. He can think about it as an organization, designed for particular purposes – presumably to propagate Christian beliefs and to pay suitable worship to the Christian God. He can think of the form of the organization and of the beliefs and of the worship as ordained by the Christ himself, and given by him to the first Christians, and handed down intact over the last two thousand years. Or he can think of them as being given by the Christ to the first Christians in germ, and worked out, and developed, and adjusted to the needs of later ages by each generation in turn. But in either case he thinks of the Church as an organization, guided and inspired, if not directed and controlled, by the power of the Spirit of the Christ.

That is one way in which a Christian can look at the Church. It is a high view, and has always been held by those who have in consequence been called High Churchmen. But under modern pressures the Christian tends to value still more highly the society of which he is a member, and to regard it as more than an organization, however august. Following a line of thought in the New Testament, he thinks of the Church as an organism – in some ways comparable to the human body – of which he and all other Christians form interdependent parts. He therefore regards his fellow Christians not simply as fellow members of a club which all have joined, nor even as fellow members of a family, into which each has been somehow

3. As evidence for this change of view compare, for the Church of England, A. G. Herbert, *Liturgy and Society*, London, 1935; for the Church of Rome, Theodore Wesseling, *Liturgy and Life*, London, 1938.

spiritually reborn. Blood relations, and still more club members, still retain their separate individuality. But he regards his fellow Christians as limbs of one body, parts of one organism, distinct but not finally separate. And he maintains that the organism is not something impersonal; but that it actually embodies the Christ himself, and enables him to carry out his functions in the contemporary world.

There is much in the Christian centuries to embarrass a Christian who expresses such views in a post-Christian world. The secular wars between Christian nations, the religious wars between different types of Christian, the exploitation of the divine character of the Church for secular ends, the demoralizing effect of a divinized institution upon its own rulers – all this a Christian freely admits and deplores. But he would claim that these horrors might have been prevented had the Christians of those days believed, not less about the Church, but more; had they not been content with viewing the Church as an organization, which in some sense acted as vicegerent for an absent Christ; but had rather regarded it as an organism through which the Christ was expressing himself, in so far as he was not hindered by the sins of those who made up his body.

Now a Christian's attitude toward liturgy is determined by his view of the Church. For liturgy is the way in which the Christian society functions, when it meets to propagate its faith and to worship its God. If he holds a low view of the Church, he will have a utilitarian view of the liturgy, as exposition of true doctrine and exhortation to sound morals. If he holds a high view of the Church, he will have a supernatural view of the liturgy, as the preaching of a living Word and as the dispensing of life-giving sacraments. But if he regards the Church as in some real sense the Body of Christ, then he will view the liturgy as an activity of the Christ himself, embodied in his Church and functioning in it and through it. He will see in the reading and the preaching and the praising and the celebration of the sacraments the Christ himself, still at work in the world, still teaching the minds and stirring the hearts of men, still worshipping his Father and leading men to worship him, as in the days of his earthly life.[4]

The liturgy of the Christian Church is centred round two principal functions, baptism and communion or Eucharist. Both of them are thought to convey benefit to the individual who receives them. But both of them are primarily social functions. Baptism is the rite which admits individuals to membership of the society. The Eucharist is the supreme act by means of which the society worships its God, and by taking part in which the individual maintains his membership. Those who have not been baptized are excluded from it. For it is the function of a society to which they do not belong. Those who have been baptized, but no longer behave like Christians, are excluded from it. For they have excommunicated themselves, or have been excommunicated, from the society, and are therefore disqualified from communicating in its Eucharist. The rules of the later canon law in this matter merely express the social character of the Church's liturgy.

But a higher view of the Church will inevitably heighten the view taken of baptism and the Eucharist. If the Church is regarded as the Body of Christ, then baptism does not merely admit the individual to the Christian society; it makes him in some sense a member of that Body, a member of the Christ himself. Again, if the Church is the Body of Christ, then the Eucharist is not merely the supreme act by means of which the Church worships. It is in some sense the Christ himself, appearing before God in his Body, Head and members alike adoring the Christian God, members uniting themselves with God and with each other by sharing in the one Christ. Those who have not been baptized therefore and those who are excommunicate are not merely outside a human society; they are in some way excluded from a share in the activities of the Christ in his Church and from a participation in his gifts. To the high Churchman the social functions of the earthly society thus become supernatural mysteries or sacraments, rites which can

4. For such a view see Karl Adam, *The Spirit of Catholicism*, revised edition, London, 1934.

be seen and heard, but which admit to heavenly realities beyond themselves.

Such a view of the Church and sacraments does not necessarily imply a narrow view of God's activity toward men. It asserts what it believes God does through the Church in the sacraments. It does not assert that he does not work in other ways, outside the Church, apart from the sacraments. God is not bound by his sacraments. He can deal with each man as he pleases. But he has placed the sacraments within the Church for men to use; and those who are members of the Church are therefore committed to their celebration.[5]

5. See Bernard Leeming, *Principles of Sacramental Theology*, London, 1956, p. 5.

One

The Origins of the Liturgy

It is claimed by Christians that baptism and the Eucharist were instituted by the Christ himself. Such a claim does not necessarily make them wholly discontinuous with the rites of other religions. Many religions have contained similar rites – washings, anointings, impositions of hands, sacrificial meals. It is asserted that in all religions there is an underlying pattern of thought and practice which governs such ritual expressions; and that any religion that is to make sense to human beings must express itself in these ways. Consciously or unconsciously, therefore, the Christ would have instituted rites of this sort, and the Church would have perpetuated them. This would be equally true whether it is held that the rites were delivered to the first Christians in detail, or whether they were delivered in germ, and subsequently developed and worked out by the Church.

The institution of the sacraments by the Christ himself was self-evident in the days before Biblical criticism. Difficulty might be encountered in providing proof-texts for such rites as confirmation and ordination. But in the case of baptism and the Eucharist there could be no doubt. In Matthew 28.19 the Christ is recorded as saying, 'Go ye therefore and make disciples of all nations, baptizing them in the name of the Father and of the Son and of the Holy Ghost'; and in I Corinthians 11.24,25 St Paul relates that the Christ performed certain actions with bread and cup at the Last Supper, and said, 'Do this in remembrance of me'; 'Do this, as oft as ye shall drink it, in remembrance of me'. But to the critical eye the evidence is by no means conclusive. The scene on the mountain in Galilee is not a piece of historical description; it is an aetiological myth. It is excellent evidence for the fact that the writer of the Gospel firmly believed that the baptism which was practised in his own day was derived from the Christ himself; but it is not evidence that the Christ had instituted baptism some fifty years before. Again, the words recorded by Paul are excellent evidence that St Paul believed, at the time when he wrote to the Corinthians, that the Christ had instituted the Eucharist. But St Paul was not present at the Last Supper; he was not converted until at least a year after the Supper had taken place; and he did not write to the Corinthians until some twenty years after his conversion. St Mark, who provides us with our other account of the Last Supper – for Matthew is wholly dependent at this point upon Mark, and Biblical scholars cannot agree about the text of Luke – makes no mention of the command 'Do this in remembrance of me'. Nor is there anything in his narrative which directly suggests that the Supper was ever to be repeated in the future.[1]

The critical scholar nowadays would probably base the sacraments, not upon the Christ's command, but rather upon his example.[2] Both at the beginning and at the end of his public life he is recorded as being engaged in a ritual action, which is seen to give meaning to his mission. At the beginning comes his baptism in Jordan at the hands of John. This event is placed first in the narrative of Mark. And although Matthew and Luke prefix stories about his childhood to their gospels, it is the baptism with which either gospel really opens. And although John places a theological prologue at the head of his Gospel, the first witness that he calls to his theology of the Christ is John Baptist, who is made to testify to the descent of the Spirit upon the Christ, presumably at the baptism in Jordan.[3] The baptism then stands at the beginning: and at the end stands the Supper. This is depicted by the first three evangelists as a deliberate, premeditated performance, upon which

1. Mark 14. 22–26; Matthew 26. 26–30; Luke 22. 14–20.

2. See W. F. Flemington, *The New Testament Doctrine of Baptism*, London, 1948, Chapter 9.

3. Mark 1. 9–11; Matthew 3. 13–17; Luke 3. 21, 22; John 1. 29–34.

the Christ sets great store. It leads directly into the Passion – the Christ leaves the Supper table for the garden where he is arrested. It forms part of the Passion narrative, and is in some way part of the Passion. Both baptism and Supper stand where they do in the Gospels to interpret the Christ's mission.

How the Christ himself thought of his baptism we can never know. But to a Palestinian Jew of the first century baptizing with water would have certain obvious meanings. Water is the universal means of washing, and in Palestinian Jewry was in constant use for both physical and ritual cleansing.[4] Water is a symbol of death, more especially to those who, like the Christ and his disciples, have experience of storms at sea. Water is a symbol of life, as is obvious to all who, as in first-century Palestine, live in agricultural communities. Further, the Christ was almost entirely educated on the Old Testament Scriptures; and the great sagas and prophecies of the sacred books would have reinforced the symbolic meanings of water derived from nature. The cleansing of Naaman in the waters of Jordan,[5] the destruction of the old world in the waters of the Flood,[6] the life-giving properties of the four rivers of Paradise[7] or of the river that flowed from the Temple in Ezekiel[8] – these are some of many examples that would have filled the mind of any educated Jew. It is therefore not impossible that the Christ in undergoing John's baptism conceived of himself as undergoing a vicarious cleansing and as consecrating himself to a life-giving death on behalf of his people. And this is in fact the way in which the evangelists suggest that he understood it.[9]

As with the baptism, so with the Supper. What the Christ thought he was doing we can never know. But the Supper, whether it was the Passover meal or not,[10] was eaten at the time of the Passover festival, and was inevitably associated with

4. Compare John 2. 6.
5. 2 Kings 5.
6. Genesis 7.
7. Genesis 2. 10 ff.
8. Ezekiel 47. 1–12.
9. Matthew 3. 15. Compare also Luke 12. 50.
10. See A. J. B. Higgins, *The Lord's Supper in the New Testament*, London, 1952; J. Jeremias, *The Eucharistic Words of Jesus*, English translation, Oxford, 1955; A. Jaubert, *La Date de la Cène*, Paris, 1957.

Passover ideas – the slaughter of the victim, and the deliverance of the people from the destroyer by the power of the sprinkled blood. It was also apparently associated with ideas derived from the making of the Covenant at Sinai. The Christ is depicted as saying, 'This is my blood of the Covenant,'[11] which is an echo of the remark of Moses in the Exodus narrative, 'Behold the blood of the Covenant.'[12] It was in the power of the sprinkled blood that Moses and his companions were enabled to go to the top of mount Sinai, and to see the God of Israel, and to eat and drink in his presence. If these were the ideas which filled the Christ's mind at the Supper, then it is not unlikely that he regarded the Supper as the consecration of himself to a life-giving death, which would deliver his people from the power of the destroyer and would admit them into the presence of God.[13]

The books of the New Testament do not provide us with a handbook to the life of the Church of the first century. For the most part they are occasional writings, each produced to meet some particular set of circumstances. They were all of them, or almost all of them, written to be read exclusively by Christians, people who were living the life of the Christian society and were wholly familiar with its liturgical functions. It is what the New Testament writings presuppose therefore that is of greater importance than what they actually describe. In the Epistles of St Paul it is assumed that everyone becomes a Christian by being baptized; and in his first Epistle to the Corinthians the Eucharist is also apparently taken for granted. It is alluded to in a discussion whether Christians might eat meat from the heathen sacrifices; and it is a matter for regulation because irregularities have occurred during its celebration.[14]

The only book in the New Testament which professes to give some picture of the life and growth of the early Church

11. Mark 14. 24. Compare 1 Corinthians 11. 25.
12. Exodus 24. 8.
13. See A. H. Couratin, 'The Sacrifice of Praise', *Theology*, August 1955.
14. 1 Corinthians 10 and 11.

is the Acts of the Apostles. But here we are faced with a difference of opinion as to its value as history. Some scholars would maintain that, although it was written as long as fifty years after some of the events it describes, it nevertheless gives a reliable account of those events. Others would argue that, although it undoubtedly contains passages of unquestionable history, it is nevertheless largely an idealized picture of the way in which the Church spread across the Mediterranean world, from Jerusalem to Rome.[15] It may however be claimed as reasonably certain that by the time the Acts of the Apostles were written baptism was the only means of admission to the Christian Church; and as equally sure that the celebration of the Eucharist was the purpose for which Christians met together on the first day of the week.

The liturgical scholar is faced with further difficulties in surveying the New Testament evidence. He is ignorant of the liturgical practices of the early Church, with which both the writers and their readers were familiar. There may therefore be allusions in the New Testament text to liturgical practices and even to liturgical phrases which escape the modern reader. Again, he does not know how far the descriptions of the Christ's baptism and of the Last Supper are genuine attempts to preserve the historical sequence of events; or how far they have been adjusted by their authors, consciously or unconsciously, to square with current liturgical patterns. Again, he cannot tell what to make of the suggestion that has been made, that the signs and wonders attributed to the Christ in the Gospels have been written up against the background of the administration of the sacraments, in order to illustrate the spiritual effect they were thought to produce.[16]

15. C. S. C. Williams, *The Acts of the Apostles*, London, 1957; E. Haenchen, *Die Apostelgeschichte*, Göttingen, 1956.

16. See Oscar Cullman, *Early Christian Worship*, London, 1953.

Two

The Pre-History of the Liturgy

The first writer who professes to give a clear description of the administration of the sacraments is Justin Martyr. In the middle of the second century he addressed his *Apology* to the Emperor Antoninus Pius. He was writing in Rome, but his description may represent the practice of other places besides. For he was born and bred in Syria, and is said to have spent part of his life at Ephesus. More difficult to assess is the completeness of the account he gives of baptism and the Eucharist. He may have been endeavouring to convince the authorities of the harmlessness of Christian rites by giving a simple and straightforward description. On the other hand he may have set out to tell the authorities no more than they already knew, and to disarm their suspicions about nameless orgies, while carefully concealing important elements in the Christian mysteries which might give a false impression and which the authorities were unlikely to discover.[1]

His description of baptism is apparently simple.[2] The convert fasts and prays for the forgiveness of his sins, and the Church fasts and prays with him. He is then taken to some place where there is water and undergoes a bath, while someone names over him the Father and the Christ and the Spirit. (In view of later practice the naming is probably a questioning, 'Dost thou believe in God the Father', etc.) He is then introduced into the assembled Church, common prayers are said for Christians everywhere and especially for the newly baptized, and the kiss of peace is given.[3] The baptismal Eucharist then begins at once. Nothing but the bath with the accompanying use of the name

1. See E. C. Ratcliff, 'Justin Martyr and Confirmation', *Theology*, April 1948.

2. *Apology* 61.

3. ibid. 65.

is described, together with some prayer for the newly baptized and the kiss of peace. The benefits conferred by the rite are said to be forgiveness of past sins and the new birth, and the promise of 'the eternal salvation', if the candidate perseveres in good living. No mention is made of the gift of the Holy Spirit, so closely connected with baptism in the New Testament and in the later liturgies of the Church.

Fifty years later we find a number of allusions to the administration of baptism in the writings of Tertullian. He was writing in Africa, and he was scarcely two generations away from Justin; yet he presupposes a rite of a much fuller kind. There is the preparatory fasting and repentance; there is the washing with water and the three-fold act of faith, and this is thought to secure the remission of sins. But the rite continues with an anointing, with a signing with the cross and with a prayer with hand outstretched over the candidate.[4] Further the Spirit of God is closely associated with the rite. The Spirit descends upon the water in order to effect the remission of sins;[5] and the Spirit descends upon the candidate when the prayer is made and the hand outstretched in order that the Spirit may be given.[6]

Scholars disagree about the relation between Justin's description and Tertullian's. Many would argue that at the end of the second century the rite of baptism was elaborated, and that a number of edifying ceremonies were added to the simple washing, to some of which spiritual efficacy was attributed. So we find anointings and signings and laying-on of hands attached to baptism, just as a drink of milk and honey was added to the reception of bread and wine in the baptismal Eucharist. The milk and honey was a symbol, derived from the Old Testament, signifying the Promised Land, to which the candidate had attained by baptism. So also with the ceremonies at baptism mentioned by Tertullian. They should be regarded as decorative additions to the washing, which alone was neces-

4. *De resurrectione carnis* 8.
5. *De baptismo* 4; compare 6.
6. ibid. 8.

sary to effect admission to the Church and its accompanying benefits.[7]

Others however would argue that the case does not admit of so easy a solution. They would claim that the rite of baptism in Justin's time was as full as it was in Tertullian's. Justin, they would say, was not concerned to give the Roman Emperor a complete account of the Christian sacraments. He was only going to tell him what every educated person already knew about the mysteries, and to contradict current stories about cannibalism and incest. He is apparently frank about the Eucharist, and explains that the Body and Blood received at it are bread and wine. But he does not mention the fact that Christians regarded the rite as a sacrifice, although he insists on this elsewhere in his writings. A sacrifice would suggest slaughter to a pagan. So also with baptism. He describes the bath with apparent frankness. But he omits all reference to subsequent ceremonies and any mention of the giving of the Spirit, for fear of exciting suspicions of magic.[8]

It is further argued that practices alluded to by Tertullian, which subsequently find their place in the later baptismal rites from the fourth century onwards, may perhaps be presupposed by the New Testament writers themselves. St Paul for instance says that 'he that stablisheth us with you in Christ, and anointed us, is God, who also sealed us, and gave us the earnest of the Spirit'.[9] St John says that 'ye have an anointing from the Holy One and ye know all things'.[10] It is commonly asserted that such expressions are figurative, and do not imply an anointing with material oil. But it is difficult to be confident about this, in view of the constant use of oil with bathing in the ancient world. Again, the author of the Apocalypse, following Ezekiel, speaks of the servants of God receiving the seal of God in their foreheads. Maybe the reference is to a figurative

7. See G. W. H. Lampe, *The Seal of the Spirit*, London, 1951, Chapters 6 and 7.

8. See E. C. Ratcliff, 'Justin Martyr and Confirmation', *Theology*, April 1948; A. H. Couratin, 'Justin Martyr and Confirmation', *Theology*, December 1952.

9. 2 Corinthians 1. 21.

10. 1 John 2. 20.

sequence Baptism → Eucharist

sealing – a figure later taken up and transformed in liturgical practice into a physical signing with the cross on the foreheads of the newly baptized. But it may be that the signing was already practised in the first century, and is alluded to by the author of the Apocalypse.[11]

It can also be pointed out that the New Testament evidence is ambiguous about the giving of the Holy Spirit in connexion with baptism. Baptism is apparently connected everywhere with the giving of the Spirit. In many places it seems to be assumed that baptism conveys the gift of the Spirit. But elsewhere it is categorically stated that the Spirit is given, as Tertullian asserted, not in baptism, but through a subsequent laying-on of hands.[12] Again, the narratives of the Christ's baptism point in the same direction. It has already been suggested that these may well have been written up against the background of current liturgical practice. The descriptions in Matthew and Mark are ambiguous.[13] The Spirit descends upon the Christ 'as he comes up out of the water'. This may mean 'as he emerges from the water'. In that case the gift of the Spirit is associated with baptism. Or it may mean 'as he steps out of the water on to the bank'. In that case the gift of the Spirit is associated with a later moment in the rite. In Luke however it is only after the Christ has been baptized and is now praying that the Spirit descends.[14] If the description in Luke is influenced by contemporary liturgical practice, it presupposes a rite such as that alluded to by Tertullian, in which baptism is first administered, and the Spirit is later given by prayer, presumably with laying-on of hands.

It is a rite of this type which emerges from the liturgical pre-history of the first three centuries into the bright light of the fourth. But it is a rite which is subject to variation. In the Roman West the two actions that stand out of the developed ceremonial complex are washing with water and prayer with the laying-on of hands. In the East also two actions stand out, but here they are washing with water and anointing with oil.

11. Apocalypse 7. 2–4.
12. Acts 8. 14–19.
13. Mark 1. 10; Matthew 3. 16.
14. Luke 3. 21, 22.

Here again there is variation in the pattern. At Jerusalem the newly-baptized was first washed and then anointed. In Syriac-speaking Syria he was anointed first and then washed with water.[15]

Puzzles such as these intrigue the liturgical scholar, whose sole interest is to establish and where possible to interpret the facts. To the theologian endeavouring to establish a theology of the sacraments they form an embarrassment. So long as it is thought that the Christ laid down regulations for baptism and the Eucharist, that embarrassment is liable to continue, especially if it is believed that spiritual benefit is tied to the exact performance of external rites. But we must not attribute a clerical mind to the Almighty. If the Christ is embodied, present and active, in his Church, he can be presumed to effect his purposes through the rites that are performed in his name. And this becomes easier to believe, if we do not think of baptism and the Eucharist as rites directly instituted by the Christ; if we rather regard them as symbolic acts whereby he consecrated himself to his Father, by imitating which we ourselves receive from him a similar consecration.

We must return to the pre-history of baptism. After whatever pattern it was administered, it was always followed by the Eucharist. In fact it would be true to say that in the liturgical tradition the Eucharist was an integral part of baptism – of the rite which made a man a member of the Christian society and so a member of Christ himself. The Eucharist was the final moment of baptism, the only part of it that could be repeated. And it was repeated everywhere every Lord's Day, every first day of the week. So far as we can discover, the first day of the week was called the Lord's Day, not merely because the Christ rose from the dead on Sunday, but also because on Sunday alone the Lord's Eucharist was normally celebrated.[16]

15. For a general survey of these rites see T. Thompson, *The Offices of Baptism and Confirmation*, Cambridge, 1914.

16. Compare Acts 20. 7; compare also Apocalypse 1. 10 and 4. 1. The visions seen in Chapters 4 and 5 on the Lord's Day appear to have a Eucharistic background.

Justin therefore gives two descriptions of the Eucharist.[17] First he describes the Eucharist which formed the climax of baptism; then he describes the normal Sunday Eucharist. There is little difference between the two. We do not know how the baptismal Eucharist began. For the Christian society is already assembled by the time the newly baptized person is introduced and the prayers begin. The Sunday Eucharist on the other hand begins with Scripture reading, which continues until the entire congregation is assembled. It seems likely that the baptismal Eucharist began in the same way; that the Scriptures were read in the Christian assembly until the baptism had been completed elsewhere, and ceased when the newly-baptized and those who had baptized him arrived. It should be noted that in the early Church baptism was never administered in the presence of the congregation. Decency forbade adults taking a bath in a mixed assembly. In the earliest days converts were baptized in a local bath-house, or in some pool or river; at a later date they were bathed in a specially constructed baptistery, apart from the church building. After baptism they were brought fully clothed into the place where the Church was assembled, in the early days in some large private house, at a later date in a specially constructed 'church'.

The Sunday Eucharist, once the congregation was assembled, opened with a sermon from the chairman of the assembly. Who exactly took the chair at this period we do not know. It was in all probability, as at a later date, the bishop. Then followed both on Sundays and also apparently at the baptismal Eucharist, the common prayers of the Church. Christians in those days were conscious of themselves as a holy people, set apart not only for the worship of God, but also for the redemption of the secular world. It was their duty therefore, before they embarked upon the Eucharist itself, to intercede with God for the Church and all its members, for those who were under instruction, for the heathen world and its rulers, and for all those in distress of any kind. Every member prayed, in the silence of his own heart. It was the business of the clergy merely to suggest

17. *Apology* 65 and 67.

the subjects for intercession, and perhaps to round off each period of short silence with a short prayer. This at any rate is what the later evidence suggests.

The Eucharist itself followed roughly the pattern of the Last Supper. Bread and a cup of wine was brought – the wine mixed with water, as always in the ancient world – and the chairman said grace over them. The Last Supper had included a full meal, as well as the bread and wine to which the Christ had attached particular meaning. The full meal still formed part of the Eucharist twenty years later, when St Paul wrote his first letter to the Corinthians. And if Jewish practice was followed by the Christ and by St Paul, the actions with the bread came near the beginning of the meal and the actions with the cup came at the end, and together constituted the grace before and the grace after the meal.[18] When the full meal disappeared, we do not know. The traditional story is that St Paul separated the sacramental bread and cup from the meal as a remedy against scandals like that at Corinth.[19] It seems safe to assume that practically everywhere by the end of the first century the Eucharist was no longer celebrated in connexion with a meal. With the disappearance of the meal the separate graces over bread and cup coalesced; and one thanksgiving was uttered over both the elements together.

What sort of prayer did the celebrant say over the bread and cup in Justin's time? It was a long prayer;[20] it was an extempore prayer;[21] but it was apparently framed on a fixed pattern. It consisted in the main of thanksgiving, so much so that, after it had been uttered, the elements were termed 'thanked-over' or 'thanksgiving', and were regarded as the Body and Blood of the Christ. It thanked God for the creation of the world for man's sake, and for the redemption of mankind from the power of evil through the Incarnation and the Passion of the Christ.[22] It effected the offering of the bread and cup as a memorial of the Passion,[22] and this offering was presumably expressed in words.

18. See F. L. Cirlot, *The Early Eucharist*, London, 1939.

19. Augustine, *Epistle* 54.

20. *Apology* 65.

21. ibid. 67.

22. *Dialogue* 41 and 70.

Eucharistic prayer

It also thanked God for our being accounted worthy of these things from him.[23] The prayer was made to the Father through the name of the Son and of the Spirit,[23] and the whole congregation said Amen to it.[24]

This account of the Eucharistic prayer is produced by piecing together stray references from Justin's writings, and by arranging them in a certain pattern. The pattern is derived from a text of a Eucharistic prayer said to have been composed in Rome some sixty years after Justin's time. The author is thought to have been Hippolytus, a traditionalist who wrote a handbook to regulate church life at the beginning of the third century.[25] The text, like many liturgical texts, has suffered badly in transmission.[26] But we find in it a thanksgiving for the redemption of mankind from the powers of evil through the Incarnation and Passion of the Christ; we find in it an offering of the bread and cup in memory of the death and Resurrection; and we find in it a thanksgiving for being accounted worthy to stand before God and minister to him. An ascription of glory to the Father through the Son with the Holy Spirit concludes the prayer, and at the end comes the Amen, which is presumably assigned to the congregation.

It is difficult to resist the conclusion that behind the battered text of the prayer in Hippolytus lies the type of prayer that Justin heard in Rome in the middle of the second century.[27] Attempts have been made to track back the pattern from the second century into the first. But it is impossible to identify the allusions in Holy Scripture. When the author of I Peter says

23. *Apology* 65. 24. ibid. 65 and 67.

25. For an edition of the text, *La Tradition Apostolique de Saint Hippolyte. Essai de reconstitution*, Dom Bernard Botte, Münster, 1963.

26. For a criticism of the Eucharistic prayer see E. C. Ratcliff, 'The Sanctus and the Pattern of the Early Anaphora I', *Journal of Ecclesiastical History*, April 1950. For another view see B. Botte, 'L'Épiclèse de l'Anaphore d'Hippolyte', *Recherches de Théologie ancienne et mediévale*, October 1947. The present writer accepts Professor Ratcliff's estimate of the text.

27. For another view see J. M. Hanssens, *La Liturgie d'Hippolyte*, Rome, 1959.

that Christians have been called out of darkness into God's marvellous light, is he alluding specifically to baptism? When he says that they have been constituted a royal priesthood to proclaim the mighty acts of God, is he alluding to the eucharistic thanksgiving for creation and redemption?[28] Is St Paul for that matter alluding to the Eucharistic prayer that he was accustomed to use when he says that we proclaim the Lord's death whenever we eat the bread and drink the cup?[29] And is he giving us a reminiscence of the sort of thanksgiving he uttered over the bread and cup, when in Philippians 2 he speaks of the Christ being in the form of God, yet taking upon him the form of a servant, and humbling himself to the death of the cross, and being exalted by his Father? And when the four and twenty elders in the Apocalypse thank God because he has created all things,[30] and thank the Christ because he has redeemed them by his blood, and because he has made them a kingdom and priests,[31] is there an allusion to the pattern that appears later in Justin and Hippolytus?[32]

Again, is the author of I Peter alluding specifically to the Eucharist when he says that Christians are a holy priesthood to offer up spiritual sacrifices acceptable to God through the Christ?[33] And is the author of Hebrews making a similar allusion, when he tells Christians to offer a sacrifice of praise through the Christ to God continually, and is the fruit of lips that confess to the name of God specifically the Eucharistic prayer?[34] For Clement, who was writing within the New Testament period, the sacrifice of praise is connected with Jesus Christ who is the high priest of our offerings,[35] and these are made in the Church by the hands of the appointed ministry.[36] But it is generally agreed that in these matters the first century keeps its secrets to itself.

28. 1 Peter 2. 9.
29. 1 Corinthians 11. 26.
30. Apocalypse 4. 11.
31. ibid. 5. 9, 10.
32. See G. A. Michell, *Landmarks in Liturgy*, London, 1961, pp. 86–9.
33. 1 Peter 2. 5.
34. Hebrews 13. 15.
35. 1 *Clement* 35. 12; 36. 1.
36. ibid. 44. 4.

Liturgy

Whether the Eucharistic prayer over the bread and cup was of the same pattern throughout Christendom in the early centuries is a matter of debate. In the fourth century there are similarities and there are differences in the traditions of East and West. Such evidence may be read in opposite ways. Either the similarities are evidence of an early universal pattern, and the differences show divergences developing later in different parts of Christendom. Or alternatively the differences are evidence of original plurality of patterns, and the similarities are to be explained as the result of a later tidying-up. The fourth century was a time when the text of the creed and the text of Holy Scripture were both being subjected to a smoothing-out process. It seems plausible that the sacramental rites underwent a similar treatment.[37]

The only liturgical texts which we possess for the second and third centuries from the eastern end of Christendom are unreliable guides, since they derive, not from the Christian Church, but from Gnostic sects which in many ways ran parallel to it. The shape of the rites described is certainly the same as that set out by Justin. There is for instance no trace of a meal attached to the Eucharistic rite. But only bread is used. It is claimed that this is evidence for the existence in the early Church of a Eucharist celebrated with bread alone. But more likely it merely proves that the sects which used such rites were of a puritanical type, which objected to the use of wine as to other pleasures of the flesh. The Gnostic prayers bear little resemblance to the thanksgivings presupposed by Justin. But this is scarcely surprising. For members of these sects commonly denied that the Father created the world and that the Son had become true man and suffered death upon the cross. They would therefore have found it impossible to thank God for the creation of the world or for the Incarnation and Passion of the Christ.[38]

37. See G. Dix, *The Shape of the Liturgy*, London, n.d., p.p. 208 ff.

38. Such texts are most easily accessible in *The Apocryphal New Testament*, newly translated by M. R. James, Oxford, 1924, pp. 250, 268, 388, 422.

There can then be no final answer to the question whether there was one pattern of Eucharistic prayer in the apostolic Church. But one thing is certain. The Christ and his apostles were Jews. Thanking God for his mighty acts in creating the world and in delivering his people was a Jewish way of praying. A thanksgiving then for creation and redemption, with an offering of bread and cup as a memorial of the Passion, would not have been an unusual way for Christian Jews to pray. Even a reference to the Christ's supposed command 'Do this in remembrance of me' would not have been out of character in a Jewish prayer. But here we are in the realm of conjecture rather than of established fact.[39]

Another problem is raised by the universal presence in the later Eucharistic prayers of the song of the Seraphim, 'Holy, Holy, Holy,' etc, which we call the Sanctus. It appears first in Isaiah and later in the Apocalypse of John; but in neither place has it any obvious connexion with the Eucharist, though at some time it found a place in the liturgy of the Synagogue. The first evidence for its inclusion in the Eucharistic prayers of Christendom comes from the fourth century, when it is found at Jerusalem and in Egypt, and slightly later at Antioch. The fourth century was a time when the Synagogue was no longer a danger to the Church, and when borrowings from the Old Testament were frequent. The sceptical scholar therefore is inclined to assert that, except possibly in Egypt, the Sanctus is a piece of fourth-century decoration, attached to Eucharistic prayers throughout Christendom without rhyme or reason, appearing at different points in the prayers of different Churches.[40]

The speculative scholar on the other hand is inclined to take the chant more seriously. He can point to a number of references to the Sanctus and to the heavenly beings who sing it in writers throughout Christendom in the first three centuries; and he may claim that these references are indications of the

39. See G. A. Michell, *Eucharistic Consecration in the Primitive Church*, London, 1948.

40. See G. Dix, *The Shape of the Liturgy*, pp. 537 ff.

presence of the Sanctus in the Eucharistic prayer. His main difficulty will be to explain why the chant attached itself to a prayer such as we find in Justin, and what position it occupied in the prayer itself. There is nothing specifically heavenly about giving thanks for the creation of the world and for the redemption of mankind over the bread and cup, or in offering them to God in memory of the Passion and Resurrection of the Christ. Our scholar will probably want to start from Justin's thanksgiving for being accounted worthy and from Hippolytus's phrase 'giving thanks to thee that thou hast accounted us worthy to stand before thee and minister to thee'. Those who stand before God and minister to him in heaven are the angels, and according to the writer of the Apocalypse they do so by singing the hymn of God's glory, the Sanctus. Could the connexion between the Eucharist and the Sanctus therefore be this, that by means of the Eucharist the Christian society is taken up to share in the worship of heaven? [41]

Such a notion may seem very far removed from the Last Supper, at which the Christ consecrated himself to a life-giving death and associated his disciples with his self-consecration. But he is said to have declared the cup to be the New Covenant in his Blood, or his Blood of the Covenant. Such a phrase to a Jew would bring with it the whole story of the making of the Old Covenant between God and man in Exodus 24. Moses, we read, sprinkled the people with the blood of bulls and goats, which he called the Blood of the Covenant, and in virtue of the Blood, and of the covenant made by means of it, Moses and his companions went up into the mount of God, and saw the God of Israel, and ate and drank in his presence. If the Christ used, or was thought to have used, such a phrase with regard to the cup, the notion of going up to heaven, and of entering into the divine presence, and of eating and drinking the bread and cup before God, would easily be associated with the repetition of the Supper. Reference therefore to the angels and to the hymn that they sing would come naturally into the

41. E. C. Ratcliff, 'The Sanctus and the Pattern of the Early Anaphora II', *Journal of Ecclesiastical History*, October 1950.

Eucharistic prayer, which would be thought to introduce the Christian society into the immediate presence of God.[42]

Another piece in the jig-saw, a scholar of this type would maintain, is the heavenly altar, or the altar on high. This symbol occurs in various places in the later Eucharistic texts from the fourth century onwards.[43] It apparently signifies the focus of the worship of heaven. It is not merely a place where the prayers and praises of angels and men are accepted by God. It is also connected with the Eucharistic oblations of bread and wine. Irenaeus, a traditionalist theologian of the late second century, maintains that 'there is an altar in the heavens, for thither our prayers and our oblations are directed';[44] and the references in the later liturgies make the same connexion. There are further references to a minister at the heavenly altar, sometimes described as an angel,[45] sometimes declared to be the Christ himself.[46] But in the early centuries it was not unusual to use the term Angel of the Christ,[47] and there is therefore no contradiction between the two ways of talking. A heavenly ministry of the Christ is certainly alluded to in Hebrews, where he is said to be a minister of the sanctuary and of the true tabernacle;[48] and in the first epistle of Clement, where he is called the high priest of our oblations, through whom we fix our gaze on the heights of the heavens.[49] The symbolism therefore in some measure goes back into the first century.[50]

What is the meaning expressed by the symbolism of an altar

42. A. H. Couratin, 'The Sacrifice of Praise', *Theology*, August 1955.

43. Ambrose, *De Sacramentis* IV, 6, 27; F. E. Brightman, *Liturgies Eastern and Western*, Oxford, 1896, pp. 23, 129.

44. *Adversus Haereses*, ed. W. W. Harvey, Cambridge, 1857, IV. 21. 5.

45. As in the canon of the Roman Mass.

46. See F. E. Brightman, *Liturgies Eastern and Western*, Oxford 1896, p. 23.

47. See Justin, *Apology* 63; *Dialogue* 93.

48. Hebrews 8. 2.

49. 1 *Clement* 36. 1.

50. For another view of the Angel see A. Fortescue, *The Mass*, London, 1926, pp. 350 ff.

in the heavenly sanctuary, in the sight of God's divine majesty, before which the Christ ministers as high priest, and presents the prayers and the oblations of the Church to his Father? The Christians who make up the Church can only approach God in worship because he has made them worthy to do so.[51] This has been effected in the mystery of baptism. They bring with them their thanksgivings for his mighty acts in creating the world and in redeeming mankind. But as a token expression of their gratitude they also offer bread and wine, in accordance with the Christ's command.[52] They offer these as a thank-offering for the creation of the natural world, since the bread and wine are regarded as its first-fruits and as the means of sustaining natural life.[53] But they also offer them as a thank-offering for the redemption of the human race, since the bread and wine are regarded as the Body and Blood of the Christ, the symbols of his Passion and Resurrection, by which the human race was redeemed. These are the thankofferings which Christians offer to the Father through the hands of the Christ in the place where God is, under whatever image that may be conceived. In virtue of his intercession they are introduced into the heavenly worship, they see God face to face, and they eat and drink in his presence. If such an interpretation of the celebration of the Eucharist was current in the early Church, it is easy to see how the references to the angels and the singing of the Sanctus became associated with the Eucharistic prayer.

Such a reconstruction of early Eucharistic theology and of the framework of the early Eucharistic prayer is not mere speculation. It is built up out of numbers of small pieces of evidence. It cannot be proved or disproved. But it may be the best interpretation of such evidence as there is. This is not a question of piecing together correctly all the bits of a jig-saw puzzle. It is rather a question of piecing together such bits

51. Justin, *Dialogue* 116 and 117; compare *Apology* 65 and Hippolytus, *Apostolic Tradition* 4.

52. Justin, *Apology* 41.

53. Irenaeus, *Adversus Haereses*, IV. 29. 5.

as remain, knowing that many of the bits are irretrievably lost.

The reader must forgive this lengthy discussion of the pre-history of the Eucharistic prayer. But it is a kind of liturgical philosopher's stone, which has fascinated scholars ever since the critical study of liturgy began in the seventeenth century. It is not without interest to ecclesiastical controversialists, who may appeal against the doctrine and practice of their opponents to the 'usages of the primitive Church'. And at a time when the Churches of Western Christendom, Catholic and Reformed alike, are taking stock of their liturgical traditions, it is thought to afford some basis for liturgical reform. It is also seen as a means of by-passing the controversies of the medieval and reformation periods and of securing some sort of *rapprochement* between divided churches. The reader must judge for himself whether it is capable of what is expected of it.

The Eucharistic prayer was apparently the only prayer in the pre-historic Eucharist. The bringing of the bread and wine to the celebrant, the breaking-up of the bread, the distribution of bread and cup to the congregation, were all actions performed in silence; or at most some words accompanied the distribution. In the West there is no certain evidence that anything was said at this point; but in the East a prayer was apparently developing which asked that the communicant might receive the fruits of communion. The texts in which such prayers appear are second-century and third-century Gnostic writings; but since in other respects the rites described correspond to those of the contemporary Christian churches, it may be assumed that similar prayers were in use there also. This would account for the invocations, or Epicleses, which stand at the end of the Eucharistic prayers of the Eastern churches, when pre-history gives place to history in the middle of the fourth century.[54]

One last point may be noted in connexion with the primitive

54. On this subject see E. C. Ratcliff, 'A Note on the Anaphoras Described in the Liturgical Homilies of Narsai', *Biblical and Patristic Studies in Memory of Robert Pierce Casey*, Freiburg, 1963.

Eucharist. The bread and cup were held to convey the spiritual benefit of union with Christ in his Church when received outside the context of the celebration of the Eucharist. Or perhaps it would be more true to say that they in some sense carried the context of the Eucharistic celebration with them and could not be divorced from it. In consequence those Christians who were unable to be present at the Sunday Eucharist were not thereby excluded from communion. The servants of the Church, the deacons, having distributed the elements to those who were present, proceeded to distribute them to those who were not present.[55] At a time when many Christians were slaves and were not free to assist at the weekly Christian assembly, the numbers of those receiving in this way may well have been large. But the reception of communion week by week was regarded as the means whereby union with Christ was maintained, and Christians could not therefore be deprived of it. Again, the elements were further reserved by those who wished to receive communion on weekdays. At this period the Eucharist was normally celebrated only on Sunday, the Lord's day, the day of the Resurrection. But this did not exclude the possibility of receiving communion on other days. Apparently any Christian who wished might take away the bread from the Sunday Eucharist and might keep it in his house or about his person, so as to be able to receive it each day, until the following Sunday.[56] In parts of Christendom the petition of the Lord's Prayer 'Give us this day our daily bread' was interpreted as referring to daily communion; and the way was thus prepared for the introduction of the Lord's Prayer into the Eucharistic rite in the fourth century as an immediate preparation for communion.

55. Justin, *Apology* 65 and 67.

56. See Tertullian, *Ad uxorem* 2. 5; the treatise by an unknown author *De spectaculis* 5; G. Dix, 'The Mass of the Presanctified', *Laudate*, March 1935.

Three

Baptism before the Middle Ages

With the fourth century the pre-history of the liturgy may be said to end, and the history proper to begin. Not that complete liturgical texts are immediately available, containing the words to be spoken and the actions to be performed in the various rites. But references to the baptismal and Eucharistic liturgies become more frequent as Christian literature grows in size; and a number of lectures given to the newly-baptized have survived from the second half of the fourth century onwards. The Christian Church, though no longer subject to persecution, reserved a full knowledge of the Christian mysteries to the baptized. Candidates for baptism therefore could be given no detailed instruction concerning the rites they were to undergo. Their formal instruction in the faith they were to profess took place during the weeks before Easter which we now call Lent. But when they presented themselves for baptism at the Easter Vigil, they still did not know what was going to happen to them. Only after they had received the mysteries were they given, during the week following Easter Day, instructions on the sacraments they had already received. It is principally from such instructions, a number of which have come down to us, that we can gain some knowledge of what was said and done.

Baptism could of course be received at any time in case of necessity. But as early as the time of Tertullian it was associated with Easter;[1] and Easter baptism everywhere became the norm. It appears that in early times there were only two festivals in the Christian year – the annual Christian Passover festival, or Easter, and its weekly counterpart, Sunday. The annual Easter festival commemorated both the death and resurrection

1. Tertullian, *De baptismo* 19. 1.

EASTER

of Jesus Christ in one service, as the one saving act of God. The death was not commemorated separately on the Friday and the Resurrection on the Sunday, as at present. Easter commemorated the death and Resurrection. Baptism caused the candidates to die and rise with Christ. Inevitably then the great baptism of the year took place at Easter. Cyril of Jerusalem, or maybe John, his successor, gives us some account of what went on at Jerusalem. John Chrysostom and Theodore describe how things were done at Antioch. Ambrose tells us what happened at Milan; and since he remarks that he desires to follow the Roman Church in all things, it is usually thought that his account also holds good for Rome. Less than a century later Narsai recounts what was done at Edessa, in the Syriac-speaking Church outside the confines of the Roman Empire.[2]

It is in this remote part of Christendom that a baptismal pattern survived which seems strange to those who have been brought up in the Western tradition. The pattern was certainly in existence in the East during the third century, and may even go back into New Testament times. The candidate renounces the devil and all his works, and makes an act of faith in God. He is then anointed on the head by the bishop with the consecrated oil, and the anointing is continued all over his body by the deacon, a deaconess performing the same service for a female candidate. He is then baptized in water by the bishop or the presbyter. Both the anointing and the baptism are accompanied by a naming of the threefold name, Father, Son and Holy Spirit. The candidate is then clothed with new garments, and is immediately introduced into the celebration of the Eucharist and given a share in the Eucharistic bread and cup.

The pattern seems strange to those who are familiar only with the Western tradition. For in the West, as we have already seen in Tertullian, the water was given first, and was thought to cleanse the candidate from his sins; and the laying-on of the hand came second, and was thought to give the Holy Spirit to

2. These authors may be conveniently consulted by the non-specialist in E. C. Whitaker, *Documents of the Baptismal Liturgy*, London, 1960.

the candidate. To give the Spirit first in the anointing, and then to baptize with water, appears to put the cart before the horse. But this is only because the effect of the two signs was differently interpreted in East Syria and in the West. In the West the candidate was cleansed from sin by baptism with water: in the East he was cleansed by the Spirit given through the anointing with oil. In the West he was consecrated by the Spirit, given through prayer with the laying-on of the hand, and making him a temple of the indwelling Spirit: in the East he was consecrated by the invocation of the Divine Name, when he was baptized with water, and became a son of God. In each tradition similar effects were attributed to the rite as a whole; but the effects were differently distributed between the outward signs.[3]

It may be asked how both the laying-on of the hand with prayer and the anointing with oil came to be regarded as equivalent signs of the giving of the Spirit. Such an equivalence could be accounted for, if it were assumed that the rite developed by stages, in some such way as this. In the earliest stage the laying-on of the hand with prayer was the only rite practised, and was unaccompanied by any anointing with oil. It was however interpreted as conveying the non-material anointing with the Holy Spirit. In the second stage the interpretation was illustrated by attaching a decorative anointing with material oil to the laying-on of the hand with prayer. But the laying-on of the hand with prayer was still interpreted as conveying the Spirit. In the third stage the anointing with oil was regarded not merely as an illustration of what was effected by the laying-on of the hand with prayer, but as the actual sign by means of which the Spirit was conveyed. In the fourth stage therefore the laying-on of the hand with prayer was either reduced to a mere preface to the anointing with oil, or omitted altogether. There is some evidence that such a development took place in the East Syrian tradition. In a third-century reference to baptism the bishop lays his hand upon the candidate's head at the beginning

3. E. C. Ratcliff, 'The Old Syrian Baptismal Tradition and its Resettlement under the Influence of Jerusalem in the Fourth Century', in *Studies in Church History* II, 1965.

of the unction, which is completed by others.[4] This might be taken as evidence of an intermediate stage, in which the anointing had been attached to the laying-on of the hand, but had not yet supplanted it.

It is sometimes claimed that the East Syrian pattern – the giving of the Spirit followed by the baptism in water – is assumed in some New Testament passages referring to baptism. St Peter is described as giving baptism with water to Cornelius and his household, after the Spirit had been given by a miraculous illapse.[5] St Paul himself is said to have received baptism after Ananias had laid his hands upon him.[6] St Paul parallels with the Christian sacraments the experiences of the Israelites escaping from Egypt; and declares that they were all under the cloud and all passed through the sea, and were all baptized into Moses in the cloud and in the sea.[7] St John speaks of three that bear witness, the Spirit, the water and the Blood;[8] and this passage has been thought to refer, first to the giving of the Spirit, then to baptism with water, and finally to the Blood of the Eucharist. But, as we have seen, other passages apparently imply the reverse order. St Luke describes the Spirit descending upon the Christ, after he had been baptized and while he was now praying.[9] St Peter and St John are said to have given the Spirit to the Samaritans by means of the laying-on of hands with prayer, after they had been baptized by Philip.[10] St Paul is described as baptizing the disciples of St John Baptist at Ephesus first, and then as laying hands upon them.[11] St John, who speaks of the Spirit, the water and the Blood, also speaks of being born again of water and the Spirit,[12] and indeed says that out of the side of the dead body of Christ there came forth Blood and water.[13] A strict interpretation of this last symbolism would demand the administration of the Eucharist before baptism. All claims to find this or that pattern for the performance

4. *Didascalia Apostolorum*, ed. R. H. Conolly, Oxford, 1929, p. 146.
5. Acts 10. 44–48.
6. Acts 9. 17–19.
7. 1 Corinthians 10. 1, 2.
8. 1 John 5. 8.
9. Luke 3. 21, 22.
10. Acts 8. 14–17.
11. Acts 19. 5, 6.
12. John 3. 5.
13. John 19. 34.

of the sacraments in the New Testament fall to the ground. They were being administered before ever the New Testament was written. The method of their administration may be reflected in different passages in the New Testament; and there is no guarantee that they were administered everywhere in the same way. Passages in the New Testament may subsequently have influenced the method of their administration. But those who originally administered them had nothing in the way of Scripture to guide them, except the Old Testament.

The teaching and practice of the Churches of the Near East towards the end of the fourth century is well documented. We not only have the lectures of Cyril of Jerusalem, of John Chrysostom, and of Theodore of Mopsuestia; we have a Church Order, a manual telling how to perform the sacraments, known as *The Apostolic Constitutions*. This is unfortunately not the service book of any particular church; it merely lays down the way in which the author thought the sacraments should be administered. But he was presumably building upon and modifying a rite with which he was familiar; and his work may take its place alongside the lectures as evidence of the West Syrian tradition in the last quarter of the fourth century.

A comparison of the documents seems to show that the liturgy of baptism at this time and in this area was on the turn. Behind the rite described by all these writers lies the old East Syrian pattern – anointing with oil, baptism with water, participation in the Eucharist. This is still the pattern described by John Chrysostom in the last decade of the century.[14] But already by A.D. 350, if we may attribute to Cyril of Jerusalem the lectures that bear his name, an anointing had been introduced at Jerusalem after baptism and before the Eucharist, and was being interpreted as the outward sign of the gifts of the Spirit.[15] *The Apostolic Constitutions*, which may be dated as early as A.D. 375, also prescribes an anointing after baptism as well as an anointing before, but attributes to the pre-baptismal unction the effect of imparting the Spirit.[16] Theodore of Mopsuestia, the

14. E. C. Whitaker, op. cit., p. 32, 33.
15. ibid., pp. 26, 27.
16. ibid., pp. 27, 28; 28–32.

life-long friend of John Chrysostom, nevertheless describes a rite similar in pattern to that of *The Apostolic Constitutions.* But he follows Cyril in ascribing the gift of the Spirit to the post-baptismal unction, and like Cyril explains it with reference to the descent of the Spirit upon the Christ after his baptism in Jordan.[17]

How can this change in the Eastern pattern of baptism be explained? Clearly the older Syrian pattern was being modified under the impulse of some outside influence. The most plausible explanation is that by the beginning of the fourth century the Western tradition was making an impact on the East. It is tempting to attribute this impact to the circulation in the East of the treatise known as *The Apostolic Tradition*, to which we have already referred. There has been and continues to be a great deal of discussion about the authorship and provenance of this work.[18] But the commonly accepted story is that it was written by Hippolytus, a presbyter of the Roman Church, at the beginning of the third century; that it was written as a protest against innovations which were being introduced into Church life there at that time; and that, since the author was plainly conservative by temperament, and since he professes to maintain the older tradition,[19] his treatise may be accepted as witnessing to Roman practice toward the end of the second century. Hippolytus himself was apparently rejected by the Roman Church, and his treatise had little or no effect on the later Roman liturgy. But it had a wide circulation in the East, in company with other Church orders of Eastern provenance, and may reasonably be thought to have had a wide influence there.[20]

The text of the treatise however must be received with caution. Liturgical texts are peculiarly susceptible to alteration in transmission, and are constantly being affected by the practice

17. ibid., p. 36–42.
18. Compare J. M. Hanssens, *La Liturgie d'Hippolyte*, Rome, 1959.
19. *The Apostolic Tradition* 1.
20. See B. Botte, *La Tradition Apostolique de Saint Hippolyte*, Münster, 1965, pp. xi–xxviii.

of the areas in which they are being copied. It is therefore uncertain whether a text which presumably left Rome in the first half of the third century would remain unaltered by the time it was circulating in the East a hundred and fifty years later. That is why little use was made of *The Apostolic Tradition* when the pre-history of the liturgy was being explored. It may in many places represent the text that Hippolytus wrote. But in other places it is obviously inconsistent with his own views and those of his contemporaries. Any passage in the treatise therefore should be carefully scrutinized before it is claimed as evidence for Roman practice in the second and third centuries.[21]

The rite of baptism as it appears in *The Apostolic Tradition* follows the developed Roman pattern, as it is found in the lectures of Ambrose and in the later Roman liturgical books. The water is blessed; the candidates renounce the devil and are anointed with oil; they are baptized in water three times, in conjunction with a three-fold act of faith in God, Father, Son and Holy Spirit; they are anointed on the head with consecrated oil; and all these actions are performed by the presbyters, with the assistance of the deacons. Finally the bishop lays his hand upon them, that is to say, stretches out his hand over them, and says a prayer; after which he pours the consecrated oil from his hand and lays his hand upon the head of each, and signs him with the sign of the cross upon his forehead, and gives him the kiss of peace.[22]

How far can this description be accepted as the work of Hippolytus, and as testimony to late-second-century practice at Rome? Tertullian was a contemporary of Hippolytus, and the connexion between Rome and Africa was close. Elements in the baptismal rite of *The Apostolic Tradition* which are mentioned in Tertullian may therefore perhaps be thought to be original. Like *The Apostolic Tradition* Tertullian mentions prayer over the water, but gives the impression that the prac-

21. E. C. Ratcliff, 'Christian Worship and Liturgy', in *The Study of Theology*, ed. K. E. Kirk, London, 1939, pp. 422–5.

22. E. C. Whitaker, *Documents etc.*, pp. 2–7.

tice was novel. It has been suggested that by the beginning of the third century the older custom of baptizing in the running water of rivers and streams was being abandoned in favour of baptizing in the static water in tanks in houses, and indeed in specially constructed baptismal fonts, as church buildings developed. The consecration of the water may perhaps be an innovation connected with this development. Like *The Apostolic Tradition* Tertullian mentions the renunciation of the devil; but he does not apparently know of any anointing at this point. Like *The Apostolic Tradition* he mentions the threefold baptism in answer to the threefold act of faith. Neither writer alludes to any such formula as 'I baptize thee' or 'N. is baptized' 'in the name of the Father and of the Son and of the Holy Spirit'. Like *The Apostolic Tradition* Tertullian mentions the anointing after baptism, and the laying-on of the hand, accompanied by a prayer for the gift of the Spirit. He also knows of a signing with the sign of the cross, but implies that it was done before the laying-on of the hand, and not after it, as in *The Apostolic Tradition*; nor does he mention any final unction in connexion with the laying-on of the hand. But otherwise the rite set out in *The Apostolic Tradition* is almost identical with the rite presupposed in the writings of Tertullian.[23]

The text of the prayers in *The Apostolic Tradition* is compatible with the explanation of the rite given by Tertullian. The candidates must renounce the devil; they must make the profession of faith, which is as integral to the act of baptism as the water; and in baptism they receive the remission of sins. The anointing after baptism in *The Apostolic Tradition* is administered 'in the name of Jesus Christ', that is to say, Jesus the anointed one; and in Tertullian is explained with a reference to the anointing which the Christ received from his Father. It is only in the final stage that differences of interpretation seem to arise. Tertullian is emphatic that water is the sign of the remission of sins, and that the laying-on of the hand with prayer is the sign of the gift of the Spirit. *The Apostolic Tradition* is thought to be inconclusive on this point. The text of the prayer

23. ibid., pp. 7–9.

is uncertain.[24] One reading seems to imply that the Spirit has already been given in baptism. The other seems to look forward to the giving of the Spirit in the anointing which follows. It is at this point, and perhaps at this point only, that one might suspect that *The Apostolic Tradition* had been readjusted in Syrian surroundings.

It is against the background of Tertullian and of *The Apostolic Tradition* that the baptismal rite described by Ambrose must be seen.[25] Ambrose was in a peculiar position with regard to the liturgy. He was only a catechumen when he was elected bishop of Milan. He was baptized and consecrated bishop in the space of eight days; and from that moment onwards was responsible for administering baptism and the Eucharist, with both of which he had only recently become acquainted. Further, he presided over a city where a succession of bishops from the East had ruled before him, and therefore probably inherited a liturgy which was partly orientalized. He himself professes in his lectures his desire to follow the Roman Church in all things; but he admits that he allows some non-Roman customs to prevail.[26] His description of the rites of baptism as practised at Milan in the last quarter of the fourth century may therefore be taken, with some exceptions, as good evidence for contemporary Roman practice.

In his lectures Ambrose was explaining to the newly-baptized the mysteries through which they had passed during the Easter Vigil. At the entrance to the baptistery they had been anointed with oil, and they had renounced the devil and the world. The anointing is interpreted as the preparation of Christ's athlete for a wrestling match with the devil, as wrestlers were anointed in the ancient world. The candidates had then advanced to the baptismal tank, and the bishop had blessed the water, calling upon the Trinity to descend upon the font, and quoting the command to baptize from St Matthew's Gospel. Each candidate had then gone down into the font, and was asked, 'Dost

24. B. Botte, op. cit., pp. 52–3.
25. E. C. Whitaker, *Documents etc.*, pp. 117–23.
26. Ambrose, *De Sacramentis* III, 1, 5.

thou believe in God the Father Almighty?', 'Dost thou believe in Jesus Christ?' etc., and 'Dost thou believe in the Holy Spirit?'; and each time he said 'I believe', he had been dipped in the water. The going-down into the water signified death and burial with the Christ, the coming-up again signified resurrection. On emerging from the font each candidate had been anointed with sweet-smelling oil, which signified admission to the royal priesthood.

At this point a ceremony had occurred which was unknown to the Roman Church. The bishop and his presbyters had washed the feet of the candidates. Ambrose admitted that, although he desired to follow Roman customs, he had nevertheless retained this ceremony, and appealed in justification to the words of Peter, himself bishop of Rome, on the occasion of the feet-washing in the Gospel. That Ambrose should retain an edifying ceremony of this kind is understandable; but that he should ascribe to it a sacramental efficacy seems to us incomprehensible. Yet this is what he does. He maintains that in baptism all the candidate's past sins are forgiven and washed away; but that in the feet-washing the poison in human nature inherited from the fall of man is similarly washed away.[27] It is difficult to understand how a theologian like Ambrose could make such an assertion. For, if pressed, it would mean that those baptized at Rome only received forgiveness of their own past sins, but still laboured under the taint they were thought to have inherited from Adam.

After their feet had been washed, the candidates had been clothed in white garments, and had received as the completion of their baptism what Ambrose calls the Spiritual Seal. Unfortunately he does not describe the rite in detail. It was administered by the bishop; it included a prayer invoking the coming of the Spirit upon the candidates, and the prayer almost certainly contained a reference to the sevenfold gift of the Spirit, which according to the prophecy of Isaiah would rest upon the Messiah.[28] The rite is comparable with that referred to by Tertullian, in which the laying-on of the hand is accompanied by

27. ibid., III, 1, 7.

28. ibid., III, 2, 8; compare Isaiah 11. 1–3.

an invocation of the Spirit upon the baptized. But the reference to the seal may suggest something more than a laying-on of hands with prayer. The word 'seal', when applied by ancient writers to the ceremonies of baptism, is of indeterminate meaning.[29] One writer may say that the seal is the water; another may identify it with the oil: but the most obvious ceremony to which the word can be attached is the sign of the cross. It may be assumed then as probable that after Ambrose had laid his hand upon the candidates and had invoked upon them the outpouring of the sevenfold Spirit, he made the sign of the cross upon the forehead of each one of them. Whether the signing was accompanied with a final anointing is unknown.

If this is so, then the baptismal rite described by Ambrose is all but identical in shape with that set out in *The Apostolic Tradition*, with the obvious exception of the feet-washing, which was admittedly no part of Roman practice. The renunciation of the devil and the anointing before baptism; the baptism itself to the accompaniment of the threefold act of faith; the bishop's laying-on of the hand with prayer – the shape up to this point is identical in *The Apostolic Tradition*, in Ambrose and in the later Roman rite. Only in what follows the laying-on of the hand with prayer is there any radical difference. Tertullian had apparently known of nothing further at this point. After the laying-on of the hand the Eucharist followed immediately. *The Apostolic Tradition* on the other hand prescribes first an anointing with imposition of hand, and then a signing with the cross. Ambrose probably knew of a signing with the cross at this point, but we have no means of knowing whether he anointed the candidates at the same time. The later Roman rite prescribes that after the bishop has laid hands upon the candidates with a prayer for the descent of the Spirit, he shall sign each one of them upon the forehead with his thumb dipped in chrism – oil mixed with balsam.[30] It is tempting to see an orderly development at this point from Tertullian through Ambrose to the

29. G. W. H. Lampe, *The Seal of the Spirit*, Chapter XI.
30. E. C. Whitaker, *Documents etc.*, p. 178.

later Roman rite, the laying-on of the hand with prayer in Tertullian being amplified with a signing of the cross in Ambrose and this in its turn being elaborated with a final unction in the later Roman books. If this is what happened, then the rite in *The Apostolic Tradition* must have been remodelled at this point under the influence of another pattern.[31]

The term 'laying-on of the hand', or 'of hands', should perhaps receive attention. In the earliest liturgical texts the phrase cannot mean that the celebrant placed his hand or hands upon the head of each person individually. The text of the prayer in *The Apostolic Tradition* to be said when the bishop lays his hand upon the newly-baptized is phrased in the plural, while the subsequent formulae for anointing and signing are phrased in the singular.[32] This can only mean that the bishop effected the laying-on of the hand during the prayer by stretching out his hand over the candidates. Presumably when the rite was being performed for one candidate only, the bishop would place his hand upon the candidate's head during the recitation of the prayer. Since however normally the rite was being performed for a number of candidates, it was thought sufficient to stretch out his hand over their heads – to overshadow them, as Tertullian puts it. The gesture could be used for an ordinary blessing. A prayer can be labelled 'The laying-on of hands upon the people', and can begin with the words 'I stretch forth the hand over the people, and I pray',[33] etc. A theologian can write,

31. On the whole subject of unction in connexion with baptism and confirmation see Lionel L. Mitchell, *Baptismal Anointing*, London, 1966.

32. E. C. Whitaker, *Documents etc.*, p. 6. It may be argued that the reference to the laying-on of the hand in the opening rubric of Chapter XXIII refers only to the laying-on of the hand during the anointing, and not to the preceding prayer. The present writer does not accept this view, but would be inclined to see in the unction in the threefold Name an adjustment made to the text under the influence of Syrian practice.

33. *Bishop Sarapion's Prayer Book*, translated by John Wordsworth, second edition, London, 1923, p. 65.

'What is the laying-on of the hand but prayer over a person?'[34] Perhaps this gives the explanation of the sign. The prayer uttered asks God for the appropriate gift, whether in baptism, ordination, absolution or blessing. The hand, laid or outstretched, indicates the person or persons for whom the gift is asked. Or maybe this is a rationalization of something more primitive, and less theologically respectable.

We have talked about the bare bones of the rite of baptism as it stood at the beginning of its history. But, clothed in the ceremonial and architectural splendours of the period, it must have been a most moving spectacle and a most affecting experience. Although children could be baptized, and were usually baptized with their parents, the candidates were normally adult. They had often undergone several years of loose attachment to the Church as catechumens; and when they had finally made up their minds to adopt the new religion, they were put through six weeks of intensive preparation – intellectual, by way of instruction, and ascetic, by way of fasting and prayer and exorcism. They were ignorant of the mysteries through which they were to pass, but they believed that by means of them they would receive salvation; and this was a gift which was passionately desired and sought after by the people of the ancient world.

At Easter the Christians would be keeping the all-night vigil, in which they celebrated annually the true Passover, the dying and rising of the Son of God. This they viewed against the background of the Old Testament Scriptures – the new creation in Christ against the first creation set out in Genesis; the salvation of Christians by water in the ark of Christ's Church against the salvation of the human family during the flood in Noah's ark; the sacrifice by the Father of his well-beloved Son against the sacrifice by Abraham of his only son Isaac; the deliverance of

34. Augustine, *De baptismo* 3. 16. The *manus impositio* referred to in this passage is in fact that which took place in the absolution and reconciliation of heretics. But it suggests a view of the sign of the laying-on of the hand which goes far beyond anything here envisaged by Augustine.

the People of God from the powers of evil, by the sacrifice of the true Passover lamb, against the deliverance of the old People of God from the tyranny of Pharaoh, by the blood of the Paschal victims; and so on through the Old Testament Scriptures.[35] Assembled in the halls of the great new basilicas, glittering with the newly kindled light of many lamps, they listened all night while these Scriptures were recited from the reading desk or ambo. Toward daybreak the bishop and his ministers left the basilica for the baptistery, a spacious and splendid building, comprising not only the hall containing the font, but also dressing rooms for the candidates, and a separate chapel for the rites preceding baptism, and another for the confirmation which followed it. The font itself was not an inconspicuous basin, but a large tank, often of fine marble, sunk into the floor of the building, into which the water might pour from jets along the sides. For the candidates were to stand in the water, and water was to pour over their bodies. In these surroundings the candidates stripped; they renounced the devil; they were anointed for the final struggle with evil. They then descended into the font; they made the threefold act of faith and received the threefold pouring of the water, showing the threefold Godhead and the three days' burial in the tomb. Coming up out of the water, they were anointed with the chrism, as being now kings and priests and in some sense Christs, since they shared his Resurrection and his Sonship. They then put on their white baptismal robes, and went before the bishop for the gift of the Spirit. The bishop prayed with hands outstretched over them; he implored the Father to send upon them the sevenfold Spirit of the Messiah, proclaimed by the prophet Isaiah. Having thus confirmed, or completed their baptism, he put the mark of Christ, the sign of the cross, upon their foreheads, and admitted them for the first time to the kiss of peace. In solemn procession the bishop and his ministers and the newly-baptized returned to the waiting congregation in the basilica, and the Mass of the Christian Passover began in the full light of Easter Day.

35. Compare the lessons of the Paschal Vigil contained in *Missale Romanum* up to 1951.

The grandeur of the rite, even in surroundings less imposing than the great churches of Rome, could not fail to impress the candidates and to convince them that they had received the desired salvation; that they had experienced a new birth, and a death and resurrection, and that they had passed out of this world into the next.[36]

36. See J. G. Davies, *The Architectural Setting of Baptism*, London, 1962, Chapter I.

Four

The Eucharist before the Middle Ages

The once-for-all salvation which the newly-baptized had attained was not secured merely by participation in the baptismal Eucharist. It demanded also regular participation in the Eucharist that was celebrated every Sunday, as being the weekly Passover, or Easter, of the Church. This was as true in theory after the Peace of the Church as it was before. It is therefore astounding to find that before the end of the fourth century the communion of the laity in the Sunday Eucharist had virtually disappeared, except on the great festivals. This is apparently equally true of the East, where Chrysostom notes it with dismay,[1] and of the West, where Ambrose makes the same complaint.[2] Only in old-fashioned churches like Rome did the older custom prevail.

What was the reason for this amazing change in the habits of the laity? It is commonly attributed to the laxity that invaded the Church when persecution was suddenly replaced by imperial patronage. But this cannot be altogether true. Candidates for baptism were no doubt more numerous, now that baptism was no longer the gateway to martyrdom, but might even be a stepping stone to imperial favour. But the practice of the catechumenate remained, and the font was still reasonably fenced. The penitential system of the Church was also in force, and the penalties for grave sin after baptism were severe. No doubt the life of a Christian in the fourth century was easier than it had been before, but it was still subject to a rigorous discipline.

Imperial toleration, and then the imperial establishment, of Christianity could not of themselves affect the sacramental life

1. *In Hebraeos* 17, 4.

2. *De Sacramentis* V, 4, 25.

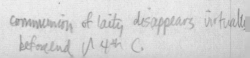

and liturgy of the Church. They did however produce a climate in which a double standard of practice developed. The same is true of the rising tide of asceticism which affected the Church in this period. From New Testament times there had been an ascetic attitude in the Church toward property and toward marriage. In a closed religious society which thought the end of the age to be imminent, people invariably sat lightly to the good things of this life, however highly they might be recommended in the Old Testament scriptures. With persecution and martyrdom always possible, if at times remote, people found it less unnatural to practise detachment from the things of the world. And so long as Christians kept themselves apart from the main stream of secular life, they were not confronted with the full-blooded wickedness of the pagan world. But once Christianity had become a lawful religion, and set out on the road to establishment, Christians were faced with a society which was blatantly immoral, not least in the sexual field. The result of this confrontation can be seen in various ways.

First of all, there was the cult of celibacy, always present in Christianity, but now more widespread than before. This found expression in the public consecration of virgins, in the flight of the hermits to the desert, and later in the establishment of religious communities of either sex. Next, there was the growing pressure on the clergy to live the celibate life, and the consequent confusion of the clerical with the monastic vocation, which has bedevilled the Christian ministry in large parts of Christendom ever since. Finally, there was the demand for temporary celibacy on the part of communicants, both clerical and lay, for some fixed period before the reception of communion.

The formal establishment of the ascetic or religious life within the Church need not concern us here. It had an effect on the liturgy of the Church, in the matter of the development of the Divine Office. But it did not immediately affect the liturgy of the sacraments, which is what we are now considering. But the tendency to assimilate the clergy with the ascetics drove a wedge between the clergy and the laity. The line should have clergy ident. w/ ascetics

been drawn between the ascetics, whether clerics or laypeople, who withdrew from society, and the rank and file of Christians, whether clerics or laypeople, who remained within it. Instead it was drawn between the ascetics and the clergy on the one hand, and the laity on the other.

But it was the growing demand for continence on the part of communicants which was probably the immediate cause for the decay of the communion of the laity. The demand was probably based on Old Testament precedent, to which appeal was increasingly made from the fourth century onwards. Origen a century earlier had seen in the Eucharist a fulfilment of the shewbread, which was set forth before God under the Old Covenant.[3] The shewbread was duly consumed by the Levitical priests during their period of duty,[4] during which they abstained from the use of marriage.[5] It could therefore easily be argued that those who received the shewbread of the New Covenant were no less bound to temporary continence before receiving it. The growing separation of clergy from laity would no doubt suggest that the reception of the Eucharist was mainly a clerical duty, since the priesthood of the clergy was being overemphasized at the time, and the priesthood of the laity was beginning to fall into the background. The demand for continence before communion continued in the Western Church until the sixteenth century, when it disappeared under Jesuit influence; but it is said to persist to this day in the East. It has left its mark on liturgical history. For in the West a daily celebration of the Mass is maintained by a celibate priesthood; while in the East the Eucharist is celebrated only upon Sundays and other Holy Days, and the priesthood is married.

In the fourth century also a new way of talking about the Eucharist appears in the East. Cyril of Jerusalem calls the time when the Eucharistic prayer is being said 'that most terrifying hour', and the elements themselves 'the holy and most terrifying sacrifice'.[6] There had always been, from New Testament times,

3. *In Leviticum* XIII, 3.
4. Leviticus 24. 5–9.
5. Compare 1 Samuel 21. 4, 5.
6. *Mystagogical Catechesis* V, sections 4 and 9.

R	F	F
D1	F	F
D1	F	F
D1	F	F
D1	F	F
R	F	F
D1	F	F
D1	F	F
D1	F	F
R	F	F
D1	F	F
D1	F	F
D1	F	F
R	F	F
D1	F	F
R	F	F
R	F	F
R	F	F
D1	F	F
D1	F	F
D1	F	F
D1	F	F
D1	F	F
D1	F	F
D1	F	F

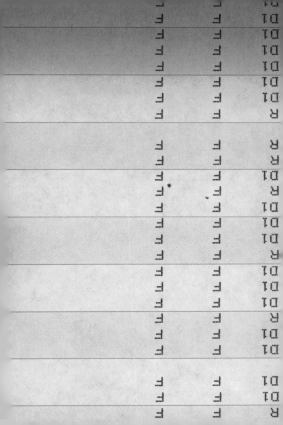

a terror of unworthy communion, based on St Paul's attribution of sickness and death among Corinthian communicants to this cause.[7] But the terror was attached, not to the elements themselves, but to receiving them unworthily, and so being guilty of the Body and Blood of the Lord.[8] From Cyril's time onward terror language about the sacrament itself is found in Eastern liturgies, and there is a growing tendency in the East to withdraw the celebration from the eyes and ears of the congregation. Veils surrounded the sanctuary; and later a screen with doors prevented the people from seeing the performance of the liturgy. Prayers which used to be sung out loud were now said secretly, and only occasionally did the celebrant raise his voice for the people to hear.[9]

It is at this time, also in the East, that the beginnings of ceremonial appear. It was inevitable that worship in a publicly recognized body should be conducted in a more formal manner than was possible in the days before the Peace of the Church. The entry of the celebrant and his deacons was turned into a formal procession, not without resistance from the older clergy.[10] The wearing of special clothing by the celebrant was beginning at Jerusalem[11] and at Antioch[12] in the course of the fourth century. By the middle of the fifth, in East Syria at any rate, both clothing and ceremonial had reached a pitch that was not reached in the West until the later Middle Ages.[13] The Roman Church, and Churches which followed Roman customs, tended to stand aloof from such developments. The clergy apparently wore their ordinary clothes in church, at least until after the death of Gregory the Great. They wore the formal dress of the period, and behaved in the churches in much the same way as the magistrates in the law courts. This is probably the explanation of the lights and the incense carried before the

7. 1 Corinthians 11. 30. 8. 1 Corinthians 11. 27.

9. Edmund Bishop, *The Liturgical Homilies of Narsai*, ed. R. H. Conolly, Cambridge, 1909, Appendices II and V.

10. Compare Canon 56 of the Council of Laodicaea.

11. Theodoret, *Ecclesiastical History* II, 27.

12. F. E. Brightman, *Liturgies Eastern and Western*, p. 14.

13. Edmund Bishop, *The Liturgical Homilies of Narsai*, Appendix I.

bishop in the procession of the entry. Carried originally before the secular magistrates of the later Empire, they were transferred to the bishops, who in many places were dignitaries of comparable rank. There is a secular sobriety about the Roman tradition of behaviour in church at this period which contrasts strongly with the religious extravagances of contemporary Eastern, and later Western, developments.

The shape of the Eucharistic rite, both in East and West, remained basically that of the Eucharist of the first three centuries – Scripture reading, preaching, intercession; and then the Supper proper, the placing of the gifts, the prayer of thanksgiving over them, the breaking of the bread, and the reception of the bread and wine. But the balance of the rite began to be seriously upset at this time, when intercessions were associated with the Eucharistic prayer. This association was based on a doctrine of the Eucharistic Sacrifice which is first expressed by Cyril of Jerusalem. He taught that great benefit was derived by those for whom prayer was put up while the holy and most terrifying sacrifice was set forth before God upon the altar.[14] He was speaking primarily of prayer for the dead in this connexion, but his argument is equally applicable to prayer for the living. Sacrificial language has, as we have seen, been used in the Eucharist from the first century onwards. From the second century at least the Eucharistic prayer had apparently included an offering to the Father of the bread and cup as a memorial of the Passion, as well as a thanksgiving for creation and redemption. But the Eucharist was primarily thought of as a sacrifice of praise and thanksgiving; it was offered to praise God for his great glory and to thank him for his mighty acts, even its notions of securing propitiation for sin and other benefits were not wholly excluded. But now the balance shifted. The obtaining of forgiveness for sin becomes prominent. As Cyril puts it, 'we offer Christ slain for our sins, propitiating the merciful God both for them,' that is, the dead, 'and for ourselves'.[15]

In the next fifty years intercessions attached themselves to

14. *Mystagogical Catechesis* V, 9.   15. ibid., 10.

Eucharistic sacrifice

the Eucharistic prayer in all the liturgical traditions in Eastern Christendom and in the Roman tradition in the West. Sometimes, as in the developed Syrian rites, they stand at the end of the prayer, before the rite moves on to the fraction and the communion.[16] Sometimes, as in Egypt, they invade the prayer itself, and become incorporated in it.[17] Sometimes the intercessions after the Scripture readings and the sermon remain intact, and the intercessions in the Eucharist are additional to them.[18] Sometimes the intercessions in the earlier part of the service atrophy, and the only substantial intercession that remains is in the Eucharist itself. At Rome the older intercessions disappear by stages over the next three hundred years; the new intercessions in the Eucharistic prayer are largely restricted to the naming of the names of those who have offered the bread and wine for the rite, and of those on whose behalf they have offered;[19] and the naming of the names of the dead for whom prayer was to be made was only later included as a regular feature in every Mass.[20] This interpolation of intercessions into the Eucharist proper inevitably interrupted the flow of the rite. Their inclusion into the Eucharistic prayer inevitably distorted the shape of the prayer. The association of intercession with the celebration of the Eucharist inevitably unbalanced the purpose and the doctrine of the sacrament, especially at a time when the laity were abandoning the practice of reception and the clergy were beginning to be thought of as mediatorial priests.

The teaching of Cyril of Jerusalem also marks a development in the doctrine of the consecration of the Eucharist. Second-century writers, as we have seen, attributed to the Eucharistic

16. Compare F. E. Brightman, *Liturgies Eastern and Western*, pp. 55 and 89, for the Liturgy of St James; p. 331 for the Byzantine Liturgy.

17. Compare ibid., pp. 126 and 165 for the Liturgy of St Mark.

18. Compare ibid., p. 158.

19. i.e., the two prayers *Memento* and *Memento etiam*, and on occasions the prayer *Hanc igitur*.

20. See Edmund Bishop, *Liturgica Historica*, Oxford, 1918, pp. 109–15. For a different view see Michel Andrieu, *Les Ordines Romani du haut moyen âge*, Volume II, Louvain, 1948, pp. 274–8.

thanksgiving as a whole the consecration of the bread and wine, which were declared to be 'thanked-over', and were indeed called 'thanksgiving' or Eucharist.[21] In the West by the end of the second century the consecration was apparently being associated specifically with the recital within the prayer of the Lord's words at the Supper.[22] In the East by the fourth century it was being associated with an invocation upon the bread and cup. God is called upon to fill the oblation with his power.[23] He is asked to allow his Word to descend into the oblation, that it may become the Body of the Word.[24] He is prayed to send his Spirit into the oblation, that all who partake may be filled with Spirit.[25] But Cyril apparently produced a form of invocation which was more theologically precise than any of these forms, and was to become the basis for later development. The prayer he describes calls upon the Father to send the Holy Spirit upon the oblation, in order that the Spirit may change the bread and cup into the Body and Blood of Christ.[26] Invocations were being attached to the Eucharistic thanksgiving in the East at the beginning of the fourth century, if not long before. It was Cyril's achievement to put the whole weight of the prayer on to the invocation. If his lectures have come down to us intact, without alteration or omission, then we may say that he shows little or no interest in the thanksgiving, or the Sanctus with which it concludes; he concentrates his whole attention upon the consecratory invocation which follows it, and upon the intercessions, which are then made effectively in virtue of the propitiatory sacrifice made present by the invocation.

21. But it should be noted that for Justin the bread is 'thanked-over' with no ordinary thanksgiving, but 'by means of a word of prayer that comes from' Christ.

22. Tertullian, *Adversus Marcionem* 4, 40.

23. *Prayer of Oblation of Serapion the Bishop* II, 11.

24. ibid., IV, 15.

25. Hippolytus, *The Apostolic Tradition* 4. The present writer shares the view of the late Professor Ratcliff that the text edited by Dom B. Botte represents the form current in the closing years of the fourth century.

26. *Mystagogical Catechesis* V, 7.

The narrative of the institution on the other hand is apparently a late arrival in Eastern Eucharistic prayers. It is not alluded to by Cyril, nor does it appear in the oldest East Syrian rite that has come down to us.[27] Yet by the end of the fourth century it has found a place in the rites of the period, attached to the end of the Eucharistic thanksgiving, and placed between the thanksgiving and the invocation in Syria, or after both thanksgiving and invocation in Egypt. If one inquires why the Eastern rites introduced the narrative at this period, one may assume that they borrowed it from the West, where it had long been established in the Eucharistic prayer. If one were to conjecture the occasion of the borrowing, one might ascribe it to the circulation in the East of the text of *The Apostolic Tradition.* It may be significant that the earliest Syrian prayer that contains the narrative is full of textual reminiscences of *The Apostolic Tradition.*[28] The narrative was normally followed as in the West by an offering of bread and cup to the Father in memory of the Passion and Resurrection.

The later Eucharistic prayers of Eastern Christendom seem to us to lack any clear sequence of thought. The reason for this is made clear, if we compare the later prayers with those of the fourth century. The later prayers are structurally telescoped, for the sake of brevity and to avoid repetition.[29] The fourth-century prayers exhibit the various items as they have been placed, one after another, on the end of the Eucharistic thanksgiving – narrative, oblation, invocation, intercessions – as changing fashion dictated.[30] The singing of the Sanctus further complicated the pattern. At Jerusalem the custom obtained of performing it at the beginning of the prayer, and this practice was largely, though not universally, followed elsewhere. But

27. The Liturgy of the Holy Apostles Addai and Mari. See F. E. Brightman, *Liturgies Eastern and Western*, pp. 283–8.

28. The so-called Clementine Liturgy of *The Apostolic Constitutions*, Book VIII. See F. E. Brightman, op. cit., pp. 14–23.

29. The Liturgy of St James and the Liturgy of St John Chrysostom. See F. E. Brightman, op. cit., pp. 50–8 and 321–37.

30. The Liturgy of *The Apostolic Constitutions*, Book VIII, and the Liturgy of St Basil. See F. E. Brightman, op. cit., pp. 14–23 and 321–37.

as often as not the place of its performance was arbitrarily chosen, and any function that it may once have performed in the prayer is now unrecognizable.

Considerable, if not inordinate, attention has been given to the Eucharistic prayer and its development in the Eastern liturgies, because of its unique importance in the Eucharistic rite. But from the fourth century it ceases to be the only prayer. One of the earliest additions was the Lord's Prayer. To us it seems odd that a prayer claiming to have been composed by the Lord himself should have found no place in the rite for the first three centuries. But it was only by the middle of the fourth century that the Lord's Prayer was first introduced,[31] and it does not appear to have been universally used, even in the first decades of the fifth.[32] It was introduced as an immediate preparation for the reception of the elements. The petition 'Give us this day our daily bread' was applied to the sacrament. The petition 'Forgive us our trespasses, as we forgive them that trespass against us' was thought to express the proper dispositions for reception. It was therefore everywhere recited after the great thanksgiving had been uttered by the celebrant, and after the bread had been broken up for distribution. Only at Byzantium was it sung before and not after the breaking of the bread. But in due course the orthodox churches of the East conformed to the usage of the imperial capital. In the West the Roman Church adopted the Byzantine position for the prayer under Gregory the Great;[33] and in adopting the Roman rite, the other churches of the West also followed the Byzantine use.

From the fourth century onwards all rites tended to elaboration at four different points.[34] (1) The entry of the celebrant became a liturgical moment. It was covered by a chant. It became an occasion for ceremonial pomp. It was rounded off

31. Cyril of Jerusalem, *Mystagogical Catechesis* V, 11.

32. Augustine, Epistle CXLIX, 16. *Fere omnis ecclesia.*

33. Epistles, Book IX, 12.

34. For the term of the development at Rome in the eighth century see *Ordo Romanus Primus* in Michel Andrieu, *Les Ordines Romani du haut moyen âge*, Volume II, Louvain, 1948, pp. 67–108.

4 pts. of ceremonial elaboration
1) entry of celebrant

with the singing of a canticle, and in the West by the recitation of a prayer. Only then did the reading of the lessons begin, divided by the psalmody between them. (2) The laying of the table lost its simplicity. It is not known whether in earlier times the bread and wine for the Eucharist were provided by the congregation, or by the clergy responsible for the celebration. But the setting of bread and cup upon the table was apparently a plain function of a utilitarian kind. From the fourth century onwards this was gradually changed. At Rome the elements were brought by the congregation and were collected after the first part of the service was over, when the Eucharist was about to begin. Part of the bread and wine was set upon the table for the sacrament; part was placed on one side, presumably for the subsequent use of the clergy and the poor. In the East, on the other hand, if the elements ever were brought by the congregation, they were apparently collected before the first part of the service began; and were placed, either upon the holy table itself, or else in a sacristy within the church building.[35] Then, when the Eucharist was about to begin, the elements on the holy table were solemnly unveiled; or, alternatively, the elements were solemnly borne from the sacristy to the altar. Accompanied with lights and incense, the deacons carried the bread and cup in pompous procession, while the choir sang anthems representing the song of the Cherubim. The procession was interpreted, either as the Christ coming forth to his passion and resurrection, which was to be mystically re-enacted in the Eucharist which was to follow; or as the dead Christ being carried to his burial on the altar, where he was to re-enact his resurrection at the time of the consecration.[36] (3) In the same way the breaking of the bread became a moment for ceremonial elaboration. In essence a utilitarian operation – the

35. See G. Dix, *The Shape of the Liturgy*, pp. 120–3.

36. ibid., pp. 282–91. See also *The Testament of our Lord*, translated into English from the Syriac, with introduction and notes by James Cooper and Arthur John Maclean, Edinburgh, 1902, p. 73, where, in the institution narrative, 'Do this in remembrance of me' is translated as 'When ye shall do this, ye make my resurrection'.

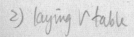

breaking-up of the one loaf among the many communicants[37] – it early attracted to itself a symbolical meaning of the Lord's body broken in death.[38] In the non-Roman rites of the West the broken pieces of bread were sometimes arranged on the plate, or paten, in the form of a man, and later of a cross.[39] In the East the bread and wine was mingled to represent the shedding of the Blood over the Body, or to illustrate the unity of Body and Blood when received by the communicant; and the giving of bread and wine together, by means of a spoon, became customary in many oriental rites. (4) Finally, the distribution of communion ceased to be the conclusion of the rite, but developed into a separate section of the service. In the East, as in some parts of the West, the celebrant blessed the people before communion. The sacrament was elevated with the formula 'The holy things for the holy people'. It was carried out of the sanctuary with some pomp, and a psalm was sung during the distribution. The procession then returned to the sanctuary, and a prayer of thanksgiving and a prayer of blessing were recited, before the people were finally dismissed. At Rome a similar pattern was followed with less exuberance. A psalm was sung during the distribution of the sacrament, after which the celebrant recited a prayer of thanksgiving and a prayer of blessing, and the deacon dismissed the congregation.

From the fourth century, church buildings had been divided up by the use of screens or balustrades.[40] The seats of the bishop and his clergy were protected in this way from the congregation, as the seats of the magistrates had been protected from the concourse of people in the law courts. So also the altar, if it stood in the middle of the church building, away

37. But compare 1 Corinthians 10. 16, 17.

38. The original text of 1 Corinthians 11. 24 was apparently 'This is my body which is for you'. But many manuscripts read 'This is my body which is broken for you', a statement difficult to reconcile with John 19. 36.

39. L. Duchesne, *Christian Worship, Its Origin and Evolution*, fifth edition, London, 1919, pp. 218–20.

40. Eusebius, *Ecclesiastical History*, X – the sermon preached at the consecration of the church at Tyre.

4) distribution & communion

from the seats of the clergy, might be similarly protected. But all such screens were low, and in no way prevented the congregation from seeing and hearing what was done during service time. Sometimes these screens were of a more elaborate kind, with columns and architraves, on which statues might be placed and from which lamps could be hung.[41] It was out of these larger screens that the iconostasis was developed, which has dominated the worship of the Eastern Orthodox Church from the Middle Ages onwards. This is no open screen, over which or through which the congregation can see and hear what the clergy are saying and doing. It is a solid screen, covered with the icons or pictures of Christ and the saints, as its name implies. It cuts off the altar and its sanctuary completely from the body of the church building, and so separates the choir and congregation from the clergy and their performance at the altar. It is pierced by three sets of doors, the middle ones leading into the sanctuary and the altar, the side ones respectively into the vestry and into the chapel where the elements are prepared for the Eucharist.

The development of this screen profoundly affected the worship of the Eastern Orthodox Churches. It expressed the logical conclusion of a way of thinking which we first noticed in the teaching of Cyril of Jerusalem. The Eucharist is a terrifying mystery; it is best performed, and indeed received, by the professional clergy; its prayers should be recited silently; its ceremonies should be carried out invisibly; only at certain great moments should it be displayed to the laity. The splendid screen is central to the majestic drama which is played out before and behind it. The doors provide the entrances and exits for the processions of the clergy – with the Gospel book at the entry, and again at the reading of the Gospel lesson, with the unconsecrated elements at the offertory, with the consecrated sacrament at the communion. At times the choir and clergy combine to further the service. At times the choir sing, while the priest and deacon continue in silence behind the

41. For this and other such matters see J. G. Davies, *Early Christian Church Architecture*, London, 1952.

screen. At times the choir and deacon sing litanies before the screen, while the priest continues the service alone. From time to time the voice of the priest is heard from behind the screen by those in the body of the church.

The splendour of the domed churches, the lights and the incense, the glitter of the vestments and of the icons on the screen, and the beauty of the music with which the rite is now clothed – all this makes the worship of Eastern Christendom an unforgettable experience for the Western Christian. In spite of its clericalized form, in spite of the absence of preaching, and in spite of the infrequency of the communion of the laity, it is a highly popular devotion, in which the congregation participate unselfconsciously, and are caught up and given a sense of eternal truths. It is not yet apparent whether it has the inner vitality which will enable it to adapt itself to the needs of the present age. Indeed there are those who would maintain that it can best serve the spiritual restlessness of the modern world by remaining exactly as it is.

The stage upon which the Roman rite was played out from the fourth century onwards underwent no such transformation as that upon which the Byzantine rite developed. Church buildings with central domes were not unknown in the West. But the older type of building known as the basilica provided the Church with a pattern for its halls of assembly, which persisted far into the Middle Ages. Screens in church buildings were not unknown in the West. But they were never used to cut the service in two, or to divorce the action of the clergy from the participation of the laity. The screens which later divided choir from nave in the great medieval churches of Northern Europe were not designed to exclude the laity from the service of the choir. They divided the buildings into two churches. In the choir the service was performed with splendid elaboration by the members of the monastery or of the cathedral chapter with their assistants. In the nave the same service might be performed in a simpler manner, for the benefit of lay-persons who might need such provision.

The basilican form of church building consisted of a hall

with an apse at one end. It normally formed part of a complex of buildings, which, apart from the baptistery, had no immediate liturgical purpose, and need not therefore concern us here. It was approached from the street through a porch, which led into a forecourt, surrounded by colonnades and containing a fountain, on the further side of which was the basilica or hall. This might consist of an aisleless nave, or of a nave flanked with two or four aisles, separated from the nave by rows of columns. This was the part of the building occupied by the congregation and, after bodies of singers had been instituted, by the choir. At the end of the nave was the apse, the floor of which was raised above the level of the nave. This contained what were normally the only seats in the building – the bishop's throne, the symbol of his authority to govern the Church, and on either side the benches for the presbyters who formed his council. Deacons, inferior clerics, singers and congregation stood or knelt throughout the service. The apse was generally protected by a low balustrade, to prevent the congregation crowding in upon the clergy. Behaviour during divine service in those days did not accord with modern standards of decorum. For the reading of the lessons a high pulpit or ambo was required, from which the lessons and the responsorial psalms might be chanted. The use of a chant instead of the natural voice was not merely a hieratic custom common to religions in the ancient world. It was also a method of making the voice carry through a large building in the absence of modern methods of amplification. The ambo was in modern terms a lectern and not a pulpit – a place from which lessons were read, not a place from which sermons were preached. The bishop preached from his throne, sitting, as was the custom of teachers in the ancient world. Apart from the ambo, which was needed for the first part of the service, the only other piece of furniture required was the altar, which was needed for the second part. To begin with this was apparently a movable wooden table, which could be placed in the basilica when there was to be a celebration of the Eucharist, and removed afterwards. But it soon became a fixed stone structure, and was increasingly associated with the relics of a martyr, which would be buried beneath it. Its position in the basilica varied from place to place. But it came more and more to be sited at the head of the nave, and even within the balustrade of the apse. The choir and congregation stood in front of the altar, the clergy performed their functions from behind. To give the altar distinction, a canopy resting on four columns was often raised above it. In the richer churches the pillars were of marble and their capitals were gilded. The floors were covered with marble and the walls with mosaic. The wooden roofs were decorated with colour. But in the midst of all this splendour the building remained simple in its lay-out – the nave and the apse, the ambo, the throne and the altar. Such divisions as were introduced by means of balustrades were there for purposes of good order and nothing more.

Music at the celebration of the Eucharist apparently developed earlier in the West than in the East. Before the fourth century there was little room for singing in the liturgy. It is possible that between the lessons in the first half of the service a psalm was sung. This would probably have been sung responsorially; that is to say, the soloist would have sung a verse of the psalm, and the people would have repeated it with the same musical inflexion; the soloist would then have continued with further verses of the psalm, and after each the people would have repeated the original verse. In the second half of the service the Eucharistic prayer would have been chanted by the celebrant; and if at this period the Sanctus formed part of the prayer, and if the congregation joined with the celebrant in singing it, it would have been sung as a continuation of the chant of the celebrant. Up to the fourth century, and indeed during most of that century in the West, there was little that could be called music in the Eucharist. But in the early years of the fifth century we find music being introduced to cover liturgical actions. A psalm was sung to cover the movement of the congregation, as they came to make their offerings of bread and wine at the offertory. Again, a psalm was sung to cover the movement of the clergy, as they went to distribute communion to the congregation.[42] By the end of the century a third covering chant had been introduced, a psalm to cover the entry of the celebrant and his ministers. All these were sung by a professional choir maintained by the bishop as a provision for orphan children, and as a training school for the large number of inferior clergy employed in a city diocese. They were not sung by the congregation, who at the offertory and the communion were otherwise employed. In time the responsorial psalm between the lessons was taken over by the professional choir, and indeed became the most elaborate musical performance of the rite. By the end of the fifth century 'Glory be to God on high' was on occasions being sung after the entry of the celebrant and before the lessons began;[43] and by the end of the seventh century 'O Lamb of God' etc. was being sung during the breaking of the bread.[44] But these remained popular numbers, sung like the Sanctus to simple inflexions, probably by the whole congregation. Even *Kyrie eleison*, which entered the rite at the end of the sixth century, was not elaborated musically until after the changes of the ninth. Up to that time the choir sang the four elaborate pieces – at the entry, between the lessons, during the offertory and during the communion. The people apparently sang *Kyrie eleison*, 'Glory be to God on high', the Sanctus with 'Blessed is he' etc. and Hosanna, and 'O Lamb of God'.

We possess an account of the ceremonial of the Roman Mass, as it was performed toward the end of the eighth century. But apart from certain features which are known to have entered the rite in the intervening period, the ceremonial described may well be as old as the time of Gregory the Great. From this account it is possible to construct a probable picture of the Eucharist, as it was performed at Rome in the period under discussion.[45]

The celebrant enters, preceded by lights and incense, and

42. Augustine, *Retractationes* II, 37. See also *Liber Pontificalis*, ed. L. Duchesne, Tome I, second edition, Paris, 1955, p. 230.

43. ibid., p. 263.

44. ibid., p. 376.

45. *Ordo Romanus Primus*, as above.

accompanied by the deacons and the inferior clergy, and passes up the nave of the basilica between the assembled congregation, and then between the ranks of the singers, until he comes before the altar. Having said his prayers, he goes to his throne in the apse, where the presbyters are awaiting him on either side of the throne. During the procession the choir has been singing the elaborate Anthem of the Entry. But when the Bishop finally reaches his throne, *Kyrie eleison* with its litany is sung, and then 'Glory be to God on high'. This latter was probably first introduced only on Easter Day. Later it was sung on Sundays and Saints' Days, when the Bishop was celebrating. Finally it was used even when the celebrant was only a priest. But it never became a permanent feature of the rite, but always remained something which was introduced on special occasions. The processional entry, with the singing that succeeded it, is finally rounded off by the bishop saluting the people, and singing the opening prayer of the Mass, which we call the collect.

The Scripture readings and the chants between them follow. But the singing of the lesson from the Gospel is made the occasion of a second procession, this time of the Gospel book to the ambo, from which the lesson is to be read. From the fourth century the book of the Gospels had been treated as a symbol of the Christ. It was laid upon the head of those who were being consecrated bishop. It had been enthroned in the middle of the assembly at the Council of Nicaea. And now, as it is carried to the ambo, it is preceded by incense and lights in the same way as the celebrant at the entry, and is kissed by all as a mark of reverence when the lesson from it has been read.

Preaching in the Roman rite appears to have been the prerogative of the bishop, who in the small sees of Italy was the normal celebrant on Sundays and festivals. But it was apparently regarded as a right rather than as a duty. While bishops like Leo I or Gregory I exercised it frequently, there is no evidence that all bishops preached every Sunday. Nor is there anything to show that presbyters, when they celebrated,

Scripture / chants / sermon

ever preached at all.[46] When the bishop preached, he did so sitting on his throne, surrounded by his clergy, and addressed himself to the congregation standing in the body of the basilica.

When the Gospel or sermon is over, the Eucharist proper begins at once. The Prayers of the Faithful, which originally occurred at this point, disappeared toward the end of the fifth century, and were replaced by a litany at the beginning of the service. A hundred years later the litany also was falling into disuse; and in another hundred years had been replaced by *Kyrie eleison*.[47] The Eucharist therefore begins without more ado. The bread and wine are collected and placed upon the holy table, while the choir sings the Anthem of the Offertory; and the celebrant concludes the action by reciting a short prayer, known as the Prayer over the Offerings.

The offertory at Rome during this period was in one respect an elaborate ceremony, intended to bring home to the worshippers one truth – the unity of the Church in Christ. Everyone was expected to bring bread and wine for the sacrifice – the laity, men and women alike, the inferior clergy, the deacons, the presbyters, the celebrant himself. Each brought to the service common bread and wine from home; each presented his bread and wine at the offertory, the laity to the deacons, the clergy to the celebrant. Most of what was presented was put aside for charitable purposes. But some bread and wine from each order in the Church had to be placed upon the holy table for the sacrifice. The collection was a lengthy and complicated affair. But the notion that lay behind it was simple, and the point was well taken. The Roman Church has always been noted for the importance it has attached to unity.[48]

The offertory concluded, the celebrant at once begins the Eucharistic prayer, or canon of the Mass. The opening section, or preface, is recited out loud, and this leads into the singing of the Sanctus. The remainder of the prayer, which later

46. Sozomen, *Ecclesiastical History VII*. 19.

47. B. Capelle, 'L'Intercession dans la Messe Romaine', *Revue Bénédictine*, 1955, pp. 181–91.

48. 1 *Clement* 3–5.

offertory / E. prayer / Sanctus

appropriated to itself the name of 'canon', came to be recited silently. At what date this practice started is unknown. But the custom of reciting the Eucharistic prayer silently was already in force in the Syriac-speaking East by the fifth century, and was coming into use at Constantinople in the sixth; and it may well be that it was introduced into Rome at about the same time.[49] The purpose behind it was apparently to withdraw the mysteries from the laity, who were coming to be regarded as in some sense second-class Christians. The same purpose was effected in the East by the introduction of veils and screens. But in the West these were unknown; and the laity could still see the performance of the Eucharist, although they could no longer hear its most important prayer. The canon itself is not at this period accompanied with ceremonial such as developed in the later Middle Ages. The celebrant, who is of course facing the people across the holy table, can be seen in all probability to take the bread and cup into his hands during the narrative of the institution, and certainly with the help of the deacon to elevate both bread and cup during the doxology at the end of the prayer. But that is all.

The fraction, or breaking of the bread, follows. This is of necessity a lengthy performance, at any rate on days when the bulk of the laity communicates. It is not however performed by the celebrant alone, or indeed, at the great public masses, at all. After the canon is ended, and after Lord's Prayer has been said and the kiss of peace given, the celebrant leaves the altar and goes with his deacons to the throne. The bread is taken from the altar on patens or plates or in linen cloths, and carried to the throne, and to the presbyters who are ranged on either side of it round the apse. The celebrant gives the signal for the bread to be broken; and the assisting clergy carry out the actual breaking up of the bread for distribution in the full sight of the congregation. Originally the bread was broken in silence, as the offertory and the communion were performed in silence. But in the early Middle Ages the action was covered

49. Edmund Bishop, *The Liturgical Homilies of Narsai*, ed. R. H. Conolly, Appendix V.

by the chant *Agnus Dei*, 'O Lamb of God, that takest away the sins of the world, have mercy upon us'.

Next comes the distribution of the sacrament. From the beginning of the fifth century, if not earlier, it was preceded at Rome by the giving of the kiss of peace. The ceremony to modern devotion symbolizes the peace and mutual charity which should exist between Christians, particularly when they are about to receive communion. Such a meaning was undoubtedly attached to it in some parts of the Christian Church at this time. But at Rome it was thought to signify the consent of the congregation to all that had been said and done in the rite.[50] When the Lord's Prayer was introduced into the Mass, it was apparently recited after the fraction and before the kiss of peace. When Gregory the Great moved the Lord's Prayer to a position after the canon and before the fraction, the kiss of peace was moved at the same time. The Lord's Prayer and the kiss of peace therefore precede the fraction and the communion, and the whole order of this section of the Mass has been in confusion ever since.[51]

Communion is given in both kinds, the celebrant and the presbyters distributing the bread, and the deacons the cups. While the people are communicating, the choir sings the Anthem at the Communion. When all have received, the remains of the sacrament are removed to the sacristy, and either reserved or consumed. The rite meanwhile comes to a swift close. The celebrant sings a last prayer, or post-communion, and on occasion a prayer of blessing, and the deacon dismisses the congregation with the cry *Ite, missa est*.

The Eucharist at Rome during the period under review was still simple in structure and straightforward in movement, although complications begin to appear at the end of the period, largely under Eastern influence. The principal change, the recitation of the canon in silence, has already been noted. The origin of this prayer is a matter of dispute. St Ambrose, who

50. Innocent I, *Epistle* 25, Chapter 1.

51. B. Capelle, *Travaux Liturgiques II*, Louvain, 1962, pp. 287 ff., 'Le Rite de la fraction dans la Messe Romaine'.

the distribution

claimed, it will be remembered, to follow the Roman Church in all things, was using at Milan in the last quarter of the fourth century a prayer not unlike the later canon.[52] It is commonly held that at this time the Roman Church was changing its liturgical language from Greek to Latin, and was at the same time overhauling its liturgical tradition.[53] It is therefore thought that the section of the Eucharistic prayer quoted in his lectures by St Ambrose represents a prayer newly come into use at this time; and that the canon found in the later Mass books is a developed form of the prayer. Such a theory is open to objections. It supposes that Greek was the only liturgical language in the Roman Church in the first three centuries. But during this period the Church in Rome consisted of a number of scattered house churches, and catered for a number of different national groups. It seems unlikely that such groups would not have worshipped God in their own languages and according to their own traditions. The shape of the primitive rite – readings, sermon, prayers, followed by the Eucharistic action – would have been uniform, but not the language in which the rite was celebrated. From earliest times there would almost certainly have been a group of African Christians in Rome, and these would have performed the liturgy in Latin. If in the second half of the fourth century the Roman Church was set upon developing a uniform Latin liturgical tradition, it is far more likely that it took over a tradition already existing in Africa and in Rome than that it translated and adapted a previously existing Greek tradition.

The Eucharistic prayer of the Roman Church, the preface and canon, as it has been called for centuries, opens with the traditional versicles and responses – 'The Lord be with you', 'And with thy spirit'; 'Lift up your hearts', 'We lift them up unto the Lord'; 'Let us give thanks unto the Lord our God', 'It is meet and right so to do'. The preface then sets out to state that it is truly meet and right to give thanks to God at all

52. Ambrose, *De Sacramentis* IV. 5. 21, 22, 23, 27.

53. Noële Maurice-Denis et Robert Boulet, *Eucharist ou La Messe dans ses variétés, son histoire et ses origines*, Paris, 1953, pp. 338 ff.

times and in all places through Christ. The context leads one to suppose that a preface in the older sense of the word is about to follow, that is to say, a telling forth of the mighty acts of God. But certainly from the time of Gregory the Great no such telling forth has taken place in the prayer, except on the great feasts of the Christian year. For most of the time the preface has ceased to be a preface in the old sense of the word, and has now become a mere preface, something which is said beforehand, before the real business of the prayer begins in the canon. The place which in all probability was once occupied by the great thanksgiving is now filled by the passage which refers to the angels and leads into the angelic hymn of the Sanctus. Before Gregory's time there was probably a variable preface in all Masses, and not merely on great feasts. But this was apparently always followed by the passage about the angels and the Sanctus. No one knows when the preface was transformed in this way or why. If originally the great thanksgiving stood at this point, as the opening words of the preface seem to imply, one can understand how it could come about that thanksgiving was restricted on particular festivals in a growing calendar to the particular mighty act of God which was being celebrated on that particular day. This would account for the replacement of the one long preface by a number of proper prefaces, and the use of these might well have been extended to cover not only the great feasts of the Christian year, but also the commemorations of the martyrs. But it would not account for the introduction of the passage about the angels and the singing of the Sanctus, which is irrelevant alike to what goes before and to what comes after, and actually cuts the Eucharistic prayer in two.

The opening words of the canon, that is to say of the second half of the prayer, may perhaps be claimed as evidence that it once followed directly after the thanksgiving for creation and redemption. For the text runs: 'Therefore, most merciful Father, through Jesus Christ thy Son our Lord we humbly pray and beseech thee to accept and bless these gifts' etc. Following as they do upon the singing of the Sanctus, and of the Benedictus and Hosanna which have been added to it, the words are inconsequent. But if they were designed to follow immediately upon the thanksgiving, they at once gain meaning. It is truly meet and right that we should give thanks, for the creation of the world and for the redemption of mankind through Christ. Therefore through Christ we ask God to accept these gifts of bread and wine as the expression of our thanksgiving, as our thankoffering. The thought underlying the prayer at this point is that of Irenaeus in the second century. God does not need any gifts from us. But we need to offer him a gift, as an expression of our gratitude. We must not come before him empty-handed, for fear we should seem to be ungrateful.[54] And indeed this way of looking at the Eucharist goes back into the first century. For the celebrants are described by Clement of Rome as those who 'offer the gifts'.[55]

It is at this point that the run of the prayer is again upset, this time by the interpolation of intercessions. It has already been pointed out that in the fourth century there developed in Eastern Christendom a fashion of praying for others in connexion with the Eucharistic prayer. The theology of Cyril of Jerusalem and its effect on Eastern liturgies has already been explained. Apparently the Roman Church also was affected by this fashion, and added intercessory prayers to its Eucharistic thanksgiving. But it did not place them, as in the Syrian and Byzantine liturgies, at the end of the prayer, after the consecration and before the communion. It attached them to the offering of the gifts, at the beginning of the canon. By the beginning of the fifth century the custom was well established at Rome of praying for the living at this point.[56] At a later date a prayer for the dead was added, but was inserted, with a fine inconsequence, into the later part of the canon.

Once the intercessory material is discounted, the run of the prayer becomes clearer. For the section after the intercessions

54. Irenaeus. *Adversus Haereses*, IV. 29. 5.

55. I *Clement* 44.

56. Innocent I, *Epistle* 25, Chapter 2; see also B. Capelle, article cited in footnote 47.

continues the petition that God will accept the oblation and ratify it. If he does this, then it will become what the Lord promised it would be, his Body and his Blood. There is therefore no specific petition for the consecration of the gifts. God is asked to accept them, and is reminded of the Lord's command – 'Do this in remembrance of me' – and of the Lord's promise – 'This is my body'. The narrative of the institution is recited; and since the command has been obeyed, it is assumed that the promise has been kept, that the Lord has effected the consecration.

God is thought in this way to provide his Church with a sacrifice, by the offering of which it can do him acceptable service; and this notion finds expression in the prayer which follows the narrative of the institution. The holy people, having in remembrance the redemptive act, that is to say, the Lord's Passion and Resurrection, offer the sacrifice which God has provided for them to offer. It is the pure offering of which the prophet Malachi had spoken, by means of which God's name should be glorified among the nations, which Justin and Irenaeus in the second century are already claiming to be the Eucharist. It is identified with the self-offering of the Lord in his Passion, it is the Bread of Life, of which the evangelist speaks as given for the life of the world.[57] The connexion between the Passion and the Eucharist in the Roman rite is very close. Cyprian in the third century declares that the Passion is the Lord's sacrifice which we offer; that the Lord offered his Passion at the Last Supper, when he offered the bread and cup which were the symbols of his Passion; and that we offer the same sacrifice, when we offer what he then offered.[58] It is for this reason that the narrative of the institution in the canon begins, not with the Scriptural words 'who in the same night in which he was betrayed', but with the phrase 'who on the day before he suffered'.

The canon continues with the request that God will accept the Church's sacrifice as he accepted those offered in the Old Dispensation. But here we are surprised to find that those

57. John 6. 35, 48, 51.

58. Cyprian, *Epistle* 63, passim.

cited are not the sacrifices offered under the law of Moses, but the earlier offerings of Abel, Abraham and Melchizedek. This selection points to an early date for the tradition underlying the text. During the second century Christians were in acute controversy with the Jews, and claimed that God had rejected the Mosaic sacrifices, and only accepted the Christian sacrifice of the Eucharist, as indeed he had foretold in Malachi.[59] It was impossible therefore to cite the Mosaic sacrifices as examples of sacrifices which God had accepted; and a selection of pre-Mosaic sacrifices is therefore given instead. The selection provides suitable types for the Eucharist. Abel had offered a lamb; Christians offer the Lamb of God. Abraham offered his only son Isaac; Christians offer the only-begotten Son of God. Melchizedek had offered bread and wine; Christians offer the holy bread of eternal life and the cup of everlasting salvation.

The canon continues with the request that God will command that the bread and cup be carried up by the hands of the holy angel to the altar on high in the presence of God's divine majesty. The petition is to be understood by reference to the ideas and language of the second century. Irenaeus, as we have seen, taught that there is an altar in the heavens, toward which our prayers and our oblations are directed. The altar is the locus of the heavenly worship, offered to God by the angels and the glorified saints, to which we obtain admission by means of our prayers and our oblations. But who is the angel who presents them on our behalf in the presence of God? The most plausible explanation is that he is the Lord himself. In the second century it was possible to refer to the Lord as the angel, the messenger; and he was identified with the Angel of mighty counsel spoken of by the prophet Isaiah.[60] The explanation is borne out by a phrase of Clement of Rome. He calls the Lord the High Priest of our oblations, and places his ministry in the heights of the heavens.[61]

How the canon originally ended we do not know. The petition that we may be filled with grace as a result of receiving communion follows oddly upon the passage about the heavenly

59. Justin, *Dialogue* 117. 60. LXX *Isaiah* 9. 6. 61. I *Clement* 36. 1.

altar which precedes it. On the other hand the next petition seems to continue the thought of the prayer. For it asks that we may have some part and fellowship with the Apostles and martyrs. Once it is recognized that the heavenly altar is the scene of the worship of the saints and angels, the connexion is clear. We are asking that, as God has accepted our prayers and our oblations at the Lord's hands, so he will also accept us, and grant us admission to the heavenly worship. And if the passage about the angels, leading into the singing of the Sanctus, was an original part of the prayer, it would follow on most naturally here, and would form the climax and the doxology of the canon.

The preface and canon of the Roman rite has been dealt with at some length for a variety of reasons. It is the Eucharistic prayer most widely used in the world today. It has continued in use, practically unchanged, from the end of the sixth century, if not from the end of the fifth. It was already in existence, as a liturgical tradition as opposed to a fixed text, during the second half of the fourth. And it reflects the Eucharistic teaching of the first three centuries – of Clement of Rome, of Justin, of Irenaeus, of Hippolytus, of Tertullian and of Cyprian. It was too old a tradition to bear the weight of the late medieval teaching. But it was too venerable to be adjusted to express the later developments.

Five

Baptism in the Middle Ages

The transformation of the baptismal rite in the West is associated with the medieval period, between the death of Gregory the Great and the outbreak of the Protestant Reformation. But the causes of its disintegration, if such it was, were present already during the earlier periods, and were already producing exceptional practices, which ultimately became the norm in Western Christendom.

Baptism, as depicted in the New Testament, is a rite intended for adults. It demands a candidate who has sins to be repented of and to be washed away. It also demands a candidate who is capable of making an act of faith in the lordship of Christ – of saying, in fact, 'Jesus is Lord', or of replying to some such question as 'Do you believe that Jesus is the Son of God?'. No doubt children were baptized, along with their parents, in New Testament times as in the second century. The accounts of the baptism of households seem to presuppose this. But the rite itself was geared to those who were capable of repentance and faith.

When children were baptized with their parents in the second and third centuries, the acts of repentance and faith were made on behalf of the children by their parents.[1] When the children of those already baptized were brought to baptism – whether during the Paschal Vigil, or immediately after birth – the same custom no doubt obtained. The importance of the act of faith in the rite at this period has already been noted. It was not, in the West at any rate, a preliminary to the act of baptism, but an integral part of that act. The three questions, 'Dost thou believe' etc., and the three replies, 'I believe', were the words

1. Hippolytus, *Apostolic Tradition*, 21.

which accompanied the pouring of the water, and were as necessary as the water to the administration of the sacrament. To make an act of faith, that is to say an act of personal committal, on behalf of another person seems to the modern mind to be impossible, and to regard such an act as binding to be immoral. But the solidarity of the family, and the relation between parents and children, in the ancient and the medieval world made the practice plausible. It remained unchallenged in the administration of baptism until the time of the Reformation, and still obtains in the greater part of Christendom to this day.

There is evidence that in the third and fourth centuries many Christian parents postponed the baptism of their children until they were of age to commit themselves. But this was not apparently because of any scruple about the propriety of baptizing infants. It was rather for fear that their children, having received the one baptism for the remission of sins, before it was strictly speaking necessary, might fall into grave sin in adult life, and have no means of remission available. The absolution of sin after baptism was indeed a possibility in the early Church. But it was only given once, and then after gruelling penance. The postponement of baptism therefore was dictated by prudence rather than by principle. The habit was widespread, and accounts for the number of prominent figures in the fourth century who were still unbaptized catechumens.[2]

Gradually however all Christian parents came to have their children baptized in infancy. In part no doubt this was due to the teaching of theologians like Augustine of Hippo, who held that all who died without baptism were eternally lost. But since the custom of infant baptism was practised before Augustine's time and in areas where his teaching had little or no influence, it cannot account for the universality of the practice. No doubt the breakdown and the transformation of the penitential system removed the earlier motive for postponement;

2. F. E. Brightman, 'Terms of Communion', in *Essays on the Early History of the Church and Ministry*, ed. H. B. Swete, second edition, London, 1921.

and Christian parents naturally desired to secure for their children admission to the Church, and all the spiritual benefits attached to it, at the earliest opportunity. With the establishment of Christianity as the religion of the Empire, and with the conversion of the barbarians within and without its boundaries, the Church finally consisted, with few exceptions, only of those who had been baptized in infancy.

The baptismal rite, as we have studied it from the fourth century onward, was clearly meant for adults. The period of instruction and fasting and exorcism which preceded it, the acts of renunciation and faith, the baptism for the remission of sins – all these made excellent sense, when the majority of the candidates were adult; and any infants who were baptized alongside them might be thought to derive from the sacrament such benefits as they were capable of receiving. When however all the candidates for baptism were infant, it might be expected that the rite would be adjusted to the changed situation. But nothing of the sort was done. The setting of the rite remained the same. During Lent the infants were brought to church, and were given token instruction and exorcism. At the Paschal Vigil they were carried to the font, they were questioned about their renunciation of Satan and their faith in God, and they replied by proxy. They received baptism for the remission of sins, they were confirmed, that is to say completed, by the laying-on of hands with prayer, followed by signing with chrism, and they were finally given communion.[3]

The only material change that occurred was in the actual administration of baptism. The threefold act of faith came to be made, no longer in combination with the pouring of the water, but immediately before it. The water was then poured with the familiar form, 'I baptize thee in the name of the Father', etc. A similar form had been in use in the East for centuries. It was presumably borrowed in the West as a concession to the changed situation. But its use loosened the connexion between baptism and personal faith, and increased the liability of the sacrament to a magical interpretation.

3. E. C. Whitaker, *Documents etc.*, pp. 156 ff.

Doctrinal development with regard to the fate of the unbaptized may not have played much part in securing the universal baptism of infants. But it rendered plausible the admission of infants to baptism. No doubt the water had always symbolized new creation and new birth; but it could scarcely be separated from the mystical washing away of sin. The question was therefore bound to occur: Since infants are not of age to commit actual sin, from what sort of sin are they cleansed in the waters of the font? Augustine and his successors supplied the answer in the doctrine of original sin. Believing that the human race was physically descended from Adam and Eve, and that the story of their disobedience and expulsion from Paradise was literal history, theologians taught that the sin of our first parents affected all their descendants, that is to say the whole human race. Every child therefore born into the world was tainted with a disease known as original sin including both Evil Desire and Guilt. Evil Desire was not removed by baptism, since it is notorious that the baptized as well as the unbaptized are in a state of moral disorder. Every child, however, was also in some sense guilty of the disobedience of Adam, since he was included seminally in Adam at the time when Adam sinned. The Guilt thus incurred demanded damnation, or at least exclusion from the presence of God; and it was this Guilt which is washed away in baptism. Such a doctrine is no doubt unacceptable to the modern mind; but it provided a cogent reason for the admission of infants to baptism for the remission of sins.[4]

The establishment of Christianity not only procured the universality of infant baptism. It also led to a modification of structure in the local church. In the earlier period Christianity had been largely a religion of the towns. That is why the word 'pagan', which only means countryman, acquired the meaning of 'heathen'. The local church was normally a closely knit group of people living in one town. They were under the leadership of their bishop, who was assisted by his presbyters

4. N. P. Williams, *The Ideas of the Fall and of Original Sin*, London, 1927, Chapters 4 and 5.

and deacons. It was the bishop who was responsible for the teaching and the worship and the discipline of the local church; and he carried out his duties, either personally, or by delegation through his presbyters and deacons. Since baptism was the most important function of the Christian community, and was only administered at Easter, or at most at Easter and Pentecost, the bishop naturally presided over the whole rite in person. He blessed the water himself, he might depute the baptizing, and the anointing before and after baptism, to his presbyters and deacons; but he reserved to himself the prayer for the Spirit with the laying-on of hands, and the final signing with chrism; and he himself celebrated the Eucharist which followed.

But when the Church moved out from the city into the surrounding countryside, the pattern inevitably changed. Presbyters had no doubt been put in charge of smaller groups of Christians within the city in earlier times. But all converts, and all children born to Christian parents, had still been brought to the bishop for baptism. But now presbyters and deacons were put in charge of villages round about the city; and it proved impossible to bring all candidates for baptism into the city to be baptized. Presbyters therefore administered baptism in the villages. But, although they performed all other parts of the rite – the blessing of the water, the baptizing and anointing, and the baptismal Eucharist – they apparently omitted the prayer with laying-on of hands, and the final signing with chrism. The omission is already noted by Jerome at the end of the fourth century, and is ordered by Innocent I at the beginning of the fifth.[5]

It is not within the scope of this essay to discuss the relation of presbyter to bishop in the course of Christian history. It seems to have differed widely, not only in different ages, but also in different areas. But in connexion with baptism, whereas the competence of the presbyter to perform all other parts of the rite has never been questioned, the laying-on of hands with

5. Jerome, *Adversus Luciferianos*, 9; Innocent I, *Epistle* 25, Chapter 2.

prayer has normally been restricted to the bishop alone. In the third century those who were baptized in sickness were required, if they recovered, to receive the laying-on of hands from the bishop.[6] The same was required at a later date of those who were baptized by presbyters in the absence of the bishop. But Jerome already notes that in his day many persons in the country districts never received the laying-on of hands at all;[7] and the same must have been true of large numbers of Christians in the West during the Middle Ages.

In the East, as we have already noted, by the fourth century Cyril of Jerusalem is associating the gift of the Spirit with the anointing which follows baptism. He does not say whether this anointing was administered by the bishop, nor does he know of any subsequent laying-on of hands with prayer or signing with chrism. His teaching is characteristic of the later Eastern baptismal rites, even where, as in Egypt, a laying-on of hands with prayer was retained, or introduced. The chrism for the anointing after baptism has always been consecrated by the bishop, who in this way may be thought to retain some connexion with the rite. But the administration of both baptism with water and anointing with chrism has passed wholly to the presbyter, and the unity of the rite has in this way been retained. Further the newly-baptized, even though infants, are given communion at once, and the primitive outline of the service has thus been kept.

In the West however at the beginning of the Middle Ages two contrary tendencies are at work.[8] In Spain and Gaul, and even in North Italy, where the bishops presided over large areas, it was impossible for them to take part in every baptism throughout their dioceses. Moreover the less organized state of the Church, and at times the exigences of the missionary situation, required a more frequent administration of baptism

6. Cyprian, *Epistle* 73. 9.
7. Jerome, as above.

8. The evidence for the outline given in the following paragraphs may be conveniently found in J. D. C. Fisher, *Christian Initiation: Baptism in the Medieval West*, London, 1965. See also, for a more detailed study, T. C. Akeley, *Christian Initiation in Spain, c. 300–1100*, London, 1967.

than at the solemn feasts of Easter and Pentecost. The presbyter therefore baptized and anointed and communicated the candidates, most of whom would be infants, and the gift of the Spirit was attributed to the anointing after baptism, as in the East. This arrangement may be said to be characteristic of those non-Roman Western rites for which evidence remains. Even at Milan, where in the time of Ambrose the climax of the rite had been the giving of the Spiritual Seal by the bishop, by the tenth century the anointing after baptism, with the feet-washing, was all that remained in the rite between the baptism and the communion.

At Rome on the other hand, and in churches which were subject to Roman influence, the bishop's connexion with baptism was strenuously maintained. In the small dioceses of central Italy this presented little difficulty. Even in the large city of Rome itself it was not impossible, since there were commonly other bishops present in the city beside the Pope himself. Further, Rome retained the tradition of restricting baptism to the feasts of Easter and Pentecost, and of baptizing at other times only in cases of emergency. By administering baptism on one or two occasions in the year, the churches which followed Roman customs could normally secure the presence of the bishop. He would generally preside over the rite in his own church, and could fulfil what was regarded as his peculiar function in the administration. In the Roman rite therefore the candidates continued to receive baptism with its anointings, and the laying-on of hands with prayer, followed by the signing with chrism and first communion, in the traditional manner. The only exceptions were those who were baptized by presbyters or deacons in emergency, and there was little difficulty in bringing these to the bishop within a short space of time for the completion of the rite.

These are the two tendencies at work in the medieval Church of the West. On the one hand the non-Roman Western tradition, a rite consisting of baptism, anointing and communion, administered by the presbyter, thought to be complete in itself, and increasingly administered as occasion required, without reference to the baptismal feasts of Easter and Pentecost. On the other hand the Roman tradition, a rite administered only once or twice in the year, normally by the bishop himself, containing not only baptism, anointing and communion, but also the bishop's prayer with laying-on of hands, and signing with chrism. As the influence of the Roman rite was gradually extended over the whole of Western Christendom, and especially at the time when Charles the Great was endeavouring to impose it upon his dominions, the two traditions react upon one another, and produce the later medieval pattern, which was inherited by the Protestant Reformers.

The problem facing those who sought to bring the non-Roman Western tradition into conformity with Roman customs was twofold. There was the liturgical problem of introducing the bishop's prayer with laying-on of hands and signing with chrism into the presbyter's rite of baptism, anointing and communion; and there was the theological problem of explaining why a prayer for the coming of the Spirit, with its accompanying ceremonies, was needed in a rite which had already given the Spirit in the anointing after baptism. A number of liturgical patterns were tried. The bishop's prayer was inserted into the rite in its Roman position, after the anointing and before the communion. Or the bishop's prayer was added to the existing pattern, and was placed after the communion. Or the bishop's prayer was made into a separate service, and was given on a subsequent occasion. When baptism was administered on great occasions in the presence of the bishop, one or other of the first two patterns might be followed. But any attempt to restrict baptism to the great feasts or to the see cities would have proved impracticable. The areas were vast, the bishops were comparatively few, and the local custom was against it. The bishop's prayer with laying-on of hands was not therefore restored to the baptismal rite, but became a separate rite of confirmation, and posed a problem for the medieval theologians to solve.

So long as the rite of baptism was administered as one whole and was treated as a unity, curious theological questions were avoided. The rite as a whole was thought to convey the baptismal gifts – cleansing from sin, new birth, spiritual death and resurrection, the royal priesthood, the indwelling Spirit, eternal life. Preachers might dwell upon one particular ceremony, and connect it with one particular gift. The same preacher might give different devotional interpretations of the same ceremony on different occasions. But, theologically speaking, before the performance the candidate was outside the Body of Christ; and afterwards he was incorporated into it, and had received all the benefits of such incorporation. But once the rite was broken into two, theological questions were asked. The historical accident of separation has given the theologians a field-day ever since.

So we find divines of the eighth and ninth centuries asking why the Spirit is given twice, first in baptism by the presbyter's anointing, and then in confirmation by the bishop's laying-on of hands and signing with chrism. The sure warrant of Holy Scripture was invoked to justify the double gift. The fourth Gospel represents the Lord as giving the Spirit to his Apostles on Easter Day. The Acts of the Apostles depicts the Spirit descending upon the Apostles fifty days later, after the Lord's ascension into heaven, on the day of Pentecost. An uncritical combination of the two passages was thought to prove that the Apostles had received the Spirit twice. But it was more difficult to distinguish between the two gifts. If in baptism the candidate is cleansed, and in the anointing is occupied by the indwelling Spirit, what further gift of the Spirit can he need? Theologians surmised that additional strength was needed, in order to bear witness to Christ in the world; and similar explanations of the confirmation gift are given throughout the Middle Ages.

The way in which the late medieval Church was organized, in Northern Europe at any rate, did not favour the practice of the Roman tradition of baptism, which had been accepted in theory. Bishops presided over dioceses which were inordinately large; Oxford for instance was in the diocese of Lincoln, and there were only three dioceses in the whole province of York. It was therefore impossible for parents to bring their children to the see city for baptism and confirmation. Moreover many bishops were engaged in secular affairs, either at the royal court or even overseas, and were seldom in their see cities at all. The traditional baptism and confirmation in the presence of the bishop could not take place very frequently.

Even in the parishes the custom of restricting baptism by the parish priests to the great feasts was gradually falling into disuse. Two tendencies can be seen pulling in opposite directions between the tenth and the fourteenth centuries. On the one hand, there is the desire, presumably on the part of the ecclesiastics, to maintain the ancient rule, and apart from Easter and Pentecost to baptize only those in danger of death. On the other hand, there is the desire, presumably on the part of the parents, to bring all infants to baptism as soon as possible after birth. It was argued, in defence of the newer practice, that all young children were in danger of death, and should therefore be baptized for safety's sake. By the time of the Reformation this was the prevailing custom. The baptism of Queen Elizabeth I illustrates the current practice. She was baptized by the Archbishop of Canterbury three days after birth in the September of 1553. But since she was baptized by a bishop, she was confirmed at the same time.

Less-privileged infants however were baptized by their parish priests within eight days of birth. The ancient rites were still performed, but in an abbreviated form. The prayers and exorcisms and other ceremonies, which, even in the case of infants had still been performed during Lent in preparation for the Easter baptism, were now telescoped and compressed into a short service at the church door. In the font the water was always ready. It had been blessed during the solemn vigil of the preceding Easter or Pentecost, and was reserved throughout the year, under lock and key as a precaution against theft for purposes of witchcraft. At the font therefore the devil was at once renounced, and the child anointed; the acts of faith were made, and the child baptized with water and anointed with chrism, clothed in a white robe and given a lighted candle. In some liturgical books it is still supposed that the child would be immediately confirmed and communicated. In others no mention is made of confirmation, but communion follows immediately on baptism. In others neither confirmation nor communion appear at all.

Confirmation, since it was administered only by a bishop, could only be received when a bishop was available. It was therefore a matter of chance when it was received. A bishop might be in the neighbourhood soon after a child was baptized; or he might not be in the neighbourhood for a number of years. The canons enacted in the thirteenth and fourteenth centuries still impose penalties upon those who fail to have their children confirmed within so many years of their baptism. But in spite of this many children were not confirmed until long after their baptism, and some were never confirmed at all.

The rite itself was administered in a variety of circumstances. It might take place in a church, or in a private house, or at the roadside, wherever and whenever a bishop could be secured. Being in origin simply the final moment of the baptismal rite, it consisted only of the prayer for the coming of the Spirit and the signing with chrism, to which a final prayer and a blessing might be added. But even this meagre performance was considered too long for busy bishops on their travels. The rite might therefore be reduced simply to the signing with chrism, which the bishop could administer without dismounting. It has already been noted that in the East the laying-on of hands with prayer was apparently replaced at an early date by anointing with oil or chrism. A similar transference of emphasis is discernible in the Roman rite of confirmation. The signing on the forehead with chrism, which follows the prayer with outstretched hands for the coming of the Spirit, was presumably in origin a decorative addition to it. But it gradually came to be regarded as the sacramental moment. With typical conservatism, however, the Roman rite retained both the prayer with the laying-on of hands, and the anointing with chrism, and so left the door open for a change of interpretation, if this were thought desirable, at some future date.

It is not surprising to find that a sacrament which was so casually administered tended in many places to lose its value in the eyes of the laity. But among the theologians also confirmation, now that it was almost always divorced from baptism, and was no longer universally received, began to be devalued. Since numbers of Christians lived and died without it, it could scarcely be regarded as 'necessary to salvation'. As early as the fourth century Jerome was making this point. From the ninth century, as we have seen, attempts were being made to define the purpose of the sacrament, and the peculiar gift that it conveyed. By the thirteenth century it was becoming generally agreed that it provided an increase of the Spirit, which strengthened those who received it to fight against sin and to bear witness in the world. Since such an increase was not needed by infants, but only by those who were capable of sin, and were approaching adult life, theologians now began to ask whether confirmation ought to be given to infants, or whether it ought not to be kept for those who were of an age to need its gifts, and would profit by receiving it consciously. The newer view gradually prevailed, and the restriction of confirmation to those who had attained years of discretion became universal in the West, except in Spain, by the end of the sixteenth century. In this way the accidental postponement of confirmation led to a new doctrine of the sacrament; and in turn the new doctrine gradually brought about the abandonment of infant confirmation.

The practice of communicating the newly-baptized underwent a similar transformation during the Middle Ages, but for a different reason. Originally, as we have seen, baptism, confirmation and communion constituted one rite, which made the candidate a Christian, and which was given indifferently to adults and infants alike. When confirmation by the bishop became separated from the rite, for the reasons we have described, the parish priest baptized, and communicated, the candidates, who by this time were almost always infants. The practice of communicating infants regularly, and not only on the occasion of their baptism, was common form in the early

Church, and continues to this day in the East. It was thought that communion, no less than baptism, was necessary to salvation. For the Lord is depicted in the fourth Gospel as saying, 'Except ye eat the flesh of the Son of man and drink his blood, ye have no life in you'. But during the eleventh century disputes with regard to the nature of the consecrated bread and cup led to a more precise doctrine of the sacrament of the Eucharist and to greater care in the handling of the consecrated species. In consequence the practice was questioned of giving them to infants, who might have difficulty in swallowing them, and might even vomit them. The same tendency which led to the withdrawal of the cup from the laity led also to the abandonment of infant communion. In some places it was thought too dangerous to give the bread to infants, but they continued to receive the wine. The priest dipped his finger into the cup, and the child sucked the sacrament from his finger. But sooner or later even this compromise was abandoned, and by the end of the thirteenth century the practice was virtually dead. It was left to the theologians to explain away the Lord's saying in John.

The baptismal practice which was inherited by the English Reformers can best be seen in the rubrics of the liturgical books in use at the beginning of the sixteenth century.[9] Infants born within eight days of Easter or Pentecost are to be baptized solemnly during the vigil of these feasts. All other infants are to be baptized as soon after birth as possible. They are to be baptized in the font of the parish church, with the anointings before and after baptism, and the giving of the white robe and the lighted candle. Then comes the rubric: 'If the bishop is present, it is right for the child to be baptized at once; and, if his age demand it, to be communicated'. Infant confirmation is still contemplated, in the unlikely circumstances of a bishop being present. The new teaching had not yet affected the liturgical tradition at this point. But infant communion is not permitted. The qualification of age has been inserted into an older rubric.

9. e.g. *Manuale Sarum*, ed. A. J. Collins, H.B.S., 1958.

It seems strange to us that the bulk of the Reformers did not question the practice of infant baptism, with its vicarious act of faith, made by the godparents on behalf of the unconscious candidate. But in the Church of England it was declared to be 'the custom of the Church – to be commended, and in any wise to be retained in the Church';[10] and, at a later date, to be 'most agreeable with the institution of Christ'.[11] No attempt was made to restore the solemn baptisms of Easter and Pentecost. But in order to emphasize the public character of the rite, it was ordered to be administered in the presence of the whole congregation, on Sundays or other holy days, during Divine Service.[12] Infants were to be brought to baptism not later than the Sunday after birth.[13] The rite with which they were to be baptized was in appearance a simplification of the late medieval rite. Its text was materially altered. Ceremony however was more important to the man in the street than text. He could see a ceremony, and might understand what it meant. But the old service had been in Latin, which he did not understand; and the new service was in literary English, to which he was not accustomed.

Like its predecessor, the new service did not begin at once with the baptism of the child. A series of prayers and exhortations, drawn in the main from continental Protestant sources, replaced the prayers and ceremonies performed in the older rite at the church door.[14] The acts of repentance and faith were made by the godparents in the traditional form; but the prayers derived from the old blessing of the font were interpolated between the act of faith and the application of the water, and the theological meaning of the sacrament was still further obscured. The child was dipped in the water with

10. Article 28 of the Articles of 1553.

11. Article 27 of the Articles of 1563.

12. The Book of Common Prayer 1552. The Ministration of Baptism to be used in the Church.

13. ibid. Of them that be baptized in private houses in time of necessity.

14. For details see F. E. Brightman, *The English Rite*, Volume II, pp. 724 ff.

the traditional form; but the anointings before and after baptism were omitted, together with the white robe and the lighted candle. The ceremony however was not reduced to the pouring of the water, and nothing more. With curious conservatism a signing on the forehead, but without chrism, was retained as the finale of the rite, to be a scandal to more thorough-going Protestants at home and abroad.

It might be thought that, in view of the unsatisfactory history of episcopal confirmation during the Middle Ages, the English Reformers would have abandoned the practice, even though they retained the office of bishop. We are therefore surprised to find that a rite of confirmation was provided.[15] It was only to be administered to those who had attained years of discretion. It was firmly linked in practice with catechizing, and was indeed to be preceded by an examination of the candidates. It was further to be the gateway to communion. The old rule that only the confirmed might communicate was revived. The rite itself was little longer than its unreformed predecessor. But the prayer for the Spirit was altered, so as to express the later medieval view of the confirmation gift – an increase of the Spirit for purpose of strengthening. The traditional prayer had run, 'Send upon them the sevenfold Spirit, the holy Paraclete, from heaven'. The new prayer ran: 'Strengthen them, we beseech thee, O Lord, with the Holy Ghost the Comforter, and daily increase in them thy manifold gifts of grace'. The final signing with chrism was omitted, as being a corrupt following of the Apostles, upon whose practice the new rite was somewhat precariously based.[16] Instead, the bishop laid his hand upon each candidate individually, with a new formula demanding an increase of the Spirit.

The Anglican transformation of the medieval rites of baptism and confirmation was in many ways a crystallization of late medieval thinking and practice. Infants must be baptized as soon as possible after birth. The doctrine of Original Guilt

15. ibid., pp. 776 ff.

16. Compare the phrase 'after the example of thy holy Apostles' in the final prayer of the rite.

was firmly held.[17] They could make the acts of repentance and faith through their godparents. Anabaptist teaching in this matter was firmly rejected. They were not to be confirmed until they reached years of discretion. Baptism was complete in itself, and did not need to be perfected by confirmation. Yet they were not to be admitted to communion until they had been confirmed. But this was not because they were imperfect Christians until they had been confirmed. It was because confirmation was the climax of instruction, and the occasion of personal repentance and faith. The restriction of communion to the confirmed was not a theological, but a pastoral matter. The only elements that seem to be misleading in the Anglican arrangements are the retention of the traditional confirmation prayer, even in an altered form, and the restriction of the rite to the bishop. This may have been due to an innate conservatism on the part of the English Reformers. But it must also be remembered that the Reformation in the Church of England failed to reach its term, owing to the Catholic reaction under Mary I.

A hundred years later the Church of England was reorganizing itself after the period of suppression under the Commonwealth. Many people had not secured baptism as infants during that period; and with the opening up of the New World converts were expected from among the 'natives in our plantations'. A new service had therefore to be devised for the baptism of adults.[18] Based on the service for infant baptism, it is a composition of little interest, apart from its final rubric: 'It is expedient that every person thus baptized, should be confirmed by the Bishop, so soon after his Baptism as conveniently may be; that so he may be admitted to the holy Communion'. Such a confirmation cannot be thought of as a purely pastoral matter. The adult candidate has already been instructed before baptism. He has already made his personal acts of repentance and faith when he was baptized, and does not need to renew

17. Article II of 1553.

18. F. E. Brightman, *The English Rite*, Volume I, p. 33; Volume II, pp. 761 ff.

them before admission to communion. He does not therefore need confirmation in the Reformed sense of the word. In the case of adults therefore confirmation can only be thought of as a solemn admission to communion, and nothing more. But it should be remembered that the provision for adult baptism and confirmation was made by those under the influence of the Caroline divines. From their study of Christian antiquity they tended to regard confirmation as a sacramental act no less than a pastoral occasion.[19] Had the English Reformers themselves made provision for the baptism of adults, it is unlikely that they would have allowed for adult confirmation at all.

19. Compare, for instance, Anthony Sparrow, *A Rationale upon the Book of Common Prayer of the Church of England*, London, 1668, pp. 303 ff.

Six

The Eucharist in the Middle Ages

The transformation of the Eucharistic rite in the West, like the transformation of the rites of baptism, is associated with the medieval period. In both cases it followed much the same pattern. The older texts were largely retained, and only decorative and devotional additions were made. But the manner of performing the rites was so changed that in either case the meaning of the rite seems to have been transformed, or at least thrown out of proportion. In baptism, for instance, so long as it was administered to all candidates only at Easter and Pentecost, emphasis was placed upon the corporate nature of the rite, and upon its connexion with the saving acts of God in Christ. When once it was given to each candidate within eight days of birth, the emphasis was shifted to individual salvation, and the connexion with the saving events was obscured. So also with the Eucharist. So long as it was celebrated, at Easter and on all the other Sundays of the year, as the solemn assembly of the Christian Church before God, the corporate nature of the Eucharistic sacrifice was apparent, and its connexion with the Passion and Resurrection of Christ clearly demonstrated. But when weekday celebrations, which could be called private, became common, and when finally private Masses were being celebrated in ever-increasing numbers, the whole conception of the Eucharist became distorted, and its practice corrupted.

As in the case of baptism, the antecedents of later Eucharistic practice may already be found in the earlier periods. In the second century Justin only speaks of the baptismal Eucharist and of the regular Sunday Eucharist. But a contemporary document, *The Martyrdom of Polycarp*, suggests that the funerals / weddings

Eucharist was already being celebrated at the graves of the martyrs on the anniversary of their deaths.[1] By the third century this was the common practice, and led to the later observance of Saints' Days. But such a celebration was always a public celebration, the whole church meeting at the cemetery instead of the usual meeting place. The commemoration of the local martyr therefore, and later of the saints of other churches, merely increased the number of public Eucharistic assemblies held in the course of the year. It was however the first step in the dissociation of the Eucharistic liturgy from the Lord's Day, with which it had been associated since New Testament times.

But another type of celebration in the cemeteries was from the first essentially private. This was the celebration of the Eucharist at funerals. Pagan funerals commonly included a banquet, which was in some sense an act of communion between the survivors and the departed. Christian funerals therefore naturally came to include a celebration of the Eucharist, by which the living expressed their communion with the dead in Christ. The funeral banquets of the pagan world were celebrated by an intimate group, that is to say the family and friends of the departed. So also the funeral Eucharists of the Christian Church came to be celebrated by an intimate group of family and friends. Here we may find the origin of the private Mass of later history. The weddings of Christian couples provided a similar occasion. The more solemn marriage ceremonies of the pagans included a sacrifice, and the sharing of sacrificial food by the bride and bridegroom. So the Christian Church, in taking over these ceremonies, substituted for the pagan sacrifice the Eucharist, which included the sharing by the bride and bridegroom of the bread and cup. But such a performance was essentially private, only the families and friends being present. The celebrations at funerals and weddings are the first examples of the votive Masses, which became so popular in the Middle Ages.

But pastoral necessity also played its part in modifying the public celebration of the Sunday Eucharist. In the second

1. *Martyrium Polycarpi* XVIII, 3.

century at Rome everyone was apparently expected to attend the one celebration. To those who were unable to do so the elements were brought from the celebration by the deacons.[2] But sooner or later it became necessary, in a large city like Rome, to provide other celebrations on Sunday. The bishop, or his deputy, presided at the principal Mass, and was assisted by the deacons of Rome, and by such presbyters as were free to attend, and by the body of singers, once they had been instituted. But individual presbyters presided at secondary Masses in other churches of the City, assisted by one or more of the inferior clergy. Inevitably the performance was of a simpler kind than that of the principal Mass. In the absence of the choir the elaborate anthems were presumably omitted. The presbyter himself was compelled to perform the duties of the deacon as well as those of the celebrant. Since by this time the reading of the Gospel was restricted to those in holy orders, he himself read the Gospel, while one of the inferior clergy read the Epistle.[3]

With the conversion of the countryside and the establishment of churches in the villages which were presided over by presbyters, the pattern was still further modified. Celebration by a presbyter became the normal method of celebration throughout the Church, and celebration by the bishop became a comparative rarity. In the larger country churches the presbyter would possess a staff which would include deacons as well as inferior clergy, and perhaps a body of singers. The Sunday Mass in such places could be performed with as much pomp as when a presbyter took the bishop's place at the principal Mass in the city. Mass was also performed with similar pomp in the great collegiate and monastic churches throughout the Middle Ages. But in remote places, and in missionary areas, the presbyter might find himself with very little in the way of liturgical assistance, and might even be obliged to read the entire text, and perform all the actions of the Mass himself.

2. Justin, *Apology* 65 and 67.

3. J. A. Jungmann, *Missarum Solemnia*, New York, 1951, Volume I, pp. 195–259.

In this way the various methods of celebrating Mass insensibly developed – pontifical high Mass, capitular, conventual and parochial high Mass, sung Mass, and finally low Mass.

How much of the text could be recited depended of course on the books available. Originally, as we have seen, even the Eucharistic prayer itself was extempore, the celebrant composing freely upon fixed themes. By the end of the fourth century and the beginning of the fifth, the text of the canon was beginning to crystallize at Rome,[4] and had reached approximately its present form by the time of Gregory the Great. The preface inevitably remained fluid longer than the canon, owing to its variation with the occasion, and newly composed prefaces still appear from time to time. The canon would be known by heart; the preface would be written out together with the other variable prayers of the Mass – the collect, the prayer over the oblations at the offertory, and the post-communion. Whether the sheet on which they were written out was taken into the church, or whether it was left in the sacristy, and its contents were recited from memory in church, is unknown. Sooner or later collections of such sheets were made for celebrants, and bound together, with perhaps a text of the canon, and in this way liturgical books came into being. So long as the various parts of the Mass were performed by their proper ministers, they were written out in separate books, one for the celebrant, one for the deacon, one for the other readers, one for the singers. But when all the parts of the Mass were performed with increasing frequency by the celebrant alone, they came to be written out in the appropriate order in one book, and so the missal had its origin.

In those areas of the West which did not follow Roman customs, a similar process was at work. The celebrant's prayers, which began as free compositions, gradually crystallized into written texts. But in the non-Roman Western rites the number of prayers which varied from one day to another was greater. Not only were there more variable prayers throughout the service, but the Eucharistic prayer itself consisted of a series

4. Ambrose, *De Sacramentis* IV, as above.

of variables. As in the Roman rite, the preface which leads into the Sanctus was subject to variation. But the prayers before and after the narrative of the institution, which in the Roman rite are fixed and form the canon, were also variable. Such rites existed in Gaul and Spain for centuries. In Gaul the native rite was first assimilated to the Roman, and finally, in the time of Charles the Great, largely replaced by it. In Spain the local tradition lasted longer, and did not finally disappear until the twelfth century. The prayers of the non-Roman Western rites are composed in an undisciplined rhetorical style, very different from the sobriety of the Roman texts which superseded them. But it was largely the prestige of the Roman see, and not the intrinsic excellence of the Roman rite, which finally led to its adoption throughout the West.

The Roman liturgical tradition began by providing proper lessons, chants and prayers for the Sunday Masses from Christmas to Pentecost, the period when the great events of the Redemption were being commemorated. It also provided texts for the penitential seasons of the year – the Ember days and the forty days of Lent – and for the feasts of the great Roman saints. It finally came to include texts for the remaining Sundays of the year and for the feasts of the non-Roman saints, and in this way provided for all the public Masses throughout the year.

But it must not be supposed that mass was said only on Sundays and fast days and Saints' Days, as in the East. Weekday celebrations were common from the third century onwards, and in some places Mass was celebrated daily. But such celebrations were strictly speaking private, that is to say for specific groups within the Church, whether for a particular family at a wedding or funeral, or for a pious household in a domestic chapel. Nor were they celebrated only for a private group of persons; they were also for a private intention. At a wedding Mass was said for the bride and bridegroom; at a funeral for the departed person; on other occasions for a person who was sick, for a person who was going on a journey, and so on. Alternatively, Masses could be said to express private devotion to some particular saint. A chapel might be erected in his honour, either in a private house, or, later, alongside a church building. Here perhaps his relics might be housed, and Mass said in his honour, quite apart from his annual commemoration.

But it was chiefly in connexion with the dead that private Masses began to increase at the beginning of the Middle Ages. Theologians like Gregory the Great were more certain than their predecessors about the state of the departed and their need of Masses. Cyprian in the third century had refused to allow a celebration for those who had not behaved virtuously during their lifetime. In the medieval period the less virtuous the departed had been, the more celebrations they were thought to need. Monasteries undertook to have Masses said for the departed members of other monasteries. Departed benefactors were rewarded with Masses for their repose; and the living were repaid with votive Masses for their safety in this world. Private individuals meanwhile might ask for particular votive Masses to be said for particular needs. The parish clergy, who on Sundays and other feast days performed the public Eucharist of the Church, were kept busy on weekdays with these requests for private Masses, and were often obliged to celebrate several times a day.

The practice of saying private Masses not only unbalanced the presentation of the Eucharistic liturgy. It also became involved in undesirable financial arrangements. The laity had of course been taught the duty of providing board and lodging for the ministry from New Testament times, and in this way had come to support a professional clergy. In connexion with the Eucharist they had produced the bread and wine Sunday by Sunday; and what was not required for the service could be used to support the clergy and others dependent on the Church. At a domestic or private celebration those who had requested the Eucharist supplied the bread and wine required; and any that was supplied in excess would naturally be given to the celebrant. At a later stage, when unleavened bread had taken the place of common bread in the Eucharist, the celebrant began to supply the bread and wine for the private Mass himself; and those who had asked for the Mass recompensed him by giving him money. Thus, imperceptibly, the system of paying for Masses crept in, which later led to such disastrous consequences.[5]

In these ways the Eucharistic rite became transformed so as to be almost unrecognizable. The local community still assembled before God on Sundays. But the assembly was no longer presided over by the bishop, assisted by his council of presbyters and by his deacons. The bishop was now a faraway official. The college of presbyters had been broken up into a number of independent parish priests, to each of whom one or more deacons might be allotted. The local community assisted at the Sunday Mass, but they no longer communicated, except at Easter. By the thirteenth century they could only be induced to do this by the threat that otherwise they would be refused Christian burial. The Eucharist was no longer the function of the whole Christian people, even at the parish Mass on Sundays. It was the function of the priest. He had the duty of providing the Mass which his people must hear, and was bound to say it on their behalf, with their intention. On weekdays he could supply them with private Masses, to suit their individual needs.

Since the Mass had become the function of the priest, and was on the way to producing a large part of his income, and since the demand for votive Masses was steadily increasing, the numbers of the clergy inevitably increased to meet the demand. It was this increase that led to a transformation in church architecture from the ninth century onwards, north of the Alps, in the dominions of Charles the Great. More priests and more Masses meant more altars. For it was the custom in many places to use an altar only once a day. The building of oratories or chapels to house the additional altars near the church, which had been the older custom, was expensive. The placing of altars here and there in a church building constructed to hold one altar proved clumsy. A new type of church

5. G. A. Michell, *Landmarks in Liturgy*, London, 1961, pp. 121–6.

building was therefore evolved, which still gave prominence to the one altar for the public celebration, but also provided a series of side-chapels for the celebration of the private Masses. Chapels could be constructed in a ring round the apse, others could be inserted in the aisles of the transepts. In the great Romanesque churches the high altar remained prominent, and the side altars secluded. But in the Gothic period the side chapels became more and more open to the body of the church; and by the end of the Middle Ages little chantry chapels had sprung up all about the nave, and even in the choir.

Throughout the Middle Ages the text of the canon remained virtually unchanged. The disposition of the collects and of the other prayers of the Mass might differ from place to place; and new prayers were composed from time to time, to meet the demands of new commemorations. The piety of individual celebrants introduced a number of private devotions into the saying of private Mass; and these were later introduced into the saying of the public Mass on Sundays and festivals.[6] But, in spite of the preponderance of private Masses, no attempt was ever made to adapt the canon or the prayers of the Mass to suit the circumstances in which by this time they were most frequently recited. All the prayers remained in the plural. The prayer over the offerings still presupposed that the people had offered, the prayer after communion still presupposed that they had communicated. But the incongruity passed largely unnoticed, since all the prayers, and indeed all lessons and chants, were still recited in Latin. No attempt was made to translate them into the vernacular, to suit the needs of the peoples north of the Alps, where the bulk of the laity knew no Latin, and numbers of the clergy knew very little.

In the circumstances it is not surprising to find that the first part of the Mass lost its character as a service of instruction. The lessons were read in Latin, and were therefore unintelligible to the people. The sermon in the Roman tradition was regarded as the prerogative of the bishop, and was no longer thought of as an integral part of the Mass, which was now

6. P. Batiffol, *Leçons sur la Messe*, Paris, 1927, pp. 12–29.

normally celebrated by presbyters. In periods of spiritual revival, as in the reign of Charles the Great, presbyters were encouraged to preach, but their sermons at Mass were inevitably expositions of Christian doctrine rather than homilies on the lessons, although the homilies of the Fathers might be read by those who did not possess the authority to preach. By the end of the Middle Ages the sermon tends to lose its connexion with the Mass, and to be preached on other occasions instead.

The first half of the Mass therefore, having lost its real character, was transformed into a service of music and decorative ceremonial; and in some places the offertory of the Eucharist proper was anticipated during it. The body of singers during the earlier period had been responsible for singing the elaborate anthems at the entry and at the offertory and at the communion. But the people had sung to simple tunes the response to the psalms between the lessons, and the Sanctus, and, once they had been introduced, the *Gloria in excelsis Deo* and the other fixed chants. But the singers had first appropriated the singing between the lessons; and in the ninth century elaborate melodies began to be composed for the remaining pieces. The later introduction of proses and other sequences between the lessons completed the series. Introit, *Kyrie*, *Gloria*, Gradual psalm, Alleluia, Sequence together formed a varied musical performance, which only needed an elaborate ceremonial to transform it into a splendid theatrical function.

The older Roman tradition had provided an austere ceremonial for the first half of the Mass. The procession of the celebrant and his ministers to the altar had been accompanied with the lights and the incense, derived in all probability from the procession of the civil magistrate. The passage of the Gospel book from the altar to the ambo had later been similarly distinguished. But once the tradition had been transplanted to the north of the Alps, it speedily lost its austerity on French soil. The incense was no longer used, along with the lights, as a processional ornament. The altar was incensed, the celebrant was incensed, the Gospel was incensed, the oblations were incensed. For it was not thought necessary to wait for the offertory before preparing the altar for the Eucharist proper. The bread and wine could be carried in during the singing of the *Kyrie*; the altar could be spread, and the chalice prepared, and the bread and wine placed on the altar and incensed, during the singing between the lessons. The rite which had originally been a service of Bible reading and preaching was now transformed into a magnificent, if somewhat meaningless, pageant. Played out on the splendid stage of the larger Gothic church, lighted from jewelled windows of stained glass, clothed in the sumptuous late-medieval vestments, with the flames of the candles flickering and the sweet-scented smoke of the incense ascending, it presented a complex of light and colour and movement, which engaged the heart, if not the head, of the medieval Christian.

The second half of the Mass was less spectacular during the earlier part of the Middle Ages. The offertory had been one of the great moments of the old Roman tradition. The bread and wine had been brought up by the people, and had been collected and disposed upon the altar by the clergy. But with the decay of the people's communion the reality went out of the offertory; and, with the substitution of wafers for ordinary bread in the Eucharist, the presentation of bread and wine for the sacrifice was replaced by the presentation of money and other gifts, which were inevitably out of context in the Eucharistic rite. The offertory itself therefore, that is to say the preparation of the table for the Supper, was reduced to the placing upon the altar of a single wafer and of a small quantity of wine and water in the chalice, and was further obscured by the elaborate incensing of the elements and of the altar and of the clergy which followed. The prayer over the offerings, which formed the conclusion of the offertory, was by this time recited silently, and only its final words were sung out loud, that the people might say Amen to it.

The Eucharistic prayer opened with the preface and with the singing of the Sanctus and Benedictus; but after that the rite lapsed into a long period of silence, while the celebrant recited the canon. Ceremonial signs of the cross and other gestures had been attached to the prayer; but these were invisible to the congregation, since by this time the celebrant had ceased to face the people across the altar, and now faced the altar with his back to the people. The change had taken place in different areas at different times. In the great basilicas of Rome, and in a number of other places, it has never been made at all. It is said to have been due to the placing of the relics of the saints on, and above, and behind, the altar. This dislodged the celebrant from his traditional position, and drove him to the other side of the table.[7] But whatever its cause, the change of position typified the changed conception of the priesthood of the celebrant. He was no longer the father at the head of his family, the leader of the priestly people, all of whom were engaged in offering the Eucharist, each in his own order. He was now the mediatorial priest, standing between God and man, personally endowed with the supernatural power of offering sacrifice, and capable of using that power on behalf of any he wished to benefit.

In the silence he consecrated and offered. He then sang out loud the Lord's Prayer, in silence broke the bread and communicated, while the choir sang the old anthem of the fraction. But the breaking of the bread was no more than the snapping of a single wafer, and the communion no more than its consumption and the draining of the chalice. Both of these moments were reduced to vanishing point; and neither of them could be seen by the people.

The whole weight of the second half of the Mass now rested upon the consecration, since the offertory and the fraction and the communion had virtually disappeared. The consecration, upon which depended the presence of Christ's flesh and blood and its presentation to the Father, took place invisibly and inaudibly at the altar. A devotional explosion was inevitable, and it is to be wondered at that it was delayed so long. For it is not until the beginning of the thirteenth century that we first find the ceremony of the elevation of the host. The theologians of the early Church had taken for granted the supernatural

7. Edmund Bishop, *Liturgica Historica*, p. 20–39.

presence of Christ's Body and Blood in the sacrament. Justin was content to say that the bread is the flesh of Christ.[8] Irenaeus simply said that there is an earthly thing and there is a heavenly thing in the Eucharist, and left it at that.[9] Tertullian said that the bread represents the Body, or is a figure of the Body;[10] and this way of talking was used for centuries in the West. But in the East a new way of talking begins with Cyril of Jerusalem – that the bread is changed into the Body.[11] This in due course became normative in Eastern theology, and began to cause controversy in the West. In the ninth century, and again in the eleventh, disputes broke out among Western theologians about the relation of the bread to the Body. Such disputes had no direct effect upon the liturgy of the Mass; but they concentrated attention upon Christ's presence in the sacrament, rather than upon the purpose for which he was present. The moment of consecration was not in doubt. Already in the second century Tertullian apparently connected it with the recital of the Lord's words at the Last Supper;[12] and by the fourth century Ambrose was teaching that the Lord's words consecrate.[13] But it was not until the beginning of the thirteenth century that the moment of consecration received liturgical recognition in the ceremony of the elevation of the host. Priests began to raise the newly consecrated bread above their heads, that the people might see and adore; and this elevation became the heart of late-medieval religion.

The silence of the canon provided the occasion. The disputes about the Eucharistic presence provided the interest. But the actual cause of the introduction of the elevation was a decree of the bishop of Paris. Either he was afraid that the people might see and adore too soon, before the consecration had taken place, and might so be guilty of idolatry. Or he was

8. Justin, *Apology* 66.
9. Irenaeus, *Adversus Haereses*, IV. 31. 4.
10. Tertullian, *Adversus Marcionem* 1, 14; 4, 40.
11. Cyril of Jerusalem, *Mystagogical Catechesis* V, 7.
12. Tertullian, *Adversus Marcionem* 4, 40.
13. Ambrose, *De Sacramentis* IV, 4, 14.

settling a theological dispute. Was the bread consecrated by the recital of the Lord's words about the bread? And was the wine consecrated by the Lord's words about the wine? Or were both bread and wine consecrated together by the Lord's words about both? Theologians were doubtful. But the bishop of Paris apparently knew the answer. He made it clear that the bread was consecrated before the wine, by ordering his priests to elevate the host for the people to adore before they said the words over the chalice. It is unlikely that ordinary Christians were particularly interested in such theological refinements. But the sudden appearance of the white circle of the host, held up by the priest to be seen and adored, gripped their imagination in a way that few liturgical gestures, before or after, have ever done. Gradually the whole Mass came to centre upon the elevation. Bells were rung to attract attention to the great moment. Torches were held that the people might better see the host. Incense was offered, but care was to be taken that the smoke did not obscure the view. The Mass was thus given a new climax, which it had come to need. The steady movement of the Eucharist from offertory to consecration, from consecration to fraction, from fraction to communion had disappeared from the late-medieval Mass. Its place was taken by a swift progression to the moment of the elevation, and an equally swift conclusion, once it was over.[14]

The Reformers made short work of the Mass as they inherited it. They retained the reading and preaching of Scripture; the lessons were read in the vernacular, and the first half of the Mass formed the model upon which their Sunday worship was based. But their sole interest in the Eucharist proper was the communion of the people, and it was on this that they centred their rites. Luther retained a belief in an objective consecration, and in the Lord's words as effecting it. The narrative of the institution therefore forms part of the Lutheran Eucharistic prayer. Calvin rejected the Lutheran view of consecration, and the narrative appears in a Calvinist order only as a lesson before the prayer begins. To Luther the

14. J. A. Jungmann, *Missarum Solemnia*, Volume II, pp. 206–17.

breaking of the bread was of little moment. To Calvin it was of great significance. In a Lutheran rite therefore the fraction has little or no place. But it is central to the Calvinist tradition, and is often accompanied by the outpouring of the wine. None of the Reformers found any place for the offertory as a separate moment in the Eucharist, and none believed that the rite was a sacrifice in the traditional sense of the term.

Both Luther and Calvin desired that the Eucharist should be celebrated weekly. But such a celebration necessarily involved for them a general communion of the people. Here inevitably the Reformers met with opposition from the laity. For centuries laypeople had not received communion except at Easter, and then somewhat unwillingly. They were not therefore prepared to change their devotional habits, even though they had changed their religion. Further, Zwingli was teaching a purely commemorative view of the Eucharist, which seemed to demand infrequent communion. The practice he advocated suited those who had been conditioned by medieval devotion; communion three or four times a year became the discipline of Protestant Christendom; and the Eucharist in any form ceased to be the focal point of worship in the churches of the Reformation.

The English Reformers abolished the medieval Mass as thoroughly as their brethren on the continent.[15] The traditional notions of sacrifice and presence were discarded. The altars were removed, and a communion table was set up, when required, in the middle of the choir or nave. The celebrant, after reading and preaching the Scriptures and saying the prayers, gave opportunity for those who were unwilling to communicate to depart. He then conducted a series of penitential devotions with those who remained, and distributed bread and wine in remembrance of Christ's Passion. An odd conservatism re-

15. Aidan Cardinal Gasquet and Edmund Bishop, *Edward VI and the Book of Common Prayer*, revised edition, London, 1928; Francis Clark, *Eucharistic Sacrifice and the Reformation*, London, 1960. For another view see C. W. Dugmore, *The Mass and the English Reformers*, London, 1958.

tained the preface and Sanctus among the prayers in preparation for communion, and the narrative of the institution in a prayer for the communicants. But it was made clear that the narrative was not intended to consecrate in the traditional meaning of the term. For the bread and wine that remained over after the distribution was to go to the priest for his own domestic use.[16] An attempt was made to secure communicants every Sunday; but in most places they were not forthcoming. In consequence communion came to be given only three or four times a year, and the Eucharist lost its central place in the worship of the Church of England.

The Catholic reaction under Mary I prevented the English Reformers from carrying their work to its full term. When Elizabeth I came to the throne, she was not prepared to endorse it, but desired a return to more traditional forms of worship. When this proved politically impossible, she accepted the Reformers' Communion Service only after the words with which the sacrament had been distributed in the older rite had been restored.[17] The Caroline divines, from their knowledge of the ancient Church, were determined to reshape the Reformers' service, and to make it patient of a traditional interpretation. But they failed to do so in Scotland in the reign of Charles I,[18] and they failed again in England at the restoration of Charles II.[19] The text of the Reformers' service, with the one addition made by Queen Elizabeth I, remained intact. Only by adjusting the rubrics did they reintroduce something of the traditional shape.[20] In this way the offertory and the fraction were restored after a fashion; and the prayer containing the narrative of the institution was now entitled 'The Prayer of Consecration', although its text contained no petition that God should consecrate. The reverent disposal of the bread and wine after

16. Compare the Communion Service of 1552: 'And if any of the bread and wine remain, the Curate shall have it to his own use.'

17. The Communion Service of 1559.

18. The Scottish Communion Service of 1637.

19. *The Durham Book*, ed. G. J. Cuming, Oxford, 1961.

20. The Communion Service of 1662.

communion was insisted upon; and provision was made for a second consecration, if the elements failed during the distribution. Only against the background of its history can the communion service of the Church of England be understood – the Reformers being prevented from completing their work, Queen Elizabeth refusing to allow that work to go further, the Caroline divines making unsuccessful attempts to modify the Reformers' text, but successfully unbalancing their service by altering its rubrics. This is why the rite is capable of such different interpretations, and has been such a source of controversy among Anglicans ever since.

Seven

The Liturgical Movement and its Background

The reader may be surprised that the liturgies of the Reformed Churches have been treated as products of the later Middle Ages, and that the period between the Protestant Reformation and the present day has not been dealt with at all. But the truth of the matter is that the Reformation liturgies were in some sense anti-liturgies, deliberately framed by removing from the traditional rites those features which were dogmatically objectionable, rather than arising spontaneously from the life of the worshipping community. The old rite of infant baptism was retained, except among the Anabaptists; but it was stripped down to what were regarded at the time as its bare essentials. Confirmation as a sacrament in its own right, or as part of the baptismal sacrament, disappeared. (What was called confirmation was a rite in which those who had been baptized in infancy professed their faith on coming to years of discretion, and were admitted to first communion.) So too, as we have already seen, with the Eucharist. The traditional rite was modified by removing those parts which were thought to be incompatible with the new religion. Since the Eucharist proper was celebrated only when the laity were prepared to communicate, it inevitably became an occasional service. Regular Sunday worship was limited to the first part of the Mass – the lessons, the chants, the sermon and the prayers. Shorn of elaborate music and ceremonial, the service became less and less formal, and more and more at the discretion of the minister, the people's participation being secured by the singing of hymns and metrical psalms. Formal prayers gave way to prayers extempore; and in consequence the liturgical documents of the Protestant Churches consisted mainly of Church Orders, or frameworks of directions. They were not fixed liturgies, giving both the texts to be recited and the rubrics, or directions, which governed their use.

The most notable exception was the reformed Church of England, which was given, by royal authority, not a book of common order, but a Book of Common Prayer. Because of its character as a fixed liturgy, in spite of its unimpeachably Protestant character, it has frequently been mistaken for a variant of the traditional liturgy. Such a view might appear plausible in the case of baptism and even of confirmation. But it was impossible to maintain in the case of the Eucharist. And those who sought to do so were reduced to performing the Communion Office in the Book of Common Prayer clothed in a ceremonial which approximated, less or more, to that of the late medieval Mass.

It is this that explains the controversies that have arisen from time to time in the Church of England over apparently trivial points of ceremonial. The religious mind is always prone to make mountains out of molehills. But the scandal caused by the décor of the Royal Chapel at Whitehall in Queen Elizabeth I's reign, and the controversy aroused by the ceremonial changes in Durham Cathedral in the days of Charles I, and, above all, the furious reaction to the introduction of ritualism into the parish churches in the nineteenth century, are not to be explained in terms of religious triviality. Consciously or unconsciously, those who introduced the older ceremonial, and those who welcomed its introduction, were endeavouring either to assert the traditional character of the rite they were compelled to use, or to conceal its obviously untraditional character. Behind all the apparent absurdity and obstinacy and at times hysteria lay a serious theological and liturgical concern. It was the tension between the text of the rite and the doctrinal interpretation being imposed upon it which led to the exaggerated importance attached to clothing and ornaments and ceremonies.

The remedy proposed to meet the situation was a revision of the Prayer Book, which was set in motion by the Royal

Commission of 1906. It is not within the scope of this essay to trace the course of revision, from its first beginning to the final rejection of the Church's proposals by the House of Commons in 1928. It will be sufficient to give the reasons for its failure. First, the motive which lay behind the revision was a matter of ecclesiastical politics – the curbing of those within the Church who, however unjustifiably, were trying to return to older ways of worship.[1] Second, in the course of revision the advice of liturgical scholars was increasingly neglected, and the drafting of the new Communion Office passed into the hands of the ecclesiastical politicians.[2] As a result, the service which they drafted, and which Parliament rejected, commanded assent, but no widespread support, among clergy and laity, and survives only as an ecclesiastical curio. Had it expressed the genuine aspirations of the worshipping Church, it would have passed into general use, in spite of its rejection by Parliament.

The Roman Catholic Church in the period of the Counter-Reform was temperamentally averse from liturgical change. As a result of the Council of Trent the Roman liturgy was pruned of certain exuberances of text and ceremony, but expressed in essentials the worship of the medieval Church. The invention of the printing press a hundred years earlier made it possible, for the first time in Christian history, to insist upon uniformity in worship. Hitherto the liturgical texts could be produced only in manuscript, and local variations were inevitably admitted, and indeed tolerated. But now printed editions were produced with uniform texts and rubrics. Since the Latin language was retained as the medium of worship in all western countries of the Roman obedience, the same texts could be recited, and the same ceremonies performed, in the same way throughout the Catholic world. At the same time all spontaneous growth and change and adaptation of the liturgy was prevented, and the worship of the Roman Catholic Church

1. G. K. A. Bell, *Randall Davidson*, Oxford, 1935, pp. 1354–8.

2. *Walter Howard Frere, His Correspondence on Liturgical Revision and Construction*, ed. R. C. D. Jasper, London, 1954, Chapter 2.

fossilized. What has been called the Age of Rubricism set in.[3]

Further, in all communions, Catholic and Protestant alike, the main religious interest since the Reformation has lain largely in the individual soul. God may be glorified in the performance of the external cult, but it is the education of the individual conscience and the development of the spiritual life that have been the main concern of the Catholic Church. Similarly, in Protestant circles, it has been the conversion of the individual and the inculcation of the domestic and social virtues that have been the objects of preaching and instruction. The reception of the sacraments in both traditions has been largely thought of in terms derived from the medieval Church, the appropriation by the individual of spiritual grace and power. The Church itself has been conceived of as an organization to promote individual salvation. The ministry has been thought to be a class of officials supernaturally endowed to administer the sacraments and commissioned to preach the Word to the individual members of the Church. The public liturgy of the Church, against such a background, has come to be regarded as of secondary importance.

The liturgical movement of the present century is not therefore primarily a liturgical movement at all. It has not arisen from a desire to put back the public worship of the Church into some ideal period, as the Romantic movement of the nineteenth century led to an attempt to restore the worship and the décor of the Gothic age. It is essentially a theological movement. It is active alike in the Roman Catholic Church,[4] in the Church of England[5] and in the other Protestant

3. Theodor Klauser, *The Western Liturgy and its History*, tr. F. L. Cross, London, 1952.

4. Compare, for instance, *Cours et Conférences des Semaines Liturgiques*, Tome VII, *Le Canon de la Messe*, Louvain, 1929; B. Capelle, *Travaux Liturgiques* I, 'Doctrine', Louvain, 1955; L. Bouyer, *Life and Liturgy*, London, 1954.

5. G. Herbert, *Liturgy and Society*, London, 1935; *The Parish Communion*, ed. G. Herbert, London, 1937; G. Dix, *The Shape of the Liturgy*. The theology of this last work is as important and as controversial as its history.

Churches.[6] It did not start with a reconsideration of the controversies of the Reformation period – infant baptism, episcopal confirmation, the Eucharistic Presence, the Eucharistic Sacrifice. It began with a revival of the theology of the Church as the mystical Body of Christ, of which clergy and laity alike are equally members. It has gone on to reconsider both baptism and Eucharist in the light of that theology. It inevitably studies the history of liturgical development throughout history, with particular reference to its relation with contemporary society and culture. But it is in no sense an antiquarian movement, although it seeks to profit by the lessons of history. It is prepared to ask radical questions; indeed they are posed by a knowledge of liturgical history. But it is not prepared, even in its most extreme form, to break with history and to start all over again. For it possesses no ascertainable principles upon which to base a new deal. Only a knowledge of the past can enable it to adapt the liturgy to the needs of contemporary society today. And this is not to be done by changing the décor or by altering the language or by any other superficial means. It can only be achieved at a point where theology and liturgy and psychology and sociology meet.

Since the Second Vatican Council the Roman Catholic Church has begun to abandon the use of Latin in public worship, and is faced with the task of translating its liturgical texts into the vernacular. At the same time the Church of England seems determined to abandon the hieratic English of the Book of Common Prayer, and to ask its Liturgical Commission to produce revised services in contemporary English. The rites of baptism and confirmation which were produced by the Commission in 1958 in simplified Cranmerian language[7] were returned to the Commission, and have since been rewritten in what is regarded as a popular style. The Roman Catholic Church is in the matter of the vernacular in a stronger position

6. Max Thurian, *L'Eucharistie*, Paris, 1959.

7. *Baptism and Confirmation*, A Report Submitted by the Church of England Liturgical Commission to the Archbishops of Canterbury and York in November 1958, London, 1959.

than the Church of England. For it has not inherited a vernacular liturgy of outstanding literary merit. It is therefore faced with straight translation from Latin into English, and not from one kind of English into another. The Roman Catholic revisers therefore find little difficulty in addressing God as You, whereas the Anglicans do not find it easy to abandon calling him Thou. The translation of the Canon of the Mass published in 1967 runs far more smoothly than the new Communion Service finally put out for experimental use in the same year.[8] There is however increasing cooperation between the two Churches, and there is good hope that a common translation will be adopted by both of such texts as the Lord's Prayer, the *Gloria in excelsis* and the Creed, which are common to Catholic and Protestant alike.

Such cooperation is also taking place between the Protestant Churches themselves. The Scripture readings of the first half of the Communion Service in the Book of Common Prayer are derived from lectionaries which, however venerable, are no longer completely relevant, and are based on a calendar in need of adjustment, to modern conditions. The Church of England and the Free Churches have been working together to produce a common list of Scripture readings – of Old Testament lessons, Epistles and Gospels – for use in the Sunday service.[9] If such a scheme is finally adopted, it will mean that in spite of divisions the same lessons from Scripture will be read each Sunday in Protestant churches throughout the country.

Inevitably the revision of services involves a reconsideration of the doctrine underlying them. The Roman Catholic Church is seeking to restore the balance of its Eucharistic teaching, by insisting on the character of the Mass as the function of the Christian community. Priests are therefore encouraged to celebrate together rather than to say private

8. *Alternative Services, Second Series*, 'An Order for Holy Communion', London, 1967.

9. *The Calendar and Lectionary*, A Reconsideration by the Joint Liturgical Group, edited by R. C. D. Jasper, Oxford, 1967.

Masses. Lay people are encouraged to receive communion within the Mass, rather than outside of Mass by means of the sacrament reserved. The exposition of the reserved sacrament for purposes of adoration is being more carefully regulated. But there are apparently no signs of departure from the traditional doctrines of the Eucharistic Sacrifice or of the Real Presence.[10] In the matter of confirmation on the other hand there have been for some time signs of doctrinal questioning. Baptism in infancy and communion only at the age of reason are not being questioned, although infant communion is practised in oriental Churches in communion with the Roman See. But some new doctrinal and pastoral significance is being sought for confirmation, which is still largely without meaning in the Roman Catholic Church.[11]

In the Church of England the administration of baptism and confirmation and of the Eucharist is under review. The practice of indiscriminately baptizing all infants brought to the font has been called in question. At a time when the country was nominally Christian, and the Church of England more than nominally established, the practice was defended on the grounds that all children would certainly receive a Christian education. At the present time the situation has so changed that indiscriminate baptism is thought by many Anglicans to be sacrilegious. A number are going further, and are questioning the whole theological basis upon which infant baptism rests, as the Anabaptists did at the time of the Reformation. They not only objected to the baptism of the children of non-practising Christian parents, but also to the baptism of any children at all. They argue that such commitment of unconscious infants has no authority in the New Testament, and is indeed offensive to the rights of the individual. In many places baptism is no longer administered apart from the public services of the Church, as a rite conferring individual salvation.

10. *Sacra Congregatio Rituum*, Instructio de cultu mysterii Eucharistici, Rome, 1967.

11. B. Leeming, *Principles of Sacramental Theology*; C. Davis, *The Making of a Christian*, London, 1964.

It is performed, as indeed the Book of Common Prayer demands, at a principal service on Sundays, as a rite of admission to the Church which is Christ's Body. Confirmation also, in a number of dioceses, is given by the bishop at the principal Communion Service on Sundays, and the candidates receive not only confirmation, but also first communion, at his hands, along with the rest of the local congregation. Any candidates who are unbaptized will often be baptized as well as confirmed and communicated by the bishop at the same time.

The Liturgical Commission produced in 1958 a series of services to provide for the changed situation.[12] The rite of baptism, confirmation and communion was first of all set out as one whole, and was then separated out into infant baptism and adult confirmation and communion. But the novelty of the liturgical approach, and the traditional character of the language, led to its being returned to the Commission. The services have however now been republished in a new and more acceptable form.[13] The language has been modernized; the structure has been simplified; and a greater share in the services has been given to the congregation. But it is significant that the liturgical approach to the rites, which ten years ago was thought to be revolutionary, is apparently not now questioned. Whether experiment will prove that the services are practically usable and pastorally effective remains to be seen.

The Liturgical Commission was from the start instructed to make a radical revision of the Communion Service, rather than tinker with the Reformation rites of 1549 and 1552, as was done in 1662 and 1928. In effect it produced a new service altogether. Owing to the growth of a more radical approach within the Church of England, and perhaps owing to more careful preliminary propaganda, the service obtained a more favourable reception than baptism and confirmation in 1958. But, in order to obtain the support of the less radical, a good many features of the old service were introduced by way of

12. See above, note 7.

13. *Alternative Services, Second Series,* 'Baptism and Confirmation', London, 1968.

alternatives, and the resulting draft, viewed as a liturgical document, was untidy in the extreme. Further, a doctrinal clash between the parties in the Church of England, which had largely been avoided in the case of baptism and confirmation, broke out in connexion with the wording of the Eucharistic prayer. As a result the new service has restored the traditional shape of the Eucharist – Scripture lessons, sermon, intercessions; offertory, consecration, fraction, communion. But in the present wording of the Eucharist prayer, it stands firmly outside the main tradition of Christian antiquity and of the modern Greek and Latin Churches.[14]

One other liturgical venture deserves mention, although strictly speaking it falls outside the scope of this essay, which has been restricted to a consideration of baptism, confirmation and the Eucharist. This is the Ordinal proposed by a joint committee of Anglicans and Methodists, to be used in both Churches during the first stage of their scheme of union.[15] Forms of conferring the three traditional orders of bishop, presbyter and deacon are included in the draft. Here again a return has been made to the traditional shape of the rite of ordination; and this is apparently proving acceptable to large numbers in both Churches. The ground for such a revision had been prepared by the production of a new Ordinal for the Church of Scotland in 1931,[16] and of an Ordinal for a similar scheme of reunion between Protestant Churches in South India.[17] It is interesting to note that, whereas the Eucharistic liturgy of the new Church of South India exercised comparatively little influence upon the recent revision of the English Communion Service, the Ordinal of that Church has very greatly affected the composition of the Anglican–Methodist Ordinal. At the same time the language of the new Ordinal

14. See above, note 8.

15. *Anglican Methodist Unity*, Report of the Anglican Methodist Unity Commission, Part I, 'The Ordinal', London, 1968.

16. *Ordinal and Service Book for Use in the Courts of the Church*, second edition, Oxford, 1954.

17. *The Church of South India. The Ordinal*, Oxford, 1958.

has been strengthened throughout, and both its structure and its language make it less susceptible to Roman Catholic criticism than that of 1662.[18]

The reader may rightly complain of breathlessness, if he has persevered to the end of this essay. But the writer also has cause for complaint; for he was set an impossible task. It is not easy to career through nineteen hundred years of Christian history, and it has only been achieved by constantly narrowing the subject – first of all, by limiting the inquiry to baptism and Eucharist alone; next, by restricting to the West the account of medieval developments; and finally, by showing a disproportionate interest in the Church of England among the Churches of the Reformation. It has also been achieved only by indulging in unbelievably loose statements and impossibly broad generalizations; but these, though offensive to the scholar, are inevitable, if the essay is to be intelligible to the ordinary reader. The writer would like to express his gratitude to those who over the years have taught him all that he knows; but he is prevented from mentioning them by name, for fear of connecting them in any way with his work.

18. *Anglican Orders*, The Bull of His Holiness Leo XIII, 13 September 1896, and the Answer of the Archbishops of England, 29 March 1897, London, 1932; *The Apostolic Constitution, Sacramentum Ordinis*, A.A.S. XL (1948).

The Study
of Modern
Ecclesiastical History
since 1930
by John Kent

Introduction

The history of modern Christianity – a period which stretches from the Reformation and Counter-Reformation to the present day – ought not to be studied only in terms of the Christian Church, as though such matters as the rise and fall of Calvinism, the amazing resilience of the Papacy, or the Anglican obsession with episcopacy, exhausted the subject. The recent history of Christianity is part of the history of the religious life of modern man, a history which shows signs of culminating in a totally non-religious culture, at any rate as 'religion' has been understood in the past. For centuries, Christianity played a vital role in Western culture, so that art, science and literature all drew to some extent on religious sources, but at least as early as the sixteenth century, institutionalized Christianity began to lose its social authority, and a culture began to form – and is still forming – which makes little use of Christian ideas, symbols and rituals. Western Christian institutions struggled to retain their former ascendancy in society even after the French Revolution of 1789, but without much success, and so in the twentieth century Christianity is fighting for spiritual quite as much as for institutional survival, and events like the Second Vatican Council, or the emergence of an American school of Protestant theology which starts from the proposition that God is dead, have to be seen in this historical perspective. The most useful work of the modern Church historian is to make Western man's religious biography intelligible, and to relate his experience to the experience of those nurtured in the other great religions of the world. (This attitude has recently transformed the traditional, hagiographical, Church-centred missionary history, as we shall see later.) Church historians often think of themselves as servants of the Church when they should be thinking of themselves as independent students and interpreters of human religious behaviour.

It has to be admitted that some at least of the Church historians discussed in this essay (which covers the Church history which has been written since about 1930) have thought of themselves primarily as servants of the Church. The 1930s was not a healthy decade in which to write Church history (or theology, for that matter). The First World War and its aftermath had left Christian opinion shocked at the weakness of Christianity and anxious to be reassured that the traditional picture of the Church as the primary divine agency in the present world could be sustained. In such circumstances the Church historian was naturally tempted to assume the role of a propagandist, to write as a Defender of the Faithful, to varnish a little the story of what the Church had done in the world. It was hardly surprising that the best-known English book on Church history written at the time was *Church and State in the Eighteenth Century* (1934), by N. G. Sykes, who discovered unexpected welcome virtues, even religious feeling, in an eighteenth-century Church of England which for more than a century had been the almost undefended target for attack by Anglo-Catholic and secular historians.

This apologetic tendency was strengthened as time went on by the powerful influence of a German school of theologians whose leader, Karl Barth, for example, often wrote as though after the death and Resurrection of Jesus Christ human history had no meaning at all. A Christian interpretation of history, at once pessimistic and supranaturalistic in the sense that the only discernible meaning in history was said to be revealed to faith, and not to reason, became both familiar and popular after 1945. Karl Löwith wrote that 'the problem of history is unanswerable within its own perspectives. Historical processes as such do not bear the least evidence of a comprehensive and ultimate meaning. History as such has no outcome. There never has been and never will be an immanent solution to the problem of history, for man's historical experience is one of steady failure. Christianity, too, as a world-religion, is a complete failure.'[1] Statements like this were often made by theologians like Barth and Niebuhr, men who were not practising historians; more rarely, a professional historian echoed them, as did, for example, Herbert Butterfield in *Christianity and History* (1953), a book which was widely read and which summed up accurately the post-war mood of exhaustion and despair in which political programmes (if one had been interested in politics), the idea of progress (if one believed in humanity), liberal theology (if one had cared about the existence of God), were alike repudiated by Christians who grasped eagerly at Butterfield's exhortation that 'they hold fast to Christ, and for the rest be totally uncommitted.'[2]

Side by side with this tendency to dismiss human history – and with it the day to day history of the Church – as of no significance, was a new theological emphasis on the importance of the Church, a theological attempt to reassert the indispensability of a declining institution. What was rejected was the nineteenth-century liberal individualistic view of the Church, classically described by Adolf Harnack in *What is Christianity?* (Berlin, 1900): 'We are well aware that in the interests of order and instruction outward and visible communities must arise . . . but we do not hang our hearts upon them, for they may exist today and tomorrow give place, under other political and social conditions, to new organizations; let anyone who has such a church have it as though he had it not.'[3] What was affirmed was the direct opposite: the idea of the Church as a corporate society, supernaturally founded and endowed, with a right to the obedience of the individual member, and assured of historical continuity. And so the Church historian was sometimes tempted to think of his subject as a special case, of the

1. Karl Löwith, *The Meaning of History*, Chicago, 1949, p. 191.
2. H. Butterfield, *Christianity and History*, London, 1953, p. 146.
3. A. Harnack, *What is Christianity?*, English translation 1901, pp. 276–7.

Church as somehow withdrawn from normal history. Significantly, a renewal of interest in the Reformation period produced excellent studies of sixteenth-century theology, but contributed little to the study of the social, economic and political matrix of the Reformation.

More recently, there have been signs of a return to the tradition in which Mandell Creighton, the Victorian founder of the study of modern Church history in this country, said that ecclesiastical history was just like constitutional history or economic history, and must be pursued in exactly the same way, and in exactly the same spirit, as any other branch of history. Studies of the clash between Christianity and non-Christian cultures, of the Protestant revivalist tradition in the United States, of the structure of the French Catholic Church in the eighteenth and nineteenth centuries – to take only a few examples – have suggested that a healthy secularization of the subject is once more under way.

The plan of this essay is as follows. In the opening chapter I have discussed the recent general histories of the modern Church, and in doing so have suggested that the optimistic slant of some of them is less reliable as history than the more critical attitude adopted, for instance, by A. R. Vidler. Then, instead of treating the whole period since the Reformation on a strictly chronological basis, I have started with the history of Christian missions in the modern era, a field which has been revolutionized since 1945 by the growth of a school of historians who are prepared to question the motives, the methods and the results of the missionaries, and to look at the missionary movement as much from the point of view of the missioned as from that of the missioner.

The third chapter, 'The Reformation and the Sixteenth Century', discusses the state of the controversy about the place of religion in the rise of Western capitalism; the new Roman Catholic historical scholarship which takes a positive view of the Protestant Reformation and which treats the work of the Council of Trent as something human and fallible; and the general renewal of interest in the fringes of the Protestant world, the Anabaptists and Socinians. This is followed by a chapter on seventeenth-century America and England which is chiefly about Puritan and Nonconformist history.

One of the more neglected areas of modern Church history, at any rate as far as British and American scholars are concerned, is the history of the continental Churches since about 1550. This is dealt with in Chapter Five, which includes books on European Church history between 1550 and 1789. Much more has been written about the eighteenth-century Church in England, and in Chapter Six I have given some account of work done on Hanoverian Anglicanism. One feature of Church historical writing since 1930, moreover, has been the rapid increase in the number of studies of John Wesley and of the history of the Methodist Church, and so I have dealt with these separately in Chapter Seven.

The remainder of the essay is given over to various aspects of nineteenth-century and twentieth-century Church history. Here it seemed necessary to begin with a general introduction on what I have described as the 'Anglican Mythology', because the study of nineteenth-century English Church history is still deeply influenced by attitudes and interpretations which have hung over from the Victorian period itself. One has to put aside the assumptions involved in this traditional way of looking at the recent past before one can see the Victorian Church in a more accurate perspective. The extent to which a new perspective exists is then looked at in three separate chapters: Chapter Nine discusses recent books on Anglo-Catholicism, John Henry Newman, and Catholic Modernism; Chapter 10 covers the Anglican Evangelical tradition; Chapter 11 groups together books about Liberal Protestantism and Christian Socialism. These are very broad headings; they are themselves a product of the Victorian past; they certainly do not exhaust the ways in which nineteenth-century English Church history can be approached; but they cover the majority of the approaches which have been made to the subject so far. I have added to the section on Christian Socialism another – Chapter 12 – on some excellent studies of American social Christianity;

this leads into a chapter on the nineteenth-century and twentieth-century European Churches.

The last long section of the essay – Chapter 14 – is on the importance of the sociology of religion for the Church historian, and on some of the results, in the way of the study of popular religion, that have already been achieved. Some of the most interesting of these I have distinguished in a separate chapter on American Revivalism. The final chapter is no more than a brief note on the impossibility of writing serious history about the Ecumenical Movement at the present time. In the Conclusion I have summed up my impressions about the state of the Church history as a discipline in the light of what has happened since 1930.

One

General Histories of the Modern Church

That optimism is the occupational temptation of the Church historian becomes evident when one reads the general histories of the modern Church which have been published over the past forty years. The standard general history remains the *Histoire de l'Église*, edited by A. Fliche and V. Martin (Paris, 1934–). The work, planned in twenty-six volumes, of which twenty-one have been published, is unfortunately largely unavailable in English; a translation, by E. C. Messenger, stopped at the fourth century. As it happens, however, this Roman Catholic series is less good on the modern than on the medieval period, though there is a fine volume by Roger Aubert on the pontificate of Pius the Ninth (1952). Also originally in French, but now appearing in English, is the late Émile Léonard's *Histoire Générale du Protestantisme*. This came out in three volumes: *La Réformation* (Paris, 1961), which ended in 1564; *L'Établissement* (1961), which covered the years 1564–1700; and a posthumous volume, published in 1964 and only partly by Léonard himself, *Déclin et renouveau*, which brought the story down to the present. Even in the French version, these volumes had many bibliographical and printing faults; in addition, Léonard was thin on the history of British Protestantism. When a translation of the first volume, by Joyce H. M. Reid, was issued in 1966, H. H. Rowley corrected the bibliographies. The second volume, which was published in 1967, was hardly a book for the general reader. Even the title, *The Establishment*, did not exactly convey the intention of the French, which suggests the settling down, or establishment, of classical

Protestantism; the text was still full of errors, especially where names were concerned.[1]

In English, the most famous historian in our period has been Kenneth Scott Latourette, Sterling Professor of Missions and Oriental History at Yale University, who has published *A History of the Expansion of Christianity* (seven volumes, 1938–45), and *Christianity in a Revolutionary Age* (five volumes, 1959–63). Latourette's great virtue was that Europe was not the permanent and only possible centre of his historical universe; with his volumes may be compared Stephen Neill's *History of Christian Missions* (1964, the sixth and final volume of the Pelican History of the Church), another study of Christian expansion as a whole and a kind of pocket Latourette. For England alone, the best recent general study is *A History of the Church in England* (1953), by J. R. H. Moorman; for Scottish Church history since the Reformation one may consult J. H. S. Burleigh's *A Church History of Scotland* (1960); for Ireland there is the three-volume *History of the Church of Ireland* edited by W. A. Phillips (1932); there seems no equivalent for Wales.

Of all these writers Latourette is at once the best known, the most widely ranging and the most optimistic. In both the works mentioned above he advocated a 'wave theory' of Christian history, according to which Christianity, after an unpromising beginning, has progressed by a series of pulsations of advance, retreat and advance. Each advance, according to Latourette, has carried the tide of Christianity further than its predecessors, while each major recession has been shorter and less marked than the one which preceded it. In the mid twentieth century, in fact, according to Latourette, Christianity is more of a force than it has ever been, an optimistic view in which a European is likely to see reflected the self-confidence of the United States of America both as a political power and as one of the few remaining areas in which classical Christian institutions appear to flourish. Latourette, however, is innocent of irony. One

1. H. H. Rowley was again the editor; the translator R. M. Bethell. Léonard was himself a French Protestant.

should compare his view of the strength of modern Christianity with that of another, more sophisticated American Church historian, W. D. McLaughlin, who, in *Modern Revivalism* (1959), an analysis of the revivalist system in the United States, said that 'even if revivalists could be credited for the fact that America today has proportionately more church members, more church wealth, and more church activity than any other nation in the world, it would not be an enviable achievement. For in spite of, or perhaps because of, this quantitative religiosity, America has also acquired a reputation as the most materialistic and secularistic nation in the world.'[2]

Here, however, Professor Latourette's professionalism has fought a losing battle with his piety, perhaps because he cannot quite believe that a religion can be declining spiritually if it can be shown to be growing statistically. Few secular historians, however, would be likely to accept a 'wave theory' of Christian history according to which the Christian Church has in the long run steadily increased its strength in human society. In terms of such an idea one is bound to doubt Latourette's grasp on the central concept of a 'revolutionary age' and of its effect on Christianity. In these general histories, in which the emphasis must lie on the interpretation of the detail rather than on the details themselves, the question of perspective is vital, and it is a very unsatisfactory state of affairs if one feels obliged again and again to turn to the secular historian for a more convincing interpretation of the mass of facts which writers like Latourette collect. E. J. Hobsbawm, for example, writing about Europe after 1789, said:

> The bourgeoisie ... remained divided in its ideology between a minority of increasingly frank free-thinkers and a majority of the pious, Protestant, Jewish, and Catholic. However, the new historic fact was that of the two the free-thinking sector was immeasurably more dynamic and effective. Though in purely quantitative terms religion remained immensely strong and . . . grew stronger, it was no longer (to use a biological analogy) dominant but recessive, and had remained so to this day within the world transformed by the

2. *Modern Revivalism*, New York, 1959, p. 529.

dual revolution (in France and America). The most obvious proof of this decisive victory of secular over religious ideology is also its most important result. With the American and French Revolutions major political and social transformations were secularised. The issues of the Dutch and English revolutions of the sixteenth and seventeenth centuries had still been discussed and fought out in the traditional language of Christianity, orthodox, schismatic or heretical. In the ideologies of the American and French, for the first time, in European history, Christianity is irrelevant.... The ideology of the new working-class and socialist movements was secularist from the start. . . .[3]

Here Hobsbawm seems a more reliable guide to Church history than Latourette with his facile optimism. This is the kind of secular judgement which a Church historian must either accept or refute if he is to offer any serious interpretation of ecclesiastical history in the post-Reformation period. Another example would be A. J. P. Taylor's view that by the 1930s England had ceased to be significantly Christian, an event as important, he thought, as any in English history since the conversion of the Anglo-Saxons.[4]

The authors we are discussing, however, do not start from such a basic interpretation. Their reasons differ. By Anglo-Saxon ecumenical standards Émile Léonard's French Protestantism was of a nineteenth-century individualistic kind, deficient in a proper understanding of the Church as an institution. Léonard would not have minded the criticism. He interpreted sixteenth-century Protestantism as at least potentially a layman's Christianity in which both priest and Church were optional; he interpreted twentieth-century Western society's attitude to religion as anti-clericalism combined with indifference to Church structures: if Protestantism learned once again to travel light both theologically and ecclesiastically it might

3. E. J. Hobsbawm, *The Age of Revolution, 1789–1848*, 1962, p. 220.

4. A. J. P. Taylor, *English History 1914–1945*, 1965, p. 168. Taylor gave little space to the event, however, perhaps because he thought that 'the weakening of Christian dogma had little immediate result other than the decline of church attendance.... England remained Christian in morality, though not in faith' (p. 169).

still, he thought, offer itself successfully as a layman's religion to laymen.

Léonard did not come to terms with the twentieth century's alienation from Christianity, even in its more extreme Protestant forms; J. R. H. Moorman is equally determined to be hopeful about the future. Despite, or perhaps because of, its title, *The History of the Church in England* is a traditional history of the Church *of* England – in his account of the nineteenth-century, for example, the Nonconformists appear principally as people who do not want to pay Church rates, and it is probably not an accident that he defines the Church of South India as a union of the Church of England 'with other Christian bodies in South India, Presbyterian, Congregationalist and Methodist' (p. 421). For Moorman the Church of England of his 1958 edition had, one gathered, weathered the storms of the previous hundred years. Theological Modernism was in full retreat, no longer either modern or progressive; parochial worship was improving; what Church membership had lost in quantity had to some extent been made up in quality; and even the great increase in divorce might be said to have 'stimulated interest in the Church's responsibility for those who seek the sacrament of Holy Matrimony' (p. 428).

The later volumes of the Pelican History of the Church, on the other hand, give the impression of a franker, more objective reaction to the course of modern Church history. These volumes (which will be discussed in more detail in connexion with the periods which they describe) are *The Reformation* by Owen Chadwick (1964), which comes down to 1648, *The Church and the Age of Reason* by G. R. Cragg (1960), which covers 1648–1789, and *The Church in an Age of Revolution* by Alec R. Vidler (1961), which ended in the mid twentieth century. The division of the series at the French Revolution accepted a secular convention. No doubt any dividing line could be criticized, but the movement of spiritual renewal which spread from the seventeenth-century French Catholic Church, through German Pietism into eighteenth-century Anglo-Saxon Evangelicalism did not exhaust itself until the mid nineteenth century. In this sense it is arguable that the natural break in modern Church history comes at about the time of the publication of Charles Darwin's *Origin of Species* in 1859. The reaction of the Church to the French Revolution was one of outraged aggression, a counter-attack which still appealed confidently to the past; but by the mid nineteenth century the note was changing as the Church went over to the defensive, a posture which it has retained.

In his Epilogue to the Pelican History of the Church A. R. Vidler recognized all this, and broke decisively with the optimism which the Church historian has so often seemed to feel the obligatory attitude of his métier:

> All in all, while the Churches have survived and their future is still open, it can hardly be said that they have revived in such a way as to offer an assurance to the dispassionate observer that they will not become mere survivals in a world that will have no further use for them ... Christopher Dawson once observed that 'men today are divided between those who have kept their spiritual roots and lost their contact with the existing order of society, and those who have preserved their social contacts and lost their spiritual roots'. To survey the history of the Church since the French Revolution is to be made aware of this schism in the soul of modern man. It does not enable one to say with confidence whether or not the schism can be healed.

Two

The History of Christian Missions in the Modern Era

The history of Christian missions is the most recent and in some ways the most promising branch of modern Church history. The swift Communist triumph in China in the late 1940s, the slower but equally impressive post-war emergence of a self-governing black Africa, the withdrawal of the British from the continent of India, were events that had not really been anticipated in missionary circles before 1939. The removal of the protecting European powers closed an era in missionary history which had begun in the 1790s: it also left the actual results of missionary work (as distinct from the glowing propaganda accounts of the past) a little cruelly exposed. Once again it is perhaps Vidler, in *The Church in an Age of Revolution*, who is most explicit about the limits of what the missionary societies achieved in the nineteenth century:

> In most areas of the world Christian missions got only quite a small footing proportionately to the total population. Between the wars, for example, the Christians numbered only two per cent of the population of India, in China one per cent, in Japan half per cent. Admittedly, in many countries the Christians were able to exercise more influence through their schools and other institutions and the quality of their converts than their actual numbers would suggest. But the nineteenth-century missionary movement had serious weaknesses and imperfections, apart from those which mark all human enterprises. (p. 251)

And Vidler goes on to suggest that the nineteenth-century missionaries were compromised in the eyes of those to whom they went by what seemed too close a connexion with Western imperialism; were not as skilful in converting members of the ruling classes and higher castes as they were in fostering Christian movements among the poorer social groups; were powerfully inspired for much of the nineteenth century by the belief that the heathen had to be saved from the certainty of eternal damnation but could not derive equal inspiration from later, more liberal forms of Christianity; and were very slow to realize that Christianity in Africa, India and elsewhere need not be strait-jacketed in Western institutions and conventions of worship. It might also be added that the nineteenth-century assumption that all non-Christian religions were 'lower' forms of religious activity which would wither away in the near future turned out to be a total misreading of the situation.

Comments of this kind are based on the missionary history which has been written since 1945. Some missionaries themselves have been anxious to find out why more had not been accomplished in order to modify missionary policy in the newly independent states; professional historians – in America as well as in Europe – found a new field in the study of Victorian imperialism. To others it seemed that the mission fields, objectively considered, offered an excellent context in which to examine the relation between society and religion, and to analyse the role of society in religious behaviour, for Christianity entered non-European cultures as a new, competitive religious movement whose communicability, influence and basic meaning could all be studied against a background which was not soaked in centuries of Christian assumptions. And so a new branch of Church history has gradually been developing which has transformed the study of missions from what it was as recently as 1939, an excuse for not very exacting biographies and for self-applauding narrative accounts of the various missionary societies.

The history of Christianity in modern China, for example, has been the subject of a number of excellent recent studies. The quantity of earlier material had not been matched by quality, for there was obvious anxiety to justify the missionaries against Western criticism, and therefore a strong tendency to see the history of missions in China as one phase of missions all over the world. This Western-centred approach still characterized K. S. Latourette's *History of Christian Missions in China* (1929), which gathered up the then existing material.

Since the Second World War, however, and especially since the Communist take-over in China, scholars have increasingly concentrated on Chinese history for its own sake, and have attempted to study the Christian mission fields from the point of view of Chinese, not European, or even 'ecumenical' history. American scholars have predominated, although one of the best books on modern Chinese history, *The Boxer Uprising* (1963), by Victor Purcell, was written in England. Among the most important studies are: *Imperial Government and Catholic Missions in China, 1784–1785*, by Bernard H. Willeke (St Bonaventure, New York, 1948); *Missionary and Mandarin. The Jesuits at the Court of China*, by Arnold Rowbotham (Berkeley, 1942); and *Apostolic Legations to China in the Eighteenth Century*, by Antonia Sisto Rosse (Pasadena, 1948). Both these last books discuss the Rites Controversy, and Cardinal de Tournon's mission to Peking in 1705. For the mid nineteenth century there is a valuable French work, *La Politique missionaire de la France en Chine, 1842–1856*, by Wei Tsing Sing (Paris, 1960), important because of the preponderance of Roman Catholic missionaries in China before 1860. There is also *Christian Influence upon the Ideology of the Taiping Rebellion*, by Eugene Boardman (Madison, 1952), to which may be added his paper, 'Millenary Aspects of the Taiping Rebellion, 1851–1864', in *Millennial Dreams in Action*, a symposium published by the journal *Comparative Studies in Society and History* (The Hague, 1962). Boardman's was the first serious attempt to penetrate the haze which had always obscured the relationship between the Taipings and Christianity. More recent studies of the mid nineteenth century include *The Last Stand of Chinese Conservatism, 1862–1874*, by Mary Clabough Wright (Stamford, 1957), a book which is partly concerned with the events leading up to the massacre of Christians in Tientsin in 1870; and *China and Christianity,*

1860–1870, by Paul Cohen (Harvard, 1963). A related study was *Wang T'ao*, by H. McAleavy (1953).

The most studied period of Chinese mission history, however, is the Boxer troubles of 1900. The Chinese Communist Government has published large quantities of primary source material relating to the Boxer period, for in modern China the Boxers are regarded as the leaders of a people's revolt against the encroaching Western powers. Some of these documents were used by Chester Tan, in *The Boxer Catastrophe* (Columbia, 1955), and he was followed by Victor Purcell in *The Boxer Uprising* (1963). There is Edmund Wehrle's *Britain, China and the Anti-Missionary Riots, 1891–1900* (Minnesota, 1966). Another remarkable American book completes this review of recent Chinese history with a Christian slant, *Missionaries, Chinese and Diplomats, the American Protestant Missionary Movement in China, 1890–1952* (Princeton, 1958), by Paul A. Varg. It is not an unimportant point that these later books have superseded in large part George Steigner's *China and the Occident. The Origin and Development of the Boxer Movement* (New Haven, 1927), which was written without the benefit of the recently published Chinese sources. Peter Fleming's *The Siege at Peking* (1959) throws no useful light on missionary history, and Dom Columba Cary-Elwes' *China and the Cross* (1957) is a depressing example of the older style of missionary writing, an account of the withdrawal of Protestant missionaries from China after the final defeat of Chiang-kai-Shek which regards the successful evacuation of the Europeans as a wonderful instance of Divine Providence but shows little interest in the fact that the Chinese Christians themselves had, after all, to remain behind.

The verdict of these secular historians is not very encouraging for the admirers of the missions. Cohen, Purcell and Wehrle, for instance, would accept the view of Joseph Needham that

four times in history was China offered the possibility of adopting organised Christianity ... but the missions always failed, and the fact must be faced by Westerners that the Christian religion in its organised forms has been decisively rejected by the Chinese culture ... this necessarily followed from the highly organic structure of the Chinese humanistic morality which could not but view with distaste a religion placing so tragic an emphasis on transcendence, and which was therefore so dogmatic and ecclesiastical. (Quoted in Purcell, op. cit.)

Cohen, moreover, has shown in some detail that a Chinese tradition of anti-Christianity goes back to the seventeenth century (some of whose anti-Christian writings were actually widely used again in the nineteenth century) so that hostility to the nineteenth-century missionaries cannot simply be explained as a by-product of Chinese hatred for the Western powers (including the United States) which were exploiting China. In fact, the Roman Catholics had suffered a severe persecution in 1784–5. The statement made in 1900 by the Protestant missionary societies that 'there is no evidence that the persecution of the Christians and the attacks on the Christians have any religious basis such as was so prominent a feature in the Indian Mutiny' cannot be taken at its face value. The Boxers *were* anti-Christian.

The historian would not accept this missionary failure as an eradicable failure in technique, but would see it rather as a blind collision between two mutually uncomprehending bodies. Even in defending themselves against criticism the Protestant missionary societies quoted above still talked about China's need for Christian civilization, and dismissed Chinese society as a 'huge anachronism'. Wehrle says that there is no doubt that some British missionaries hoped to see the Yangtze valley incorporated into the British Empire as a step towards civilization, though partition of China was never an aim of British official policy in the nineteenth century. Many missionaries saw no more in Confucianism than a Chinese pharisaism, an incubus; they attacked the Confucian gentry with the verbal aggressiveness of a Griffith John, the late nineteenth-century Nonconformist missionary; while Cohen points out that even a more tolerant man, like Timothy Richards, was deeply committed to changing Chinese society.

The nature of the change demanded should not be misunderstood, for it is one of the main points of P. A. Varg's book that until 1945 – until in fact it was too late – the missionary societies had not regarded the economic and social problems of China as part of their business, and so were taken by surprise by the strength and still more the popularity of the Marxist thrust. In fact, of course, as in Africa, the missionaries had less faith in the value of Western culture as a whole than they sometimes asserted; it was an ideal, and not an actual, Christian civilization which they sought to make out of China; at times they resembled the Puritans of the seventeenth century, who went to America to build a perfect Christian community which should be untainted by European corruption. As a Chinese intellectual, Wen Chung, pointed out about 1900, they did not encourage independence of thought in their converts, but kept them as long as possible to a Chinese equivalent of the medieval Christian world picture. It is significant, as Purcell says, that the education offered by the missionaries in the later nineteenth century failed to offer the stimulus or the information that the Chinese reforming party – such as the group surrounding the young Emperor, Tsai T'ien, deposed for his pains in 1898 – would have needed in transforming the Manchu governing class. Purcell underlines the extraordinary nature of Timothy Richards' choice of *The Nineteenth Century, A History* (1880), by a Scottish journalist from Dundee, Robert Mackenzie, as the book best calculated (in 1893) to convey to Chinese readers in translation the essence of Western achievement. Perhaps a million copies of this all too mediocre work were circulated in the late nineteenth century, and it was a principal source of Chinese information about Europe at the time. What it (temporarily) concealed was the existence of powerful non-Christian traditions in Western culture itself.

The missionaries did not see the irony contained in the verdict of the British Representative in China in 1870, Sir Rutherford Alcock (who would have liked to be empowered to confine their efforts to the coastal cities): 'What 30,000 pulpits and preachers cannot do in Great Britain at the present day, is not, so far as human means are concerned, to be accomplished by 200 or 300 teachers of an alien race, and of differing and conflicting sects and churches, however earnest they may be as men' (quoted in Cohen, op. cit.). This remained true in 1900, when the number of Christian workers had mounted rapidly to just over 2,800. At the same time the missionaries indirectly helped to destroy the authority of the Manchu government – for on the one hand they made it impossible for the British Government to preserve the 'informal imperialism' which guided their actions in China, while the Chinese xenophobia which resulted made it equally hard for the Chinese Government to fulfil its treaty obligations, a failure which further weakened the Manchu dynasty.

Here, as in other parts of the world, much remains for historians to do to break down the over-simplified concept of a 'Christian missionary' who preaches 'the Gospel', and to replace it with a pattern which reflects the complex interaction of missionaries who often preached something other than 'the Gospel' (if this can be defined at all) and alien, self-sufficient societies. In a recent discussion of the relationship between the well-known cargo cults of the South Pacific and missionary Christianity, Mircéa Eliade, the famous Rumanian social anthropologist, gave a brilliant analysis of how this confrontation might on occasion actually take place:

> If so many cargo cults have assimilated Christian ideas, it is because the natives have rediscovered in Christianity their old traditional eschatological myth. If the natives came to feel disappointed in the missionary, if the majority of the cargo cults ultimately turned anti-Christian, it was not on account of anything in Christianity itself, but because the missionaries and their converts did not appear to conduct themselves as true Christians. The disillusionments that the natives suffered in their encounter with official Christianity were many and tragic. For what attracted the natives to Christianity the most powerfully was the preaching of the renewal of the world, the imminent arrival of Christ and the resurrection of the dead; it was the prophetic and eschatological

aspects of religion that awakened in them the most profound echo. But it was precisely these aspects of Christianity that the missionaries in practice seemed to ignore or not take seriously. The millenarist movement became savagely anti-Christian when their leaders realised that the missionaries, who had indirectly inspired them, did not really believe in the arrival of the ships of the dead bearing gifts, that in effect they did not believe in the imminence of the Kingdom, the resurrection of the dead, or the establishment of Paradise. (*Millennial Dreams in Action*, ed. S. L. Thrupp, The Hague, 1962, p. 143)

This is certainly not what the older school of missionary historians meant by missionary history. They were chiefly concerned about the development of the missionary societies, and were too close to their material to grasp how bizarre an episode was the invasion of the South Pacific by evangelizing mid-Victorians. We, however, at a greater distance of time, can see that the inner content of the religious behaviour stimulated by the intervention of the missionaries in the existing native cultures mattered far more than what happened to the missionary societies themselves.[1] We are also in a position to see how many different strands were woven into this religious behaviour, and how easily the Victorian missionaries deceived themselves about the degree of Christianity reached by their converts.

Valuable documentation of this may be found in *The History of the Tahitian Mission* by John Davies, an important original source which was reprinted by the Hakluyt Society in 1961. This account of the Protestant missionary activity in the islands covers the years 1799 to 1830; at no point does Davies show himself fully aware of the degree to which his presence had altered the Tahitian situation and contributed to the decline of a civilization. Another recent Pacific study is *From Mission-*

1. The missionaries, that is, estimated their success in terms of the rate at which they set up and expanded a new, separate Church; modern critics are much more interested in the fate of the whole new society, Christian and non-Christian, which the missionaries helped the administrators and businessmen to form.

field to Independent Church (1958), by Hendrik Kraemer, but the historical value of this discussion of Dutch missionary work in Indonesia is limited by the author's preponderant interest in missionary theology and technique.

In the study of India and Ceylon recent historical research has been concerned less with the missionary societies themselves than with the role of Christianity in the development and collapse of British rule in the East. As for the societies pure and simple, *The Church of South India* (1954), by the Swedish scholar, Bengt Sundkler, is a straightforward account of the movement towards Church unity in Southern India; *Bishops and Societies*, a study of Anglican colonial and missionary expansion, 1698–1850, by H. Cnattingius (1952), is a discussion of the long Anglican controversy over the place of episcopacy in missionary work – should the bishop go as a pioneer to found a new diocese, or should the bishop be called in only after missionary societies had already established Christianity? – and *The Church at the Gateway of India* (Bombay, 1960), by J. H. Gense, is really the only history of Roman Catholic missions in India, but is very traditional in approach.

On a broader and much more significant field, a series of studies has illuminated the official role of Christianity in eighteenth-century and nineteenth-century India and Ceylon (the problem of religious behaviour has not been so carefully investigated). Among these are *Charles Grant and British Rule in India*, by Ainslie Embree (1962); *Reformers in India 1793–1833*, by Kenneth Ingham (1956); *The English Utilitarians in India*, by Eric Stokes (1959), which discusses Anglican Evangelical as well as Benthamite influences; *British Attitudes towards India, 1784–1848*, by George Bearce (1961); S. B. Chauduri, *Civil Rebellion in the Indian Mutinies*, a book which is important when one is considering how far India was suffering general discontent in 1857, and what part the missionary societies had played in early nineteenth-century India; Thomas Metcalfe's very interesting study, *The Aftermath of Revolt in India, 1857–1870* (Princeton, 1964); and *Clemency Canning*, by Michael Maclagan (1962). In the case of Ceylon there is K. M. de Silva's excellent book, *Social Policy and Missionary Organisations in Ceylon, 1840–1855* (1965).

Taken together, these studies (and others like them) necessitate a revision of the older account according to which the Christian missionary societies had gradually made triumphant headway against a combination of the darkness and idolatry of Hinduism and the cynicism and obstruction of Government. (This version still appears without radical change in Stephen Neill, op. cit., who dismisses the Indian Mutiny as an unimportant interruption in the steady advance of the Gospel in India.) In fact, as Ainslie Embree shows in *Charles Grant and British Rule in India*, this whole picture of India as a land of moral darkness and idolatry owes much to the efforts of Charles Grant and his friend William Wilberforce, who perhaps succeeded better in moulding the average Englishman's opinion of India and the Indian peoples than they did in converting the Indians to Anglican Evangelical Christianity. Charles Grant's 'Observations on the State of India among the Asiatic Subjects of Great Britain' had an influence beyond its author's wildest dreams. He wrote the original essay in 1792, when he was trying to ensure that the new Charter of the East India Company should include what was called the Pious Clause, which would have obliged the Company to take active steps to Christianize India; Wilberforce popularized Grant's arguments in England; the essay was printed in 1813 and by 1820 it was the Evangelical source-book and final authority on India and Indian policy. Grant denounced Indian society as corrupt and traced all its evils to the Hindu religion; the evangelization of India was a necessary preliminary to its good government. He said that there was no foreseeable future 'in which we may not govern our Asiatic subject better than they can be governed by themselves', but that the Indians could not be expected to suffer British rule indefinitely unless they were Christianized. All this material was given great publicity in 1813 when the East India Company's Charter came up for renewal. Grant and Wilberforce, who wanted the legalization of the entry of missionaries into India and the appointment of an Anglican bishop, mobilized British public opinion in a campaign of a type that was to be repeated again and again in the Victorian period. Those who opposed the work of the missionaries were said to be ready to trample on the Cross of Christ. A journal, *The Missionary Register*, was started, full of vilification of Hinduism and praise for the missionaries. An unprecedented number of petitions was gathered, and the Government gave way to Wilberforce, but much more important than this local victory was the fact that the kind of propaganda used in this struggle was to affect the British attitude to India for generations. Something of the long prestige of Grant's opinions is evident when one realizes that the so-called 'Christian policy' (see below) which was advocated in mission circles after the *débâcle* of 1857 was little more than a *réchauffé* of his views.

The most interesting analysis of the situation created for Christianity by the Mutiny is to be found in Thomas R. Metcalfe's *The Aftermath of Revolt in India, 1857–1870*, which shows that once the Mutiny had been put down there was general agreement in non-missionary circles that Dalhousie's well-meant reforms had been mistaken and that the spread of Christianity, which had had the apparent support of the British administration, had thoroughly alarmed both Hindus and Muslims for the future of their own religions. These conclusions, which meant that official opinion held the missionary societies partly responsible for the Indian rebellion, were denied by the missionaries at the time. They repeated Grant's argument that British rule in India required the Christianization of the country (without seeing that this meant a British withdrawal, since the Christianization of India was improbable in any likely future); they said that Indian Christians had remained loyal to Britain in the rising, which they attributed to the failure of the administration to support Christianity more openly. They demanded a more vigorous pro-Christian policy, just as Grant had done after the Vellore Sepoy Mutiny of 1807, and said that the Government should ignore all caste distinctions, sever all connexion with the rites and customs of Hinduism, introduce the Bible into Indian schools as a class-book, and take whatever other steps were needed to propagate the faith of the occupying power. This policy was advocated by famous missionary leaders like Alexander Duff. In practice, however, the administration drew quite the opposite conclusion from the revolt (official opinion would have agreed with S. B. Chauduri's diagnosis of considerable civil as well as military discontent in 1857, in *Civil Rebellion in the Indian Mutinies*). The Indian Mutiny, in fact, marked the end of the real power and influence of Christian opinion in India, a power which had depended far more on the Evangelical Anglican laymen who held prominent positions in the Punjab, for example, than upon the efforts of the missionaries themselves. From the 1860s official circles, when liberal at all, agreed with Matthew Arnold's brother, Henry, that Britain held India in trust for the Indians themselves, and had no special mission to change the religious behaviour of the country.

The primary impression given one by these studies of nineteenth-century Protestant Evangelical effort in China and India is that of the self-confident aggressiveness of the Evangelical world, and the impression is deepened by K. M. de Silva's book, *Social Policy and Missionary Organisations in Ceylon, 1840–1855*. De Silva shows in great detail how after 1805 consistent Anglican Evangelical pressure, directed more especially by James Stephen from his central position in the London Colonial Office, achieved, against the better judgement of the British administration on the spot, a complete severance of the links, dating from the Kandyan Convention of 1815, between the ancient Buddhism of Ceylon and the newly arrived British Government. 'Stephen's attitude on this subject', de Silva said, 'is a study of the darker side of Evangelicalism – its confident assumption of moral superiority, its intolerance and its bigotry.' Central to the Evangelical position was the assertion, first made in the case of India, that a Christian government ought not to associate itself in any way with an idolatrous religious system, such as Buddhism was held to be. In the background lay the belief of the missionaries that the withdrawal of what they claimed to be official recognition of Buddhism would accentuate its decline in Ceylon. De Silva contrasts this campaign, sustained over a long period and absorbing much energy, with the comparative lack of interest which the same missionary societies showed in Ceylon's social problems: caste, slavery and immigrant Indian labour. 'It was unhappily characteristic of the missionary movement in Ceylon at this time,' he concluded, 'that they seldom interested themselves in a social problem if it was not likely to bring a dividend of converts.'

In the case of Africa a similar general pattern has emerged. Over the past decade the process of reassessing the significance of the Western missionary movement has gathered speed. There were a few purely historical studies, of which the most important, and also the best book on modern Africa and Christianity, was *Independent African – John Chilembwe* (Edinburgh, 1958), by G. Shepperson and T. Price, a description and analysis of the Nyasaland native rising of 1915, a movement, quickly enough snuffed out at the time, which combined African nationalism, Christian eschatology, American Negro influence and a strong impulse to break with any form of Christianity which was identified with Europe or Britain: not much noticed in the midst of the First World War, John Chilembwe was a portent of the future of much of Africa. Christopher Fyfe's vast, idiosyncratic *History of Sierra Leone* (1964) also threw much light on missionary developments; *Mackenzie's Grave* (1962), by Professor Owen Chadwick, contained an interesting reappraisal of David Livingstone. Other books were prompted by the anxiety of the missionary world itself to understand what had happened in what had often seemed their most hopeful continent. An early, influential example of this was *The Missionary Factor in East Africa*, by Roland Oliver (1952); in retrospect, however, Roland Oliver seems to have been too sanguine about the influence of the missionaries, as appeared from J. V. Taylor's carefully documented study, *The Growth of the Church in Buganda* (1958), as well as

Christians of the Copperbelt (1961), which Taylor wrote in conjunction with Dorothea Lehmann. By 1958 it was possible – and, indeed, necessary – to say openly that much missionary work had been ineffective, over-Westernized and complacent. What this meant can be seen from a less critical work, *The Roots of Ghana Methodism* (1965), by F. Bartels, a former headmaster of Mfantsipim School, the oldest school in Ghana, and an actor in the events which set up an autonomous Methodist Church in Ghana in 1961, after 126 years of tutelage under the British Methodist Conference. Bartels was most interesting in what amounted to asides. As far back as 1880, he said, the European Methodist Chairman of Ghana recommended the complete Africanization of the mission, but nothing came of his proposals. The policy of making African Christianity an English religion meant that as late as 1950 *Pilgrim's Progress* was the one religious classic available in the vernacular to the African catechist who bore the greatest part of the pastoral care of the Church, and for three Sundays out of four in the towns 'the literate were found in the transepts of the church, the illiterate in the nave, silent spectators for the best part of the service' (p. 214). There was a similar conflict between the African religious world which had never been destroyed and the new Christian religion: 'there were in the Church men and women who were trying to live in two worlds, the world of a personal God and the world of the protecting influence of ancestral spirits and their forces of good against those of evil' (p. 233).[2]

In the meantime the Ibadan School of History had begun its own examination of the evidence. Two extremely interesting and scholarly studies have appeared: *Christian Missions in Nigeria, 1841–1891*, by J. F. A. Ajayi (1965), and *Missionary Enterprise and the Evolution of Modern Nigeria*, by E. A. Ayandele (1966), books which overlapped with one another and with J. B. Webster's *The African Churches among the Yoruba*,

2. The same point emerges even more clearly in *The Presbyterian Church of Ghana, 1835–1960*, by Noel Smith (1966): cf. especially Chapters 5 and 11.

1888–1922 (1964), an account of the independent African Churches which set themselves up in West Africa. In these books Henry Venn, Secretary of the Evangelical Anglican Church Missionary Society 1842–72, emerged as an African hero, rejected and betrayed by his own missionary society. Ayandele said of him that 'if any individual is to be credited with originating Nigerian nationalism', Venn was the man. He made an African, Samuel Crowther, Bishop of the Niger Mission in 1864, an experiment not tried elsewhere, and so Crowther became a 'romantic figure, the symbol of the Negro race, its ability to evangelize and its capability to rule' (op. cit., p. 182). After Venn's death the British C.M.S. missionaries on the West Coast turned sharply against his policy, which was really to create an indigenous Church as rapidly as possible; Crowther was disgraced in 1891, no African appointed to succeed him, and his alleged failure used for years afterwards as proof that Venn's policy was wrong in principle. This has become a highly controversial issue, and it is interesting to see that while Stephen Neill, in *Colonialism and Christian Missions* (1966) was still very loath to admit that the C.M.S. tradition was misleading, Canon Max Warren, on the other hand, in his *Social History and Christian Mission* (1967) felt bound to say that Venn's critics were 'missionaries of lesser vision' (p. 129). The change in missionary attitude which was implied here was in line with the general hardening in the attitude of the British towards their subject races in the generation after the Indian Mutiny (cf. *Africa and the Victorians*, R. Robinson, J. Gallacher and Alice Denny, 1961).

It is as well to bear this in mind when reading one of the few American sallies into African history, *Christian Missionaries and the Creation of Northern Rhodesia, 1880–1924*, by Robert I. Rotberg (Princeton, 1965). He concluded:

occasional successes there were, but total victory eluded and has continued to elude the missionaries. From the start, the missionaries compromised their message. As absolute power supposedly corrupts absolutely, so the isolation of their stations and their own heightened sense of moral and racial superiority tended to corrupt the attitude of the missionaries and to perpetuate the apparent tension between sermon and action. . . . They thus resembled white settlers, traders and officials in their inability to come to terms with the aspirations of Africans and the African mental environment. In this respect the experience of most of the missionaries in Northern Rhodesia differed decisively from that of their colleagues in neighbouring Nyasaland, where the Scottish Churches seem successfully to have recruited a cadre of exceptionally well-qualified representatives. (op. cit, pp. 145–6)

Independent African Churches were to appear in Rhodesia as a reaction to all this, as they did in East Africa (cf. *East African Rebels*, a study of some Independent Churches, by F. E. Welbourn, 1961), and in South Africa (cf. *Bantu Prophets in South Africa*, by B. G. M. Sundkler, 1948).[3]

All these studies are of great value for a future properly ecumenical Church history. There is also a historical question about the historical effects of nineteenth-century Western missionary expansion which will have to be answered, though it will not be answered very successfully if the task is left to men convinced that they have a duty to save the credit of God and the missionary societies, and that serious criticism of the societies is intolerable. No complete assessment of the over-all results of nineteenth-century Christian missions has yet been made, but there are grounds for the assertion that the final outcome of Victorian missionary aggression on East–West relations was disastrous, and that the full consequences of the mistakes that were made have not yet been seen. Such a conclusion might even be tolerable theologically to those who believe that human history has no significance in the eyes of God since the death and Resurrection of Christ, but is much less easily stomached by those who hold what may be termed a Christian humanist position.

3. For a general study, cf. *Post-Christianity in Africa*, by G. C. Oosthuizen, 1968.

Three

The Reformation and the Sixteenth Century

There have been perhaps three major developments in the study of sixteenth-century Church history since 1930. First, the destruction of the orthodoxy about 'religion and the rise of capitalism'; second, the emergence of Roman Catholic scholars prepared both to accept the Protestant bodies on their own terms and also to historicize the Council of Trent; third, the renewed interest in, and comparative respectability of, the outer fringe of the Protestant Reformers, the Anabaptists and Socinians.

The economic and social history of the sixteenth-century Church has been more carefully examined than that of subsequent centuries, and for many years it has been taken for granted that some special relationship existed between the Protestant Reformation and the rise of modern capitalism. This theory was first advanced by the German historical sociologist, Max Weber, in *The Protestant Ethic and the Spirit of Capitalism* (1904), of which an English translation appeared as recently as 1930. Weber suggested that modern capitalism was a by-product of the Protestant ethos; in 1926, R. H. Tawney, in *Religion and the Rise of Capitalism*, gave even wider currency to the thesis that Calvinism prospered by adapting itself to the capitalist spirit. Either way, Protestantism became somehow (the causation was never demonstrated very clearly) guilty of the sins of modern capitalist society. Both theories were rendered almost untenable by K. Samuelsson in *Religion and Economic Action* (English translation by E. G. French, ed. D. C. Coleman, 1961), who showed in full historical detail how institutionalized religion, Catholic as well as Protestant, resisted the growth of the new economic order. As Professor G. R. Elton summed up:

> It was not Calvinism that freed men from the restraints of the traditional moral concepts in economics, but emancipation from religion and theology in general which enabled men, pursuing the logic of palpable economic fact, either to ignore the thunders of their clergy or ultimately to persuade some clergy to come to terms. The late medieval schoolmen had suffered the same fate. ... In the face of the long, ramifying controversy sadness is the only proper thing: sadness at so much misguided effort, and sadness at the willingness of historians to worship the graven images set up by the sociologist. (*Reformation Europe, 1517–1599*, 1963)

Elton's book was the best general introduction to the period; for its Church history in particular, the best recent text-book was *The Reformation Era, 1500–1650*, by H. J. Grimm (New York, 1954); the relevant volume of the Pelican History of the Church, *The Reformation* by Professor Owen Chadwick (1964), also ran down to the middle of the seventeenth century.

The change in the Roman Catholic attitude to the Reformation and to Martin Luther came slowly but surely. For centuries Luther had simply been regarded as the heretic who destroyed the unity of the Church and endangered countless souls. Personal attacks on him were common, and neither Heinrich Denifle, whose *Luther und Luthertum* was published in Mainz in 1903, nor Hartmann Grisar, whose three-volume *Luther* appeared in Freiburg in 1911–12, the two most prominent Catholic scholars of the Reformation at the beginning of the present century, was able to take Luther seriously as a religious figure. The scholar most responsible for changing this situation was Joseph Lortz, whose most important *Die Reformation in Deutschland* (Freiburg, 1939) has just been translated into English. Lortz, though inclined to regard Luther as unduly subjectivist, nevertheless described him as an unwilling rebel, a man whose grasp of the core of true Catholicism was frustrated by an institution which itself was not completely representative of Catholicism. Breaking with the judgement of the past, Lortz held that the Roman Church could not avoid some share of the responsibility for the division between Catholicism and Protestantism. Lortz's views did not win immediate assent, but a younger generation of German Catholic scholars, A. Bradenburg, Erwin Iserloh and Hubert Jedin, for example, have continued to build on the foundations he laid. One is bound to add, however, that there is no corresponding Catholic interest in, or fresh appreciation of, John Calvin.

The Roman change of attitude towards the Council of Trent, however, is at least as important as the change in the interpretation of Luther. It is closely associated with the name of Lortz's pupil, Hubert Jedin. As long ago as 1931 he wrote a book called *Die Erforschung der Kirklichen Reformations Geschichte seit 1876* which was a review of modern Roman Catholic interpretations of the Reformation, in which he dismissed both Denifle and Grisar (see above) as inadequate. Jedin made the Council of Trent his special study, and in 1937 published *Cardinal Seripando*, a biography of the Papal Legate at the Council (English translation 1947). Three other Trent biographies may be mentioned here: *The Cardinal of Lorraine and the Council of Trent*, by H. O. Evenett (1930), *Reginald Pole, Cardinal of England*, by W. Schenk (1950), and *Jacopo Sadoleto*, by R. M. Douglas (Harvard, 1959). Jedin has since begun a *History of the Council of Trent*, of which two volumes have so far been translated into English, in 1957 and 1961, bringing the story down to about 1547.

What Jedin and other Catholic scholars did was to abandon the idea that Trent had fixed for ever the norms of Catholic theology, spirituality and administration; instead, they tried to put the work and results of the Council into their historical context, to historicize them, to make clear that what the Council achieved was essentially only a temporary solution to problems which in a modern form might need a different answer. Jedin's work should not be thought of as a triumph for a 'Protestant' view of the Council: it was the gradual acceptance of the historical approach in the Roman Church itself which led both to this new way of looking at the Council and to the toleration (however unwilling at times) of the more liberal positions maintained at the Second Vatican Council. Among the other powerful forces which helped to bring all this about was the modern Roman Catholic liturgical movement, which sought to restore the vitality of the parish as a spiritual community, but whose scholars found that the prevailing individualism of Roman liturgical practice drew much of its theory and prestige from the Tridentine system. The Council's decree on the Scriptures (1546), for example, is now often criticized on the ground that it has had the effect of pushing the Bible into the background in later devotion, and of fostering an individualistic concentration on the Eucharist. This gradual entrance of historical relativism into the Roman Catholic analysis of its own tradition was of the greatest importance, analogous to the shock that the Church of England suffered when John Henry Newman applied a similar technique to the Thirty-Nine Articles in the famous *Tract Ninety* (1841), though Newman at that time treated Trent as a fixed point and saw only the Anglican Articles as subject to the pressure of their historical environment. This process is bound to lead to sociological criticism of specific Councils, and in fact Hubert Jedin's account of Trent has already been criticized on the ground that he emphasized the ecclesiastical and political history but neglected the Council's sociological context. As long as the concept of a once for all revelation of truth persists, the Church historian is a paper tiger; but grant the possibility of dogmatic change and development, and the tiger puts on flesh.

'From all sides,' wrote G. H. Williams, 'we are coming to recognize in the Radical Reformation a major expression of the religious movement of the sixteenth century. It is one that is as distinctive as Lutheranism, Calvinism and Anglicanism, and is perhaps comparably significant in the rise of modern Christianity' (*Spiritual and Anabaptist Writers*, 1957, p. 19). This radical Protestantism, sometimes called 'the left wing of the Reformation', might be roughly described as consisting of those religious groups which rebelled not only against the authority of the Church of Rome but also against the authority of Luther, Zwingli and, later, Calvin. This radical movement took several forms, from Anabaptism to anti-Trinitarianism, but all shared a common disappointment with the moral results of early Protestantism. They also united in 'a common resistance to the linking together of Church and state, a relationship which the Reformation espoused in principle and the Counter-Reformation acquiesced in for reasons of expediency. . . . They would not tolerate the trespassing of pope, town council, prince or king upon the rights of the loyal subjects of the King of Kings' (Williams, op. cit., p. 21). As for dogma, the dissidents often rejected the practice of infant baptism and sometimes rejected the doctrine of the Trinity; most held firmly to the idea of the place of human free-will in the process of sanctification, as distinct from the unyielding determinism of both Luther and Calvin. Indeed, it is this passion for freedom, freedom of the spirit, which often expressed itself as freedom from the power of the state, from the authority of the traditional Church, or even from the traditional idea of God, which gives the radicals their continuing attractive power. And here one has to distinguish between those radicals, the Anabaptists, for example, who at least believed in the possibility of organizing a Church on earth, and set up their own small, highly disciplined communities, and those radicals, sometimes now called Spiritualists, who despaired of establishing the Church in a fallen world, and either turned to revolutionary violence or withdrew into religious individualism.

In the sixteenth century these radical reformers were dismissed by Protestant as well as Catholic as fanatical, anti-social and heretical. All the great reformers wrote against them, while insisting that they were unworthy of serious theological attention. Their rehabilitation, still only partial, has taken place in this century, and was especially promoted by the famous German sociologist of religion, Ernst Troeltsch, who in *The Social Teaching of the Christian Churches and Sects* (Tübingen, 1912, English translation, 1931) argued that it was the sixteenth-century radical sects, rather than the Lutheran and Reformed Churches, which broke with the ethos of the medieval world; it is in this tradition that one finds Professor Williams claiming that the radicals 'induced currents in history and the interpretation thereof which pulsate today in diverse conceptions of history ranging from explicitly Christian theologies of history, through democratic progressivism, to Marxism' (op. cit., p. 25). There came a reaction against Troeltsch's views in the 1920s, however, when Reformation scholars like Karl Holl and Henrich Boehmer reproduced the older picture of the Anabaptists as violent revolutionaries. Moreover, the twentieth-century pressure towards Church reunion caused some Protestant scholars to insist that the Reformation of the sixteenth century was not committed to such ideas as theological toleration, or 'the right of private judgement', or 'the invisible Church'. Such writers might rediscover the radicals, but they did not enthuse over them. They implied (and here they had Luther, Zwingli and Calvin behind them) that the radical fringe was not a part of the true Reformation, but a mistaken deviation from its proper course, and in saying this they emphasized the radicals' rejection of the sacramental solidarity of the Church and accused them of reducing the idea of the Church to a vague, voluntary association of Christian believers. It was left largely to American scholars, some of whom were connected with the American Mennonite Church, which can trace its history back to the sixteenth-century Anabaptists, to assert the positive value of this tradition. (Indeed, *The Mennonite Encyclopaedia*, 4 vols., Scottdale, Pa., 1955–9, ed. H. S. Bender and C. H. Smith, is an indispensable tool of scholarship in this field.) Among these American writers were John Horsch, who published *The Hutterian Brethren, 1538–1931* (Goshen, Ind., 1931), and *The Mennonites in Europe* (revised ed., Scottdale, Pa., 1950); Harold Bender, who wrote a biography of *Conrad Grebel* (Goshen, Ind., 1950); and Franklin Littell, whose book *The Anabaptist View of the Church* (second ed. Boston, 1956) offered a brilliant introduction to the whole movement. For the anti-Trinitarian radicals, Professor R. H. Bainton (whose study of Luther, *Here I Stand*, 1952, is probably the best popular account of the great reformer) contributed a life of Servetus called *Hunted Heretic* (Boston, 1953); there is also a very solid

History of Unitarianism, Socinianism and its Antecedents (1945), by another American scholar, E. M. Wilbur. Finally, Professor G. H. Williams attempted at least an interim summary of the state of scholarship in *The Radical Reformation* (1962), an immense work which traced the history and doctrine of all the sixteenth-century sects down to about 1580. *The Radical Reformation* was meant as a companion volume to the anthology of texts published in *Spiritual and Anabaptist Writers*, which Professor Williams edited with Professor A. M. Mergal in 1957. This valuable collection of translations included a bibliography of all the primary works of the radical Reformation available in English, supplemented rather than duplicated what had already been done, devoted a large section to the writings of the little-known Spanish reformer, Juan de Valdes, and offered in general an excellent entry into the ideas of the radical world.

This renewal of interest in the radical Reformation has overtaken the British revival (from the 1930s) of Luther and Calvin. This is especially associated with the Methodist scholar, Professor E. G. Rupp, author of *Luther's Progress to the Diet of Worms* (1951), and *The Righteousness of God* (1953), and with the Presbyterian scholar, Professor T. F. Torrance, who has written *Calvin's Doctrine of Man* (1949), *Kingdom and Church* (1956), and *The School of Faith, the Catechisms of the Reformed Church* (1959), as well as encouraging a new translation of Calvin's Biblical commentaries. It is not uncharacteristic of modern Reformation scholarship that this revival has undoubtedly served, not only the interests of pure scholarship, but also the existing ecumenical and theological situation. The Methodist Church in England and the Presbyterian Church in Scotland had become deeply involved in negotiations for union with the Church of England. The leaders of both Churches were aware of the hesitation which many Anglicans, especially Anglo-Catholics, had about non-episcopal Churches, doubts which to some extent originated in the view that all such bodies had developed from one-sided interpretations of the Gospel, and so could not be regarded as possessing the wholeness, or

'Catholicity', of Christianity. A century of Anglo-Catholic criticism, moreover, had left Anglicans more conscious of the weaknesses of Luther and Calvin than of their theological stature: Calvin's part in the murder of Servetus, for instance, was certainly better known than his doctrine of God, which helped to explain his action. The Anglo-Catholic view of the Reformation, a view which owed more to tradition than to historical scholarship, was embodied in *Catholicity, A Study in the Conflict of Christian Traditions in the West* (1947), the report of a commission of which Gregory Dix and A. G. Herbert were the secretaries.

A non-Anglican appeal for a better understanding of the Reformation, or at any rate of the Reformation as Luther and Calvin defined it, was therefore opportune: here was a theological inheritance of vast potential, so that it is not surprising that the editors of the one major Free Church statement of faith drawn up in the course of the ecumenical debate called it *The Catholicity of Protestantism* (ed. R. N. Flew and R. E. Davies, 1950). The aim of this ecumenical Reformation scholarship was to show that, contrary to Roman and Anglo-Catholic tradition (as exemplified, for instance, in the writings of Dom Gregory Dix – *The Shape of the Liturgy*, 1945, and a contribution which he made to *The Apostolic Ministry*, edited by K. E. Kirk, 1947), belief in the One, Holy and Catholic Apostolic Church was integral to the faith of Protestantism; that Protestants did not regard incorporation into the Church as an optional extra which could be dispensed with by men of unusual spiritual stature, but believed that outside the Church there was no salvation. And this reassertion of one aspect of Reformation ecclesiology also bore witness to a theological (rather than historical) attempt to recover, through the study of the writings of Luther and Calvin, the existential impact of a theocentric Gospel (similar to that proclaimed by the Swiss theologian, Karl Barth, whose influence was at its most potent in the years 1930–50), which would exorcise, it was hoped, the spirit of nineteenth-century liberal individualism which was widely believed to have corrupted the Church.

These prior considerations meant that much of what was written seemed theological rather than historical. No new English life of Calvin replaced that by R. N. Carew Hunt (1933), though the best of continental scholarship was translated in *Calvin, the Origins and Development of his Religious Thought*, by François Wendel (Paris, 1950, English translation 1963). Wendel, incidentally, offered the standard defence of Calvin's behaviour towards Servetus (to which reference has already been made), saying that 'it is contrary to a sound conception of history to try to apply our ways of judging and our moral criteria to the past. Calvin was convinced, and all the reformers shared this conviction, that it was the duty of the Christian magistrate to put to death blasphemers who kill the soul, just as they punished murderers who kill the body' (op. cit., p. 97). In as much as the Reformation was a theological battlefield Calvin's position was made more accessible in such books as *Calvin's Doctrine of the Word and Sacraments* (Edinburgh, 1953) and *Calvin's Doctrine of the Christian Life* (Edinburgh, 1959), both by R. Wallace. The Library of Christian Classics also published a group of Calvin's *Theological Treatises* in translation (ed. J. K. S. Reid, 1954); a selection of *Commentaries and Letters* (ed. J. Haratounian, 1958); and a two-volume version of *The Institutes of the Christian Religion* (1961), edited by John T. McNeill, whose *History and Character of Calvinism* (New York, 1954) was more strictly a work of Church history, though he did not enter sufficiently into the causes of Calvinism's decline in the seventeenth and eighteenth centuries. *Reformed Dogmatics* (1965), edited by John W. Beardslee, contained translations from the writings of Continental Calvinists, Wollebius (1586–1629), Voetius (1589–1687) and Turretin (1623–87), valuable in themselves, but needing more editorial matter to make them significant to the general reader whom the Library of Protestant Thought has claimed to have in mind. Light was also thrown on the later history of European Calvinism by the famous Dutch historian Pieter Geyl, whose *Revolt of the Netherlands* (second ed. 1958) is indispensable.

For many of these writers, however, what mattered was not so much the Church history as the attempt to restore the theological prestige of the Calvinist tradition, shattered almost irreparably in the course of the eighteenth and nineteenth centuries. Luther, on the other hand, has never counted for so much in the history of the British Churches, and the attempt to engender a theological renascence from a study of his thought was correspondingly less successful. Nevertheless, in a period when theologians were at last having to accept the fact that they could no longer appeal directly to the Scriptures properly understood as an absolute authority the appeal to a classical Protestant interpretation of the Scriptures seemed to hold out some hope of a fresh beginning. Luther, moreover, had the literary gifts to communicate across the centuries, as was evident, for example, in the Elizabethan translation of his Commentary on *Galatians* (ed. P. S. Watson, 1953), which caught the vitality of the original: 'Hereby we may see who be very saints indeed. They be not stocks and stones (as the monks and schoolmen dream) so that they are never moved with anything, never feel any lust or desires of the flesh: but, as Paul saith, their flesh lusteth against the Spirit, and therefore they have sin and can sin' (p. 508).

Not all modern translations succeed so well. In the Library of Christian Classics there have appeared: *Luther: Letters of Spiritual Counsel* (ed. T. G. Tappert, 1955), a less exciting volume than might have been expected; the early *Lectures on Romans* (1961), edited by another American scholar, Wilhelm Pauck; and a selection of Luther's *Early Theological Works* (ed. T. F. Torrance, 1962). Those who want an English text of such vital Lutheran texts as 'The Pagan Servitude of the Church' and 'The Appeal to the Ruling Class of German Nationality' can find them in *The Reformation Writings of Martin Luther*, translated and edited by Bertram Lee Woolf (2 vols., 1953, 1956). To the expository books mentioned above might be added *The Revolt of Martin Luther*, by R. H. Fife (1957), *Luther's World of Thought*, by Heinrich Bornkamm (English translation 1958), and *Ottoman Imperialism and*

German Protestantism, 1521–1555, by S. A. Fischer-Galati (1959). Luther probably reached a wider public, though with less religious impact, through John Osborne's play, *Luther*, for which the author drew heavily on a psychoanalytic study of the reformer, *The Young Luther*, by Erik Erikson (1959). Erikson made a gallant attempt to fit Luther's theological development into psychological categories, but two comments might be made. First, it seems extraordinarily difficult to apply the psychoanalytical method to someone who is dead; there must be grave danger of assimilating the individual to theoretical models of development. Second, this sort of assimilation is all the more difficult to check if the historical facts about the subject are uncertain and few in number: in Luther's case, the shortage of material compelled Erikson to treat as reliable evidence which most Church historians would regard as untrustworthy. Nevertheless, Erikson's book provided a salutary shock for anyone who thought that Luther's theological development consisted only of (a) an intellectual-emotional search for religious certainty which the existing Roman system could not satisfy, and (b) a moment of supernatural illumination.[1]

It is hardly surprising that Zwingli, the third of the principal reformers, should not have benefited much from this revival of interest in the theological Reformation. In English, one has still to make do with Oscar Farner's short study, *Zwingli the Reformer* (Zurich, 1917, English translation 1952), and with a more recent popular Swiss study, *Zwingli, Third Man of the Reformation* (Paris, 1959, English translation 1964). In the Library of Christian Classics he shared a volume, edited by G. W. Bromiley (1953), with Bullinger, the reformer who succeeded Zwingli as chief pastor in Zurich in 1531. Still untranslated are the four volumes of O. Farner's great biography, *Huldrych Zwingli* (1943–60). An American scholar, C. Garside, has written a very interesting study, *Zwingli and the Arts* (Yale, 1966), of the way in which Zwingli moved from an early

1. James Atkinson's *Martin Luther and the Birth of Protestantism* (1968) appeared too late for more than mention here.

enthusiasm for music and other arts to a rigid exclusion of them from the worship of God.

Perhaps the best accounts of the religious changes which took place in England in the sixteenth century may be found in the books of those who have on the whole subordinated the ecclesiastical history proper to the general, and especially political, history of the country, as has for instance G. R. Elton in *England under the Tudors* (1955) and *The Tudor Constitution, Documents and Commentary* (1960), or J. E. Neale in *The Elizabethan House of Commons* (1949) and *Queen Elizabeth I and Her Parliaments* (2 vols., 1953). To these must be added the brilliant account of the English Reformation given by A. G. Dickens (1964). (A good short account from a more ecclesiastical point of view was *The English Reformation to 1558*, by T. M. Parker, 1952.) These authors did not hesitate to accept the sixteenth century's own understanding of itself on the fundamental issue of what happened to the Church of England at the 'Reformation': they rejected the Church historian's temptation to impose a particular religious interpretation on events. Thus G. R. Elton wrote of the Elizabethan religious settlement:

> It now consisted of an act of supremacy enforcing the renewed break with Rome and the queen's position as supreme governor of things temporal and spiritual, and an act of uniformity enforcing a protestantism not so quite clearcut as that of 1522 but much more extreme than that of 1549. It is usual to call this settlement a compromise, and so it was – but not quite in the sense supposed. Contemporaries did not think that the Established Church rested halfway between the rival denominations: they thought this was a protestant Church. ... It was only the further development of puritanism ... as well as Elizabeth's diplomatic suggestions to a number of deliberately blind Spanish and French emissaries that her protestantism was after all quite like catholicism, that disguised the nature of the settlement. (*England under the Tudors*, pp. 273–4)

This was all very well, but the sixteenth-century religious changes still have too much effect on twentieth-century ecclesiastical politics for all Church historians to let the matter rest there. The growing *rapprochement* between Rome and Canterbury has not completely transformed the Roman interpretation of the past, if only because the nineteenth-century Papal condemnation of Anglican ministerial orders (in 1896) has not yet been withdrawn; indeed, as late as 1960 F. Clark powerfully restated the Roman position in *Eucharistic Sacrifice and the Reformation.* A mellowing of the Roman attitude may be traced, however, through the books of the distinguished Catholic historian Philip Hughes. In *A Popular History of the Church* (1939), he suggested that at the start of Elizabeth I's reign 'all the bishops were deposed and a new self-consecrated hierarchy of heretics took their place'; in *Rome and the Counter-Reformation* (1942) he took the more guarded line that the Elizabethan Church Settlement was the work of a minority who forced their views on a reluctant majority who would probably have preferred Catholicism. Finally, in *The Reformation in England* (3 vols., 1950–54), he gave a full-scale history of the period in which he granted that the Reformation showed the disastrous results of bad Catholicism, but not that Catholicism was wrong in principle as the Protestant Reformers maintained: his emphasis on the Elizabethan persecution of Catholics did not please his Anglican reviewers. On the emotive question of the Henrician suppression of the English monasteries there has also been a gradual softening of Catholic resentment, perhaps assisted by the return of monasticism to Anglicanism since 1840. The authoritative account of the suppression is in the third volume of M. D. Knowles' *The Religious Orders in England* (1959); G. Baskerville, in *English Monks and the Suppression of the Monasteries* (1937), took rather a rosy view of the sufferings caused by the suppression.

Quite apart from the struggle between these major traditions, there has been the contest between the Anglo-Catholic and Anglican Evangelical for possession of the Anglican past. The classical defences of the Anglican Evangelical interpretation of the sixteenth century, according to which the English Reformation was consciously Protestant, were written in the nineteenth century (see, for example, William Goode, *The*

Nature of Christ's Presence in the Eucharist, 1856, or John Harrison's *Whose are the Fathers?*, 1867, a massive reply to the Anglo-Catholic, Pusey, in which Harrison employed not only patristic sources, but also the Fathers of 'the Reformed Church of England'). The Anglo-Catholic version has dominated much of our period, though it has not impressed uncommitted writers like G. R. Elton; the scholars concerned have sometimes been American, like P. M. Dawley, whose *John Whitgift and the Reformation* (1955) might stand for many other books taking the same view. For Professor Dawley, Elizabeth in her religious settlement revived a 'Catholic' Anglicanism which had its roots in the reign of Henry VIII – and so one is back with the view to which Dr Elton was referring in the passage quoted above, according to which the sixteenth-century reformers did not intend to produce a 'protestant' Church. Dawley's views were not unlike those of earlier writers like H. Maynard Smith who, in his *Pre-Reformation England* (1938), for instance, tried to distinguish between a reformation, which the Church certainly needed, and the actual Reformation, which was a tragedy. For Maynard Smith too the essential, 'Catholic' Reformation was that of Henry VIII, while 'Protestantism' was of 'alien origin', 'not in accord with national sentiment'. *The Marian Exiles*, by M. Garrett (1938), again offered a similar religious interpretation, but her picture of the exiles taking part in a planned emigration, inspired by Cecil, from which they meant to return and overthrow the Government, has not gained general assent, though it was echoed in 1952 by T. M. Parker (op. cit.). More specifically theological was C. W. Dugmore's *The Mass and the English Reformers* (1958), an important analysis of the sources of Cranmer's Eucharistic theology. Much of the biographical work on this period is still affected by these religious attitudes. There have been many biographies since 1930, including R. W. Chambers' famous life of *Sir Thomas More*, perhaps the most over-written character of the time. There were also lives of *Tyndale* (1937), *Foxe* (1940) and *Coverdale* (1953), all by J. F. Mozley; *Ridley* (1957) and *Cranmer* (1962), both by Jasper Ridley, though the latter book did not supersede A. F. Pollard's earlier study of Cranmer (new ed. 1926); *Whitgift* (1957), by V. J. K. Brook; *Walter Travers* (1952), by A. J. Knox. Of great interest was *Erasmus and Cambridge, The Cambridge Letters of Erasmus*, translated by D. F. S. Thomson and edited by H. C. Porter (whose *Reformation and Reaction in Cambridge*, 1958, was also a useful local study); Thomson also produced a superbly printed translation of Erasmus's *Colloquies* (1965). The wider study of Erasmus continued in books like *Erasmus and the Northern Renaissance*, by M. M. Phillips (New York, 1950), and *Erasmus and the Age of the Reformation*, by J. Huizinga (English translation 1957). Another important monograph, *Erasme et l'Espagne*, by M. Bataillon (Paris, 1937), has not been translated into English. No one really tried to re-interpret Erasmus – as, for instance, the most religious of the reformers – but this was hardly surprising in a period when Luther and Calvin, traditionally accepted as more 'profound' than Erasmus, were coming back into favour as religious writers.

One cannot leave the sixteenth century without saying something about Elizabethan Puritanism. Here the way forward was shown by Professor A. G. Dickens in *Lollards and Protestants in the Diocese of York, 1509–1558* (1959), a piece of meticulous research which abandoned the sterile controversy about a Reformation seen largely in administrative terms and examined instead the growth of the popular Protestantism which gave strength to the Puritan minority in the Elizabethan House of Commons which refused to accept the finality of the famous 'Settlement'. Much of the discussion still ran on theological lines: the Congregationalist scholar Albert Peel, assisted by Leland H. Carlson, edited a series of Elizabethan Nonconformist texts, beginning with *Cartwrightiana* (1951); William Haller published *Foxe's Book of Martyrs and the Elect Nation* (1953). *The Vestments Controversy* (1960), by J. H. Primus, was closer to the ground, but the most detailed examination of the Elizabethan Puritans as a political force was *The Elizabethan Puritan Movement*, by Patrick Collinson (1967). Dr Collinson did not always resist the temptation to discover elaborate conspiracies, but he was certainly right in his view that neither religious necessity nor some sort of social determinism obliged Elizabeth and Whitgift to try to stamp out Puritanism. Their decision – which was political rather than religious – had disastrous results for the unity of British society. Such a verdict runs counter to the mainstream of the Anglican tradition, which has never accepted the idea that sixteenth-century Anglicanism was as divisive as Puritanism, and it will be interesting to see whether, over the next generation, A. G. Dickens, Dr Collinson and other scholars will be as successful in modifying that tradition with regard to the sixteenth century as Norman Sykes was in modifying its interpretation of the later seventeenth and eighteenth centuries.[2]

2. A. G. Dickens, *The Counter-Reformation* (1969) appeared too recently for comment here.

Four

The Seventeenth Century: America and England

Puritanism has continued to dominate the study of the seventeenth-century British and American Church history. This is especially true of America, where the publication of Samuel E. Morison's *Builders of the Bay Colony* (1930) marked the moment at which American historians rediscovered Puritanism as a vital ingredient in American culture. Morison added *The Puritan Pronaos* (1936), reprinted in 1956 as *The Intellectual Life of Colonial New England*: another distinguished student of Puritanism was William Haller, among whose works were *Tracts on Liberty in the Puritan Revolution* (Columbia, 1934), *The Rise of Puritanism* (1938) and *Liberty and Reformation in the Puritan Revolution* (1955). Yet another important American contribution was W. C. Abbott's edition of *The Writers and Speeches of Oliver Cromwell* (4 vols., Harvard, 1937–47). The most remarkable product of this American school, however, was the intellectual history written by the late Perry Miller, *Orthodoxy in Massachusetts, 1630–1650* (1933); *The New England Mind, the Seventeenth Century* (1939); *The New England Mind, from Colony to Province* (1953); and *Jonathan Edwards* (1948), his brilliant portrait of the early eighteenth-century New England divine who was at once the most terrifying of hell-fire preachers, the most penetrating critic of the revivalist tradition, and also, as Miller claimed, a philosopher of genius.

In America, the reconstructed Puritan theological imagination emerged as one of the intellectual foundations of the nation; Puritanism was accepted, as it never has been in England, as part of the main stream of the national culture, and this led on to an interest in nineteenth-century revivalism (see below, p. 362). In England, on the other hand, 'Puritanism' is still sometimes invoked as one explanation of what is wrong with English culture, and Anglican historians are apt to regard the Puritanism of 1558 to 1640 as an alien, non-Anglican element in the Established Church, a source of disaffection which was inevitably and properly expelled in 1662 at the Restoration. One might take as an example *Puritans and the Church Courts in the Diocese of York, 1560–1642*, by Ronald Marchant (1960), a book in which Puritanism was treated as at best an error and at worst a heresy. In such books one misses a sense of the Church of England in this period as itself a struggle for self-definition; instead, there is an assumption that 'Anglicanism' had already been defined once and for all, and that the Puritans were rebelling against the very nature of the Church. There is a similar over-drawing of the matter in the title of John F. H. New's *Anglican and Puritan, the Basis of their Opposition* (1964); New tried to distinguish his two parties theologically, though not so much in terms of strict definition as in terms of the suggestion that the 'Anglicans' *felt* the key doctrines (the Fall of Man, for instance) less deeply and rigidly than the Puritans. Such interpretations may be a product of Church history rather than Church history itself. We need a colder eye cast on this whole period, and terms like 'Anglican' and 'Puritan' used as clues to the religious aspect of a wider social struggle which lasted for more than a century and which ended in the radical division of English culture. Part of the trouble is that since 1930 secular historians have lost interest in the religious side of seventeenth-century history: they have concentrated more on social and administrative history, conjuring up a new version of Charles the Martyr, Charles the misunderstood head of an unfortunate administration. One exception to this was Christopher Hill, who wrote *The Economic Problems of the Church from Archbishop Whitgift to the Long Parliament* (1956), *Puritanism and Revolution* (1958) and *The Century of Revolution* (1961). Hill emphasized the importance of religion in precipitating the Civil War:

As in the revolt of the Netherlands and the French Revolution, revolution in England was precipitated by 'a revolt of the nobles'. Revolution happens only when the government has lost the confidence of an important section of the ruling class. But in France in 1789 the aristocracy rallied quickly to the Crown once the Third Estate put forward revolutionary demands; in England the House of Commons was split, and even in the Lords there was a considerable minority which carried opposition to the point of civil war. The difference can partly be explained by the importance of questions of religion and Church government in the English Revolution. (*The Century of Revolution*, 1961, p. 104)

British Church historians continued to study Puritanism themselves. For the earlier period one should consult the Congregationalist historian G. F. Nuttall, who wrote *The Holy Spirit in Puritan Faith and Experience* (1946), one of those books in which Church history and history of doctrine are inextricably blended together; *Visible Saints, The Congregational Way, 1640–1660* (1957); and a life of *Richard Baxter* (1966). The best work on Nonconformity after 1660 was by Professor G. R. Cragg, a Canadian Presbyterian, who published *From Puritanism to the Age of Reason* (1950) and *Puritanism in the Period of the Great Persecution* (1957). More valuable, perhaps, in the long run, was the work of A. G. Matthews, who in 1934 produced *Calamy Revised*, a revision of the standard seventeenth-century account of the numbers and sufferings of the Nonconformist ministers ejected from the State Church at the time of the Restoration; and who in 1948 followed this up with a companion volume, *Walker Revised*, a reworking of John Walker's *Sufferings of the Clergy in the Great Rebellion* (1714), the counterpart of Calamy on the winning side. These two books contained brief biographies of virtually all the Anglican and non-Anglican clergy caught up in the chaos of the mid seventeenth century and showed how the ejection of the Nonconformists in 1662 was not an act of irrational Anglican cruelty but the almost inevitable consequence of the prior ejection of thousands of Episcopalian clergy from the same livings during the Civil War. This was the Church historian's contribution to better understanding between Anglican and Free Churchman, and helps to explain why in 1962 the tercentenary of the Ejection was commemorated on an ecumenical basis: there was even a joint memorial volume, *From Uniformity to Unity, 1662–1962*, edited by G. F. Nuttall and W. O. Chadwick, which contained essays by Anglican and Free Church historians, but which was somewhat distorted by its inadequate treatment of the Methodist role in British ecclesiastical politics since the mid eighteenth century. The celebrations also saw the issue of a new denominational history, *Congregationalism in England, 1662–1962*, by R. T. Jones.

The growth of the ecumenical climate, however, has reduced the interest in denominational history by exposing its essential limitation in perspective; it has also diminished interest in a century so passionately divided by religion as was the seventeenth. An excellent new denominational history, *A History of the British Baptists*, by A. C. Underwood (1947), replaced the older history by W. T. Whitley, who had undervalued continental influences on the origins of the movement. The unabridged text of George Fox's *Journal* first appeared in 1911, edited by T. E. Harvey and N. Penney; a valuable new edition, with additional material, was published by John L. Nickalls in 1952: one cannot understand Fox without his *Journal*, and one cannot understand English Christianity without Fox. Among Anglican seventeenth-century studies were *The High Church Party, 1688–1714*, by G. Every (1956), and *The Making of the Restoration Settlement*, by R. S. Bosher (1951). R. S. Bosher not only gave an interesting account of how Charles II outmanoeuvred his Presbyterian opponents after his return; he also communicated something of the horror with which the Laudians in exile contemplated the appalling possibility that the Anglican episcopal succession might lapse altogether because of the hesitation of the surviving, ageing handful of bishops to run the risk of defying the Commonwealth by acts of consecration. The Restoration came just in time to save them from a final decision.

Anglican bishops have perhaps figured too prominently in modern Anglican writing on this period. The late Norman Sykes set a fashion in episcopal biography which might have had more exciting results if Sykes's influence had been less. The most outstanding of these books included: *White Kennett, 1660–1728* (1957), by G. V. Bennett; *Thomas Sherlock, 1678–1761* (1936), *Thomas Tenison, Archbishop of Canterbury. His Life and Letters* (1948) and *The Protestant Bishop, Henry Compton* (1956), all by E. F. Carpenter; *Joseph Glanville, Anglican Apologist*, by J. I. Cope (St Louis, 1956); *The Life and Times of John Sharp, Archbishop of York* (1949) and *William Lloyd, 1627–1717, Bishop, Politician, Author and Prophet* (1952), both by A. Tindal Hart; *A North Country Bishop* (Nicholson), by F. G. James (Yale, 1957); *Tillotson* (this was really more of a literary study), by Louis Glen Locke (Copenhagen, 1954); *Isaac Barrow*, by P. H. Osmond (1944); *The Life and Writings of Jeremy Taylor*, by C. J. Stranks (1952); *Lancelot Andrewes* (1958) and *George Abbott, the Unwanted Archbishop, 1562–1633* (1962), both by P. S. Welsby; and *Nathaniel, Lord Crewe, Bishop of Durham* (1940), by C. E. Whiting. None of these books had quite the attack of *Archbishop Laud* (1940) (new edition 1962), by Professor Hugh Trevor-Roper: a clerical reviewer said that the author's wit bordered on the blasphemous, but consoled himself with the thought that the book expressed 'a lay view' and was none the worse for that. Finally, mention should be made of B. H. G. Wormald's *Clarendon, 1640–1660* (1951).

Five

The European Church, 1550–1789

The history of the Church in Europe between the Reformation and the French Revolution has been largely neglected by modern British and American scholars. In the case of Germany, A. L. Drummond's *German Protestantism since Luther* (1951) has stood almost alone, and so we are nearly as ignorant as were our grandfathers about Pietism, the German Enlightenment and the relationship between eighteenth-century Church and State in Germany. In the case of France the situation is a little better. N. J. Abercrombie's *The Origins of Jansenism* (1936) has not been superseded, though one may consult the relevant chapters of R. A. Knox's *Enthusiasm* (1950). Jansenism, however, remains a mystery to most of the English (as, indeed, it does to most Frenchmen), and so does Fénelon (of whom there was a study by K. D. Little in 1951). In *The Opposition to Louis XIV*, L. Rothkrug held that Fénelon's overthrow by Bossuet (cf. the biography by W. J. S. Simpson, 1937) was the point at which the political opposition to French absolutism finally lost faith in the Church as an ally, and that this decided the anti-Christian character of the French Enlightenment. This anti-Christian movement, some of whose roots were to be found in English Deism, was originally explored by I. Wade in *The Clandestine Organisation of Philosophical Thought in France* (Princeton, 1938), and the inquiry was carried further in a brilliant book by J. S. Spink, *French Free Thought from Gassendi to Voltaire* (1960). The same tradition in Germany was examined by H. E. Allison in *Lessing and the Enlightenment* (Michigan, 1966). The most important aspect of the history of modern Christianity is its fight for intellectual survival, a fight which can be studied properly only on a European scale, and it is a pity that there is still no equally sober modern study of the English Deists themselves.

Among other books on the continental Church, *The Persecution of the Huguenots and French Economic Development, 1680–1720*, by Warren C. Scoville (California, 1960), threw doubt on the traditional statement that France paid a heavy economic price for the expulsion of the Huguenots; *French Protestantism and the French Revolution, 1685–1815*, by Burdette C. Poland (Princeton, 1957), explained how the gradual erosion of French Calvinist orthodoxy produced a generation of pastors who welcomed the French Revolution as a step forward towards true Christianity. The most remarkable book on French Church history for many years, however, was *French Ecclesiastical Society under the Ancien Régime*, by J. McManners (1961). This was based on a detailed study of the French cathedral town of Angers in the eighteenth century. McManners described first of all the immobility of the pre-revolutionary Church, especially the monasteries, of which there were twenty-seven in Angers: 'at a time when lay society was becoming more and more doubtful of the value of the celibate and contemplative life, the monks and nuns remained in the monasteries caught in a network of tradition and property-owning which perpetuated inequality and ineffectiveness' (p.101). In the Revolution this institutional framework collapsed quite suddenly, to the general satisfaction of most people. The National Assembly's attempt to transform the Church religiously, making it a symbol of the Enlightenment, was less successful, though a Festival of Reason took place in Angers Cathedral in November 1793. What impresses one, nevertheless, is the fury with which a section of French society turned against the Church: at the height of the Revolutionary struggle 264 priests from the Angers area were shipped off to Spain, and more than 100 others, too old or ill to travel, died later in the drownings at Nantes. The contrast between the somnolent Angers of the mid eighteenth century and the savage Angers of the 1790s gave a new depth of meaning to the Revolution and suggested what bitterness the

Church had accumulated against itself since the sixteenth century.[1]

Finally, a word about Pascal, perhaps the only seventeenth-century theologian who is still a living force in twentieth-century Western culture. There have been many Pascals. There was Chateaubriand's romantic early nineteenth-century Pascal. There was the anti-Catholic Pascal of the late nineteenth century, the darling of French anti-clerical writers. In the early twentieth century it was the turn of the editors, hard at work weaving his *Pensées* into new patterns. Recently, he was seen to have been an existentialist all the time, while in 1955 Lucien Goldmann, the French Marxist literary critic, in *Le Dieu caché* (English translation by P. Thody, *The Hidden God*, 1964), linked together Jansenism, the 'tragic vision' of Pascal, and the philosophy of Immanuel Kant as stages in the development of the dialectical philosophy of Hegel and Marx:

> The idea of a wager not only occupies a central position in Jansenist thought (wager on individual salvation) or in Pascal's ideas (wager that God exists) or in Kant's philosophy (wager on the practical postulate that God exists and that the soul is immortal). It is also at the very heart of dialectical and materialist thought under the form of the wager that, in the alternative facing humanity of a choice between socialism and barbarism, socialism will triumph. (p. 301)

Although Goldmann assumed that Marxism was an advance on Pascal's thought, he stated Pascal's central position so well that many of his readers must have found Pascal more convincing than Marx:

> Far from merely stating that it is reasonable to chance the certain and finite goods of this world against the possibility of gaining a happiness which is doubly infinite both in intensity and duration (this being merely the external aspect of the argument, aimed at allowing the interlocutor to become conscious of the human situation even on the plane farthest removed from the faith), this wager states that the finite goods of this world have no value at all, and

1. cf. *Bayeux in the Late Eighteenth Century* (1967), Olwen Hufton. Bayeux was also primarily an ecclesiastical centre.

that the only human life which has meaning is that of a reasonable being who seeks God. (And this is whether or not he is happy or miserable because he does or does not find Him, which is nevertheless something which he cannot discover until after his death.) The only life which has any real meaning is that of the being who places all his goods on the wager that God exists and that He will help him, and who shows this by devoting his life to realising a value – that of infinite happiness – which does not depend upon his own strength and of whose final creation he has no certain proof. (p. 302)

In a paragraph like this the Marxist M. Goldmann performed one of the essential tasks of the historian of religion – he made clear why in the seventeenth century some men could take Christianity seriously. It is a pity that the modern Church historian, working, for example, on the nineteenth century, does not always give a similarly sympathetic explanation as to why some men, Ludwig Feuerbach for example, found themselves unable to take Christianity seriously.

Six

The Eighteenth Century in England

The recent study of English eighteenth-century Church history was greatly influenced by Norman Sykes, whose first important book, a biography of Edmund Gibson, the eighteenth-century bishop of London, appeared in 1926. He established his reputation with *Church and State in England in the Eighteenth Century* (1934); his one major failure was his two-volume biography of the eighteenth-century Archbishop of Canterbury, William Wake (1957). Few readers felt that Wake had deserved to be commemorated on such a scale.

Of *Edmund Gibson* and *Church and State in England in the Eighteenth Century* G. V. Bennett wrote that 'taken together, they made possible a reassessment of the eighteenth-century church in England, revealing indeed its immobility and involvement in the world of patronage and politics but showing that in pastoral matters its record was not one of unrelieved torpor and neglect as had so often been asserted. His work complemented well the researches of the political historians and came to be the standard reference for them as for others.'[1]

It may be noted that in establishing this kinder view of the clergy of the eighteenth century Sykes was able to draw heavily on several journals, diaries and other contemporary sources then only recently published and all of them worth reading in their own right. Among these the best known was *The Diary of a Country Parson*, edited by J. Beresford in five volumes (1924–31), the diary, covering the years 1758–1802, of James

1. *Essays in Modern Church History in Memory of Norman Sykes*, ed. G. V. Bennett and J. Walsh, 1966, Preface.

Woodforde of Weston Longville, Norfolk, the self-portrait of a country parson; but Sykes also made much use of the less well-known but not less charming *Blecheley Diary of William Cole, 1765–1767* (ed. F. G. Stokes, 1931), the antiquarian clerical friend of Horace Walpole. He also leaned on *The Diary and Letter-Books, 1672–1709, of T. Brockbank*, edited by R. Trappes-Lomax for the Chetham Society in 1930; the *Diary of the Rev. William Jones of Broxbourne, 1777–1821* (ed. O. F. Christie, 1929) and *The Journal of a Somerset Rector, 1772–1838*, the diary of John Skinner (ed. H. Coombes and H. N. Box, 1930). To these might be added the five volumes of *Archbishop Herring's Visitation Returns, 1743* (ed. J. L. Ollard and P. C. Walker for the Yorkshire Archaeological Society, 1928–31): Sykes fully endorsed the editorial conclusion concerning the Yorkshire clergy that 'the strong impression left by these returns is that of a body of dutiful and conscientious men, trying to do their work according to the standards of their day' (op. cit., vol. i, p. xviii).

When *Church and State in England in the Eighteenth Century* was first published, Claude Jenkins, for many years Professor of Ecclesiastical History in the University of Oxford, and one who in that time rarely exposed himself to the risk of being reviewed, gave the book a cool reception, implying that it was special pleading. Special pleading, however, was exactly what Sykes demonstrated in all earlier versions of the history of the eighteenth-century Establishment (for despite his book's wide title he said little about Methodism or Dissent). For their own different reasons both Anglo-Catholic and Methodist writers had vilified the Anglicanism from which they sprang. An excellent illustration of Sykes's reply to this tradition was his criticism of an essay which S. L. Ollard had written on confirmation (in 1926); here Sykes was taking the chance to defend the bishops of the eighteenth century:

In their endeavours to grapple with the many obstacles to pastoral oversight and to the discharge of the spiritual administration of their office, the eighteenth-century episcopate merit a juster measure of appreciation than has been their lot at the hands of subsequent historians. The Georgian bench indeed has been pilloried as a byword of sloth, inefficiency and neglect. Apologists have shown a marked capacity for differentiation between the same characteristics when present in bishops of the Caroline age and in those of its successor. The biographer of Lancelot Andrewes [seventeenth century] allows that 'we know little of his distinctively episcopal work, his few extant letters making no special mention of pastoral duties'; but he is careful to add 'that the standard by which a bishop's work was measured in those days was not that of our own time'. The nicest degree of discrimination between prelates of the High and Low-church traditions is shown by Canon Ollard in his survey of confirmations. Although referring to the enquiries of Barlow of Lincoln [High-Church] concerning confirmation, he makes no mention of that bishop's complete and protracted neglect of his diocese, whereas he is at pains to note of Hoadly [Low] that 'he never visited his diocese of Bangor, nor apparently Hereford.' . . . The restriction by Bishop Bull [High-Church] of confirmations to the place near his residence, owing to his inability to visit his diocese in person and to travel through its territory to confirm, is applauded as 'an advance upon the practice which confined confirmation to the bishop's visitation'; whilst of Gilbert Burnet [Low] it is stated that in his *Discourse of the Pastoral Care* 'confirmation is not mentioned under a bishop's duties', although that prelate is allowed the credit of having been 'active in administering confirmation and in twenty years had confirmed in 265 churches in his diocese'. Finally, following a summary of the confirmation tours of Archbishop Drummond of York, who died in 1771, and without any later reference save a reference to confirmations in the diocese of Ely in 1829 and 1833, Ollard affirms that 'the evidence for the later years of the eighteenth century and for the earlier years of the nineteenth, points to the conclusion that carelessness and infrequency in administering confirmation were reaching their lowest level, comparable only to the period of neglect when Calvinism was at its height two hundred years before'. Before such a tribunal the eighteenth-century episcopate may well decline to plead its defence. (pp. 144–5)

It is not difficult to see why Sykes's reputation grew in ecclesiastical circles. Here was a ruthlessly professional Church historian prepared to argue that eighteenth-century Anglicanism, the lost century of Anglican tradition, ought not to be singled out for adverse criticism; that many of its clergy, if neither Methodists nor Anglo-Catholics, had quietly devoted themselves to their parishes; that the bishops ought not to be judged in terms of the ambitious, theological rationalist Hoadly, but Hoadly in terms of his betters – men who struggled to cope with their ramshackle, rambling dioceses and who had neither the railway nor the motor-car to lessen the strain. In later years Sykes over-identified himself with the alleged sufferings of an unfairly harassed episcopate, and in *The Interim Statement on the Conversations between the Church of England and the Methodist Church* (1958) even said that 'it was not the case that the spread of Methodism was frustrated or hindered by episcopal action ... instead a juster charge against the episcopate would be that no steps were taken to establish a corporate policy'. It was a rather desperate defence of the eighteenth-century hierarchy's reaction to the Evangelical Revival to say that the bishops did not actually do anything to hinder it and the facts do not bear out so categorical an assertion. Sykes, however, took little interest in the Evangelical side of the eighteenth century; his vision of the Establishment hardly allowed for its existence; John Wesley figured most vividly in *Church and State* as a critic whose sweeping condemnation of the Anglican priesthood could be (and rightly) rejected.

This concentration upon the Church as an ecclesiastical institution (Sykes produced little in the way of an economic or sociological study of the Church of the Enlightenment) suited the mood of the period deeply involved in efforts to unite the institutional world-Church. It characterized *Old Priest and New Presbyter* (1956), a book in which Sykes tried to influence the ecclesiastical politics of his day, and which was an extended treatment of the subjects discussed in an earlier monograph, *The Church of England and Non-Episcopal Churches in the 16th and 17th Centuries* (1948). Sykes here attempted to settle by the use of the historical method as he understood it the long controversy over the Anglican attitude to episcopacy, Presbyterianism and Papacy since the Reformation. This was very much an ecclesiastical subject: what was at stake was the Anglo-Catholic interpretation of the Anglican past.

He sought to show that between the Reformation and the early nineteenth century there was a general refusal by Anglicans of many different shades of opinion to regard episcopacy as of the essence of the Church's being; most Anglicans recognized that 'in cases of necessity it might be dispensed with'. Moreover, not only was it agreed in theory that the 'cases of necessity' argument applied to many of the continental reformed Churches, but in practice these Churches were not commonly refused 'the true nature and essence of a church', however short they might fall of 'the integrity and perfection of a church'. Sykes worked out in detail such examples as the regular employment in eighteenth-century India by the Anglican authorities of Lutheran ordained missionaries, a practice which certainly involved recognition of their ministerial orders. Having established the existence in the sixteenth, seventeenth and eighteenth centuries of what he called an Anglican norm in such matters, Sykes said that the Tractarians broke with *Anglican* tradition when they tried to substantiate an exclusive theory of episcopacy. It was the Tractarians, not the (once again) much maligned Anglicans of the Enlightenment, who had innovated. In so far as anyone could be said to have done such a thing, Sykes drove his opponents from the ground in this quiet but effective book. One may doubt whether the study of Church history can ever do what he was trying to make it do here, shatter the standing of a particular doctrine. It might be said that Sykes was ignoring the real historical nature and origin of Tractarianism, that the roots of the movement lay in an eighteenth-century sociological pattern quite different from the Biblical, patristic and philosophical material in which they seemed to grow in the 1830s, but Sykes was not trying to penetrate that ambiguous background, any more than he was asking what it was in early nineteenth-century Evangelical families which made so many of the children welcome the Tractarian theory (surely not on rational, historical grounds) once the battle had begun. What Sykes did do, however, was to show in crushing detail that if the Anglican norm could be defined by an appeal to Anglican history then all the historical facts must be given their full weight, and that taken as a whole the evidence implied that the Tractarians (as Anglicans) were, what they had always claimed not to be, innovators. And this was valuable because although *Old Priest and New Presbyter* probably failed to shake Anglo-Catholic confidence to any marked degree, it did in however limited an area (for its subject-matter was not of the first importance) weaken the grip of Anglican mythology on the writing of Anglican history.

Seven

The Eighteenth-Century Evangelical Revival and the Rise of Methodism

There has been a great increase of interest in both the Anglican and Methodist sides of the eighteenth-century Evangelical Revival since 1930. One reason for this has undoubtedly been the rapid development of plans to unite Methodism and Anglicanism into a single Church. Another reason was the comparatively late awakening of Methodist interest in the Methodist past, as though the threat of extinction was needed to make the Methodists study what their tradition contained. One has to make the same general criticism of what has been written in this field as have been made in other parts of this essay: historians of Anglican Evangelicalism and Methodism have relied too much on the biographical approach, and indeed have sometimes seemed to be contributing to a putative Protestant *Lives of the Saints*; little attention has been paid to the varieties of religious behaviour in the Revival; once again the history of the ministry has been substituted for the history of the Church; the sociological and economic understanding of what happened has been left largely unexplored; curiously little has been written about the origin of the movements. In *Church and State* Sykes himself dismissed Anglican Evangelicalism in less than three pages with the comment that 'inevitably its least satisfactory aspect lay in its retrograde intellectual influence'. The best recent study of the causes of the Anglican movement was to be found in an essay by John Walsh in *Essays in Modern Church History* (ed. Walsh and Bennett, 1966). There was a specialized account of a single area in *The Early Cornish Evangelicals, 1735–1760*, by G. C. B. Davies (1951). For the complex relationship between Anglicanism and

Methodism in the eighteenth century *The Age of Disunity*, by the present writer, may also be consulted.

Anglican Evangelicalism will be considered in a later section (see p. 330). On the Methodist side, the most notable feature of our period has been the growth of a franker attitude toward the character of John Wesley, though this could hardly have been said to dominate the recent first (eighteenth-century) volume of the official *History of the Methodist Church in Great Britain* (ed. R. Davies and E. G. Rupp, 1966), a composite work in which there was too much of the Wesleys and too little of the Methodists. The original break with the traditional picture of a flawless Wesley was made by Elsie Harrison in *Son to Susannah* (1937), in which she ignored the long-standing Wesleyan tabu on any mention of John Wesley's sexual life, and suggested that his mother, Susannah, was not the triumphant matriarch of Wesleyan mythology but a maternal failure who crippled her son's emotional development and made it impossible for him to establish a stable relationship with any woman.

Methodist writers fought shy of the issues Mrs Harrison raised, and the next considerable advance came in *The Young Mr Wesley* (1961), by V. H. H. Green, the Anglican historian and Chaplain at Lincoln College, Oxford, where Wesley himself was a Fellow. Green was the first to make extensive use of the diaries which Wesley kept as an undergraduate; he was also able to prove from the College records that John Wesley never at any time lived in the rooms at Lincoln which were solemnly restored (largely with American money) in the 1920s, and in which a long stream of pilgrims has undoubtedly been discovering his aura ever since. The book might have been called 'The Young Mr Wesley at Oxford', however, for Dr Green ignored everything else, including the two years spent in Georgia, the vital prologue to the emotional crisis of Wesley's life. Dr Green made up for this in 1964, however, in a very lively short biography, perhaps the best life so far. The only parallel was the incisive chapter on Wesley which J. H. Plumb included in his eighteenth-century volume of the Pelican

History of England (1950). Dr Green thought that Wesley's famous Evangelical conversion of 1738 was not an Evangelical conversion; he thought that Wesley's action in ordaining some of his preachers in the 1780s was quite unjustifiable. As for the Methodist Revival itself, 'the private lives of the religious societies revealed so often an atmosphere of jealousy and intrigue that it is open to wonder whether the claim for conversion and rebirth really stood the test', a point about Methodist eighteenth-century history which Methodist historians have usually failed to take sufficiently seriously. No other writer in this century has spoken of Wesley with such vigour as this:

> Ultimately John Wesley, like so many of the Christian saints, was self-regarding. He was unwearied in his pursuit of the good, unwearied in charity, unwearied in well-doing, unwearied in the saving of souls, but John Wesley had under God's providence become the real centre of his interest. His life was built round his own experience, an experience glazed and insulated from the outside world by his confidence in God and in himself. Completely selfless and yet intensely egoistic, he had come to identify himself with his own creation. The carefully kept Journal was a record of self-giving actions, but for whom was it written? If it was penned for his own edification, then he was guilty of ministering to his pride. If it was written for posterity, then he was pandering to self-glorification. The diaries form one of the most consistently complacent documents ever written, and the more religious he became the more free from human frailty he appeared to be. Apart from the period of his early life his entries are almost entirely devoid of doubt and self-criticism. Self-satisfied and self-regarding, yet by his unstinted selflessness he made himself wondrously beloved. Nothing could justify the wild attacks of the neo-Calvinists and the writers in the *Gospel Magazine*, but their fury, like his wife's rages, may have been provoked by his untouchability, the hard core of his personality.

This biting little book offered a final summary of the case – the Anglican case, at any rate – against any proposal for Wesley's canonization. The failure either to anticipate or answer such a view of Wesley has been a persistent weakness of Methodist books on the eighteenth century. The first volume of the new official history (see above) ignored the problems set by Wesley's personality altogether. Wesley, indeed, offers a good example of the influence of denominational outlook on the writing of Church history. While Methodists have normally attributed the success of the movement to John Wesley's spiritual genius, both Roman Catholic and Anglican historians have sought to show that whatever was good in Methodism really came from their tradition, and that the later development of Methodism was degeneration. Thus the Jesuit Maximin Piette, in *John Wesley and the Evolution of Protestantism* (French ed. 1926, English translation 1937), argued that the vital conversion in Wesley's life came in 1725 and was the result of studying Catholic authors like à Kempis; it involved a reaction in the direction of Catholicism and away from the chaotic spiritual individualism of Protestantism. V. H. H. Green (op. cit.), as an Anglican, regarded Wesley's career as the natural outcome of his Anglicanism, and said of the 1738 conversion experience that 'in the Moravian sense of an instantaneous change and renewal Wesley was not indeed converted.... The ideas and habits of the next fifty years were already fixed.' Few Methodist writers have agreed with these minimizing views of Wesley's conversion: one may mention the American, Humphrey Lee, *John Wesley and Modern Religion*, Nashville, 1936; and J. E. Rattenbury, *The Conversion of the Wesleys*, 1938.

It was the significance of nineteenth-century Methodism, however, that excited the secular historian. Élie Halévy's *History of the English People* began to appear in French in 1913, the English translation following from 1924. He interpreted early nineteenth-century Wesleyan Methodism as a valuable stabilizing factor in a potentially revolutionary British society, a more favourable view than that of J. L. and Barbara Hammond (*The Age of the Chartists*, 1930, and *The Bleak Age*), who regarded Methodism, together with other forms of Evangelical Pietism, as weakening the power of political resistance of the British working class, and so making their condition worse. The latter view was recently revived in E. P. Thompson's *The Making of the English Working-Class* (1963). He described Methodism as the transforming power which disciplined the emerging industrialized working class. Methodist conversions produced 'the psychic ordeal in which the character-structure of the rebellious pre-industrial labourer or artisan was violently recast into that of the submissive industrial worker. ... It is a phenomenon almost diabolic in its penetration into the very source of the human personality, directed towards the repression of emotional and spiritual energies.' I have criticized Halévy's ignorance about the facts of Methodist history, and also E. P. Thompson's romanticism about it, elsewhere (cf. *The Age of Disunity*, 1966); it is sufficient here to say that these historians seem to exaggerate the effect of denominational allegiance on behaviour; they also accept too uncritically the assumption that nineteenth-century Methodism can be treated as a single, compact, organic historical force. Methodist books on the nineteenth century include *Methodism and Politics, 1791–1854* (1935), by E. R. Taylor, who described the passage of Wesleyan Methodism from Tory to Liberal politics; *After Wesley* (1935), by Dr Maldwyn Edwards, who was inclined to agree with the Hammonds; and various studies by Dr R. F. Wearmouth into the links between nineteenth-century Methodism and working-class politics. *Methodism Divided* (1968) by R. Currie covers the whole range of Methodist history, but his sociological interpretation of it is unconvincing.

Eight

The Nineteenth Century in England: The Anglican Mythology

The history of the Victorian Church in England has still to be written. This is not to say that we do not know the surface outline of events, for indeed certain episodes, such as the story of the Tractarian Movement and of J. H. Newman's withdrawal from the Church of England to the Church of Rome, or the intellectual consequences for Christianity of the thought of Karl Marx, Charles Darwin and Sigmund Freud, have become almost too familiar. Every university examination paper on the period has a question about the Victorian conflict between science and religion and most students are prepared with their answer as though they really knew what the question was about. Nevertheless, the study of the Victorian Church remains in its infancy.

There is first the problem of perspective and interpretation. In general, English Church history in this period is still treated too much as a self-contained unit and written as though what was thought and written in these islands quite overshadowed what happened in Europe and America. There is no ecumenical approach to the problems involved. This is most evident in the way in which German nineteenth-century theology is regarded as though it were peripheral to *Essays and Reviews* (1860) and *Lux Mundi* (1889), neither of which would feature as important landmarks in a properly balanced account of the development of theology, but which are still presented as major events in most British text-books. By 'ecumenical' here I do not mean a vaguely non-denominational approach, but a point of view which grasps, for instance, that the salient facts of eighteenth-century church history as a whole were German intellectualism and Wesleyan revivalism (the latter not least in view of

Methodism's tremendous expansion in the United States and because of the part that it played in the psychological destruction of Calvinism) and that the sociological ground of these has first to be explored and then the resulting perspective applied to the understanding of early nineteenth-century British Church history. The spectacle of Anglican Evangelicals, themselves still obsessed with the sixteenth-century Reformation, denouncing the Tractarians and their successors as 'medieval', while the Anglo-Catholics themselves took it for granted that the future of theology lay in the study of the Fathers, is one that needs fresh analysis. Similarly, British ignorance of the work of the mid-nineteenth-century German school of theologians on the doctrine of the person of Christ has meant a permanent overvaluation of late nineteenth-century British forays into this field. The record has recently been corrected by the publication of *God and the Incarnation in Mid-19th Century German Theology* (1965), edited by an American scholar, Claude Welch. This volume contains translated selections from Gottfried Thomasius (1802–75), Isaak Dorner (1809–84), and A. E. Biedermann (1819–85), representatives of the orthodox Lutheran, 'mediating', and 'speculative' schools of German theology. As Welch said in his introduction:

> For rigour and vigour in working out the implications of the (kenotic) conception, Thomasius (and the German kenoticists in general) make the later nineteenth-century British ventures into kenoticism look pallid indeed. It is all very well to praise the imprecision or vagueness of the British kenoticists as theological modesty and restraint before a mystery, but the presuppositions on which the kenotic theory can really emerge are precisely those which demand pursuit to the limit of the metaphysical and even the psychological questions involved.

The British study of Victorian Church history, in fact, is still to some extent controlled by a historical tradition largely formed in the Victorian period in Anglican circles. If this tradition has not been quite abandoned it is partly because the Victorian Church is still very much with us, some of its controversies even now still undecided: too much is still at stake. This historical tradition not only tended to minimize influences from the Continent, but also depreciated, for example, the theological writings of Matthew Arnold, treating them as the marginal indiscretions of a lay amateur, whereas they offered perhaps the clearest evidence of what was going on in the minds of that large section of the later nineteenth-century Protestant laity which had abandoned the respective orthodoxies of Anglo-Catholicism and Evangelicalism but had not followed men like Leslie Stephen beyond the pale of the Church. The tradition, moreover, exaggerated the significance of the three Cambridge clerical scholars, Hort, Lightfoot and Westcott, to whom was sometimes attributed something like the intellectual salvation of Christianity. It is amusing to find Dr A. R. Vidler, in a recent essay on B. H. Westcott's Christian Socialism (in *Maurice and His Circle*, 1966), almost reaching the conclusion that Westcott was, in social theology at any rate, much less original and penetrating than might have been supposed, and then shying off suddenly with the disclaimer that 'even such a one as myself who is not an alumnus of Westcott House and who has an inveterate disrespect for bishops, feels it to be somehow irreverent to criticize Bishop Westcott'. (It is only fair to add that Dr Vidler was giving the Westcott Memorial Lecture at the time.) It was also part of this historical tradition that the British Church had 'accepted Darwinism' by the end of the nineteenth century (but see my Dr Williams Library Lecture, *From Darwin to Blatchford*, 1966, for a contrary view), and that Liberal theology had declined since about 1920.

Nor is this all. Recent study has not always kept a proper balance between Anglican and non-Anglican interests in the nineteenth century. This problem has always affected the authors of general histories of the period; they have usually been Anglican, and have not been assisted by the fact that modern Free Church historians have shown no great interest in the Victorian Church. Some of the older general histories have not yet been completely replaced, despite their being essentially histories of the Church of England. F. Warre Cornish's *A*

History of the English Church in the 19th Century (2 vols., 1910) remains a standard source for the legal and constitutional aspects of Victorian ecclesiastical history, and in as much as J. H. Overton's *English Church in the 19th Century* dealt chiefly with the years 1800–1830 no later study has yet replaced it altogether. In the 1930s two new outline histories appeared: *Church and People, 1789–1889*, by S. C. Carpenter (1933), and *Religion in the Victorian Era* (1936), by the indefatigable L. E. Elliott-Binns, whose work had the great value of providing that basic information about books and people from which a student could make his own way into the subject. All these were Anglican works, and their points of concentration were naturally the same and derived from a common historical tradition: something about early nineteenth-century Anglican Evangelicalism, more about Tractarianism and the Anglican career of J. H. Newman, the Christian Socialist movement from F. D. Maurice to B. F. Westcott (though not much after), the rise of the ritualist clergy and the consequent internal troubles of the Established Church, *Essays and Reviews* and *Lux Mundi* (the publication of which marked the climax of Carpenter's book, and which so retained its prestige that in 1961 A. R. Vidler, in *The Church in an Age of Revolution*, could still refer to 'the tide that had turned with *Lux Mundi*'), together with Church relations from the Jerusalem Bishopric and the first Lambeth Conference of 1867 onwards.

The lack of balance between Anglican and non-Anglican continued even after 1945. In *A History of the Church in England*, by J. R. H. Moorman (1953), the nineteenth-century section followed very much the traditional formula. Despite, or perhaps because of its title, this was still a history of the Church of England, and the nineteenth-century Free Churches appeared only very occasionally in its pages, objecting to Church rates in the early part of the period and to denominational schools in the latter part. Dr Moorman even reduced the Victorian controversies about disestablishment to disagreement within the Church of England about the establishment of the Anglican Church in Ireland.

For a decisive break with the historical mythology involved in all this one has to come down to the publication of *The Victorian Church, Part 1* (1967), by Owen Chadwick, the first of two volumes in which he intends to survey the history of Christian institutions in England in the Victorian period. The part so far published covers the years 1829–59, and is basically a narrative in which old friends like Tract Ninety, the Jerusalem Bishopric, the Hampden and Gorham Cases, Wiseman's Pastoral and Samuel Wilberforce (to whom Dr Chadwick is kinder than previous historians have been) rub shoulders with less familiar figures, like that squire of Helmingham in Suffolk, who stood up watch in hand if he thought that the sermon was too long; or David Jones, a simple Unitarian weaver from Llanon in Carmarthenshire who became so entangled in his struggle against dissenting disabilities that when he died in flight from the police his vicar, Ebenezer Morris, declared that he died to all appearances under the most awful judgement of God. Such events, and others like them (for the Victorian was on the whole more litigious than liturgical), were considered within the framework of a discussion of three major ecclesiastical issues of the time. First, whether representative government was compatible with an established church; second, whether Christian institutions in Britain could adjust to industrial change, population increase and overseas expansion; third, whether what organized Christianity taught was true.

The narrative of Professor Chadwick's book covers most aspects of Victorian Christianity. This is the story of what the leaders of the Churches wanted and of what they achieved. Dr Chadwick did not make the common mistake of identifying the history of the priesthood with the history of the Church. Down to about 1860, at any rate, it would be true to say that the influence of organized Christianity on Victorian society amounted to a compromise between what the world of Lord Shaftesbury wanted and what the prejudices of Lord John Russell would permit. If on the one hand Anglo-Catholic presbyters extracted concessions from their bishops by a kind of spiritual violence, Professor Chadwick's pages also brought out vividly how the urban mob, equally passionate, resisted the kind of spiritual and social control it resented by the traditional methods of physical violence. He described how the British and Foreign Bible Society had to struggle hard (and invoke Lord Shaftesbury's personal intervention) in order to persuade Prince Albert the Good to grant them the right to set up a stand at the Great Exhibition 'in an obscure back room in a side passage upstairs', and this only on the ground that recent translations were a triumph of the *modern* mind; how an Evangelical campaign (blessed by an Archbishop) drove the directors of the reopening Crystal Palace to agree to put fig leaves on their nude statuary, though 'doubtful whether they would be able to secure a sufficient quantity of fig leaves before the day of opening'; how in 1855 the London crowds (despite Peel's over-rated police force) terrorized the House of Commons into the withdrawal of a Bill which would have limited Sunday trading in the capital; and how in 1856 Lambeth Palace had to be put into a state of defence because of another popular outcry, this time against the attempt of the Sabbatarians to stop Sir Benjamin Hall's military bands from playing in the London parks on a Sunday.

Professor Chadwick did his best to present a balanced picture of Victorian religious institutions, Anglican, Roman Catholic, and Free Church. His suggestion that the Sabbatarian campaigns that he described should be interpreted as in part an attack by the older English rural society on the new urban culture helps to explain why here, as in the case of the teetotal movement, Anglican and non-Anglican were often found pursuing the same aims, even if they did so through different committees. He gave more, and more sensitive, space to Dissent than had any of his Anglican predecessors (Moorman, op. cit., left one with the impression, for example, that teetotalism emerged in Anglican circles in the 1860s, whereas Professor Chadwick dated the movement earlier, and even over-emphasized the share of Methodism in its inception).

This is not to say that there are no traces of the Anglican historical tradition in *The Victorian Church*. Professor Chadwick's rather harsh references to A. C. Tait, for example, were probably due to the lack of a modern critical study of a man who was perhaps the most liberal-minded of nineteenth-century Archbishops of Canterbury, and who brought to the office a tolerance and intelligence rare at any time: Tait, however, was black-listed by the tradition. The Anglo-Catholics never forgave his attempt to limit their freedom by the ill-fated Public Worship Regulation Act of 1875; the Evangelical Anglicans, on the other hand, did not forgive the failure of the attempt; while both groups, for different reasons, doubted the soundness of his doctrinal views. His pithy comment that the tragedy of the Church of England was that the liberals seemed to lack religion and the religious to lack liberalism endeared him to neither party.[1]

This does not mean that bishops have not continued to reap their biographical reward, but in the past thirty years the biggest, if not always the most substantial, biographies have been written about twentieth-century bishops. Thus some idea of what happened to the twentieth-century Church of England might be gathered from the archiepiscopal lives of *Randall Davidson*, by G. K. A. Bell (2 vols., 1935); *Cosmo Gordon Lang*, by J. G. Lockhart (1949); *William Temple*, by F. A. Iremonger (1948); and *C. F. Garbett* (an Archbishop of York), by Charles Smyth (1959) – the last the least convincing, probably because Garbett was the least attractive or significant of an otherwise rather formidable quartet. Other useful episcopal biographies are those of two Anglo-Catholic leaders, *The Life of Charles Gore*, by G. L. Prestige (1935), and *The Life of K. E. Kirk* (Bishop of Oxford), by E. W. Kemp (1959); there are also lives of *A. C. Headlam* (Bishop of Gloucester), who took an intimate part in the ecumenical diplomacy of the 1930s, by R. Jasper (1961), and of *A. F. Winnington-Ingram*, by S. C. Carpenter (1949). R. C. D. Jasper has also (1967) published a life of *George Bell*, Bishop of Chichester, as uncompromising in his opposition to Nazi Germany in the 1930s as Headlam was

1. P. T. Marsh, *The Victorian Church in Decline* (1969), is about Tait as archbishop.

hesitant. Future historians may yet find Ingram's long tenure of the see of London of signal importance in deciding the Anglican Church's response to the twentieth century, for he was a prime example of a new, soft-centred conception of episcopacy quite unlike that held by such men as Samuel Wilberforce, Tait, or Ingram's own predecessor in London, the sardonic Creighton. Over this period episcopal autobiography often appeared, but held only slight historical interest: bishops seemed to lack that inner need to justify themselves which made the autobiographies of generals from the Second World War both fascinating and untrustworthy. H. H. Henson's *Retrospect of an Unimportant Life* (3 vols., 1942–50) stood out, perhaps because of Henson's ambiguous prominence in ecclesiastical politics.

Nineteenth-century bishops have been rather less well served in recent study, and the stately Victorian lives with their plentiful though not always reliable quotations from letters and other documents often reveal as much if not more than later books. The vitally important Tait, the enigmatic Frederick Temple, the Alpine Harold Browne, Benson, have not been re-interpreted. There is a short book on *William Thompson, Archbishop of York 1819–1890*, by H. Kirk-Smith (1958), and there is a longer study of the formidable High Churchman, *Henry Phillpotts, Bishop of Exeter, 1778–1869*, by J. C. S. Nias (1951). There is a life of *Connop Thirlwall, Historian and Theologian*, by J. C. Thirlwall (1936): he was Bishop of St David's and for many years in the first half of the nineteenth century a brilliant if unreliable defender of intellectual freedom in the intensive Anglican controversies about Biblical criticism. Professor P. Hinchcliffe wrote a short study of *Colenso* (1964), while another portrait of an Anglican bishop in Africa, *Mackenzie's Grave* (1959), came from the pen of Professor Owen Chadwick, but neither of these cast more than incidental light on the nature of the mid-Victorian Church in England. In *Godliness and Good Learning* (1961), David Newsome was chiefly interested in Victorian ideas of education, but he included an essay on the otherwise unchronicled, disastrous first Bishop of Manchester, the sub-Christian Prince Lee; while in *The Parting of Friends* (1966) he followed the career of Samuel Wilberforce some way into his tenure of the see of Oxford. Newsome's intention, or part of it, was to dispute the unfavourable verdict which historical tradition attached to 'Soapy Sam' who, as everybody knew, ardently longed to become Archbishop of Canterbury, but who died as Bishop of Winchester, the leader of a kind of unofficial High Church opposition to his rival, A. C. Tait.

Nine

Anglo-Catholicism, J. H. Newman, and Catholic Modernism

ANGLO-CATHOLICISM

So many books have been published since 1930 about nineteenth-century and twentieth-century Church history that it seems necessary to consider them under several broad headings, beginning with Anglo-Catholicism – a subject which leads on naturally into John Henry Newman and into a brief note on Catholic Modernism. No revolutionary advances have been made in the study of Anglo-Catholicism, or for that matter in the study of its natural Anglican opposite, Evangelicalism. Both groups have been discussed in terms of their personalities, William Wilberforce, Simeon, Keble and Newman, for example; and in terms of their theology, though Evangelical theology between 1840 and 1914 has not yet been examined with the care that has been given to some of the Anglo-Catholic writers. The Anglo-Catholic adoption of a form of Christian Socialism in the later nineteenth century has been lavishly documented, and Kathleen Heasman, in *Evangelicals in Action* (1964), tried to show that the whole Evangelical world, a wider constituency than the Church of England, throbbed with social concern if hardly with social theology in the Victorian Age.

Much of this work, however, was in the shape of biography or abstract theology: the social groups concerned have been analysed less. We know very little about the kind of people who became Anglo-Catholics or Evangelicals in the course of the nineteenth century, or the extent to which they could claim to speak for a section of the Anglican laity as well as for particular bodies of clergy. Research might show, for instance, that what was called the Broad Church, or anti-dogmatic theological attitude, which was never strong among the more prominent ministers and is therefore minimized in Anglican histories of the nineteenth-century Church, was in fact the most widespread theological attitude among the laity. A related problem is how far the growth of Anglo-Catholicism and Evangelicalism was related to the nineteenth-century decline of the social status of the clergy in Britain. A further neglected problem is the structure of these religious groups: the modes of organization and common action of the Anglo-Catholics and Evangelicals have not been sufficiently examined, or compared with those of the Victorian sects proper; they have been defined and discussed too much in terms of theology and not enough in terms of institutions and political activity. Nor has anyone shown so far how the development of ecclesiastical parties in the nineteenth-century Church of England was related to the crumbling of the eighteenth-century social pattern, to which the older denominational structure characteristic of Dissent had been geared. Anglo-Catholicism and Anglican Evangelicalism emerged in response to the changing social situation of the Anglican Church, but they did not become formally and officially separated 'sects' or 'denominations' – as Methodism had done in the later eighteenth century; once again, this is not a process which can be explained entirely in theological terms, by an investigation of particular doctrines of the Church, for example.

As a study in religious behaviour Tractarianism offers a rich field and one even now not very much worked over, for with Tractarianism it tends to be Newman all the way. The centenary of the Anglo-Catholic movement fell in 1933 and was commemorated with many books, a few of which are still remembered, though perhaps only one, *Oxford Apostles* (1933), by Sir Geoffrey Faber, broke new ground. Of what was written from the movement's point of view *The History of the Anglo-Catholic Revival from 1845*, by W. J. Sparrow Simpson (1932), concentrated on the period after Newman's secession but suffered from the author's conviction that the movement was and always had been an unmixed blessing. *Northern Catholicism*, ed. N. P. Williams and C. Harris (1933), contained several historical essays whose chief value was to show how movements of a similar nature had taken place in Germany, Holland and the United States. *The Development of Modern Catholicism* (1933), by W. L. Knox and A. R. Vidler, was an essay in theological history whose aim was to show that the Liberal Catholicism in which the authors ardently believed was the natural heir of early nineteenth-century Tractarianism, which had so far restored the vitality of the Church of England that it was possible, in the later nineteenth century, for the very Liberalism against which Tractarianism had originally protested to enter into fruitful union with Catholicism itself.

These books were not so much historical writings as themselves historical evidence of the euphoria with which Anglo-Catholicism greeted its centenary. This state of mind was to be seen at its peak in *The Social Implications of the Oxford Movement* (1933), by W. G. Peck, who said that

> the Oxford Movement was part of that wider revival of Catholic thought which has now become one of the most notable features of the intellectual situation at the very time when the exhaustion of the secular adventure has produced so inclusive a confusion. To learn the right use of the world, and the satisfying structure of society in that operation, men must now return to the principles of the sacramental fellowship from which they have strayed so far. (pp. 315–16)

In reality, of course, the Catholic revival was dying down and it was the secular adventure which turned out to be far from exhausted. Nevertheless, these and other books asserted the historical judgement that the Anglo-Catholic movement saved the Victorian Church of England from collapse. This view was recently repeated by Professor Owen Chadwick (*The Victorian Church*, 1966):

> Beneath popular disesteem and public weakness they strengthened the soul of the Church of England. ... No one did more to drive Anglican worshippers out of formalism, to give them a sense that Christianity had a history and a treasure not insular, and to enable

sympathetic hearts to perceive the beauty and poetry of religion. (p. 231)

This note of approval was carried even further by historians who minimized the differences between Anglican Evangelicalism and Tractarianism, so that it became possible to speak of a 'dependence of the Tractarians on the Evangelicals'. This idea had appeared already in Yngve Brilioth's *The Anglican Revival* (1925), and was re-emphasized by him in his contribution to the centenary, *Three Lectures on Evangelicalism and the Oxford Movement* (1934). Its strongest recent expression was in *Worship and Theology in England: from Watts and Wesley to Maurice*, by D. Horton Davies. In a passage which summed up much modern opinion, he said:

It has been customary to define the relationship between the Evangelical and Tractarian parties as an antithetical one and, indeed, the later so-called 'Ritualistic Controversy' (which was, in fact, a controversy about ceremonial) was sufficiently embittered to lend force to this view. On the other hand, ceremonialism was a later development of Tractarianism, and not expressive of its early genius, at least as discoverable in the first Tractarian leaders who had a very minor and subsidiary interest in ceremonial matters. Furthermore, this mutual suspicion and partisanship may be regarded as deflecting attention from the basic loyalties shared by the Evangelicals and Tractarians within the same Church of England. The view will be maintained that ultimately the Oxford Movement is not so much an antithesis or opposition to the Evangelical wing as it is a supplementing of it with elements of thought and practice that were lost and forgotten. Certainly, there would have been no Tractarian or Oxford Movement unless the Evangelicals had revived personal religion in the Church of England, and to this extent the later movement is indebted to the earlier. ... The present demand that party cries and partisanship itself be dropped in the Church of England is a proof that the contributions of each movement were mutually fructifying. (p. 244)

There is no space here to criticize this argument in detail. One can only underline the danger that anxiety to reconcile these Anglican traditions in the present may lead to an unhistorical account of their relations in the past. The 'ritualist' phase of the Oxford movement ought not, for instance, to be treated as 'not Tractarian'; this prejudice goes back at least as far as R. W. Church, for whom Newman was all that historically mattered, and for whom the 'ritualists' were just a dilution of a pure original. Similarly, the eighteenth-century revival may have stimulated personal religion, but, historically, the first Tractarian generation reacted against what it believed to be Evangelical lack of personal religion. Nevertheless, Horton Davies' attitude may be regarded as dominant, and the same outlook coloured both Owen Chadwick's anthology, *The Mind of the Oxford Movement* (1960), and a second reader, *Anglo-Catholic Theology* (1965), edited by E. R. Fairweather. Both books might lead the unwary student to suppose that the mind of the Oxford Movement was serene, traditional, lofty and dull, whereas Anglo-Catholic theology was controversial and committed from the first blast of Keble's Assize trumpet. It is an inevitable hazard of anthologies, of course, that they tend to reinforce traditional perspectives.

At the time of the centenary there was not much criticism of the Movement. The keenest attack was that of E. A. Knox (a former Bishop of Manchester), in *The Tractarian Movement, 1833–1845*, a book now largely forgotten. Knox argued that Tractarianism was a phase in a more general revival of religion in Europe in the second quarter of the nineteenth century; it was a tragically mistaken phase, however, because the Tractarians, impressed by the 'encircling gloom' of the 1830s, found the root of all evil in the rebellion against the divine authority of the Church, the great, romantic Church of the Middle Ages, and thought that if this authority could be restored all would be well – whereas, Knox said, the true danger to Christianity lay in the liberal theology of Strauss and his successors, and to this the Oxford Movement had no answer at all:

> For this attack the Oxford Divines had made no preparation. Of German theology they had studied nothing but the Roman Catholic Symbolic of Möhler. Scientific history they had despised and done their best to discredit. While Thomas Arnold had studied the system

of Niebuhr, they had regarded his doing so as another evidence of his heterodoxy. It was ludicrous, had it not been inexpressibly sad, that against the deluge of Strauss' *Life of Jesus* the great and brilliant Newman provided nothing better for his followers in the way of historical refuge than *The Lives of the Saints*. The defence of the Church of England in the hour of peril was left to Cambridge, to Alford, Westcott, Lightfoot and Thirlwall. Oxford had not even sympathy to offer the orthodox Germans, whom W. G. Ward in his rashness had pronounced worse than atheists. (p. 356)

Oxford had no 'rational defence against a deliberate onslaught on the foundations of the Catholic Church' (p. 357).

There was much truth in this, though it could have been said just as accurately of Charles Simeon and the Anglican Evangelicals of the same period. Knox added that the Anglo-Catholics failed at what for them was the crucial point – they did not succeed in increasing the authority of the clergy over the Anglican laity, who persisted in what he called 'the national refusal to be governed by the clergy even in things spiritual' (p. 364).

For the moment discussion of the movement as a whole is limited by our comparative ignorance of what happened after 1845, of what kind of men became Anglo-Catholic priests, and of the actual power of the movement at parish level in 1860 and 1900. At the personal level, there is still no critical life of either Pusey or Liddon, and studies of secondary figures such as W. J. E. Bennett of Frome and W. J. Butler of Wantage would be valuable. Miss Georgiana Battiscombe's *John Keble, A Study in Limitations* (1963) was almost a devotional study, too brief on the twenty years through which Keble lived after Newman's secession, and unwilling, like so much Church historical writing, to face the complicated and often bitter struggles into which ecclesiastical politics degenerated. *John Keble's Literary and Religious Contribution to the Oxford Movement* (Nijmegen, 1959), by W. J. A. M. Beek, had some of the vices of an academic thesis without Miss Battiscombe's virtues. Some aspects of the Anglo-Catholic revival of monasticism have been chronicled. In 1950 T. J. Williams published a not very critical biography of *Priscilla Sellon* (second ed. 1965), whom Pusey called 'the restorer after three centuries of the Religious Life in the English Church', but also a woman whose name was so controversial that at least one of Pusey's biographers quietly omitted it. A fuller account of the monastic revival followed in 1955, in P. F. Anson's *The Call of the Cloister*; in 1958 A. M. Allchin wrote a shorter, more reflective essay, *The Silent Rebellion.*

Neither Anson nor Allchin paid enough attention to the French Catholic influences on this movement. This insularity also came out in Professor Horton Davies' view (op. cit.) that Anglican Evangelical influence on Anglo-Catholicism could be seen in the Anglo-Catholic Missions to London in 1869, whereas the inspiration of this aggressive phase was really the French Catholic 'mission', whose origin could be traced back into the seventeenth century, and which had been used vigorously in France after 1815 in the hope of rechristianizing France. The same criticism applied to an interesting book by a German scholar, Dieter Voll, *Catholic Evangelicalism* (1963), a work originally published in Munich as *Hochkirklicher Pietismus* (1960). Dieter Voll interpreted the Missions to London of 1869 and 1874 as a kind of reconciliation between Anglo-Catholicism and Evangelicalism of permanent value for the ecumenical future – once again one notices how often the writing of Church history is influenced by later ecclesiastical needs. In fact, no such reconciliation took place, but the missions carried out by the Anglo-Catholic Cowley Fathers, with their reliance on the framework supplied by the sacramental system, their use of French services such as that for 'the renewal of baptismal vows', and their appeals to lapsed believers to return to the Eucharist, were bitterly criticized by the Evangelicals, who conducted their own campaigns in revival meetings of a type familiar since the days of John Wesley and George Whitfield. Moreover, the reappearance of monasticism in a Protestant context requires more elaborate psychological and sociological study than has yet been given to it.

Another aspect of Anglo-Catholicism was its relationship to the history of nineteenth-century architecture. For the Church historian the most important study was *The Cambridge Movement* (1962), by James White, an American scholar. White took for granted the background supplied by such works as Sir Kenneth Clark's *The Gothic Revival, an Essay in the Study of Taste* (revised ed. 1950), and John Summerson's *Heavenly Mansions* (1949), as well as Henry-Russell Hitchcock's remarkable *Early Victorian Architecture in Britain* (2 vols., New Haven, 1954). *The Cambridge Movement* was a history of the Cambridge Camden Society, started in 1839, and of its periodical, *The Ecclesiologist* (1841–68), which White claimed did far more than the movement based on Oxford to bring about the changes in worship and architecture which constituted the real religious revolution of Victoria's reign, and covered England with neo-medieval churches suited only to a neo-medieval liturgy. His book contained a full bibliography of the publications of the Camden Society, and drew attention to the importance of John Mason Neale, one of the forgotten leaders of the Victorian Church. From a non-Anglican point of view *The Architectural Expression of Methodism, 1738–1840*, by G. W. Dolbey (1964), showed that Gothic was more a secular than a religious fashion: after 1848 one had the extraordinary spectacle of Methodist and other Nonconformist bodies building chapels with Gothic exteriors and meeting-house interiors; officially, the Methodists adopted the Gothic style because it was cheaper than the Grecian. Further light on all this may be found in P. F. Anson's *Church Furnishing* (1962), which illustrated how the interiors of Victorian churches altered steadily under the pressure of ecclesiastical fashion. Yet another side of the Victorian movement, its zeal for a new training of the priesthood, was discussed in *The Founding of Cuddesdon*, by Owen Chadwick (1964).

These books do not amount to a full account of Anglo-Catholicism after 1845. Some biographies must be mentioned: *Dean Church, The Anglican Response to Newman* (1958), by B. A. Smith; *Martyr to Ritualism, Father Mackonochie of St*

Alban's, Holborn (1965), by M. Reynolds; *Darwell Stone* (1943), by F. L. Cross, who in 1933 had written a book on the Oxford Movement and the seventeenth century. Cross's biography of Stone was an important source for knowledge of the late nineteenth-century Anglo-Catholic Movement. A valuable recent addition to the literature was *The Tractarian Understanding of the Eucharist*, by A. Hardelin (Uppsala, 1965). For the twentieth century biographies have included *Lord Halifax*, by J. G. Lockhart (1935–6), the *Life of Charles Gore*, by G. L. Prestige (1935), and *The Liberal Catholicism of Charles Gore* (1960) by F. C. Carpenter.

THE PROBLEM OF J. H. NEWMAN

Somehow, the central problem remains untouched: why did a section of the nineteenth-century Anglican Church move so dogmatically and successfully back to a style of religious behaviour that had seemed so entirely abandoned in England? The problem does not become simpler if one turns at last to John Henry Newman, still himself the subject of international scholarship. The outstanding modern contribution to Newman studies has been C. S. Dessain's superb and as yet unfinished edition of *The Letters and Diaries of John Henry Newman* (1961): so far volumes xi-xviii have been published, containing the letters and diaries from the beginning of his Roman period, from October 1845; Dessain proposed to publish the whole of Newman's Anglican correspondence in his first ten volumes. Other Newman manuscripts were edited by Henry Tristram as the *Autobiographical Writings* (1956); Tristram also wrote *Newman and his Friends* (1933). More recently Martin J. Svaglic has published a richly annotated edition of the *Apologia Pro Vita Sua* (1967). Many useful biographical studies have been made: *Cardinal Newman and William Froude*, by G. H. Harper (1933); two books by R. D. Middleton, *Newman and Bloxham* (1947) and *Newman at Oxford, his Religious Development* (1950); Maisie Ward's *Young Mr Newman* (1948); and *Newman's Way*, by Sean O'Faolain

(1952). There have been many background studies, among them Joseph Althoz's *The Liberal Catholic Movement in England, The Rambler and its Contributors, 1848–64* (1960); *The Wilfrid Wards and the Transition*, vol. i, *The Nineteenth Century* (1934), again by Maisie Ward, a book really about the growth of English Roman Catholicism in the Victorian Age; two works on Dominic Barberi, who admitted Newman into the Roman Church, *Dominic Barberi in England*, by Urban Young (1935), and *Father Dominic Barberi* (1947), by Dennis Gwynn, who also wrote *Lord Shrewsbury, Pugin and the Catholic Revival* (1946), and *Newman's University, Idea and Reality*, by F. McGrath (1951). Newman has not attracted much attention in England as a theologian; the best English study was Professor Owen Chadwick's *From Bossuet to Newman, The Idea of Doctrinal Development* (1957); there have been many continental studies, one of the best of which, *Newman the Theologian*, by J. H. Walgrave, was published in English in 1960. (But see J. Coulson's *Newman, a Portrait Restored*, 1965.)

Through much of this material may be traced a sustained attempt to present a consistent picture of Newman as the great modern saint of English Catholicism, the man with the key to our present religious discontents. This was broadly the approach of Miss Meriol Trevor's full-scale two-volume biography, *The Pillar of Cloud* and *Light in Winter* (1962); another, less convincing attempt was *The Life and Spirituality of J. H. Newman*, by the French ex-Protestant Oratorian, Louis Bouyer, originally published in 1952. The best expression of the case of Newman's critics was Sir Geoffrey Faber's *Oxford Apostles* (1933), a book which despite its title was really about Newman. Faber was consciously reacting against Lytton Strachey's portrait of Newman as the gentle artist *manqué* of his essay on Cardinal Manning: 'A very little first-hand knowledge blew to pieces Strachey's cynical estimate of the Movement as a game of exciting make-believe. It was evident that the Gallic method in biography purchased readability at too high a price, and that it might be thought worth while to try to understand the recent past, instead of treating it as an amusing period piece' (p. xiii). In the background, however, though not often referred to (except by Louis Bouyer, who sought to refute his thesis), was *The Mystery of Newman*, by Henri Bremond, translated from the French and published with an introduction by George Tyrrell in 1910. To estimate the present position in Newman studies one has to look at Bremond first.

Bremond (whom Bouyer dismissed as portraying Newman in his own image) made at least three statements which have left their mark on the literature even if they are not often repeated. First, he insisted on the primary importance of Newman's Evangelical Anglican conversion at the age of fifteen: 'I do not hesitate to say that this was the most important date of his life . . . the turning point of his life was not that October evening which saw him abjure Protestantism in the hands of an Italian priest. The essential conversion dated much further back. . . .' (p. 183). Second, when he came to delineate Newman's inner piety he said: 'It is only the imagination of Newman that is mystical; his heart is not so. . . . He is a stranger to those strong passions which alone could be adequate to the visions of his mind. Devotion, in his case, often difficult, sometimes very sweet, is never ardent' (pp. 268–9). And Bremond linked this with what seemed to him Newman's self-centredness, his need for love, and his inability to give equal love in return. Third, Bremond was convinced that Newman could not be called a saint in the traditional sense: he was 'too like the generality of mankind for Rome to canonize him' (p. 326); and on the last page of his book Bremond said again: 'let those who wish to find, not among fanatics, nor even among saints or mystics, but in everyday humanity, a witness of the invisible, come to Newman' (p. 358).

Faber, Bouyer and Miss Trevor were all concerned with Bremond's interpretation, and with the portrait of Newman as hyper-sensitive and the victim of unnecessary suffering for which Wilfrid Ward's biography (1912) bore some of the responsibility. It is not for Church historians to say whether or not the Roman Church should canonize Newman, but they are perhaps obliged to say that this is an issue which can only confuse the historical account of Newman himself. Thus Meriol Trevor's biography (see above) offered too sweeping a defence; one would have to read *Father Faber* (1961), by Ronald Chapman, for example, or *Cardinal Manning, His Public Life and Influence, 1865–1892*, by V. A. McClelland (1962), to realize that either of these men might have objected to being judged purely in terms of their behaviour towards Newman. Sir Geoffrey Faber, on the other hand, expanded Bremond's subdued statements about Newman's self-centredness and inability to trust himself to his emotions, and concocted a striking picture of a man emotionally crippled by his mother, a sublimated homosexual (though the term itself was not pressed), a man unable to bear the full weight of maturity and authority and so perpetually creating situations in which others, deliberately or casually, humiliated and rejected him, and a man who at the same time was a theologian who salvaged his self-respect by turning his self-imposed defeats into occasions of penitential obedience. All this was brilliantly persuasive, though Miss Trevor (op. cit.) weakened the force of some of his illustrations, as when she pointed out that Wilfrid Ward gave no authority for the statement that Newman lay all night on Ambrose St John's bed after his great friend's death, and that other known facts hardly allowed for the possibility of the incident. She also said that Faber's use of William Ward's famous dream, in which he saw a beautiful woman who subsequently turned out to be Newman, was open to the objection that the dream gave information about Ward's state of mind, and not about Newman's state of sex. Miss Trevor was less convincing in her attempt to interpret the long estrangement between Newman's Birmingham Oratory and F. W. Faber's Oratory in London as a significant matter of high principle: the unfavourable reaction of many reviewers to the publication of Newman's correspondence on this subject (cf. Dessain, op. cit.) did not arise purely from prejudice and misunderstanding, but from something in Newman's tone which explains, if it did not entirely prove the truth of, Bremond's reading of the Cardinal's character.

The problem of Newman is not the same, however, for the Catholic and the non-Catholic writer. Newman's conversion to Catholicism must seem natural to Catholic historians – even Bremond said that the idea of a Protestant Newman was impossible. Most Catholic writers have been anxious to defend Newman against nineteenth-century charges of disloyalty and unorthodoxy, to present him as the symbol of all those Catholic theologians who would like to see the Roman Church on better intellectual terms with the modern world. The non-Catholic writer, on the other hand, is bound to feel that Newman's adhesion to Rome was a less natural and therefore in a sense a more significant example of Victorian religious behaviour. He may think that Newman's willingness to accept the decree of Infallibility outweighed his opposition to some of the more extreme Catholic interpretations of the dogma. Above all, he may feel that Catholic historians have concentrated too much on the case of Newman himself, when what needs more study is the emergence in the early nineteenth century of this small but talented group of English converts; Sir Geoffrey Faber's book was sometimes open to the same criticism, that he reduced the causes of the Second Spring to Newman's complex personality.

CATHOLIC MODERNISM

In England, however, too much time has been spent on Newman and not enough on Catholic Modernism, the liberalizing movement which flowered briefly in the Roman Church at the beginning of the twentieth century, was savagely repressed by Pope Pius X, but which found some belated recognition in the limited reforms discussed at the Second Vatican Council. In English, the introductory study remains A. R. Vidler's book, *The Modernist Movement in the Roman Church* (1934); more recently, Dr Vidler edited a fresh edition of the most important English Modernist work, *Christianity at the Cross-Roads* (1963, original edition 1909), by the ex-Jesuit George Tyrrell, but this attracted little attention. The swift passage into scepticism of the leader of the movement, the Frenchman Alfred Loisy, left the Modernists with few friends in England apart from Maud Petre, whose loyalty to the defeated never faltered, who wrote *Von Hügel and Tyrrell* in 1937, and whose last book was a brief, posthumously published biography of *Loisy* himself (1944). Baron von Hügel retained his popularity (at least in part because he submitted to the Roman See), and Maurice Nédoncelle published *Friedrich von Hügel, His Life and Thought* in 1937; further interest followed the publication of Michael de la Bedoyère's *Life of Baron von Hügel* (1951), which contained much previously unpublished material. French philosophy has been as much out of favour in England as Catholic Modernism, so that it is hardly surprising that Maurice Blondel, the Catholic philosopher who was also involved in the early stages of the affair, has remained almost unknown here: Alexander Dru and Illtyd Trethowan have now produced a translation of his *Letter on Apologetics and History of Dogma* (1965). Of Italian Modernism and its leader, Ernesto Buonaiuti, there is small trace in the English literature. There is considerable French interest in the subject of Modernism (see especially *La Crise Moderniste*, by Émile Poulat, Paris, 1962), and this has resulted in recent editions of the correspondence of Blondel, Loisy, von Hügel and others. The editorial matter has to be read with caution, however, for Modernism is not yet a dead issue in the Roman Church, and there is no question for the moment of more than a partial rehabilitation of the principal personalities. Finally, one cannot leave the subject of twentieth-century Catholicism without a reference to *Ronald Knox* (1959), by Evelyn Waugh, perhaps a perfect example of the biographer's art, which is to combine charity with truth.

Ten

The Evangelical Tradition

This is not the place to enter on a definition of Evangelicalism, but it is proper to distinguish between the Anglican Evangelicals of the eighteenth and early nineteenth century and those who followed them. In his short life of *Shaftesbury* (1964) G. F. A. Best said that perhaps there never was an Evangelical 'party' worth speaking of in the first part of Queen Victoria's reign. Wilberforce and the Clapham Sect had been one thing, but once they were dead no comparably homogeneous group of leaders took their place.

> There was so much Evangelicalism of one kind and another about in early Victorian Britain that the historian cannot define it further than by noting what, in general, men who were ready to acknowledge themselves as Evangelicals believed, and by noticing how similar their reactions were to certain stimuli – Popery, Puseyism, Lord's Day Observance, Liberal Theology, slavery, overseas missions, dancing and the theatre for example. But even in these special interests of theirs, there was room for some diversity of opinion and emphasis; and on an even larger number of great political, social and intellectual questions they shared no common views at all. To speak of an 'Evangelical party' in the 1860s is not thus very helpful. (pp. 65–6)

And Best went on to point out how Shaftesbury constantly found himself unable to draw help in his crusades from an 'Evangelical' clergy who he felt ought to be willing to rush to his assistance.

This was well said, and two observations may be added. The first is that although the Clapham Sect disintegrated as G. F. A. Best observes, Anglican Evangelicalism did reform in the second half of the nineteenth century, so that a powerful pressure group of this kind existed in the late Victorian Anglican Church. The second is that if the tendency of this group was to withdraw from the great political and social questions of the time, this was partly because the new lay leadership lacked the wealth and political influence of William Wilberforce and his friends. This was the lesson of *The History of the Evangelical Party in the Church of England*, by G. R. Balleine, a book first published in 1909, and most recently reprinted in 1951, when G. W. Bromiley added a chapter which brought the account well down into the twentieth century. Balleine's book showed, almost incidentally, how Anglican Evangelicalism gradually contracted out of nineteenth-century society, how it ceased to be purely 'Anglican' and became the centre of an Evangelical 'world' with links with the Baptists, the Plymouth Brethren, and the American professional revivalists who came to Britain at fairly regular intervals after 1830. Balleine did not provide much more than a rapid résumé of names, dates and anecdotes together with book-titles, but as such the book remains indispensable to anyone entering the world of British Evangelicalism for the first time. It was, however, a tale of declining significance, and perhaps this explains why no one has really replaced a book which did not attempt to penetrate far beneath the surface. L. E. Elliott-Binns sometimes seemed on the point of doing so: he wrote *Religion in the Victorian Era* (1936), *The Development of English Theology in the Later 19th Century* (1952) and *The Early Evangelicals* (1953): these were compilations, however, and threw little new light. Among special studies *The Evangelicals at Oxford 1735–1871*, by J. S. Reynolds (1953), stood out. He said that from 1845 to 1870 the Oxford Evangelicals were at the height of their power in the university; their power declined as Oxford's reputation as the home of Anglo-Catholicism made Evangelical parents hesitant about sending their boys there. He also provided a valuable appendix containing biographical sketches of the chief Oxford Evangelicals. Valuable information about the fringe of the movement may be found in books by J. C. Pollock. *A Cambridge Movement* (1953) was an account of the growth of the late nineteenth-century student Christian movement which at first comprehended Evangelical as well as other kinds of Christian, but from which a more purely Evangelical student group broke away in 1910. The history of the Keswick Convention (*The Keswick Story*, 1964) was indispensable to anyone who wanted to understand the strange Evangelical Holiness movement which entered Britain from America in the 1860s, and penetrated Anglican Evangelicalism in the 1870s (cf. *Christian Perfection and American Methodism*, by John L. Peters, New York, 1956). *The Cambridge Seven* (1955) also shed incidental light on the internal workings of the late nineteenth-century Evangelical community.

But if no new general historian of Anglican Evangelicalism has appeared since Balleine, one still senses a change in the presentation of Evangelical history. There has been a steady drive to bring Evangelicalism into the foreground of the Victorian picture, to insist on its importance and positive value, to work out for modern Evangelicalism as distinguished a pedigree as that of Anglo-Catholicism, offering John and Charles Wesley (who were not Anglican Evangelicals, however, despite the determination of many writers, including J. S. Reynolds, op. cit., to make them such) the two Henry Venns (of whom the nineteenth-century missionary leader is emerging as much the more important), Charles Simeon and J. C. Ryle as the equivalent of John Keble, Edward Pusey and Charles Gore. In other words, the overriding purpose has been more ecclesiastical than historical, and has run parallel with the slight recovery of the Evangelical movement in the Church of England in the twentieth century.

This emphasis on the importance of the Evangelicals in the formation of the Victorian Church of England and in the growth of the characteristic pietism of a large section of Victorian society has meant a recurrence of interest in Charles Simeon (1759–1836), the Cambridge don in whom some have seen the architect of nineteenth-century Evangelicalism, and who was certainly the great-grandfather of those student religious societies which are at once the pride and bane of English university religious life. Mention has already been made of *Simeon and Church Order* (1940), perhaps the seminal work in this field. In 1959 a bi-centenary appraisal, *Charles Simeon*, was published, edited by Michael Hennell, who in 1958 had produced one of the few new Evangelical biographies, *John Venn and the Clapham Sect* (a quiet record of a quiet life), and Arthur Pollard, the leading British authority on Mrs Gaskell, the novelist, who also edited a short selection of Simeon's sermons, *His Master's Voice* (1957). The bi-centenary volume accepted Canon Smyth's dictum that Simeon's ecclesiastical genius had not been sufficiently recognized. 'He seems to me,' he said, 'to rank with Samuel Wilberforce, Bishop of Oxford, the Remodeller of Episcopate as Burgess calls him, as one of the founding fathers, or Remodellers of the Church of England in the nineteenth century,' a statement some of whose force depends upon how far one feels that the Establishment really was remodelled in the nineteenth century, and how far one attributes what was done to politicians, Dissenters and the Church Commissioners.

It is not easy to accept what has rapidly become an orthodoxy about Simeon. If he really was a founding father of the Church of England in the nineteenth century this should be obvious in the developments which followed his death. Some of the contributors to the symposium offered clues as to how far the evidence confirmed the hypothesis. In 'Simeon's Pastoral Theology', for example, Douglas Webster distinguished between Simeon's positive teaching on the Eucharist and the negative, defensive teaching of his Evangelical successors, who had been frightened by the Oxford Movement. The same suggestion of a tradition petering out was to be found in 'Simeon's Doctrine of the Church', by Michael Webster, who admitted that despite Simeon's strong emphasis on the corporate life of the Church of England his successors became far more individualistic and obsessed with anti-Roman Catholic polemic. The contrast with Simeon was not quite as striking here, however. He was a vigorous opponent of Roman Catholic Emancipation in the late 1820s, and said that 'all attempts to reform the Roman Catholic Church will be in vain and there must be an extermination of it as a Church, and any conversion must be of individuals'.

Simeon, in other words, did not mould an interpretation of Anglicanism strong enough to survive without serious distortion the impact of Anglo-Catholic teaching. Nothing in his writings or practical spirituality prepared anyone for the sudden return of religious symbolism; no spirit of prophecy rested upon him, though he lived in an important college in constant contact with young men. In the tight little Evangelical circle of which he was the centre, religious revival could only mean a continuation of what had already been achieved – a new spirit of consecrated earnestness, in contrast with the apparent formalism and partial inefficiency of the eighteenth century. Nothing Simeon said or did prepared men for a time when Evangelicalism was itself rejected as formal, and when religious revival meant a passionate return to the use of images.

This view of Simeon's importance was certainly brushed aside in *Fathers of the Victorians: the Age of Wilberforce* (1961) by an American, Ford K. Brown, a book in which laymen predominated and Simeon was hardly mentioned at all. This book aroused considerable controversy. The title suggested a study of one of the more fascinating problems of nineteenth-century church history, why so many Anglo-Catholics were men who had been brought up in Evangelical homes. The author, however, was concerned with the origins of the Victorian moral tone, and his thesis was that whereas John Wesley failed to achieve the moral and religious reformation of England, William Wilberforce organized an Evangelical pressure-group which captured the leadership of early Victorian society.

The Victorian Age escaped a heritage it might easily have had. If Wilberforce (or some equally perfect leader) had not chosen to reform his country and if the Methodists had retained their status of 1800 (there is no sign that they became a powerful reforming force) there could have been more sporting duchesses, more objectionable royal mistresses and continued lurid scenes at the Brighton Pavilion. The obscene prints and objects could have gone on being openly displayed in the shop fronts and sold in young ladies' schools and the *Town and Country Magazine* could have continued its open lubricities.

Ford K. Brown made two points which were not well received. He said, for instance, that as an old man Wilberforce abandoned Anglican Evangelicalism and adopted the High Church outlook. This statement was directly contradicted by David Newsome in *The Parting of Friends* (1966), a still more important study of the Wilberforce world. 'The truth is,' wrote Dr Newsome, who had made a special study of the Wilberforce family manuscripts,

> that Wilberforce was as firmly Evangelical in the last years of his life as he was when he first saw the light of God's grace when studying Doddridge's 'Rise and Progress of Religion in the Soul' in the autumn of 1784. The point which Mr Brown missed was that William Wilberforce, whom he represented quite erroneously as a man committed entirely to promoting the interests of a single religious party, abhorred the very name of party as applied to religion even more decidedly than he disliked embroiling himself in the concerns of political parties.

Ford K. Brown also said that when Robert and Samuel Wilberforce wrote their father's biography they tried 'to minimize, or even to conceal as far as they could, their father's adherence to the Evangelical party'. Dr Newsome granted that Robert Wilberforce, already under Newman's influence, might have been glad to tone down some of the expressions of Wilberforce's evangelical zeal, but said that neither Samuel Wilberforce nor James Stephen, to whom the book was read before its publication, was prepared to agree with this. One may safely follow Dr Newsome on the Wilberforces, though his picture of William himself would have benefited from a more serious discussion of Wilberforce's missionary politics. F. K. Brown's book had many brilliant passages, as where he said that Wilberforce attempted the impossible task of seeking 'to reform the morals and manners of a society while disturbing no elements of its socially immoral structure' – a penetrating comment on Christian social activity throughout the nineteenth and twentieth centuries.

Eleven

Liberal Protestantism and Christian Socialism

Recent Church historians have rather ignored the Broad Churchmen, the 'radical theologians' of the mid nineteenth century. There is no general account of the nineteenth-century British movement towards a more liberal theology (though much can be learned from *The Liberal Anglican Idea of History*, 1952, by Duncan Forbes). The general histories of the Victorian Church (Chadwick, op. cit., Vidler, op. cit.) made surprisingly little of them. Their picture was rather one of an early nineteenth-century Anglican revival which spread largely from Tractarian roots, profited from institutional and financial reform, was momentarily checked about 1860 by the assault of scientific and Biblical criticism, but regathered momentum in the latter part of the century, when the Church had accepted evolution and the 'critical approach', through the mediating influence of *Lux Mundi* (1889). From this point of view there was something vaguely disloyal about the Broad Churchmen and their late nineteenth-century successors, the Liberals. The traditional account never quite forgave the Broad Churchmen the publication of *Essays and Reviews* in 1860 (for which see, e.g., *More Nineteenth Century Studies*, by Basil Willey, 1956). The Church historian did not feel himself obliged to write a history of nineteenth-century religious thought, and he was tempted to believe that the Liberal tradition really belonged there, rather than in a history of 'the Church'. In fact, of course, by the time that one reaches the nineteenth century what happened on the margin or beyond the technical borders of 'the Churches' mattered quite as much for the future of Christianity and for the understanding of its history as what happened in 'the Church'. There was a 'liberal' perspective also, and it has been missing from many versions of the recent past. Books like W. E. Houghton's *The Victorian Frame of Mind 1830–1870* (Yale, 1957) offer a corrective.

Certainly it was sometimes students of English literature who discussed the mid-Victorian religious crisis with the most enthusiasm, because of its impact on the careers of such writers as Tennyson, George Eliot and Arthur Hugh Clough. Perhaps the most outstanding book of this kind was *Matthew Arnold*, by Lionel Trilling (1939). Basil Willey (see above) published *Nineteenth Century Studies: from Coleridge to Arnold* (1949), as a successor to his very popular *Eighteenth Century Background* (1940). Professor Willey always seemed more interested in religious ideas than in literary criticism; he was especially interested in what he called 'honest doubters', and must have been the first writer to discuss John Stuart Mill's *Three Essays in Theism* (1874) seriously since Leslie Stephen did so in 1900 in the third volume of *The English Utilitarians*. None of his explorations, however, touched the depths of Sir Geoffrey Faber's intensely sympathetic study, *Jowett, Portrait with Background* (1957), a biography which for once superseded the Victorian 'life and letters' which underlay it (by E. Abbott and L. Campbell, 1897).

It was time that justice was done to Jowett. He had the misfortune to live out his life in Victorian Oxford in a University which lacked some of the essential qualities of civilization, among them tolerance and magnanimity. The background may be found in *Victorian Oxford* (1965), by W. R. Ward, who gave a relentlessly unflattering picture of the university's internal politics and religious quarrels in the nineteenth century. The secularization (or reform) of Oxford required years of ugly warfare and Jowett was one of the victims, his liberal Christianity so vilified as to leave a lasting suspicion that he was dishonest about his true beliefs. Sir Geoffrey Faber summed up his interpretation of Jowett in a way which might seem at first sight to justify his unmerciful persecution by the rigidly orthodox Anglo-Catholic, Pusey, but which placed Jowett in the main stream of Christian liberalism:

Freely as his mind ranged in search of explanations and reasons, it was tethered to the peg of morality. Belief in a personal God was implanted in him when he was a child. He held fast to it all his life; but in his manhood it seemed to him to be the consequence, rather than the cause, of his attachment to the idea of the good. He became a priest because that was, in his state of life, an office he was naturally destined to fill; because he believed in the social necessity of religious institutions, in the moral content of Christianity, the logical necessity of a divine sanction for ideals which were inexplicable by mere humanism. To this belief he was constant, and his constancy justified him in remaining a priest, in spite of the fact that the various dogmatisms of the divided Christian Churches came to seem man-made stuff, and often man-made nonsense. Though he could bring himself to suspect that tabu and priestcraft had gone to shape the moral code, he not only obeyed the code, accepted and preached it, but used it as the corner-stone of faith. No Leslie Stephen could have outdone the sarcasms which he allowed himself to make privately upon the Church and its rulers, and upon the current language of belief. He went so far as to describe the term 'God' as 'the greatest *équivocque*' or ambiguous word that exists, 'the worship of the Bible' as 'a slavery of the mind and therefore worse than any falling down before outward images'; and 'the notion of God in Plato' as 'far higher than in the Old Testament'. But these expressions of intellectual freedom never, in his own mind, invalidated his clerical status. (pp. 145–6)

The passages quoted came from his private notebooks.

Jowett was honest enough, however; that was why he was pursued. He set out his frank rejection of the classical Protestant substitutionary doctrine of the Atonement in 1855, and asserted the liberal view of the authority of the Scriptures in 1860. It was because he maintained that one could hold these opinions and remain an Anglican that men like E. B. Pusey resisted his influence. His quiet retention of his clerical status was a firm assertion of the right of the ordained ministry to doctrinal freedom, a right seldom granted by the majority of the ministry themselves. Pusey's case, which unfortunately no modern biographer has put, lay in the emotion generated by the fact that Jowett could dismiss the Catholic Church, of which Pusey always spoke with reverence, as 'a figment of theologians'. Jowett's modernity is seen in his absorption in moral experience: he could not appeal, as F. D. Maurice did, to direct experience of God as a source of authority in religion, and his reason only made him conscious of flaws in the Bible, 'a claim to supplement man's blindness with divine illumination.' It is this uncertainty about the location of authority in religion which links Jowett with much recent theological writing.

It is along such lines that one might interpret F. D. Maurice's reluctance to associate himself with the Broad Church school, for Maurice believed in the possibility of direct contact between God and Man, and his belief in the authority of the whole Bible was not significantly diminished by the development of the Higher Criticism – the analysis of any book of the Bible on the assumption that we do not already know who wrote it, why he did so, or at what time. (There are few recent studies on this subject, but *The Higher Criticism in Nonconformity in the 19th Century*, 1954, by Willis Glover, is useful to the church historian; another, less satisfactory book was *Conflict in Christology*, by J. S. Lawton, 1947, a review of the changing British and American view of Christology between 1889 and 1914: Lawton was too hostile to late nineteenth-century Protestant Liberalism to produce a definitive work; for America, see also *The Impact of American Religious Liberalism*, by Kenneth Cauthen, New York, 1962.) Maurice's combination of positive qualities – his emphasis on the love, rather than the wrath and justice of God, his Christian Socialism, his confidence in the Bible as a vehicle of divine revelation, his capacity to find great value in institutions which are currently under fire, for example the establishment of the Church of England and the practice of infant baptism – have made him more and more attractive in modern Anglican circles, and much has been written about him.

A series of books more concerned with Maurice's theology paved the way for the strictly historical studies. These included *The Gospel and the Catholic Church* (1936), by A. M. Ramsey;

Maurice to Temple (1947), by M. B. Reckitt, who was especially interested in Maurice's social teaching; *The Theology of F. D. Maurice* (1948), by A. R. Vidler, a revised version of which appeared in *F. D. Maurice and Company* (1966); Vidler also edited a new edition of Maurice's most famous book, *The Kingdom of Christ*, in 1958; a second work by A. M. Ramsey, *F. D. Maurice and the Conflict of Modern Theology* (1951); and a reprint of Maurice's *Theological Essays*, edited by E. F. Carpenter, in 1957. Thus it was against a background of steadily growing interest[1] that there was published Torben Christensen's thoroughly documented book, *Origin and History of Christian Socialism* (1962), together with *John Malcolm Ludlow, The Builder of Christian Socialism* (1963), by M. C. Masterman, both of them books which stressed the importance of J. M. Ludlow's role in the formation of the Christian Socialist group in 1848–52. The revival was supplemented by biographies of other members of Maurice's circle: *The Life of Thomas Hughes*, by E. C. Mack and W. H. G. Armytage (1953), and the *Life of Charles Kingsley*, by R. B. Martin (1960). In *F. D. Maurice and Company* A. R. Vidler wrote interesting essays on other figures connected with the movement, and especially an exposé of B. F. Westcott's Christian Socialism which was the nearest thing to adverse criticism which the reputation of that rather lofty figure had encountered since his death at the beginning of the century. These books between them largely replaced the late Canon Charles Raven's *Christian Socialism 1848–1854* (1920).

What these books did, especially through the researches of Christensen and Masterman, was to demonstrate that the earlier versions of the story had overrated the importance of Maurice in the Christian Socialist group, and underrated that of Ludlow, who at times – notably in the journal *The Christian Socialist*, for instance, which he edited in 1850–51 – thoroughly rejected the ethos of Victorian capitalist society and wanted to

1. There was also the *Autobiography* of Conrad Noel (the Anglican parson who founded the Church Socialist League in 1906), which was published, ed. Sidney Dark, in 1945.

introduce a new system of industrial organization based on the idea of forming cooperative societies for production as well as distribution; once these cooperatives had been set up on a national scale, they would be able to decide on wages and prices nationally and for the public good. This enthusiasm for the national and centralized was in direct contrast with Maurice's dislike of action which went beyond the parochial level. As for the place of Christianity in the scheme which he proposed, Ludlow argued that socialism required for its success self-sacrifice and brotherhood which could grow only from religious roots; he did not think that such a religion could be provided by the Church of England as it was in 1848 – it must first be democratized, or 'Americanized', as he put it. Such ideas alarmed F. D. Maurice, who was at heart a conservative, and Ludlow's failure to convert his leader symbolized his wider failure either to democratize the Established Church or to persuade the mass of its members to accept as their personal ideal the model of society which he advocated. Ludlow recognized the need to bring the new urban factory-workers into the Church before they became confirmed non-Christians: K. S. Inglis (see below) recently reminded Church historians how middle-class, in social policy as well as in composition, the institutional churches remained even in 1900. An even more recent account of the same field was *The Churches and the Labour Movement*, by Stephen Mayor (1967).[2]

The significance of nineteenth-century Christian Social Action has perhaps been somewhat exaggerated in order to balance the admission that throughout the nineteenth century the practical influence of the British Churches on the changing forms and content of society was declining. Hence the value attached by some reviewers to *The Ten Hours Parson: Christian Social Action in the 1830s*, by J. C. Gill (1959), a biography of the Reverend George Sturges Bull, an Anglican who played a vigorous part in early attempts to obtain better working conditions for northern textile workers. Bull was a good man,

2. For the later period, see *The Christian Socialist Revival 1877–1914*, by P. d'A. Jones (1968).

deeply moved by what he had seen (as Charles Kingsley was, though much more evanescently), but his actions did not alter the general picture of Protestant acquiescence in the sufferings of the poor. The emergence of the Christian Socialist programme in the Anglo-Catholic section of the Church of England was chronicled at the time of the Anglo-Catholic centenary by A. C. Binyon in *The Christian Socialist Tradition in England*, and, more lyrically, by W. A. Peck (op.cit.).

Twelve

The Social Gospel in America

The pattern of events in the United States has been traced in two excellent books, *The Rise of the Social Gospel in American Protestantism, 1865–1915*, by C. H. Hopkins (New Haven, 1940), and *The Decline and Revival of the Social Gospel*, by Paul Carter (New York, 1956). There was more detail in Aaron E. Abell, *The Urban Impact on American Protestantism, 1865–1900* (Cambridge, Mass., 1943), and *Protestant Churches and Industrial America*, by Henry May (New York, 1945). These writers showed how the American Social Gospel arose primarily as a reaction to economic and social conditions in the high capitalist era after the Civil War, and how its theology depended upon Liberal Protestantism and not upon Anglo-Catholic sacramental theory. It was natural that enthusiasm for the Social Gospel should wane with the rapid disintegration of Liberal Protestant theology after 1918, and this process was discussed, with special reference to the prominent American theologian Reinhold Niebuhr, in *The Protestant Search for Political Realism, 1919–1941*, by Donald B. Meyer (Berkeley, 1960), a book which championed Niebuhr's pessimism about the possibility of more than limited returns from Christian social action and criticized what now seemed the naïve political expectations of Liberal Protestant social idealism. The idealism was illustrated in *The Social Gospel in America, Gladden, Ely and Rauschenbusch*, a reader edited by Robert T. Handy in 1966. Gladden and Rauschenbusch, of neither of whom is there a definitive modern study, were well known in Britain at the opening of the century, and their books can still be picked up on surviving second-hand book-stalls. Their influence in Britain has been neglected; it may well have done more than Maurice and his disciples to create a left-wing Protestant political tradition, especially in Free Church circles. Very little research has so far been done into the social policies and programmes of the British Churches between 1900 and the present day. Much the same is true of education, despite the passion which the subject aroused in the Churches between 1820 and 1944: the best British study was *Church and State in British Education, 1870 to the Present Day*, by R. Cruickshank (1963); *The Religious Issue in the State Schools of England and Wales, 1902–14*, by an American, Benjamin Sacks (New Mexico 1961), did not get beneath the surface of a very tangled situation.

Thirteen

Europe in the Nineteenth and Twentieth Centuries

There was a parallel social movement in the nineteenth-century Roman Church, though no one has yet attempted a comparative study. A. R. Vidler provided a brief introductory survey, *A Century of Social Catholicism, 1820–1920* (1964), which included references to the principal continental works which should be consulted. A more elaborate account, more about politics than economics, was *Christian Democracy in Western Europe, 1820–1953*, by Michael Fogarty (1957). In English, it is French Church history which is most represented here. The general background was given in *Histoire religieuse de la France contemporaine*, by A. Dansette (Paris, 1948–52), which was translated into two slightly abridged volumes as *The Religious History of Modern France* (1961). Dansette covered the period 1789–1939; he was deeply interested in the problems set for Christianity by urbanization and industrialization, and his untranslated book, *Le destin du Catholicisme français, 1925–56* (Paris 1959), had an excellent interpretation of the French worker-priest movement against the background of earlier French Catholic searches for a proletarian form of Christianity. The most detailed history of the worker-priests in English was in *The Church and Industrial Society* (1965), by Gregor Siefer, an English edition of a book originally published in German as *Die Mission der Arbeiterpriesten* (Essen, 1960).

Dansette's history of the modern French Church largely replaced the earlier standard work in English, *The Church in France, 1815–1907* (2 vols., 1929, 1936) by C. S. Phillips. Of more specialized studies, the most important was A. R. Vidler's *Prophecy and Papacy, A Study of Lamennais, the Church and the Revolution* (1954), which may now be supplemented to some extent by *Lamennais and England* (1966) by W. A. Roe, a book on the reception of Lamennais's extremely liberal Catholicism in England. Dr Roe showed that Lamennais's ideas did not spread widely in this country; this was perhaps because in England the major ecclesiastical problem was not the autocracy of Pope Pius IX but the ambiguity of Anglicanism, while the revolutionary year of 1848, which restored a by then almost humanist Lamennais to brief political prominence in France, produced in England neither a Chartist National Assembly nor a dictatorship dominated by a Bonaparte-like hero selected by Thomas Carlyle. Other useful biographies of nineteenth-century French Catholics include *Frederic Ozanam and his Society*, by J. Broderick (1933), and *Père Lacordaire, Leader of Youth*, by M. V. Woodgate (1939). For the Catholic Social movement in the United States the best introduction was *American Catholicism and Social Action, a Search for Social Justice, 1865–1950*, by Aaron I. Abell (New York, 1960).

It is a pity that modern British Church historians have not taken more interest in the rise of the Ecumenical Movement on the Continent. In the case of the Roman Catholic Church, even the decision of Pope John XXIII to call the Second Vatican Council together did not provoke a coherent attempt to explain how throughout the nineteenth century liberal and conservative forces had struggled for power over the Roman Church: instead, the summoning of the Council was left to appear as the almost arbitrary outcome of the election of a particular Pope, or as though the invocation of the activity of the Holy Spirit was all that was necessary to explain the process of Christian history. Even now, the best exposition of the First Vatican Council (1869–70) remains *The Vatican Council* by Cuthbert Butler (2 vols., 1930). There is little in English about the religious crisis of modern Italy: *Pio Nono*, by E. E. Y. Hales (1954); R. A. Webster's *Christian Democracy in Italy, 1860–1960* (1961); *Church and State in Italy, 1850–1950*, by A. C. Jemolo (translated 1961). *Religious Liberalism in Modern Italy*, by M. C. Casella, an Italian Anglican (2 vols., 1965–6), was disappointing, though the first volume dealt with the history of the situation since the Risorgimento.

As was said earlier, there is a shortage of British books on German Church history since the Reformation (and our acquaintance with that tends to stop about 1521). There has been no British student of seventeenth-century German Pietism, and no important German work on the subject has been translated into English. The immense prestige of Reformation Church history – or rather the prestige of Reformation theology, for the Continental Reformation as a process of change in religious behaviour has not been excessively explored by British writers – has left us, despite the strong, if often rather belated, interest in what modern German theologians have been saying, almost entirely ignorant of their ecclesiastical background. Bismarck's late nineteenth-century battle with the Church of Rome has been ignored, and A. L. Drummond's *German Protestantism since Luther* (1951) was the only general introduction available to the period. Any proper concern about both the history of the Church and the history of theology ought to show more interest than this in what happened to German Christianity in the two generations that preceded Hitler's rise to power. It is in a book like *The Politics of Cultural Despair*, by Fritz Stern (California, 1961), technically a study of German right-wing thought which discussed Paul de Lagarde (1827–91), Julius Langbehn (1851–1907), and Moeller van den Bruch (1876–1925), that one finds a description of the roots of the fantastic Germanic Christianity purified from the dross of Judaism which Hitler tried, not without success, to force into reality in the 1930s.[1] The German Church struggle with the Hitlerian régime was originally described in *The Struggle for Religious Freedom in Germany* (1938), by A. S. Duncan-Jones, of whom there was a memoir by S. C. Carpenter

1. cf. *The Rise of Political Anti-Semitism in Germany and Austria*, by Peter G. J. Pulzer (New York, 1964), which contains good chapters on the links between the Churches and anti-semitism; and *The Crisis of German Ideology*, by G. L. Mosse (1966).

(1956). Material on the period is slowly being translated: *The German Church Conflict*, by Karl Barth (1965), was not a history, but contained nine commentaries written by Barth between 1933 and 1939;[2] and two volumes of selections from the collected works of Dietrich Bonhoeffer, *The Way to Freedom* and *No Rusty Swords* (1966), contained documents from the same decade: the most useful English introduction to the work of this famous German theologian, whom the Nazis hanged in 1945, was *The Form of Christ in the World*, by John A. Phillips (1967), a book which covered far more than was implied in its sub-title, 'A Study of Bonhoeffer's Christology'. One cannot hope to understand the apparent extremism of recent German theology unless one knows something of the dark conflict in which it was written. W. S. Allen's sociological analysis of a Hanoverian town in the 1930s, *The Nazi Seizure of Power* (1966), shows what a gulf existed between the Lutheran laity, who were often Social Democrats, and their Lutheran pastors, many of whom were political nationalists who supported Hitler's drive for power because they thought that he would protect them against social revolution. Arguments about the relation of the Lutheran doctrine of political obedience to Hitler's success are academic: the attractive power of Paul de Lagarde, whose veneer of scholarship, hysterical rhetoric, and bitter attacks on the materialism of late nineteenth-century industrial civilization all helped to make violent anti-semitism respectable among the German

2. See also the cautionary observations of Paul Tillich, in *Perspective on Nineteenth and Twentieth Century Protestant Theology* (1967), who said that Barth and the German Churches did not speak against Hitler in the name of religion until they themselves were attacked by Hitler. 'This is one of the great shortcomings of the German Churches, but also of Karl Barth. But then Barth became the leader of the inner-churchly resistance against National Socialism. . . . This was quite different from his earlier position' (p. 243). Tillich was arguing that the political quietism of the Barthian movement assisted Nazism in its work of corrupting the German middle-class; this religious failure to resist nationalism and anti-semitism went back well into the nineteenth century. On the British side of German Church relations in the 1930s, cf. the life of *George Bell* (Bishop of Chichester), by R. C. D. Jasper (1967).

Protestant middle classes is a more significant topic for investigation; a French parallel would be Georges Darien (1862–1921), Protestant, novelist, nationalist and (almost certainly) professional burglar.

Fourteen

The Sociological Approach and Popular Religion

From all that has been said so far it is evident that one of the major problems of the present state of British ecclesiastical history is the comparative scarcity of books on the social and economic history of the Church, a lack which is especially serious in the case of the nineteenth century. Nothing of this sort has been written in English which can be compared with Christiane Marcilhacy's amazing description of the mid-nineteenth-century diocese of Orléans during the episcopate of the famous Dupanloup. She produced an exacting socio-historical analysis of the laity, the clergy, the diocesan institutions and its religious practice; she surveyed the bishop's programme for the re-evangelization of his diocese (a programme on a scale unknown in England at the same period), as well as his provision for the education and training of the clergy. Mme Marcilhacy wrote two volumes, *Le diocèse d'Orléans sous l'épiscopat de Mgr Dupanloup* (1963), and *Le diocèse d'Orléans au milieu du XIXe siècle* (Paris, 1964). Dupanloup was bishop from 1849 to 1878, and he directed a campaign for rechristianization which showed some results between 1858 and 1862 but which fell away after 1865. The doyen of French Catholic sociology of religion, Gabriel le Bras, commented on this failure:

> To all other causes of the final failure (which she shows was not absolute) Mme Marcilhacy adds the inability of the clergy to adapt. One is bound to feel that the clergy could not, in view of its training, its prejudices, understand the inevitable transformations of a society which were going on, and that the clergy's social condition and intellectual level would have made it impossible for them to adapt even if they had been granted the necessary insight. One feels in

any case that personal religion has been and always will be the privilege of an élite, one made up of peasants, workers, bourgeois, the naïve and the intellectual, and that this dream of a large-scale conquest (which was *a fortiori* a re-conquest) would be sufficient in itself to class Mgr Dupanloup among the romantics. (*Archives de Sociologie des Religions*, 1964, pp. 202–3)

There is no strict British equivalent here, though Diana McClatchey's *Oxfordshire Clergy, 1777–1869* (1960) made a serious attack on the problem of the social and economic position of the Anglican clergy in a particular diocese and so indicated how far they were free to adapt themselves to the changing conditions of the nineteenth century. That some degree of adaptation was not impossible in England may perhaps be inferred from a comment of Professor G. F. A. Best of Edinburgh University in *Temporal Pillars* (1964), a book in which he discussed the foundation and growth of Queen Anne's Bounty, created in 1704, and the Ecclesiastical Commissioners, established in 1736, taking the story down to their amalgamation in 1948 as the Church Commissioners, and giving at the same time an outline social history of the Anglican clergy in the eighteenth and nineteenth centuries:

It had been an article of belief with church reformers and non-reformers alike before 1830 that gentlemen would not go into the clerical profession unless its rewards matched those of other professions. Some still maintained this in the eighteen-fifties; but there was certainly much less of it by the eighteen-fifties than there had been earlier, and the examples of good clergymen, of all parties and of none, testified to its error. Before 1830 it had been taken very much for granted that the incumbents of onerous urban parishes, the disagreeable importance of which was already well recognised, would need a country living in plurality, wherein to recruit their strength and rear their family. By 1850 this was no longer true. Villiers of Bloomsbury, Hook of Leeds, Bull of Birmingham – examples of the early Victorian urban clergyman at his best – had no country retreat, and neither themselves expected, or were expected by others, to want them. They might indeed look forward to promotion or removal to less unhealthy surroundings as they got on, but that was different. Nor were they certain to want such a move. So radically was the tone of the establishment changing, that lifelong service of the most testing kind, even involving a deterioration rather than an improvement of worldly circumstances, was becoming an ideal for many of its members, to be voluntarily embraced, as it was by R. M. Benson when he founded the Society of St John the Evangelist in 1866 and by all the others who felt the 'call of the cloister'. (pp. 402–3)

This general theme of the reform of the Establishment was also considered in *Church and Parliament, the Reshaping of the Church of England, 1828–1860*, by Olive Brose (1959), a field which had been explored forty years before by the ironical pen of W. L. Mathiesen in *English Church Reform, 1815–1840*, published in 1923.

It cannot be said, however, that what a recent French writer called 'the sociology of religious belonging' has really caught the imagination of Church historians, who have usually been more interested in the history of religious institutions (and sometimes in the history of religious ideas) than in the history and analysis of religious behaviour. The pioneer work in this area was that of the French Roman Catholic school of the sociology of religion which has grown up in Paris and has fostered the periodical *Archives de Sociologie des Religions*. One member of this group, Canon F. Boulard, wrote an *Introduction to Religious Sociology* in 1955 which was translated and published in England by Michael Jackson of the Sheffield Industrial Mission in 1960. Part of the importance of Boulard's work was historical: he was able to show, for example, that in the diocese of Montauban the Lazarist missions held between 1683 and 1714 had geographical areas of success and failure which corresponded to a striking extent with present-day areas of majority and minority Catholic practice. Studies along these lines, he said, made it clear that one must go behind the French Revolutionary period to find explanations of the ways in which French rural areas differ in their religious behaviour one from another at the present time.

Church historians and theologians have both seemed sceptical of the value of the sociological approach. This is partly because they dislike the atmosphere of apparent determinism, the implication that even for individuals class, for example, may be decisive rather than faith, and partly because of the wider doubts which the sociological method seems to them to raise about the working of the Holy Spirit in human history. Nor do they take kindly to the kind of reductionism which would interpret the Nonconformist Conscience of the 1890s, for instance, as the result, not of Nonconformist moral insight, but of Nonconformist social and political aggression. A strong adverse ecclesiastical reaction took place when in 1966 Bryan Wilson published a study of the Ecumenical Movement, *Religion in Secular Society*, in which he emphasized the role played in it by the professional clergy and offered sociological (and not very flattering) explanations of their fervour: the ecumenical movement, he said, was one way of trying to halt the steady decline in social status and influence of the various professional ministries. Such contentions wounded not only those who were accustomed to take it for granted that the only significant causation of the movement must be sought in the mind of God, but also those who had been recommending Richard Niebuhr's *Social Sources of Denominationalism* ever since its appearance (1928) without apparently ever suspecting that anti-denominationalism might have its social sources also. It must be recognized, however, that the serious church historian cannot remain content with a purely theological analysis of the ecumenical movement; he knows that such ideas have been circulating for generations, and so he faces the problem of explaining why they should suddenly become institutionally effective in the twentieth century. The solution of this problem certainly involves some of the factors mentioned by Bryan Wilson.

Nevertheless, some attempts have been made to apply sociological attitudes to Church history, though the result sometimes looks more like a kind of religious social history than sociology as sociologists understand it. This was true of a pioneer work, *Church and People in an Industrial City* (1957), by E. R. Wickham, at that time organizer of an Anglican industrial mission in Sheffield, the city of his title. His survey of religious practice there began with the seventeenth century and his major conclusion was that neither classical Nonconformity nor eighteenth-century Methodism (both of which like to think of themselves as Churches of the people) had succeeded any better than the Church of England in Christianizing more than a small proportion of the city's working class. The proletariat, he said, had not left the Churches, nor had the Churches lost contact with the proletariat, but broadly speaking Church and industrial people had never been closely in contact at all. It was one of the virtues of Wickham's approach that he paid more attention to the nineteenth-century Free Churches than has often been the case with Anglican historians, and in his pages the Primitive Methodists, who did actually extend their influence among the Sheffield working class after 1850 (but who still reached only a tiny fraction of the whole), made one of their rare appearances in non-Methodist literature.

Church and People in an Industrial City was widely read because its theme chimed in with a major outbreak of anxiety about the future of organized Christianity in England. The statement that the Victorian ecclesiastical institutions had failed to Christianize at any rate the new urban working class was in itself irrefutable; it would not have surprised the middle-class leaders of the late nineteenth-century Churches, who often said as much themselves, or for that matter such observers as the early sociologist Charles Booth, who had documented a similar contention in *Life and Labour in the City of London* (third series, 8 vols., 1902), but it came as a further shock to a generation uncomfortably aware of the decline of institutional Christianity but without an accurate picture of the historical past to guide its judgement.

Few other attempts have been made to study the actual religious behaviour of the Victorian working class. The most recent book, *Churches and the Working-Classes in Victorian England* (1965), by Professor K. S. Inglis of the Australian National University, was almost entirely concerned with the last quarter of the nineteenth century and did not contain a detailed analysis of the condition, religious or otherwise, of the proletariat. The bulk of Inglis's work described the theoretical and practical aspects of the approaches which the Churches made to the urban worker once they had grasped that he had become indifferent to them. The Churches tried both direct attempts at conversion, and indirect attempts at conciliation through social work. Professor Inglis made clear that the indirect method failed – the small band of enthusiasts did not fulfil F. D. Maurice's programme of Christianizing the socialists and socializing the Christians. What mattered as much was the failure of the direct approach, which might be summed up in the question, insufficiently asked by Church historians, why did the late Victorian worker already find so little need for religious 'rituals' in coping with his daily life? In fact, despite the conviction of the Churches which Professor Inglis studied that the poor must either accept *their* form of religion or be reckoned as non-religious, it seems likely that many working-class people lived in terms of a drastically simplified 'religion', anti-institutional, centred on morality rather than on worship, and theologically defined by a flat rejection of the classical Protestant description of man as 'fallen'. An organization like the Salvation Army, to which Inglis devoted a chapter, failed to make a decisive break-through because it offered the urban poor only a vulgarization of middle-class Protestantism with a fresh set of institutions.

Surprisingly enough, the Salvation Army has attracted little attention from British Church historians. St John Ervine's often-praised biography of the founder, *God's Soldier: General William Booth* (1934), seems less valuable in retrospect than Harold Begbie's two-volume life published in 1920. How far Begbie understood what he was doing it is hard to say; he did not lack sympathy with his subject; but he provided the necessary clues – extracts from early copies of the *War Cry*, the Army paper, for example – for a sound interpretation of a movement which has been both misunderstood and overvalued as a working-class religious movement. (Even the normally acute Thomas Huxley could make little sense of his own instinctive dislike of the Army, and rationalized his reaction in a bizarre vision of the future in which the General or his successors would complete a social revolution by the seizure of political power.) More recently, Robert Sendall wrote an official three-volume history of the Army, *History of the Salvation Army* (1947–55). This printed much useful information, but by this time the mythology of the Army had developed fully, criticism of Booth had become almost unthinkable, and *Darkest England and the Way Out* (1890), Booth's plan for the elimination of late-Victorian poverty, had to be presented as a vital work. (One suspects that William Booth's son and successor, Bramwell Booth, whose biography by Catherine Bramwell Booth came out in 1933, inherited some of the hostility which critics had hesitated to release on the founder.) Sendall, however, wrote sensibly, and his account was preferable to both the centenary volumes, *The General next to God*, by Richard Collier (1965), and *A Hundred Years War, The Salvation Army, 1865–1965*, by Bernard Watson (1964) – the latter is chiefly about the present-day Army.

None of these books offered a re-interpretation of the Army's history, still less a critical appraisal of William Booth. The Army's success, one feels, sprang from the fusion of two factors in the early 1870s – the waning of official Methodist, including Primitive Methodist, enthusiasm for revivalism, which left a discontented, nostalgic minority ripe for the formation of a new body; and the brief new impulse given to British holiness revivalism by Robert Pearsall Smith the American holiness revivalist when he visited England in 1873–5. As was always clear from Harold Begbie's pages, and from the Salvation Army's earliest regulations, it was as a holiness movement based on this American teaching that the Army made its first, all-important impact, and it owed its spread, to a greater extent than has been recognized, to the prior existence of many local holiness groups. Robert Sendall (op. cit.) said little about this; he was more critical of *Darkest England and the Way Out*, though neither he nor Professor Inglis made clear that while Booth left the impression that no one had taken urban poverty seriously before him or had suggested constructive remedies for it, he was in fact taking up late in life problems which other people, inside and outside religious bodies, had been studying for years, and that his famous scheme: to use revivalism and farming to transform the destitute spiritually and physically, was an amalgam of most of the many plans which had been put forward and experimented with in the Victorian period. As for the personality of Booth himself, that still awaits its analyst.

The most important study of British sectarianism, however, was Bryan Wilson's *Sects and Society* (1961).[1] This was the first attempt to treat in depth the kind of material which the popular chroniclers of Evangelicalism, like Balleine (see above), had presented as a kind of faith-history, the *Gesta Dei per Sanctos*. Wilson provided valuable historical essays on three sects, the Elim Four Square, Christian Science, and the Christadelphians, and then offered a sociological commentary on the development of sects in England in the nineteenth century. The role of the sect, he said, was to reconcile 'the disinherited to their social and economic status by compensatory devices and by the transvaluation of social experience'. He qualified this by the suggestion that a nineteenth-century sect which had survived into the twentieth century (which was the case with the three groups he was describing) must have done so because it also had something to offer to the culturally disinherited and socially isolated; he showed himself more concerned, that is, to emphasize the relevance of psychological and cultural deprivation than to rely on the kind of economic and social causation which has often been invoked in the past to explain the growth of sects. Such explanations are rather too general, however, to explain sect-formation satisfactorily. The worst victims of nineteenth-century economic distress and cultural isolation did not, for the most part, join any sect at all, and so the problem arises why (in view of the very general explanations offered) Victorians sects attracted such small

1. cf. *Patterns of Sectarianism*, ed. B. R. Wilson (1967). Here, however, the emphasis on sects showed diminishing returns.

numbers of adherents. One reason might be that the larger denominations coped just as well as did the small sects with the factors implied in these sociological considerations.

Nevertheless, Victorian sects did multiply, and the mental attitudes which reigned in the Evangelical Pietist world, including its Anglican sector, were broadly sectarian. Bryan Wilson felt that one could not explain why a man became a member of, for example, an Adventist sect, in terms of either what the sect thought or in terms of what the theologian would call religious faith – and the majority of secular historians would agree with this sociological approach. Wilson found the answer in 'differentiated social and psychological considerations', so that sects 'recruit those for whom they can fulfil more specific social functions'. Such an argument brings one back, however, to the individual Adventist rather than to generalizations about his total economic and cultural environment, and to the individual Adventist as the subject of psychological description and explanations, a position reminiscent of Jean-Paul Sartre's attempt to combine Marxism and psychoanalysis. The Adventist, however, is not obliged to accept the reduction of his 'faith' to non-religious terms. He might say, for instance, that since in the nineteenth century the original members of a new sect were almost always people whose lives had been religion-centred to an abnormal degree, the cause of the sect's formation was to be found in a state of dissatisfaction within the 'religious world' rather than in the need to compensate for more general socio-economic deprivations. An example of this might be found in *The Sixth Trumpeter: The Story of Jezreel and his Tower*, by Philip George Rogers (1963). The Jezreelites were the followers of James Rowland White, an obscure private in the 16th Foot, who in 1875 happened to make contact with a surviving Southcottian congregation in Chatham, recognized his destiny, and became the sixth and final prophet of the Southcottian End. He took the name Jezreel (from Hosea); he composed the Flying Roll, which added little to what had already been revealed; he persuaded his followers – about 1,400 in the sect's heyday, 1885 – to provide the money with which to build near the top of Chatham Hill a massive building called Jezreel's Tower, its lofty walls decorated with stone-carved trumpets, crossed swords and scrolls. (Fantastic faiths often find comfort in the superficial solidity of architecture; a similar phenomenon can be observed in Nazi Germany.) To the non-religious world the Sixth Trumpeter seemed to be trumpeting nonsense, however: he offered no solution to its problems.

The material of popular religion, and of the revivalist tradition associated with it, has not been extensively studied in England. In the Ford Lectures for 1960, published as *The Making of Victorian England* (1962), Dr Kitson Clark argued strongly that the time had come 'to put back religion, particularly popular religion, into the picture of nineteenth-century England'. He complained that despite the pioneer work of Élie Halévy, who emphasized the links between early Victorian religion and English political stability, 'nevertheless, in recent books there is still very little about the second Evangelical Revival, little about the (revival) movement in Wales, little about Sankey and Moody, not very much about Spurgeon, nor has anyone written that history of nineteenth-century Nonconformity which is so badly needed' (pp. 22–3). Dr Kitson Clark criticized secular historians of the nineteenth century on the ground that they were obsessed with political history and striking personalities: they therefore ignored popular religion, which rarely took the centre of the stage or produced leaders of genius. He thought that many historians showed an aversion for the vulgarity and shallowness of popular religion which was illogical in view of the vulgarity and ignorance which they tolerated in much political behaviour.

It is impossible not to sympathize with Dr Kitson Clark, though Church historians have also often dismissed popular religion with a brief reference. It is an obvious criticism of the eighteenth-century and nineteenth-century volumes of the *New Cambridge Modern History* (vols. 6–12) that in each of them 'Church History' was relegated to a separate chapter. The result was not always an improvement on the original *Cambridge Modern History* (1900), whose contributors handled eighteenth-century and nineteenth-century religion with the distaste with which survivors of a shipwreck might contemplate the sea. This segregation and minimization of the subject was justified on the traditional ground that 'Church history' was concerned with the relationship between ecclesiastical and civil institutions: in the nineteenth century the collapse of the concept of 'established Church' over wide areas would be one example, the secularization of the Papal States another. From the point of view of political and economic historians, the importance of ecclesiastical institutions declined steadily after 1789, and this decline was reflected in their miserly treatment of 'Church history'. If, however, by 'Church history' one means the study of human religious behaviour, one cannot accept such a relegation of the subject. It is important to know if human religious behaviour has been decreasing in Europe since 1789, and if so, why? One must also explore the possibility that what was really happening was that more and more people were deciding not to express themselves religiously through the traditional religious institutions. Either way, the study of popular religion, which is not necessarily only a matter of the study of fringe sects with dubious habits, has to be undertaken.

In fact, much work has been done on the subject in the United States, where its value may even have been exaggerated. Dr Kitson Clark (op. cit.) himself warned against this temptation: he pointed out, for example, that it was difficult to take much Victorian popular Protestantism seriously as religion: in its back-street varieties, at any rate, it often seemed to be rooted in feelings more analogous to anti-semitism in a continental sense than to any profound spiritual phenomena. Failure to recognize this was one of the reasons why J. E. Orr, in *The Second Evangelical Awakening in Britain* (1949), failed to make out a convincing case for there having been a major Victorian Evangelical revival of religion, starting in 1859.

Fifteen

American Revivalism

In America, on the other hand, the total impact of eighteenth-century and nineteenth-century revivalistic phenomena could not be ignored. When the late Perry Miller tried to describe *The Life of the Mind in America from the Revolution to the Civil War* (1966), he began with a chapter entitled 'The Evangelical Basis' and discussed the nature of the revivalistic tradition. W. B. McLaughlin wrote *Modern Revivalism* (1959), a book partly based on his earlier study, *Billy Sunday was His Real Name* (1955), which was about the famous ex-baseball player revivalist who filled the gap between the death of D. L. Moody and the rise of Billy Graham. Both McLaughlin and Miller tried to place revivalism in the context of a wider understanding of American history, and their books formed part of the continuous effort of American scholars to decide what, if anything, is really 'American' about America. Miller called revivalism a central mode of America's search for a national identity; he pointed out how in the earlier nineteenth century revivalists wanted to save the nation as well as the individual:

> There we have it – save the country! Does the country need saving? Why the urgency? It is a shallow view of the social situation which regards the revivals as only a device in the capitalist expansion – as though revival did no more than set Max Weber's 'Protestant Ethic' on fire in primitive America and so give added incentive to the pious to work in their callings of building up a new country, even though there is, I agree, some such aspect to the movement. On the other hand, it is equally unperceptive to take the Revival as solely a religious outburst unrelated to national and economic concerns. In every cataclysm there were hundreds who

asked only, What shall I do to be saved? But over and over again, when the workers in the vineyards could be induced for a moment to lay aside their pruning shears and explain what they were about, they came back to the communal effect of their exertions. Not only the moral but the physical aspect of the community is changed by a revival, said Sprague, it 'has encouraged industry, and has caused the social virtues to look forth in smiles, where chilly selfishness, and hateful discord, or unblushing crime, seemed to have established a perpetual reign'.

In this field Perry Miller was drawing on the work of a group of American scholars, not all of whom would want to be called Church historians, but whose books fall within the definition of Church history which I have been using. A new American folk-hero, Charles Grandison Finney, has emerged from their books, a professional revivalist whose triumphs in the 1820s seemed to both Miller and McLaughlin to mark a new era in the history of American Protestantism, an era in which the newly independent United States was saved for the Reformation tradition for another half century. McLaughlin edited Finney's *Lectures on Revivalism* (1836) for a Harvard series of texts which it was claimed were fundamental to a proper understanding of American culture (1960). (It was joined in the series in 1961 by *Ten Nights in a Bar Room and What I Saw There* by T. S. Arthur, the one classic example to survive from the Himalayan heaps of teetotal propaganda that were published in the Victorian age – to have missed it is to have missed a whole dimension of popular religion. There is still little in England on this subject apart from *The English Temperance Movement*, 1933, by Henry Carter, a one-sided introduction to the topic.)

McLaughlin showed less reverence for most of Finney's successors at professional revivalism. His portrait of Billy Sunday (see above) was brilliantly ironical; he maintained that the key to Sunday's popularity was social and not religious. Late-nineteenth-century immigrants who wanted to become absorbed in American culture found themselves still unhappily European. Sunday's revivals offered them a way of integration with American culture which they gratefully followed to the very end of the sawdust trail. In the concluding section of *Modern Revivalism* McLaughlin also showed himself unimpressed by the fruits of Billy Graham; he rather unkindly compared America's twentieth-century reputation as a church-going nation with America's twentieth-century reputation as a materialistic society. Only Moody was spared (though not entirely) and this largely because Moody, despite his enormous bulk and business sense, was dull and uninspiring. Moody's dullness has harassed all his modern biographers: the best recent life was probably *Moody without Sankey* (1964), by J. C. Pollock, in which Sankey is not, in fact, noticeably absent; there have been several recent American books about Moody, but the authors have not been able to find many new facts about him, and have all seemed nervous of adopting the critical attitude which might lead to a challenging interpretation of him. This caution is not necessarily caused by religious bias: Moody, like Finney, though in a lesser degree, is an American folk hero. An *Annotated Bibliography of D. L. Moody* was compiled by W. M. Smith (Chicago, 1948).

McLaughlin and Miller both played down the role of the Baptists and Methodists in the foundation of modern America. Not all American scholars would agree that Finney deserved the prominence that he has achieved. Whitney Cross, in *The Burned Over District* (New York, 1950), an impressive analysis of revivalism, utopianism and anti-slavery in Eastern America in the first half of the nineteenth century, thought that Finney's influence had been exaggerated, and that it was difficult to believe that he succeeded in the 1820s because he had a new theological outlook. 'It is fair to question,' Cross wrote, 'whether he had at the beginning anything whatsoever which deserves the title of a theology.' Finney's genuine theological peculiarities, especially his adoption of a form of holiness revivalism, came to him in the 1830s when his prestige as a straight revivalist was declining. In 1826, when he stood at the apex of his career, his technique combined little more than personality, showmanship and threats of damnation.

Other interesting modern studies of the American popular religious tradition were: Elizabeth K. Nottingham's *Methodism and the Frontier* (New York, 1941); A. Pope's important book, *Millhands and Preachers* (New Haven, 1942), which discussed the interaction of religion, the Southern textile trade, and Marxism in nineteenth- and twentieth-century Carolina; *The Frontier Camp Meeting* (Dallas, 1955), by Charles Johnson; and a more popular book, *They Gathered at the River*, by Bernard Weisberger. As the Evangelical world became increasingly conscious of the common criticism that revivalists concentrated on saving men's souls and ignored the sufferings of their not unimportant bodies, books appeared both in America and in Britain which sought to show that revivalists were just as concerned about social problems as their Christian and humanist critics. In America there was *Revivalism and Social Reform in the mid-19th Century America* (1957), by Timothy L. Smith, and *The Social Ideas of the Northern Evangelists*, by Charles C. Cole (New York, 1954). Such work is not quite convincing, or at any rate no more convincing than would be a thesis designed to show that the plays of Noël Coward reveal a profound social conscience. The sour edge of American religiosity was well exposed in *Apostles of Discord* (Boston, 1953) by Ralph Lord Roy, and also in Norman F. Furniss's *The Fundamentalist Controversy, 1918–1931* (New Haven, 1954). Even more revealing was *Popular Religion – Inspirational Books in America*, by Louis Schneider and Sanford M. Dornbusch (1958), an analysis of religious best-sellers published in America between 1875 and 1955. The authors said that in the period under review inspirational books had become steadily more secularized; characteristically, the books promised that religion would bring by direct assault goods – such as peace of mind – which it is classically assumed can be reached only indirectly; techniques are offered, especially prayer techniques, for obtaining the desired result. The religious status of data of this kind is not easy to decide, but there is no question of its place in the study of the history of human religious behaviour.

Sixteen

The Ecumenical Movement

It is too early to speak of a history of the Ecumenical Movement, although Ruth Rouse and Stephen Neill edited a symposium with the title *A History of the Ecumenical Movement, 1517–1948* in 1954; this contained a very informative article on the nineteenth-century movement by Miss Rouse herself. At the level of public negotiation the official statements were patiently collected by G. K. A. Bell in three series of *Documents on Christian Unity* (1924, 1930, 1948); there was no commentary in these volumes. Among the first attempts to provide something more analytical were *The Social Thought of the World Council of Churches*, by Edward Duff (1956), and Bryan Wilson's controversial book, *Religion in Secular Society* (1966). There was no question, however, even of agreement on terms. As a sociologist of religion, Wilson took the increasing secularity of twentieth-century British society for granted, but David Martin, as a religious sociologist, in *A Sociology of English Religion* (1967), argued that there had been little real change since 1900. Without some more definite picture of what was happening to Christianity in the twentieth century it was difficult to make more than tentative approaches to the problem of the historical genesis of the Ecumenical Movement.

Conclusion

Since 1930, the study of Church history has been affected by various ecclesiastical factors. In the 1930s, for example, the powerful Barthian drive to re-establish classical Protestant orthodoxy led to a renewed theological interest in the Reformation period, and so to much historical writing, especially about Luther and Calvin. More recently, this conservative movement has lost its impetus, but the new theological radicals in whom the Victorian questionings of tradition have reappeared are more concerned with philosophy than with history and have not as yet stimulated a new wave of historical investigations.

A significant change also took place in the area of Christian social thinking. After 1930 the politically naïve Christian Socialist tradition steadily lost ground in favour of a Christian political realism devoted to short-term rather than long-term ends. Anxiety, both about the political behaviour of the Church and about the loss of contact between the Church and the international working class, helped to foster a wide variety of historical studies, both of Christian Socialism itself and of the political activity of the Church in the nineteenth century and after. Another interesting phenomenon here was what might be called an American humanist attempted take-over of the Puritan tradition in an effort to assess the contribution of Puritanism to the growth of America as a 'nation' with a 'national culture'. This development underlines the fact that if the official Church historians, professional historians, that is, who are in some sense committed to the Christian position, want to retain hegemony in their own dominion, they will have to stop treating the history of the Church as a special case.

They must analyse more freely the extent to which the religious behaviour, institutions and beliefs of a particular society at a particular period are deeply affected, although not totally conditioned by, the social and economic environment in which the religious community exists. If they do not do this, other historians, with different basic interests, will do it for them, as has been the case with recent studies of the role of the Christian missionary in non-Christian communities, such as British India or Imperial China. The political changes in Africa and the Far East have put an end to the old-style missionary history for ever: this has been the major revolution in modern Church historical studies.

Finally, one other potent factor in the period under review was the movement for the reunion of the divided Church, a movement which reached an early peak in the formation of the World Council of Churches in 1948. This movement offered a powerful stimulus to historical studies of the problems involved in both the division and unification of Churches, and bore out to some extent the late Norman Sykes's view that sound historical scholarship produces charity in religion. On the debit side, however, it must also be admitted that the ecumenical mood did not always lead to sound scholarship, but had sometimes a tendency to read its own eirenical spirit back into periods which were passionately intent upon division. The modern Church historian cannot accept the theologian's simple distinction between 'the sins of our divisions' – which disposes of the past, and 'the knowledge that the reunion of the Church is the will of God for our time' – which disposes of the future as well. The 'coming Great Church' will fall apart again very quickly if its leaders assume that the unity that they have achieved is somehow beyond the touch of history: it has never been so in the past.

Of course, these are questions of interpretation. We should not now subscribe to Newman's view that 'the philosophy of history is the science of which historical facts are the basis, or the laws on which it pleases Almighty Providence to conduct the political and social world': we underline the uncertainty of 'facts' and reduce the 'laws' to hypotheses. In his recent book, *The Shape of Christology*, Professor John McIntyre said that 'our theology, our Christology, is *human* thinking about God, *human* thinking about Christ. There is an element of deceit in pretending that these are not our thoughts but God's thoughts, blasphemy, perhaps, more than deceit. The danger is that we become so convinced that our thoughts are God's thoughts that we make a fair shape at reproducing the wrath of God against those who have the effrontery to disagree with us. Theology, Christology, is none the worse for being humble – and none the less true for it, either' (p. 175). Both the theologian and the historian are engaged in *human* thinking about human religious behaviour; neither should suppose that he has more than a partial human insight into either its past or its present.

Index of Names

Akakius of Caesarea, disciple of Eusebius, 81; originality of his thought, 81–2; and Cyril of Jerusalem, 94; Gregory of Nyssa and, 100

Albinus, and Middle Platonism, 43; Athenagoras and, 45; Origen and, 58; Tertullian and, 67

Alcock, Sir Rutherford, on ineffectiveness of missions, 260–61

Alexander, St, Bishop of Alexandria, 84

Alford, Henry, Dean of Canterbury, 321

Ambrose, St, Bishop of Milan, 92, 93, 100, 158, 172; and works of Origen, 55; biographical notes, 101, 165; his work, 101–2; indebted to Easterns, 116; his education, 119–20; Augustine and, 120–21, 122, 124; influenced by Greek doctrine of man, 125; and baptismal rites, 163, 165–7, 168; and feet-washing ceremony, 166; and canon prayer, 191–2; and consecration, 226

Ammonius Saccas, 43; father of Neo-Platonism, 59; Origen's disciples of, 59–60; and identity of Dionysius, 114

Ananias, 160

Anthony, St, and spiritual warfare, 61; and monastic movement, 92; and desert of Nitria, 112

Antiochus of Ascalon, 43

Aphraates, *Treatises*, 103

Apollinarius, 29

Apollinarius, Bishop of Laodicea, and a human mind in Christ, 86, 95; his theological thought, 95; a millenniarist, 96; Jerome and, 98, 117, 118; and Christological question, 104, 110; an Origenist, 118

Apollinarius the Elder, 95

Aquila, and *Hexapla*, 54

Aristotle, his influence on second-century Christian apologists, 44; Neo-Platonism and Aristotelian logic, 90

Arnobius, *Adversus nationes*, 76; influences of his work, 76–7

Arnold, Matthew, importance of his theological writings, 309; biography of, 338

Arnold, Thomas, 320

Asterius, *Homilies on the Psalms*, 87

Athanasius, St, Bishop of Alexandria, 28; and spiritual warfare, 61; resists condemnation of Marcellus, 83; biographical notes on, 84–5; his significance in Trinitarian theology, 85–6; Hilary compared with, 89–90; his successors, 93; Apollinarius and, 95; St Basil and, 97

Athenagoras, 45

Augustine of Hippo, St, 27, 28, 112; formerly a monk, 31; Tertullian foreshadows, 68; influenced by Victorinus, 91; hears Ambrose's lectures, 101; Ambrose anticipates, 102; development in modern study of, 119–20; conversion of, 120–21; importance of chronology of his works, 121; his doctrine of man, 122; and primacy of Pope, 123; his theology, 122–4; his disciples, 124; brings Origenism to West, 126; Prosper of Aquitaine and, 127; and death of unbaptized, 199; and doctrine of original sin, 201

Ausonius, Decimus Magnus, 102

Barberi, Father Dominic, works on, 325

Barth, Karl, 245, 278; and post-Resurrection history, 244; *The German Church Conflict*, 349; and Nazism, 349n.

Basil of Caesarea, St, 'the Great', 27; on teaching, 28; formerly a monk, 31; Biblical narrative and science, 83; biographical notes, 96–7; his work, 97; *Philocalia*, 97; his theology, 98; Gregory of Nazianzus and, 99; Ambrose indebted to, 102; Jerome and, 117

Baxter, Richard, life of, 289

Bell, George, Bishop of Chichester, 313

Benson, Richard Meux, 353

Index of Names

Bernard, St, 30
Best, G. F. A., on changing tone of establishment, 353
Biedermann, A. E., 308
Bismarck, Otto Edward Leopold von, Prince Bismarck, 348
Blondel, Maurice, 329
Bonhoeffer, Dietrich, 349
Booth, Bramwell, 357
Booth, Charles, 355
Booth, William, works on, 356; Huxley and, 356–7; his remedy for urban poverty, 357–8
Bouyer, Louis, 326
Bremond, Henri, on Newman, 326
Brown, Ford K., on heritage of Victorian age, 334–5; on William Wilberforce, 335–6
Bruch, Moeller van den, 348
Bull, George Sturges, 342–3
Bullinger, Johann Heinrich, 281
Buonaiuti, Ernesto, 329
Butler, Joseph, Bishop of Durham, 22
Butterfield, Herbert, 245

Caesarius, St, Archbishop of Arles, 127
Callistus I, St, Pope, Hippolytus attacks, 71, 73
Calvin, John, 15, 285; lack of Catholic interest in, 273; radical Protestantism and, 274, 275; works on, 277, 279; and Servetus, 278, 279; Anglican attitude to, 278
Cassian, John, and Valentinus, 47; biographical notes, 126; Prosper of Aquitaine and, 127
Cecil, William, 1st Baron Burleigh, 284
Chadwick, Owen, 314, 320; *The Victorian Church*, 311–13; on Anglo-Catholic movement, 318–19
Charles I, King of England, 288
Charles II, King of England, 290
Charles the Great, King of the Franks and Roman Emperor, 221, 223
Chrysostom, St John, Bishop of Constantinople, 27, 158, 172; formerly a monk, 31; pupil of Libanius, 95, 104; and Epiphanius, 96; and moralism, 106; biographical notes on, 106–7; writer and orator, 107; defends Origenist monks, 109; Cassian takes refuge with, 126; and pattern of baptism, 161
Church, Dean, 323
Cicero, Marcus Tullius, 70
Clark, Kitson, and Victorian popular religion, 360, 361
Cleanthus, 67
Clement of Alexandria, St, 27, 37, 88; *Hypotyposes*, 38; and Hellenism, 48; his works, 48, 49; and the Gnostic Christian, 49; the Logos and ancient sages, 50–51; Eusebius's work compared to that of, 81; and sacrifice of praise, 149
Clement of Rome, St, Pope, 64, 197; *First Epistle*, 39; and Logos, 50; and heavenly ministry of Christ, 153, 196; his description of celebrants, 194
Combefis, François, 26
Commodian, 77, 78
Constantine the Great, Roman Emperor, 92; consequences of his conversion, 79; and patristic literature, 80; Eusebius's view of, 81; Lactantius and, 88
Cosmas Indicopleustes, 105
Coverdale, Miles, work on, 284
Cranmer, Thomas, Archbishop of Canterbury, an early liturgiologist, 20; works on, 284, 285
Creighton, Mandell, 246
Cromwell, Oliver, work on, 287
Crowther, Samuel, 269
Cyprian, St, *Against the Jews*, 46, 65
Cyprian, St, Bishop of Carthage, 197; his classical style, 74–5; his selection of *Testimonia*, 75; *De unitate ecclesiae*, 75, 76; two poles to his theology, 75–6; *Ad Demetrianum*, 76; and the Passion, 195; and Mass for the dead, 220
Cyril, St, Patriarch of Alexandria, and Antiochene Christology, 107; and Athanasius, 109; his work, 109–10; his theology, 110; his fanaticism, 111
Cyril, St, Bishop of Jerusalem, 158, 183, 194; a Nicean, 94; his catechetical collection, 94; and baptism, 161, 203; and Eucharistic prayer, 174, 178; and bread and Body, 226

Damasus, St, Pope, Jerome and, 116, 117
Darien, Georges, 350
Davies, D. Horton, 319, 322
Didymus the Blind, 27; and Origen, 55, 93, 109; his work, 93; Jerome and, 98, 118; and Alexandrian tradition, 112; Evagrius and, 112
Diocletian, Roman Emperor, 80
Diodore, Bishop of Tarsus, an Antiochene liberal, 95; and Apollinarius, 96, 117; and Christological question, 104; his pupils, 104, 106

Index of Names

Dionysius of Alexandria, 'the Great', Origen's disciple, 62; and identity of Pseudo-Dionysius, 114
Dionysius, the Pseudo-Areopagite, identification of, 114; and Neo-Platonism and Christianity, 115
Dorner, Isaak, 308
Duc, Fronton du, 26
Duff, Alexander, 266
Dupanloup, Félix Antoine Philibert, Bishop of Orléans, 351, 352

Edwards, Jonathan, 287
Eliade, Mircéa, 261–2
Elizabeth I, Queen of England, 283, 284; baptism and confirmation of, 207; accepts Reformers' Communion Service, 229; and Reformers, 230; and Puritanism, 286
Elton, G. R., on religious emancipation and capitalism, 272; on Elizabethan religious settlement, 282
Ephrem Syrus, St, 102, 103
Epictetus, 44
Epiphanius, St, 58
Epiphanius, St, Bishop of Salamis, his *Panarion*, 96; Jerome partisan of, 117
Erasmus Desiderius, works on, 285
Etheria, *Travel Journal*, 94
Eunomius, Arian Bishop of Cyzicus, 29, 100
Eusebius, Bishop of Caesarea, and early ecclesiastical writers, 26; reports on Papias, 37; and works of Melito, 46; and Origen, 54, 88; and Hippolytus, 71; the historian, 80; his aim in *Demonstration of the Gospel*, 81; *Against Marcellus*, 83; and Homoean tradition, 87; Lactantius compared with, 88; Theodoret and, 108
Eusebius of Emesa, an exegete, 83; a scholar, 86; Diodore of Tarsus his pupil, 95
Eustathius, St, Bishop of Antioch, an exegete, 83; his orthodox theology of Incarnation, 86; deposed, 87
Eustathius, Bishop of Sebaste, 97
Evagrius Ponticus, disciple of Origen, 58, 113; biographical notes, 112; scholarly reconstruction of his writings, 113; his *Kephalaia Gnostica*, 113–14; Jerome accuses, 117; Cassian and, 126

Faber, Frederick William, 327
Faber, Sir Geoffrey, on Strachey, 326; his view of Newman, 327; his book open to criticism, 328; *Jowett, Portrait with Background*, 338; on Jowett, 339
Faustus of Milevis, 124
Felicissimus, 75
Fénelon, François de Salignac de la Mothe, 292
Feuerbach, Ludwig, 295
Finney, Charles Grandison, 363, 364
Firmilian, St, Bishop of Caesarea, 62, 97
Fox, George, 290
Foxe, John, works on, 284, 285

Garbett, Cyril Foster, Archbishop of York, 313
Gibson, Edmund, Sykes's work on, 296
Gore, Charles, Bishop of Oxford, 324
Graham, Billy (William Franklin), 362, 364
Grant, Charles, and Christianization of India, 264–5
Green, V. H. H., and John Wesley, 303–4, 305
Gregory I, St, 'the Great', Pope, 175, 193; and the Lord's Prayer, 180, 191; a frequent preacher, 188; recognizes needs of the dead, 220
Gregory, St, Bishop of Elvira, 89
Gregory of Nazianzus, St, 27, 93; orthodox theology of, 28; a hermit, 98; personality and character as a writer, 98; a rhetorician, 98–9; and Prudentius, 102; ordains Evagrius, 112; Jerome and, 117, 118
Gregory of Neo-Caesarea, 62
Gregory, St, Bishop of Nyssa, 27; on tradition of holy Fathers, 28; and Origen, 58, 100; and doctrine of *epectasis*, 61; Biblical narrative and science, 83; biographical notes, 99–100; his theology, 100–101; Ambrose and, 101; and two narratives of Genesis, 102; and Pseudo-Dionysius, 114; and Augustine, 122; influences Cassian, 126
Gregory Thaumaturgus, St (the Wonder-Worker), 97

Headlam, A. C., Bishop of Gloucester, 313–14
Hegel, Georg Wilhelm Friedrich, 294
Hegesippus, St, 39, 81

Henry VIII, King of England, 283, 284
Henson, H. H., 314
Heracleides, 56
Heracleitus, 50
Heracleon, 47
Hermas, *Shepherd*, 36, 37, 65
Hermogenes, 66
Hierocles, 59, 60
Hilary, St, Bishop of Poitiers, 88; his work expository, 89; his theology, 89–90; indebted to Easterns, 116; influenced by Greek doctrine of man, 125
Hill, Christopher, on religion and English Revolution, 289
Himerius, 98
Hippolytus, St, 197; opponent of heresy, 47; identification of, 70–71; his typology, 71–2; his interest in eschatology, 72–3; his quarrel with Papacy, 73–4; Novation and, 74; and Second Advent, 81; probable author of Eucharistic prayer, 148; and thanksgiving, 152; *The Apostolic Tradition*, 162–3
Hitler, Adolf, 348, 349
Hobsbawm, E. J., on secular and religious ideology, 251–2
Hort, Fenton John Anthony, 309
Hügel, Baron Friedrich von, 329
Hughes, Thomas, biography of, 341
Huxley, Thomas, and Salvation Army, 357
Hypatia, Synesius and, 110, 111; lynched, 111; belongs to Neo-Platonic tradition, 111

Iamblichus, and Plotinus, 60; and Neo-Platonic anti-Christian tradition, 111
Ignatius of Antioch, St, *Epistles*, 39; and heterodoxy, 40
Innocent I, St, Pope, 202
Irenaeus, St, 64, 197; influence of Melito on, 46; opponent of heresy, 47; his history, 47; *Adversus haereses*, 48; his theology of religious history, 51; Origen and, 57; Methodius faithful to, 62; Tertullian and, 66, 69; Hippolytus a disciple of, 73; and heavenly altar, 153, 196; and Eucharistic prayer, 194; and Eucharist, 195, 226

Jansen, Cornelius Otto, and Augustine's theology of grace, 122; *The Origins of Jansenism*, 292; the wager in philosophy of, 294
Jerome, St (Eusebius Hieronymus Jerome), 28, 37, 92; and early ecclesiastical writers, 26; formerly a monk, 31; and Origen, 55, 58, 118; and Epiphanius, 96; his high opinion of Gregory of Nazianzus, 98; biographical notes, 116; involved in theological disputes, 117; his expository work, 117–18; translator, 118–19; learns Greek, 120; Julian of Eclanum and, 125; and laying-on of hands, 203; and confirmation, 209
Jesus Christ, various interpretations of, 13; Bible witness to, 31; Judaism and titles given to, 41; Origen and, 57; Eusebius's view of, 81; in theology of Athanasius, 85, 86; Apollinaris and *nous* in, 95, 110; Theodorus emphasizes his humanity, 106; and baptism and Eucharist, 136; baptism of, 137, 144, 160; heavenly ministry of, 153
John, St, Apostle, and baptism of Christ, 137; on anointing, 143; and baptism, 160
John the Baptist, St, 137
John, Bishop of Jerusalem, 96, 158; and 'mystagogic catecheses', 94; Jerome at odds with, 117
John XXIII, Pope, 347
Jowett, Benjamin, Faber's study of, 338; Faber on, 339; asserts his right to doctrinal freedom, 339; his modernity, 340
Julian, Bishop of Eclanum, and Antiochene literalism, 125; teaches moralism, 126
Julian (Flavius Claudius Julianus), 'the Apostate', Roman Emperor, 111
Justin Martyr, St, 27, 35, 64, 88, 197; and Gregory of Nazianzus, 28; his history, 44; uses Greek mythology, 48; and the Logos, 50; Clement develops ideas of, 50–51; Origen and, 57; Methodius and, 62; Tertullian and, 65–6, 68, 69; gives clear description of baptism, 141–2; his guardedness in account of sacraments, 143; and Eucharist, 146, 150, 195, 215; and Eucharistic prayer, 148; and thanksgiving, 152; bread and the Body of Christ, 226
Justinian, 58

Kant, Immanuel, 294

Index of Names

Keble, John, 316, 320; works on, 321
Kingsley, Charles, biography of, 341, 343
Knox, A. E., on Oxford Movement, 320–21; and Anglo-Catholic clergy, 321
Knox, Ronald, Waugh's biography of, 329

Lacordaire, Henri Dominique, 347
Lactantius, his theology, 88–9; and subordinationism, 89–90
Lagarde, Paul Anton de, 348, 349
Lamennais, Félicité Robert de, works on, 346–7
Langbehn, Julius, 348
Laud, William, Archbishop of Canterbury, an early liturgiologist, 20; Laudians in exile, 290
Le Bras, Gabriel, on inadaptability of clergy, 351–2
Leo I, St, Pope, and Augustinianism, 127; a frequent preacher, 188
Libanius, 98; his Christian pupils, 95, 104, 106
Liddon, Henry Parry, 321
Lightfoot, Joseph Barber, Bishop of Durham, 309, 321
Loisy, Edward, 329
Löwith, Karl, on problems of history, 244–5
Lucian of Antioch, 87
Lucifer, Bishop of Cagliari, 90
Ludlow, John Malcolm Forbes, and Victorian capitalist society, 341–2; his ideals, 342
Luke, St, Evangelist, and baptism of Christ, 137, 144, 160
Luther, Martin, 15, 285; and Augustine's theology of grace, 122; Eucharist in Lutheran rite, 228; works on, 272, 276, 277, 280–81; changing Roman Catholic attitude to, 272; radical Protestantism and, 274, 275; Anglican attitude to, 278; and British Churches, 280; Erikson and psychology of, 281; Lutheran missionaries, 300; and doctrine of political obedience, 349

Mackonochie, Father, 323–4
Manning, Henry Edward, Cardinal, 327
Marcellus, Bishop of Ancyra, condemnations against, 83; his theology of Incarnation, 84; Athanasius and, 85
Marcilhacy, Christine, her works on diocese of Orléans, 351; le Bras on, 351–2
Marcion, 66
Marcus Aurelius, Emperor of Rome, and Stoicism, 44; Athenagoras and, 45
Mark, St, Evangelist, and the Last Supper, 137; and baptism of Christ, 137, 144
Marx, Karl, and Pascal, 294
Mary I, Queen of England, 229
Matthew, St, Apostle and Evangelist, and baptism, 137; dependent on Mark, 137; and baptism of Christ, 144
Maurice, Frederick Denison, 345, 356; his beliefs and positive qualities, 340; books on his theology, 340–41; and Christian Socialism, 341; alarmed by Ludlow's ideas, 342
Maximus of Tyre, Middle Platonism and, 43; Origen and, 58
Melania, St, 'the Elder', 112
Melitius, St, Bishop of Antioch, a great man, 94; and St Basil, 97; and Synod of Antioch, 99; Jerome opposed to, 117
Melito, St, works of, 45–6; his influence on Irenaeus, 46; Tertullian influenced by, 66
Methodius of Olympia, St, 58, 62
Mill, John Stuart, *Three Essays in Theism*, 338
Miller, Perry, on aim of early revivalists, 362–3
Minucius Felix, *Octavius*, 70; compared with Tertullian, 70
Montfaucon, Bernard de, 26
Moody, Dwight Lyman, 360, 362; works on, 364
More, Sir Thomas, Chambers's life of, 284
Moses, on Mount Sinai, 139, 152; controversy over sacrifices of, 196
Musaeus, 51

Narsai, 158
Neale, John Mason, 323
Nemesius of Emesa, 59
Nepos, 62
Nestorius, 29, 106
Newman, John Henry, Cardinal, 30, 307; *Tract Ninety*, 274; and Tractarianism, 317; *Lives of the Saints*, 321; works on, 324, 325–6; Bremond on, 326; Faber's view of, 327; Meriol Trevor and, 327; Catholic and non-Catholic attitudes

Newman, John—*continued*
to, 328; on philosophy of history, 368
Newsome, David, on William Wilberforce, 335
Niebuhr, Reinhold, 245, 344
Noetus, 73
Novatian, 74, 75
Numenius, and Middle Platonism, 43; Athenagoras and, 45; Origen and, 58

Origen, 27; and Fathers of the Church, 30; importance of his work, 53–4; *Hexapla*, 54; interpretation of Bible text, 55–6; his ecclesiastical tasks, 56; his theological ideas, 57–8, 82; his condemned texts, 58; and Origen the pagan, 59–60; and Plotinus, 60; basic theme of mystical thought of, 60–61; disciples of, 62; his work under criticism, 62–3; and library at Caesarea, 80; Akakius rejects ideas of, 82–3; Eustathius an opponent of, 85; Epiphanius attacks, 96; St Basil a disciple of, 97; his influence on Gregory of Nyssa, 100; and the two Alexandrian traditions, 109; Evagrius's theology follows that of, 113; Jerome and, 117; Pelagius indebted to, 125; his view of the Eucharist, 174
Origen the pagan, 59–60
Orosius, Paulus, 124–5
Orpheus, 51
Ossius, Bishop of Cordova, 90
Ozanam, Antoine Frédéric, 347

Pachomius, St, 92
Palladius, *Lausiac History*, 108
Pamphilus, St, 62, 80
Panetius, 44
Papias of Hierapolis, 36; and parable, 36–7; and traditions about apostles, 38
Pascal, Blaise, varying views of, 294; Goldmann on, 294–5
Paul, St, the 'Apostle of the Gentiles', *orig*. Saul, 64; and Dionysius, 114; and Body of Christ, 132; and Eucharist, 136, 137, 139, 147, 149; and baptism, 139, 160; on anointing, 143
Paul of Samosta, 62, 87
Paulinus, St, Bishop of Nola, 102, 117
Pelagius, and Theodorus of Mopsuestia, 106; his work condemned, 125; influenced by Origen, 125; Julian of Eclanum and, 126
Peter, St, Bishop of Alexandria, 62, 85
Peter, St, 'Prince of the Apostles', 64, 160
Peter the Fuller, 114
Peter the Iberian, 114
Petre, Maud, 329
Philo of Alexandria, and symbolism in Old Testament, 43; and the two narratives of Genesis, 102
Photius, Patriarch of Constantinople, his *Library*, 26; and Ammonius Sakkas, 59
Pierius, 62
Pius V, St, Pope, 118
Pius IX, Pope, work on, 347
Pius X, St, Pope, 328
Plato, 60
Plotinus, Origen and, 59, 60; his thought diverges from that of Ammonius, 60; Augustine and, 120; and corporeal existence of man, 122
Plutarch, 45
Pontianus, Pope, 71
Porphyry, and the two Origens, 59; and Plotinus, 60; Arnobius and, 76; Hypatia of school of, 110; and Christianity, 111; and Neo-Platonism, 112; Augustine and, 120
Posidonius, 44
Praxeas, Tertullian and, 66, 73
Proclus, and Plotinus, 60; and Neo-Platonic tradition, 111; and Pseudo-Dionysius, 114, 115.
Prosper of Aquitaine, St, 127
Prudentius Aurelius Clemens, 27, 102
Pusey, Edward Bouverie, 321; on Priscilla Sellon, 322; and Jowett, 338–9
Pythagoras, 51

Quodvultdeus, Bishop of Carthage, 124

Richards, Timothy, and Chinese society, 259; his choice for Chinese readers, 260
Ridley, Nicholas, work on, 284
Rotberg, Robert I., on overall unsuccess of missionaries, 269–70
Rufinus, Tyrannius, translation of Origen, 92, 125; Evagrius, 112; Jerome at odds with, 117

Sankey, Ira David, 360, 364
Sellon, Priscilla Lydia, 322

Seneca, Lucius Annaeus, Tertullian and, 67; Minucius Felix influenced by, 70; Novatian influenced by, 74
Servetus, Michael, Calvin and, 278, 279; work on, 276
Severus, Patriarch of Antioch, his Monophysite doctrine, 110; and identity of Dionysius, 114
Shaftesbury, Anthony Ashley Cooper, 7th Earl of, 330
Simeon, Charles, 316, 321; and Evangelicalism, 332-3; works on, 333; Smyth on, 333; and Roman Catholic Emancipation, 333-4
Smith, Robert Pearsall, 357
Socrates, Logos-inspired, 50; Theodoret indebted to, 108
Soranus, 67
Sozomen, Salmaninius Hermias, 108
Stephen I, St, Pope, 75
Stephen, James, de Silva on, 266
Stephen, Leslie, 309; and Mill's *Three Essays in Theism*, 338
Stone, Darwell, 324
Strauss, David Friedrich, considered a danger to Christianity, 320; *Life of . .Jesus*, 321
Sunday, Billy, 362, 363–4
Sykes, Norman, his importance as historian of eighteenth century Church, 296–7; defends bishops, 297-8; his high reputation, 298-9; and Evangelical Revival, 299, 302; and Church as ecclesiastical institution, 299-300; and episcopacy, 300; on effect of sound historical scholarship, 368
Symmachus, and *Hexapla*, 54
Synesius, Bishop of Ptolemais, 111, 112
Syrianus, 111

Tait, Archibald Campbell, Archbishop of Canterbury, 313, 314, 315
Tatian, 64; his *Address to the Greeks*, 45; and precedence of non-Greeks, 51; Tertullian and, 66
Tertullian, Quintus Septimius Florens, 197; early works in Greek, 64; and Christian Latin, 64–5; sources of his thought, 65–6; influence of Gnosticism on vocabulary of, 66–7; Montanism, 67; a man of wide culture, 67; attacks paganism, 68; and Biblical interpretation, 68–9; and Trinity, 69; and resurrection, 69–70; Hippolytus and, 73; Novatian and, 74; Cyprian and, 74–5; *Ad nationes*, 76; and Varro, 77; Ambrose recalls, 102; his account of baptism, 142, 163–4, 167; and Holy Spirit in baptism, 144, 166–7; and Eucharist, 226
Themistius, 98
Theodore of Mopsuestia, 158; and Fathers of the Church, 30; his *Catechetical Homilies*, 94; pupil of Libanius, 95, 104; teacher of Antioch school, 104; reconstruction of his works, 104–5; his exegesis, 105; his theology, 106; an exegete and theologian, 107; Julian of Eclanum his pupil, 125; and baptismal rite, 162
Theodoret, Bishop of Cyrus, scholar and editor, 107–8; the writer, 108–9; rejects Antiochene literalism, 109
Theodosius I, 'the Great', Roman Emperor, 93; and Gregory of Nyssa, 99–100; and Ambrose, 100, 101
Theodotion, 54
Theognostus, 62
Theophilus, Patriarch of Alexandria, 93; hostile to Origenism, 109, 126
Theophilus of Antioch, St, and Middle Platonism, 45; and precedence of non-Greeks, 51; Tertullian uses, 66
Theotecnus of Caesarea in Palestine, 62
Thirlwall, Connop, Bishop of St David's, 314, 321
Thomas Aquinas, St, 122
Thomasius, Gottfried, 308
Tournon, Cardinal François de, 257
Travers, Walter, work on, 285
Tyndale, William, work on, 284

Valentinus, 47, 48, 64
Varro, 68, 77
Venn, Henry (1725–97), 332
Venn, Henry (1796–1873), 269, 332
Venn, John, 333
Victorinus, St, Bishop of Pettau, 77–8
Victorinus Afer, Caius Marius, 90–91, 112
Vidler, Alec R., *The Church in an Age of Revolution*, 253; on future of the Church, 254; on nineteenth-century missionary movement, 255; critical of missionaries, 255–6

Ward, Wilfrid, work on, 325; his biography of Newman, 326; and Newman, 327
Ward, William George, 327
Wesley, Charles, 332
Wesley, John, in *Church and State*, 299; works on, 303, 305; varying

Wesley, John—*continued*
views on, 303–4; and Church history, 305; importance of Wesleyan revivalism, 307; and Evangelicalism, 332
Wesley, Susannah, 303
Westcott, Brooke Foss, Bishop of Durham, 321; Vidler and, 309, 341
White, James Rowland, 359
Whitgift, John, Archbishop of Canterbury, works on, 284, 285; and Puritanism, 286
Wilberforce, Robert, 335
Wilberforce, Samuel, Bishop of Winchester, 314, 315; Simeon compared to, 333
Wilberforce, William, 316, 331; and Christianization of India, 264–5; and Clapham Sect, 330; and Evangelicalism, 334; Brown and Newsome disagree over, 335; Brown on his efforts for reform, 335–6
William of St-Thierry, 30
Williams, G. H., on Radical Reformation, 274, 275, 276

Zeno of Citium, 67
Zeno, St, Bishop of Verona, 89
Zephyrinus, St, Pope, 73
Zwingli, Ulrich, 15; teaches commemorative view of Eucharist, 228; radical Protestantism and, 274; works on, 281; arts and worship of God, 282

Index of Subjects

Acts of the Apostles, value as history, 139–40
Adventists, 359
Alexandria, Alexandrian traditions, 86, 109, 112; centre of Nicaean orthodoxy, 87, 93; Didymus the Blind at, 93; and Antioch, 104; Augustine and Alexandrian allegorization, 124
Altar, symbolism of, 153–4, 196; development of, 185–6; and transformation of church architecture, 221–2; position of celebrant at, 225
Anabaptism, 271; and baptism, 231, 237; contrasted with Spiritualists, 275; Holl's and Bochmer's view of, 276; works on, 276
Anglo-Catholicism, and Christian Socialism, 316; and Broad Church attitude, 316–17; works celebrating centenary of, 317–18; and Victorian Church of England, 318–19; and authority of clergy, 321; French Catholic 'mission' and Missions of, 322
Anointing, and early baptismal rites, 143–4, 161; in Eastern baptism, 144, 145, 158–60; and Roman practice, 163; symbolism of, 165
Antioch, Council of, 62; Antiochene tradition, 86–7; varying schools of thought at, 87; Synod of, 94, 99; centre of Biblical scholarship, 94–5; and Christological question, 96; and Alexandria, 104; Theodoret and, 109; Antiochenes stress Christ's humanity, 110; literalism of, 125
Apostles' Creed, 14
Apostolic Tradition, The, authorship of, 162; text probably altered, 162–3; baptismal rite in, 163, 167, 168; Tertullian and, 164; text of prayers in, 164; Ambrose and, 167; and narrative, 179
Architecture, church, effect of screen on Eastern Orthodox Church, 182–4; basilica, 184–6; transformation from ninth century, 221–2; Anglo-Catholicism and, 323; works on, 323; fantastic faiths and, 360
Arianism, 80; Arian controversy, 17; Athanasius opposes, 84; Eustathius attacks, 86; at Antioch, 87; Ambrose and the struggle against, 101; Platonic speculations and, 123
Asceticism, in early Church, 173
Augustinianism, 126–7

Baptism, privilege of, 134; Biblical authority for, 136–7; based upon Christ's example, 137; symbolism, 138, 145; Paul's assumption about, 139; means of admission to Christian Church, 140; described by Justin Martyr, 141–2; Tertullian and, 142, 163–5; relation between Justin's and Tertullian's accounts of, 142–3; anointing in, 143–5; giving of Holy Spirit in, 144; followed by Eucharist, 145; in the early Church, 146; allusion in 1 Peter, 148–9; pattern of East Syrian, 158–62; *The Apostolic Tradition*, 163–4; Ambrose and rite of, 163–7; laying-on of hands in, 168–9; the Easter vigil followed by, 169–71; of adults, 198, 200, 212–13; baptism of infants, 198–200, 275, 340; washes away original sin, 201; administration by presbyter, 202–3, 204; in East, 203; in West, 203–4; at Rome, 204; theological questions posed by breaking in two of rite of, 205–6; church-door rite, 206–8; English practice in sixteenth century, 210–12; Anglican transformation of rite of, 212–13; emphasis shifts, 215; retained by Protestant Reformation, 231; Roman Catholic Church and, 237; under review, 237–8
Baptists, work on, 290; Evangelicalism and, 331
Benedict, Rule of St, 126
Bible, and Christian doctrine, 11, 15; interpretation of, 12–14; Fathers of

Bible—*continued*
the Church and, 15; Origen and, 54–6; early Latin versions of, 65; in Indian schools, 266
Bishops, and tradition of Apostles, 48; and Sunday Eucharist, 146, 216–17; and baptism, 158, 159, 163, 166, 167, 201–15, 206–7, 210; and laying-on of hands, 168; at Easter baptism, 170; preach from throne, 185, 189; in Roman Mass, 188; preaching prerogative of, 188–9, 222; and confirmation, 208, 210, 212, 213; and Eucharistic rite, 221; place of episcopacy in missionary work, 263; works on, 291, 313–15; Sykes and, 297–8, 299, 300
Blood, its power for Moses, 139; in Eucharist, 143, 147, 154, 160; of the Covenant, 152
Body of Christ, the Christian and, 132–3; baptism and Eucharist in, 134; in Eucharist, 143, 147, 154, 182; theological dispute about, 226; Church as, 235
Bread, *see* Elements
British and Foreign Bible Society, 312
Broad Church School, Anglo-Catholicism and, 316–17; Church historians ignore, 337; Maurice and, 340
Buddhism, 266–7

Calvinism, Eucharist in, 227–8; and capitalism, 271, 272; prestige of Calvinist tradition, 280; French Calvinism and Revolution, 293; Methodism and, 308
Camden Society, 323
Caroline divines, the, and Fathers of the Church, 30; adult baptism and confirmation, 214; and Reformers' Communion Service, 229, 230
Catholic Modernism, works on, 328
Catholic Socialist movement, works on, 346, 347
Celibacy, problems created by Church attitude to, 173–4
Chalcedon, Council of, 92; dispute culminating in, 96; Christological question subject of, 104; Theodoret's achievement at, 107; and doctrine of hypostatic union, 110; and doctrine of Incarnation, 127
Chrism, in baptism, 167, 205, 206; not mentioned by St Cyril, 203; in confirmation, 208; abandoned in baptism and confirmation, 212; Anglican transformation of rite, 212
Christadelphians, 358
Christian Science, 15, 358
Christian Socialism, Anglo-Catholicism and, 316; Maurice and, 340, 341; works on, 341, 342, 343; political naïveté, 367
Christology, importance in fifth and sixth centuries, 104; and Council of Chalcedon, 107; McIntyre on, 369
Church of England, 1662 Prayer Book, 19; Book of Common Prayer, 232; controversy over ceremonial in, 232; at present day, 235–40; attitude to non-episcopal Churches, 277–8; and Roman Catholic Church, 283; Puritanism and, 288; and Evangelical Revival, 302; and Methodism, 303
Churches of Christ, 11
Clapham Sect, 330, 333
Communion, *see* Eucharist
Confirmation, lack of proof-texts for, 136; problems of baptism leading to separate rite of, 205; theological questions posed by, 206; administered only by bishop, 208; the simple rite, 208; devaluation of, 209; postponement of, 209, 313; in Protestant Reformation, 212–13, 231; Roman Catholic Church and, 237; Church of England and, 238
Confucianism, missionary attitude to, 259
Constantinople, Council of, 92; crowns Basil's success, 97; Gregory of Nyssa at, 99; Jerome and Gregory of Nazianzus at, 117
Constantinople, Second Council of, 58; and Theodore of Mopsuestia, 104; Evagrius's and Didymus's work condemned by, 112
Corpus Scriptorum Eccliasticorum Latinorum, 26
Cowley Fathers, 322
Cross, Sign of the, in baptism, 167, 168, 170

Darwinism, 309
Dead Sea Scrolls, importance of, discovery of, 33; the 'pesher', 35
Deists, English, 292–3
Didache, background to, 33; Eucharistic prayers in, 37; translated into Latin, 65
Doctrine, formation of, 14
Dogma, meaning of term, 14–15; development of, 28

Index of Subjects

Donatism, 76
Dualism, 40–41

Easter, baptism at, 157–8, 170, 202; all-night vigil at, 169–70; Rome restricts baptism to Pentecost and, 204; baptismal water blessed at Pentecost and, 207; communion at, 228
Eastern Orthodox Church, informality within formality of, 18–19
Ebionites, 40
Ecclesiastical Commissioners, 352
Ecumenical Movement, works on, 354, 366
Edessa, 37
Ekstasis, 61
Elements (Bread and Wine), in Eucharist, 147, 150; a thankoffering, 154, 178; outside celebration of Eucharist, 156; development of ritual of, 181–2; contributed by laity, 189, 220; breaking of the bread, 190; questions about nature of, 210; payment for, 221; theological dispute about, 226–7; reverent disposal of, 229–30
Elim Four Square, 358
Enlightenment, works on, 292; Church as symbol of, 293; Tractarians and, 300
Epectasis, doctrine of, 61
Ephesus, Council of, 92; dispute culminating in, 96; Christological question subject of, 104; doctrine of hypostatic union prevails at, 110
Eucharist, the supreme act, 134; Biblical authority for, 136–7; based upon Christ's example, 137; Paul takes for granted, 139; Sunday, 140, 146; Justin Martyr and, 141, 143; expansion of ritual, 142; a symbolic act, 145; baptismal, 145, 146, 158, 160; meal disappears from, 147; New Testament allusions to, 149; distribution of elements to those not present, 156; regular communicants decrease, 172; continence before, 174; terror and, 174–5; ceremonial introduced into, 175–6; shape of rite, 176; intercessions in, 176–7; development in doctrine of consecration, 177–8; prayer in, 177–80, 189, 192–7; elaboration of rites, 180–82; development of Byzantine rite, 183–4; music in, 186–7; Roman Mass, 187–8; offertory, 189, 224; breaking of bread, 190; distribution of sacrament, 191; communion, 191, 212, 213; communicating of infants, 209–10; confirmation and, 212, 213; practice corrupted, 215; dissociation from Lord's Day, 216; at funerals and weddings, 216; presbyters preside at, 217; change in attitude of priest to people in, 225; elevation of the host, 225–7; Reformation and, 227–9, 231; Roman Catholic Church and Eucharistic teaching, 236; Church of England and, 239
Evangelicalism, Sykes and, 299; historians and, 302; works on, 302, 331; and the working class, 305; and the clergy, 317; Tractarianism, Oxford Movement and, 319–20; and Anglo-Catholic Missions, 322; bitterly critical of Cowley Fathers, 322; Newman's conversion to, 326; Best on, 330; reforms in late nineteenth century, 330–31; Evangelical Holiness movement, 332, 357; Simeon and, 332; Victorian evangelical revival, 361; and social problems, 365

Fathers of the Church, and formation of Christian doctrine, 14–15; special authority of, 25, 29; patristic studies and, 27; explanation of term, 28–9; reason for attraction of, 30, 32; and the Bible, 31; their theology and the Church, 31; theologians, 32
Fonts, 170
French Church history, works on, 346

German Church history, works on, 348
Gnosticism, 123; Gnostic library, 27, 34; and Jewish and Judeo-Christian culture, 34; *Gospel of James*, 38; Tatian and, 45; draws on Greek philosophy, 47; Valentinus and, 47; Irenaeus attacks, 48; Clement of Alexandria and, 48, 49; Tertullian and, 66, 69–70; Hippolytus and, 73; determinism of, 125; and early liturgical texts, 150; and Eucharistic prayer, 155

Helcesaites, 40
Hellenism, Clement of Alexandria and, 48; Christianity and Hellenistic imagery, 48–9; and Judaism, 51; Christians and, 52; Cyril fanatical against, 111
Higher Criticism, 340

Hinduism, Grant denigrates, 264; alarmed by Christianity, 265; Government advised to sever connexion with, 265–6
Holy Places, 94
Holy Spirit, Justin Martyr omits mention of, 142; in Tertullian's account of baptism, 142; ambiguity concerning, 144; and baptism, 158–9, 160, 167, 170; and Eucharistic prayer, 178; double gift of, 206
Homoeans, Akakius one of leaders of, 82; Eusebius of Emesa, 83; importance of Homoean tradition, 87
Homoousios, 83
Huguenots, 293
Hypostatic union, 110

Iconostasis, development of, 182–3; effect on Eastern Orthodox Churches, 183–4
Incarnation, in Irenaeus's theology, 51; late arrival of, 52; turning point in history, 52; Eusebius and, 82; Marcellus gives importance to, 83; Athanasius as theologian of, 85–6; Eustathius's orthodox theology of, 86; Lactantius and, 89; Cyril's treatment of, 110; Pope Leo I and, 127; Gnosticism denies, 150
International Congress of Patristic Studies, 27
Italian Church history, works on, 347–8

Jezreelites, 359–60
Judaism, Jewish literature, 35–6; Christianity and, 49; Greek philosophy and, 51
Judeo-Christian literature, 41; apocalypse in, 36; Testament form in, 36; parable in, 36–7; Jewish influence in, 37; other influences in, 37–8, 39; missionary literature, 39–40
Judeo-Christian theology, 41–2

Kiss of peace, in baptism, 142, 163, 170; in Eucharist, 190; symbolism of, 191

Last Judgement, 123
Last Supper, St Paul and, 136, 137; and Passover and Covenant, 138–9; Eucharist follows pattern of, 147; Christ consecrates himself at, 152
Laying-on of hands, and Holy Spirit in baptism, 142, 144, 158–60, 167, 170; in Roman practice, 163; symbolism of, 164; term clarified, 168–9; restricted to bishop alone, 202–3
Liturgical Commission, work of, 235, 238–9
Liturgy (*see also* Baptism, Eucharist *and* Mass), and history, 19–20; liturgioligy, 20; Jewish influence, 37; varying Christian attitudes to, 133–4; two principle functions, 134; modern ignorance of early liturgical practices, 140; language of, 192; Roman tradition, 219; Reformation liturgies, 231; and C. of E. Book of Common Prayer, 232; effect of invention of printing on, 233–4; twentieth-century liturgical movement, 234–6, 274
Logos, progressive revelation of, 50; special activity of, 50–51; in theology of religious history of human race, 51; importance of Incarnation of, 52; Origen and relatedness of man to, 60–61; and the soul, 61; and Incarnation in Marcellus's theology, 84

Manichaeism, Augustine and, 120
Marcionites, 68
Mass, votive, 216, 221; development of ways of celebrating, 217–18; private Masses, 219–20; payment for, 220–21; and transformation of church architecture, 221; pageantry in first half of, 223; new climax of, 227; Reformers and, 227; Reformation and, 228, 231
Mennonite Church, American, 276
Methodism, and union with Church of England, 277; and Anglicanism, 297, 302, 303; Sykes on, 299; works on, 303, 305–6, 365; Methodist Revival, 304; and Wesley, 304, 305; and the working class, 305; expansion in USA, 308; and teetotalism, 312; separate denomination, 317; and Victorian heritage, 334; and Wickham's *Church and People in an Industrial City*, 355; and Salvation Army, 357
Millenarianism, 41–2; Victorinus shares doctrine of, 78; and Lactantius's theology of history, 88; Apollinarius, 96
Missal, 218

Index of Subjects

Missionary history, change in attitude since 1945, 256; in China, 256–61; in South Pacific, 261–3; in India, 263–6; in Ceylon, 263, 266–7; in Africa, 267–70; political changes and, 368
Missionary societies, Vidler on nineteenth-century, 255; Vidler critical of missionaries, 255–6; Protestant societies on China and Christianity, 259; Varg critical of, 260; failure of education offered by, 260; make difficulties in China for British Government, 261; and Indian rebellion, 265, 266; self-confident aggressiveness of, 266; lack of interest in social problems, 267; Rotberg on, 269–70; Lutheran missionaries in India, 300
Missions to London, 322
Modalism, 87
Monastic movement, in fourth century, 92; expands, 104; Synesius hostile to, 111; work on, 283, 322; work on monasteries of Angers, 293–4
Monophysitism, at Antioch, 87; in debate with Nestorius, 96; and Christological question, 104; and Severus of Antioch, 110
Montanism, Tertullian and, 66, 67, 73
Mormons, 15
Music, development of church, 186–7; in Roman Mass, 188; in first half of Mass, 223
Muslim religion, 265

Nag Hammadi, Gnostic library at, 27, 34; Codex V of, 36, 39; *Apocryphon of James*, 36; *Gospel of Thomas*, 38; Valentinus works among manuscripts of, 47
Neofiti Codex, 34
Nestorianism, at Antioch, 87; in debate with Monophysitism, 96, 104; Theodore of Mopsuestia master of, 104
Nicaea, Council of, 80, 83
Nonconformists, 289–90

Orange, Second Council of, 127
Origenism, origins of system, 58–9; condemnation of, 93; Theophilus's hostility to, 109, 126; Evagrius's work and, 112; Augustine and Origenist doctrine, 123; Cassian, Evagrius and, 126
Origenists, of Antioch, 87
Oxford Movement, Peck on, 318; Davies on, 319; and Tractarianism and Evangelicalism, 319–20; works on, 320; E. A. Knox on, 320–21

Passion, the, the Supper and, 138; Eucharist and, 147, 195; Gnostics deny, 150
Passover, ritual use of unleavened bread, 19; Last Supper and, 138–9; celebrated at Easter, 169
Pelagianism, Jerome against, 117; Augustine's attitude to, 122; Western theology breaks with, 123; Prosper of Aquitaine denounces Cassian's, 127; Semi-Pelagianism rejected at Orange, 127
Pentecost, baptism administered at, 202, 204, 207; commemorates Redemption, 219
Platonism, 43–4; Tatian and, 45; Athenagoras and, 45; Theophilus of Antioch and, 45; Gnosticism and, 47; and Hellenistic culture, 48–9; Christianity as successor to, 49; Origen's doctrine of pre-existence, 57; Origen's philosophic background, 58; Tertullian indebted to, 67; Victorinus and Neo-Platonism, 90; Neo-Platonic anti-Christian tradition, 111; Augustine and Neo-Platonism, 120, 121, 123
Plymouth Brethren, 331
Port-Royal, Convent of, 30
Prayer, in baptism, 141, 142, 144, 159, 170, 205; and Eucharist, 146–7, 148, 155, 156, 182, 218, 224–5; over bread and cup in Justin's time, 147; pattern in early centuries, 150; thanksgiving and Jewish prayer, 151; Lord's Prayer, 156, 180, 191, 225; in *The Apostolic Tradition*, 164; intercessions, 176, 194; Eucharist prayers, 178, 192–7, 239; lack of sequence of thought in, 179–80; over the Offerings, 189; canon prayer, 189–90, 191, 218; development in Middle Ages, 218–19; in Latin, 222; 'Prayer of Consecration', 229; Reformation and, 231
Prayer Book, of 1662, 19; Book of Common Prayer, 232; attempted revision of, 232–3
Presbyterian Church, and union with Church of England, 277; Charles II and, 290
Protestantism, and capitalism, 272; radical, 274–7; importance of Church to, 278

Puritanism, works on Elizabethan, 285; Elizabeth and Whitgift and, 286; works on seventeenth century, 287, 288; accepted in America, 287; English attitude to, 288; and growth of America, 367

Queen Anne's Bounty, 352

Reformation, and rise of modern capitalism, 271; works on, 253, 272, 273, 277, 278, 282, 283, 285; and interdependence of Church and state, 275
Revivalism, McLaughlin on, 251; Evangelicalism and American revivalists, 331; and Salvation Army, 357; British Holiness revivalism, 357; works on, 362–5
Revolution, French, French Calvinism and, 293; fury against Church during, 293–4
Roman Catholicism, changed attitude to Reformation, 272; and Luther, 272–3; and Council of Trent, 273–4
Roman Catholic Church, at present day, 235–7; and Church of England, 283

Saints' Days, origin of, 216
Salvation, Origen's theology of, 57; Augustine and Pauline doctrine of, 122; Augustine's theology of grace and, 123; passionately desired, 169; Eucharist and, 172
Salvation Army, spontaneity and warmth of, 18–19; failure of, 356; works on, 357; factors contributing to success of, 357
Sanctus, and Eucharistic prayer, 151–3, 154, 179, 186; cuts Eucharistic prayer in two, 193
Second Advent, 81
Sectarianism, 358
Sin, and structure of universe, 57–8; obscures image of Logos, 61; prayers for forgiveness of, 176; absolution after baptism, 199; doctrine of original, 201
Socinianism, 271; work on, 277
Spiritualists, 275
Stoicism, its influence on Christian thought, 44; and *Epistle to Diognetus*, 45; Irenaeus and, 46, 48, 51; Tertullian influenced by, 67; Novatian and, 74; Cyprian and, 75; John Chrysostom and, 107
Stowe Missal, the, 19
Subordinationism, at beginning of fourth century, 79–80; Marcellus's theology and, 84; Church of Rome unresponsive to, 84–5; Athanasius rejects, 85; Hilary rejects, 89–90

Targum, 34–5
Throne, bishop's, 188; symbolism of, 185; preaching from, 185, 189
Tractarianism, Sykes's interpretation of, 300–301; Newman and, 317; Liberalism and, 318; Evangelicalism, Oxford Movement and, 319–20; works on, 320, 324
Trent, Council of, 271; changing Roman Catholic attitude to, 273–4; works on, 273
Trinity, 17; in second and third centuries, 28; Tertullian and, 69; subordinationism and, 79–80; Eusebius's doctrine of the word and, 82; Athanasius's significance in theology of, 85; Lactantius and, 89; Hilary and Trinitarian theology, 90; Victorinus's Trinitarian thought, 90–91; St Basil and doctrine of, 96–7, 117; Gregory of Nazianzus and, 98; Greek theology and, 123; Augustine and theology of, 123; radical Protestants and, 275

Unitarianism, work on, 277
United States of America, works on Protestantism in, 344

Vatican Councils, works on, 347
Vulgate, the, 119

Water, symbolism of, 138, 164; and baptism, 141, 142, 144, 145, 158, 160, 163; consecration of, 164
Wine, *see* Elements
Witnesses of Jehovah, 15
Word, the, Origen and, 57, 61; Eusebius's theology of, 81–2; Athanasius terms Pancrator, 85; Lactantius's theology of, 88; in Theodorus's theology, 106; Cyril and deifying activity of, 110
World Council of Churches, 368

The Pelican Guide to Modern Theology
Volume 1

Systematic and Philosophical Theology

William Nicholls

In modern times theology has run into that same crisis which has been induced in the whole of civilized culture by the advance of science. This first volume outlines the directions of thought adopted by such modern theologians as Barth, Bultmann, Bonhoeffer and Tillich in the face of scientific challenge. It reveals a liveliness and openness in modern religious thought which suggest that, whatever it may become in the future, theology is not dying.

Volume 3

Biblical Criticism

Robert Davidson and A. R. C. Leaney

In the third volume two theologians closely survey the results of modern study of the Old and New Testaments. They show how the Bible, after more than a century of critical and historical analysis, still retains a central literary position within the Christian Church but can no longer be accorded the inerrant authority of the word of God. Neither history, linguistics nor archaeology, however, have been able to settle every problem, and this volume introduces the reader to a modern Bible industry of unprecedented activity.